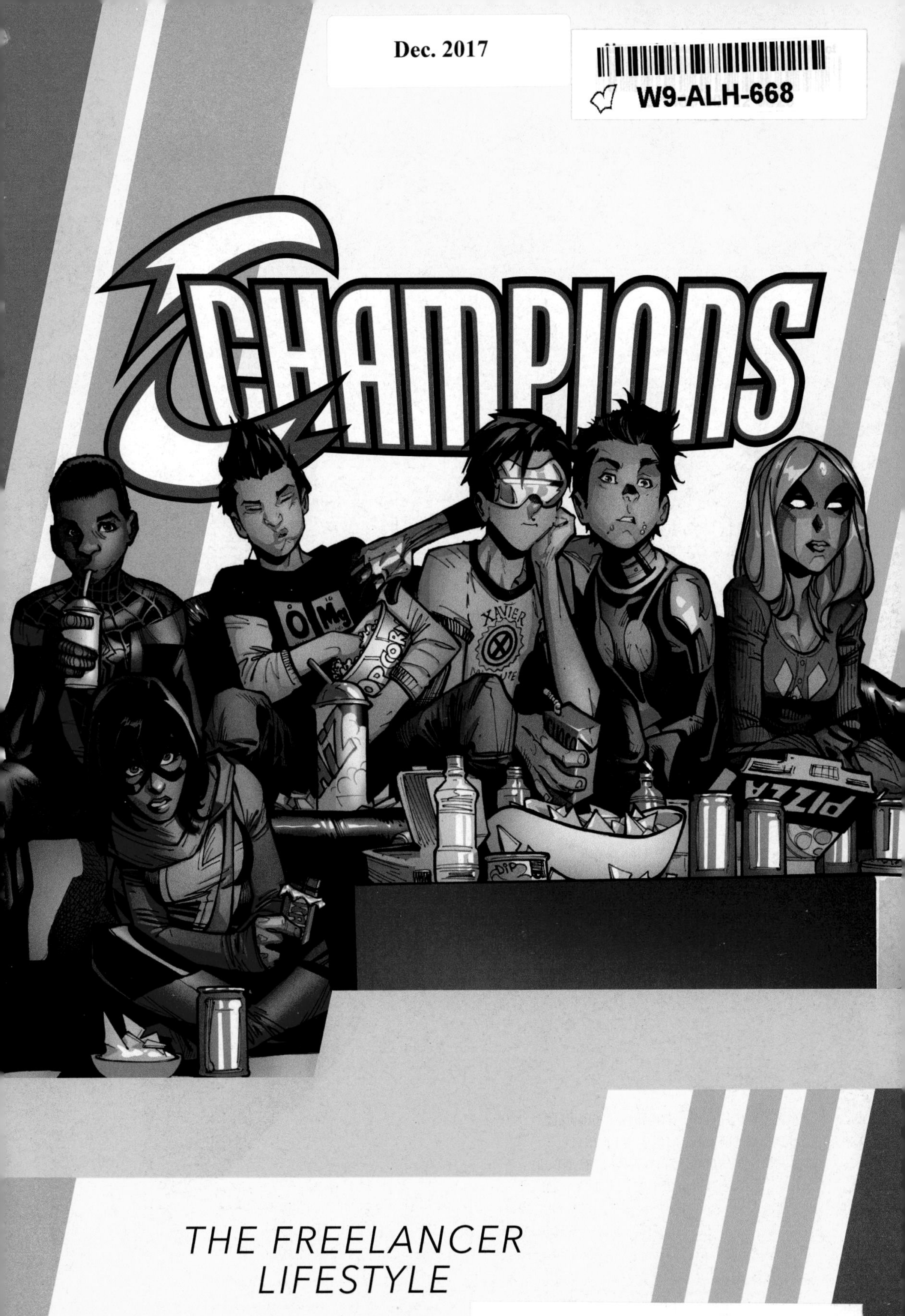
CHAMPIONS
PIZZA
DIP

THE FREELANCER LIFESTYLE

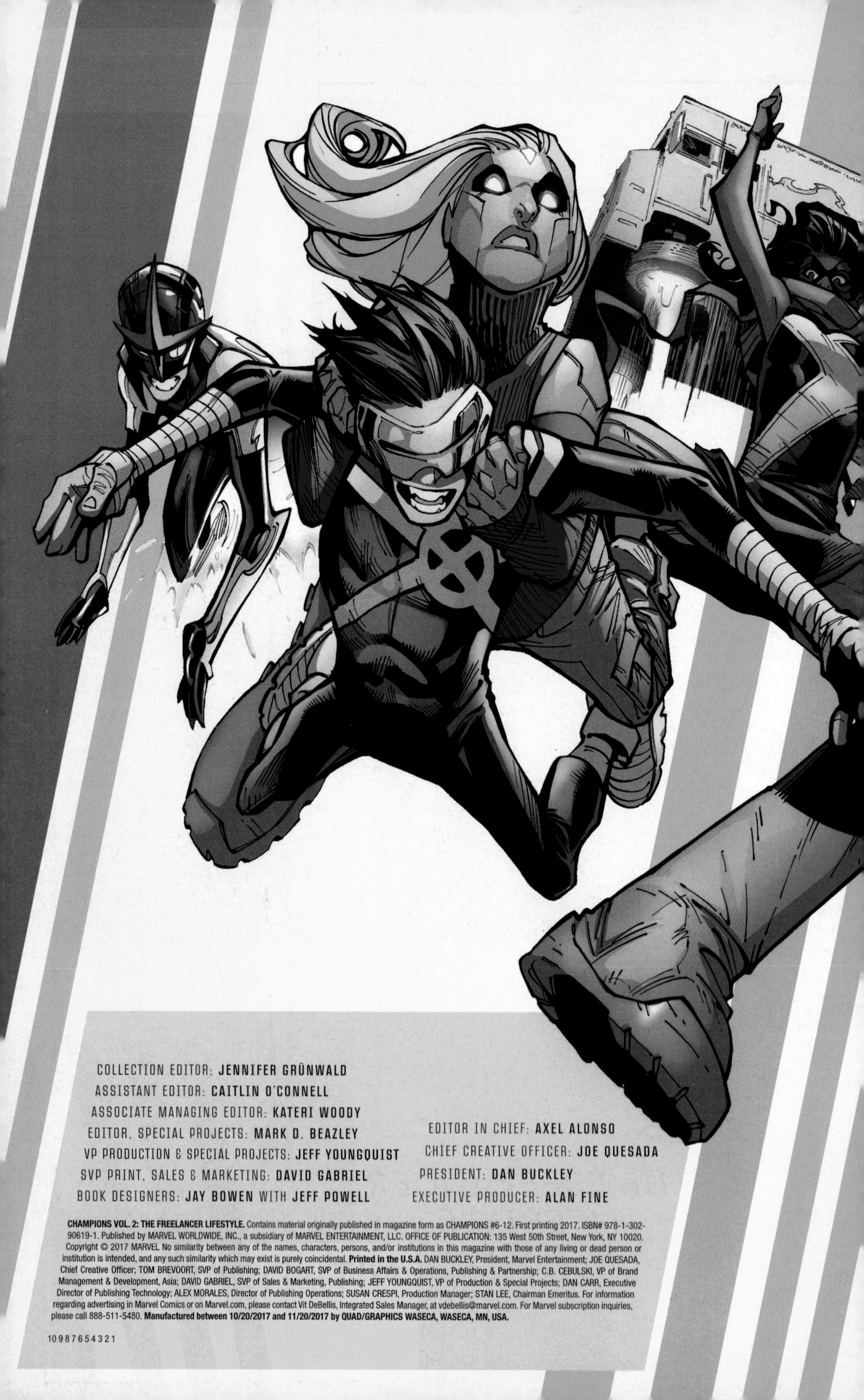

COLLECTION EDITOR: **JENNIFER GRÜNWALD**
ASSISTANT EDITOR: **CAITLIN O'CONNELL**
ASSOCIATE MANAGING EDITOR: **KATERI WOODY**
EDITOR, SPECIAL PROJECTS: **MARK D. BEAZLEY**
VP PRODUCTION & SPECIAL PROJECTS: **JEFF YOUNGQUIST**
SVP PRINT, SALES & MARKETING: **DAVID GABRIEL**
BOOK DESIGNERS: **JAY BOWEN** WITH **JEFF POWELL**

EDITOR IN CHIEF: **AXEL ALONSO**
CHIEF CREATIVE OFFICER: **JOE QUESADA**
PRESIDENT: **DAN BUCKLEY**
EXECUTIVE PRODUCER: **ALAN FINE**

CHAMPIONS VOL. 2: THE FREELANCER LIFESTYLE. Contains material originally published in magazine form as CHAMPIONS #6-12. First printing 2017. ISBN# 978-1-302-90619-1. Published by MARVEL WORLDWIDE, INC., a subsidiary of MARVEL ENTERTAINMENT, LLC. OFFICE OF PUBLICATION: 135 West 50th Street, New York, NY 10020. **Printed in the U.S.A.** DAN BUCKLEY, President, Marvel Entertainment; JOE QUESADA, Chief Creative Officer; TOM BREVOORT, SVP of Publishing; DAVID BOGART, SVP of Business Affairs & Operations, Publishing & Partnership; C.B. CEBULSKI, VP of Brand Management & Development, Asia; DAVID GABRIEL, SVP of Sales & Marketing, Publishing; JEFF YOUNGQUIST, VP of Production & Special Projects; DAN CARR, Executive Director of Publishing Technology; ALEX MORALES, Director of Publishing Operations; SUSAN CRESPI, Production Manager; STAN LEE, Chairman Emeritus. For information regarding advertising in Marvel Comics or on Marvel.com, please contact Vit DeBellis, Integrated Sales Manager, at vdebellis@marvel.com. For Marvel subscription inquiries, please call 888-511-5480. **Manufactured between 10/20/2017 and 11/20/2017 by QUAD/GRAPHICS WASECA, WASECA, MN, USA.**

10 9 8 7 6 5 4 3 2 1

In the aftermath of the second superhuman civil war, the world has become disillusioned with its heroes. The next generation has to be better. They have to be...

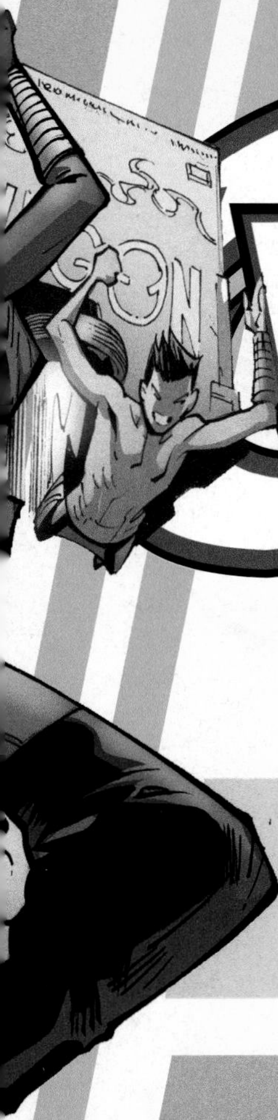

CHAMPIONS

THE FREELANCER LIFESTYLE

WRITER: **MARK WAID**
PENCILER: **HUMBERTO RAMOS**

INKER: **VICTOR OLAZABA**
COLORISTS: **EDGAR DELGADO** WITH **NOLAN WOODARD** [#6 & #8]
LETTERER: **VC'S CLAYTON COWLES**
COVER ART: **HUMBERTO RAMOS & EDGAR DELGADO**

ASSISTANT EDITOR: **ALANNA SMITH** EDITOR: **TOM BREVOORT**

CHAMPIONS

RECENTLY, THE CHAMPIONS TANGLED WITH A GROUP OF SUPER-POWERED CORPORATE MERCENARIES KNOWN AS THE FREELANCERS.

AND THEY DIDN'T LEAVE THINGS ON GOOD TERMS...

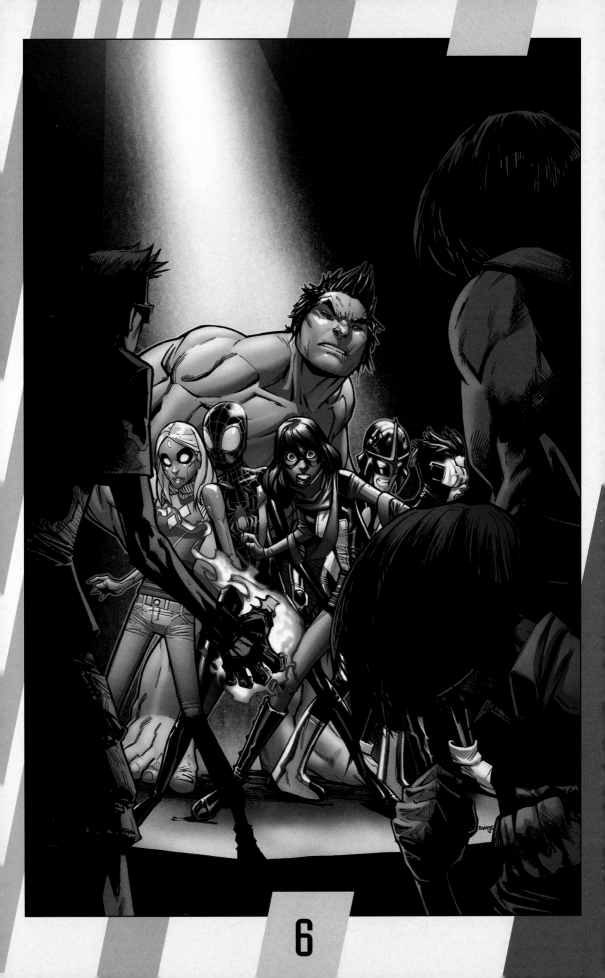

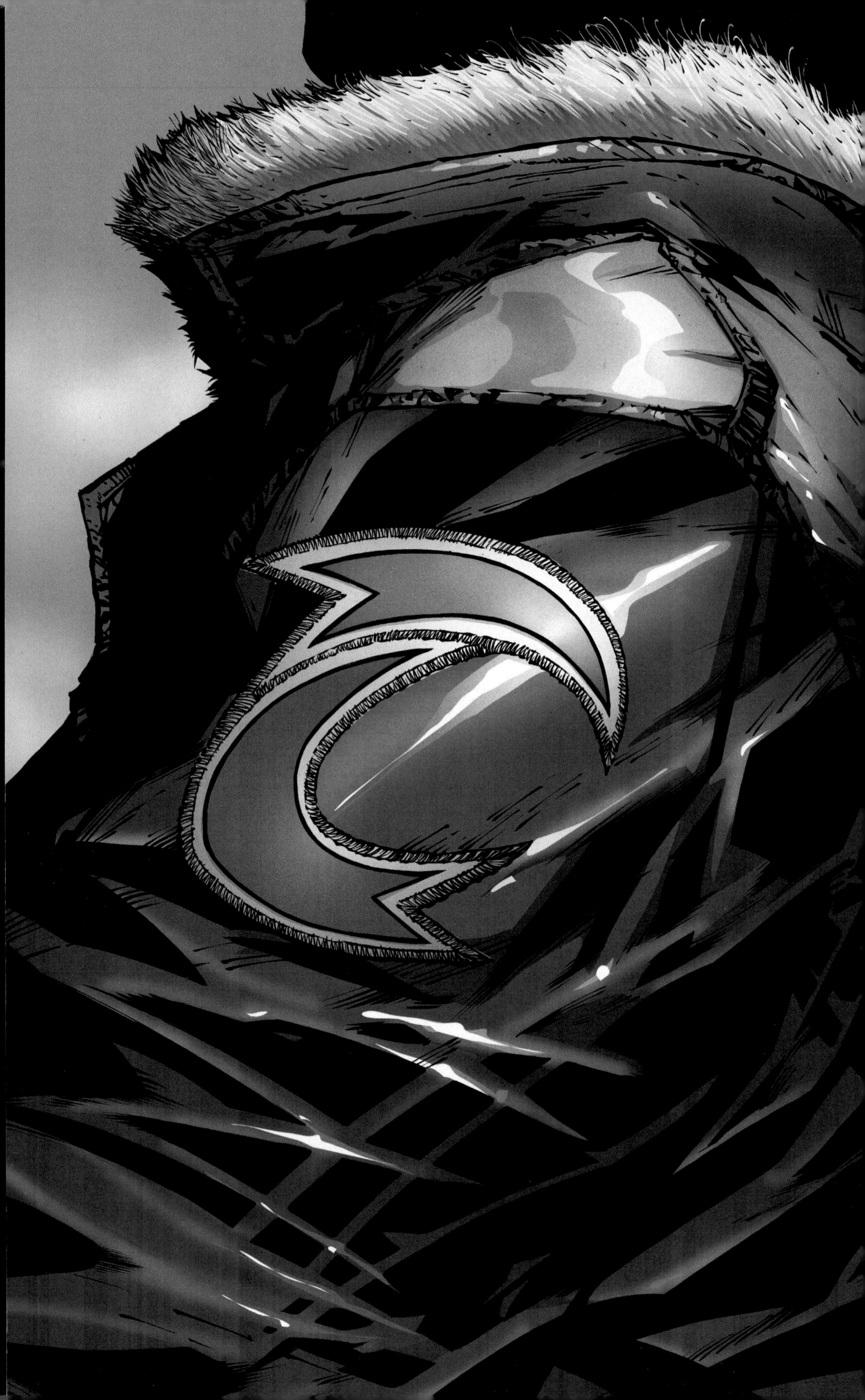

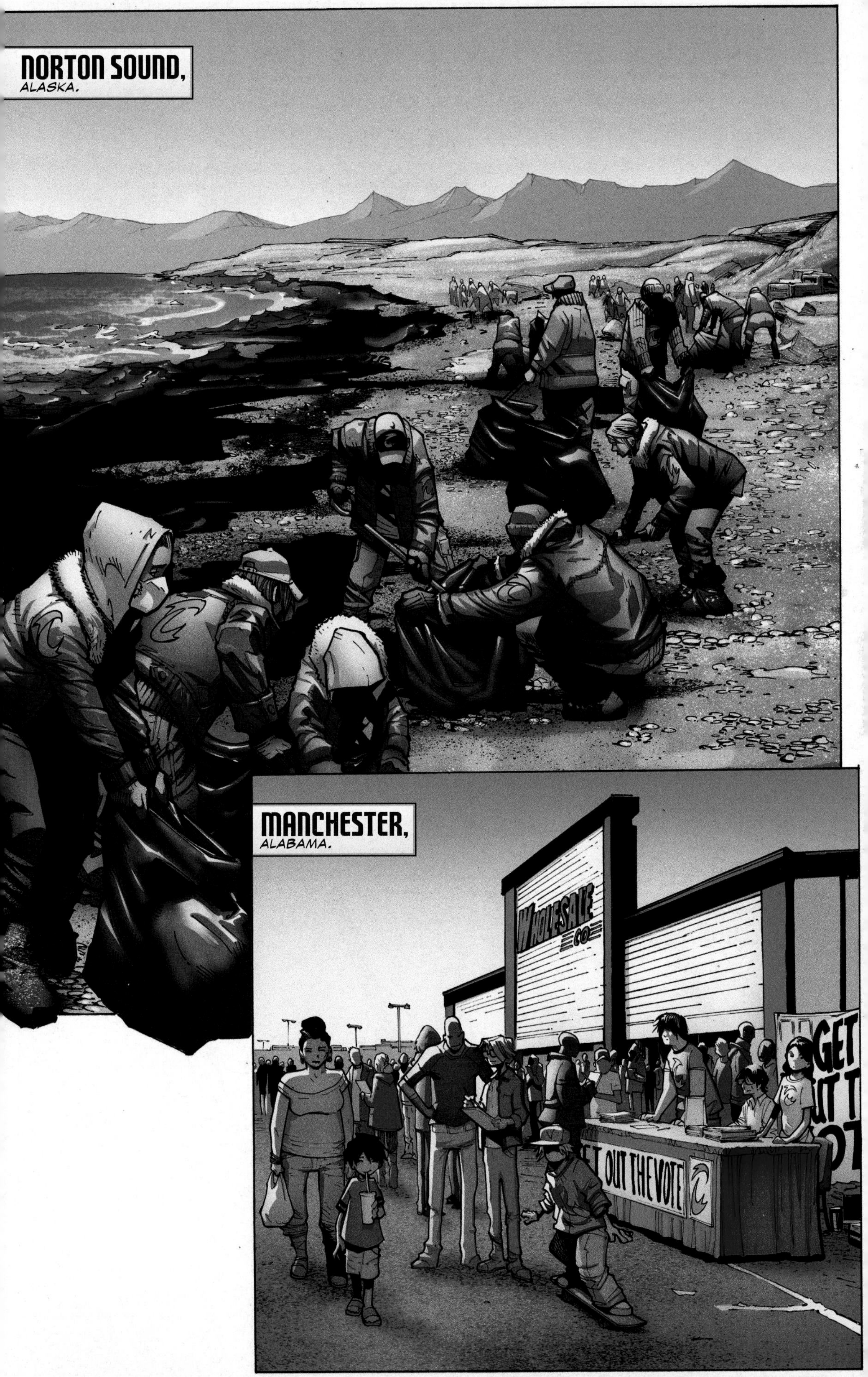
NORTON SOUND,
ALASKA.
MANCHESTER,
ALABAMA.
WHOLESALE
CO
GET
ET OUT THE VOTE

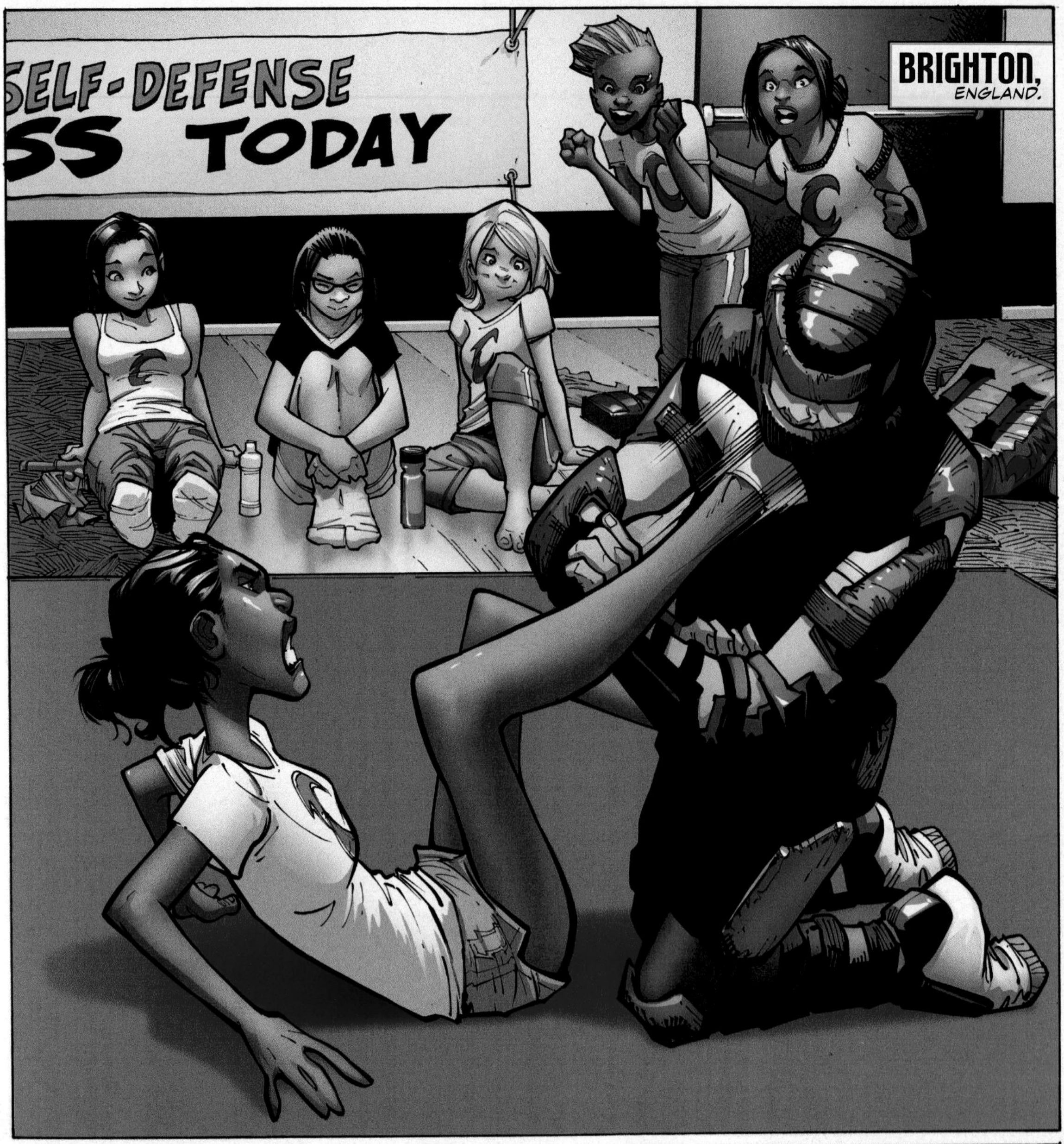
SELF-DEFENSE
SS TODAY
BRIGHTON,
ENGLAND.

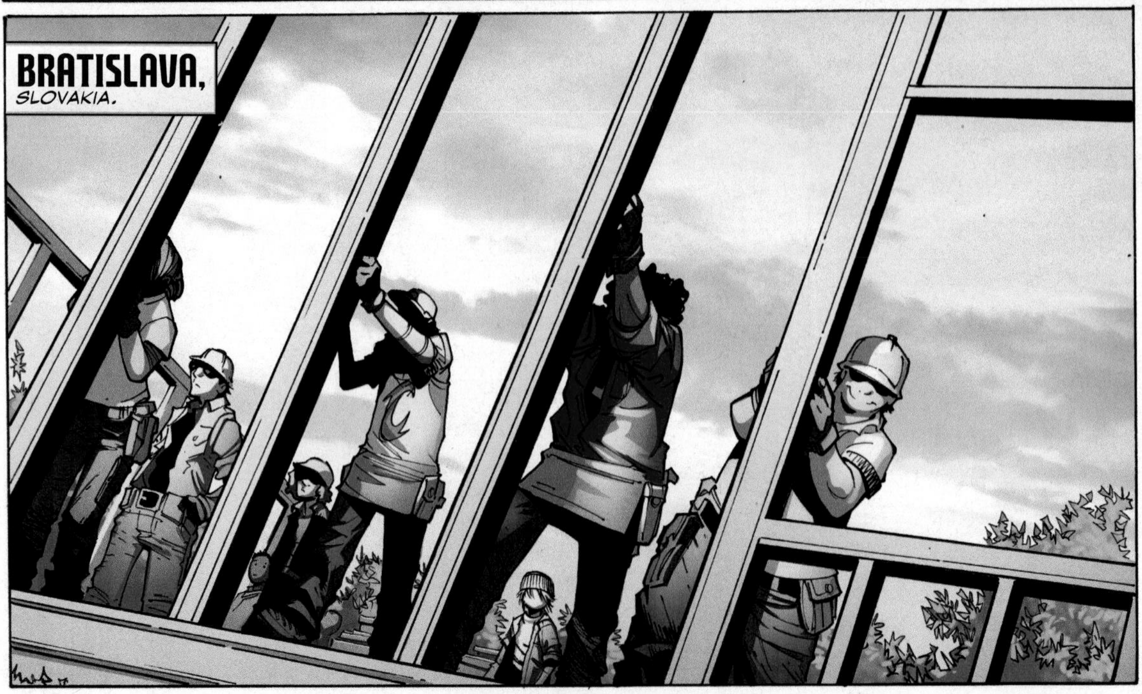
BRATISLAVA,
SLOVAKIA.

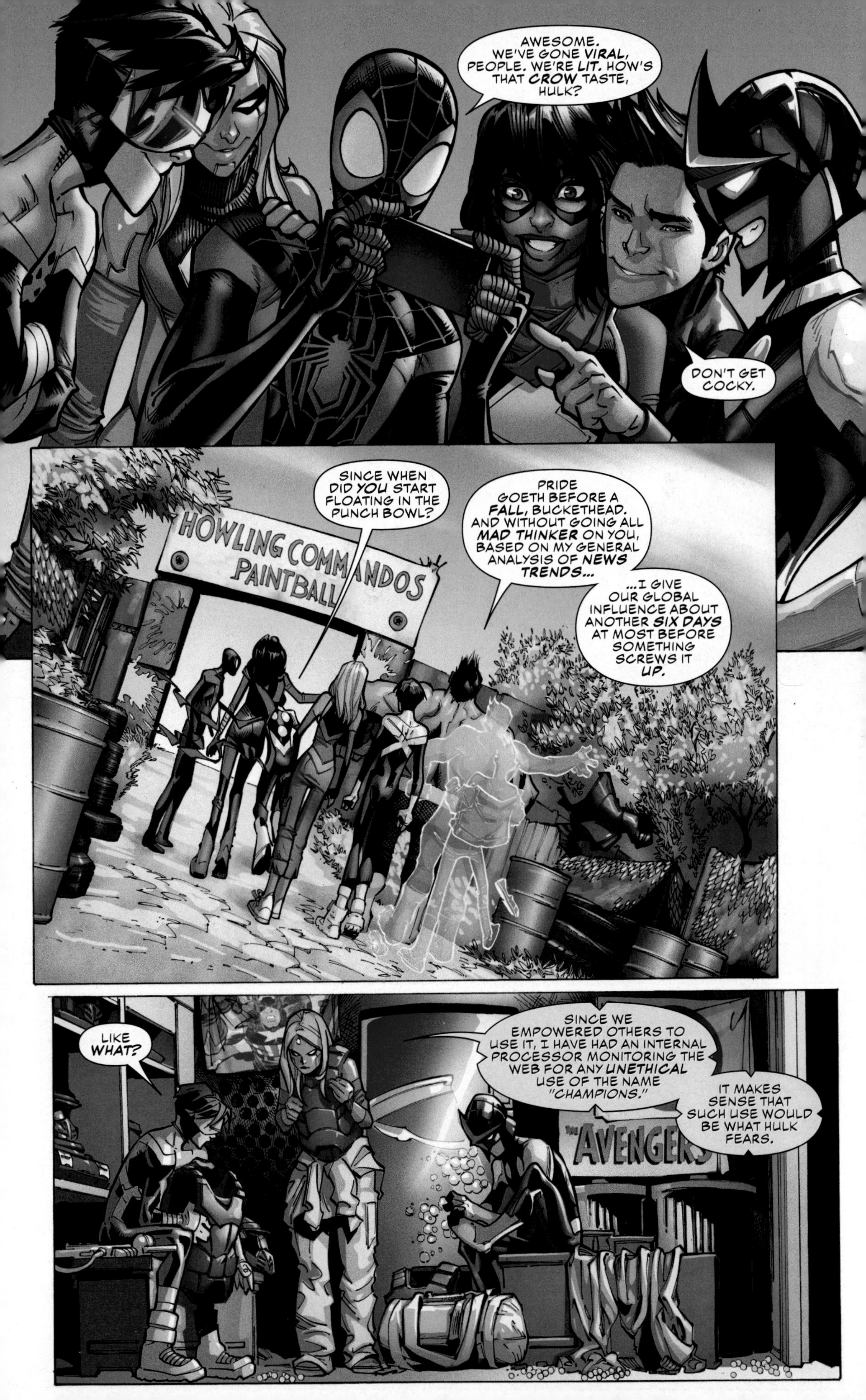
AWESOME. WE'VE GONE VIRAL, PEOPLE. WE'RE LIT. HOW'S THAT CROW TASTE, HULK?
DON'T GET COCKY.
HOWLING COMMANDOS PAINTBALL
SINCE WHEN DID YOU START FLOATING IN THE PUNCH BOWL?
PRIDE GOETH BEFORE A FALL, BUCKETHEAD. AND WITHOUT GOING ALL MAD THINKER ON YOU, BASED ON MY GENERAL ANALYSIS OF NEWS TRENDS...
...I GIVE OUR GLOBAL INFLUENCE ABOUT ANOTHER SIX DAYS AT MOST BEFORE SOMETHING SCREWS IT UP.
LIKE WHAT?
SINCE WE EMPOWERED OTHERS TO USE IT, I HAVE HAD AN INTERNAL PROCESSOR MONITORING THE WEB FOR ANY UNETHICAL USE OF THE NAME "CHAMPIONS."
IT MAKES SENSE THAT SUCH USE WOULD BE WHAT HULK FEARS.
AVENGERS

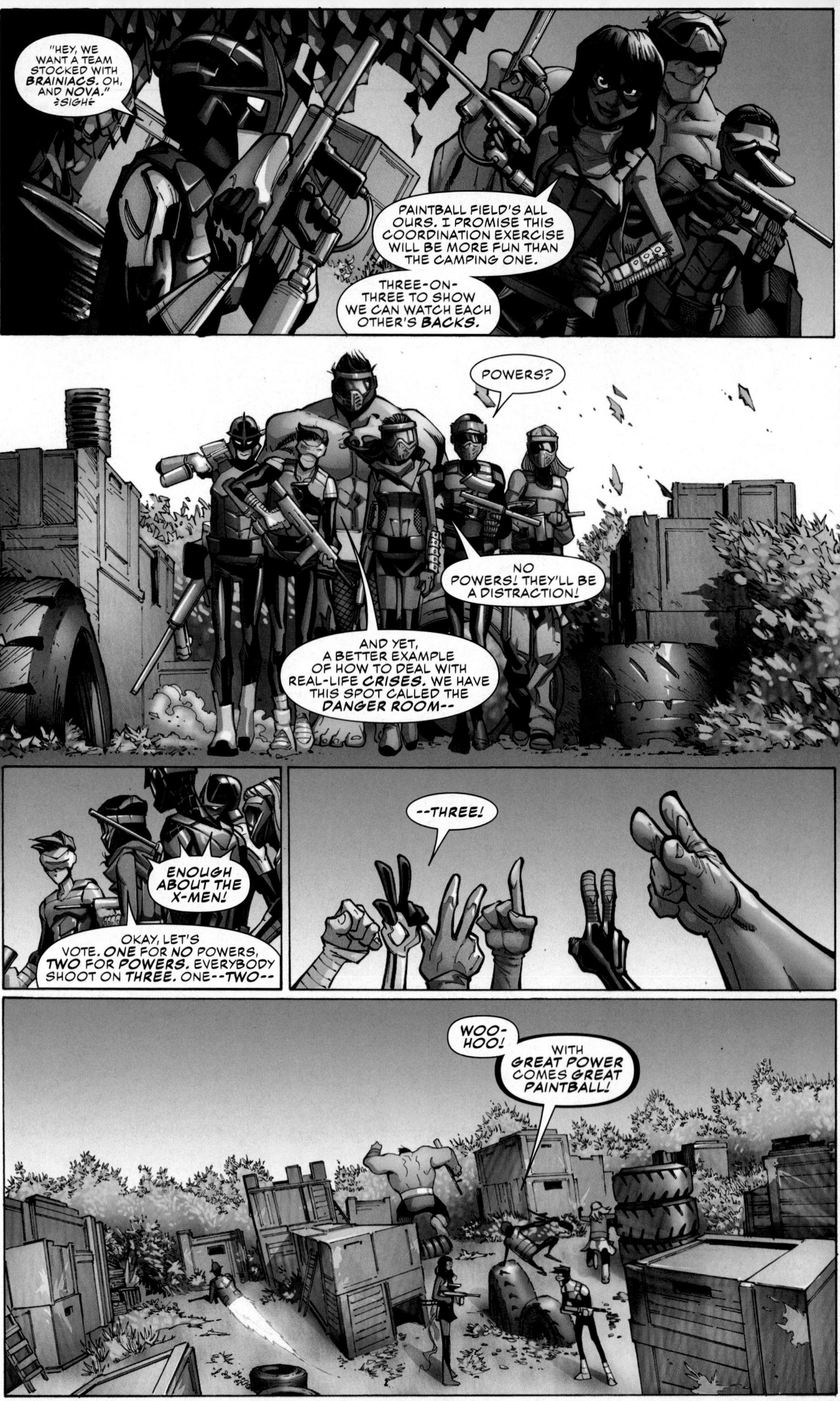

"HEY, WE WANT A TEAM STOCKED WITH BRAINIACS. OH, AND NOVA." *SIGH*
PAINTBALL FIELD'S ALL OURS. I PROMISE THIS COORDINATION EXERCISE WILL BE MORE FUN THAN THE CAMPING ONE.
THREE-ON-THREE TO SHOW WE CAN WATCH EACH OTHER'S BACKS.
POWERS?
NO POWERS! THEY'LL BE A DISTRACTION!
AND YET, A BETTER EXAMPLE OF HOW TO DEAL WITH REAL-LIFE CRISES. WE HAVE THIS SPOT CALLED THE DANGER ROOM--
ENOUGH ABOUT THE X-MEN!
OKAY, LET'S VOTE. ONE FOR NO POWERS, TWO FOR POWERS. EVERYBODY SHOOT ON THREE. ONE--TWO--
--THREE!
WOO-HOO!
WITH GREAT POWER COMES GREAT PAINTBALL!

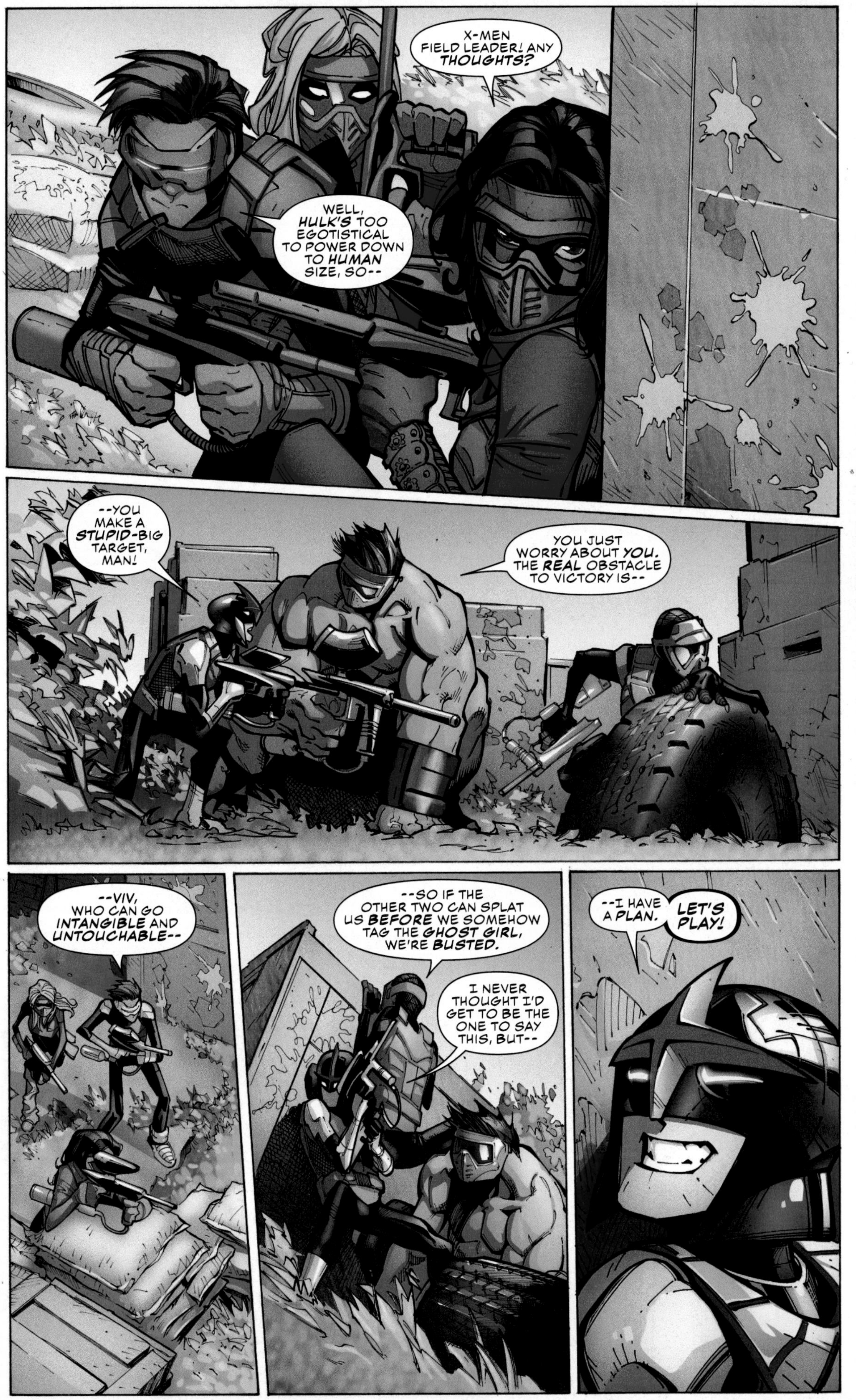
X-MEN FIELD LEADER! ANY THOUGHTS?
WELL, HULK'S TOO EGOTISTICAL TO POWER DOWN TO HUMAN SIZE, SO--
--YOU MAKE A STUPID-BIG TARGET, MAN!
YOU JUST WORRY ABOUT YOU. THE REAL OBSTACLE TO VICTORY IS--
--VIV, WHO CAN GO INTANGIBLE AND UNTOUCHABLE--
--SO IF THE OTHER TWO CAN SPLAT US BEFORE WE SOMEHOW TAG THE GHOST GIRL, WE'RE BUSTED.
I NEVER THOUGHT I'D GET TO BE THE ONE TO SAY THIS, BUT--
--I HAVE A PLAN.
LET'S PLAY!

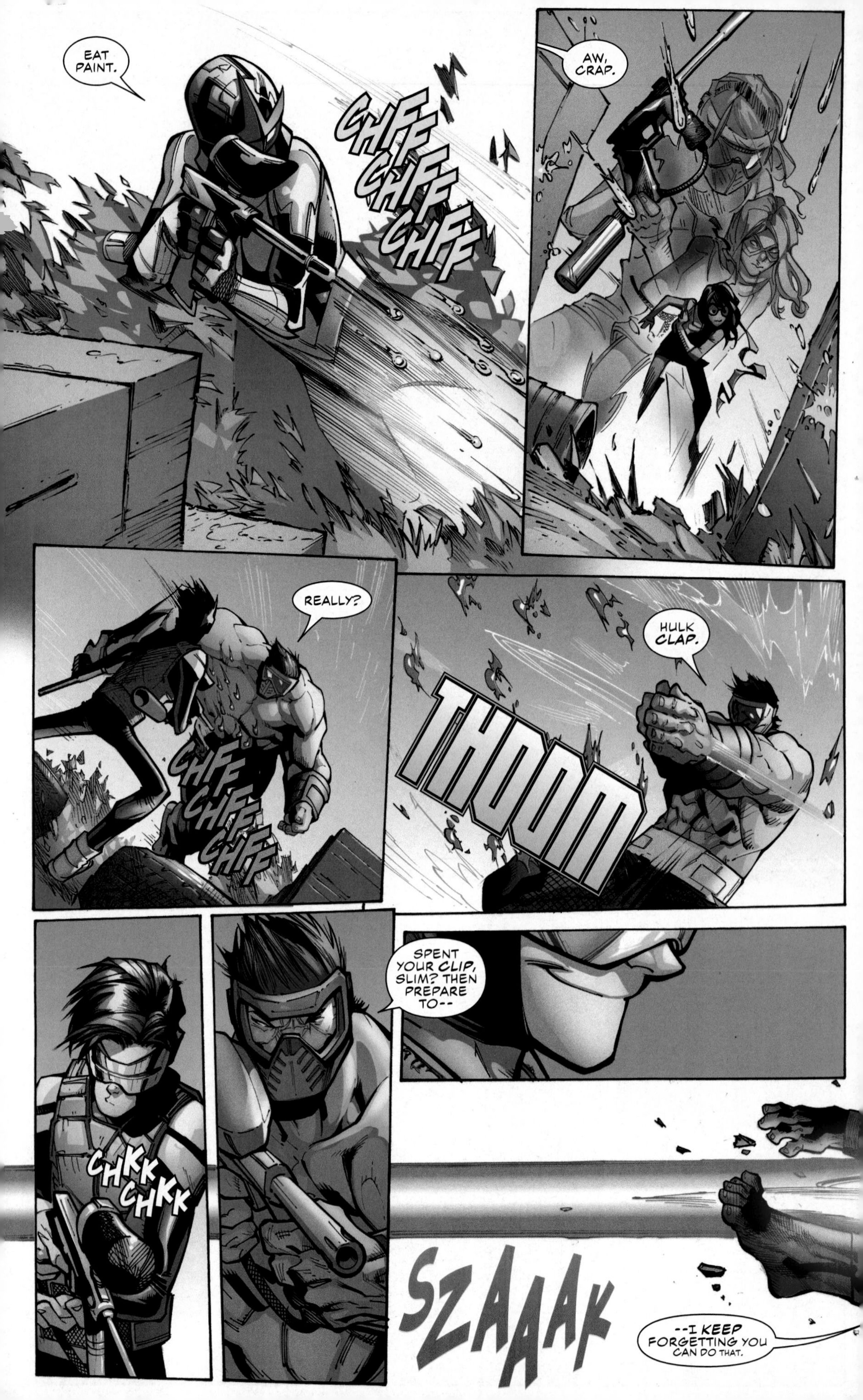
EAT PAINT.
CHFF CHFF CHFF
AW, CRAP.
REALLY?
CHFF CHFF CHFF
HULK CLAP.
THOOM
SPENT YOUR CLIP, SLIM? THEN PREPARE TO--
CHKK CHKK
SZAAAK
--I KEEP FORGETTING YOU CAN DO THAT.

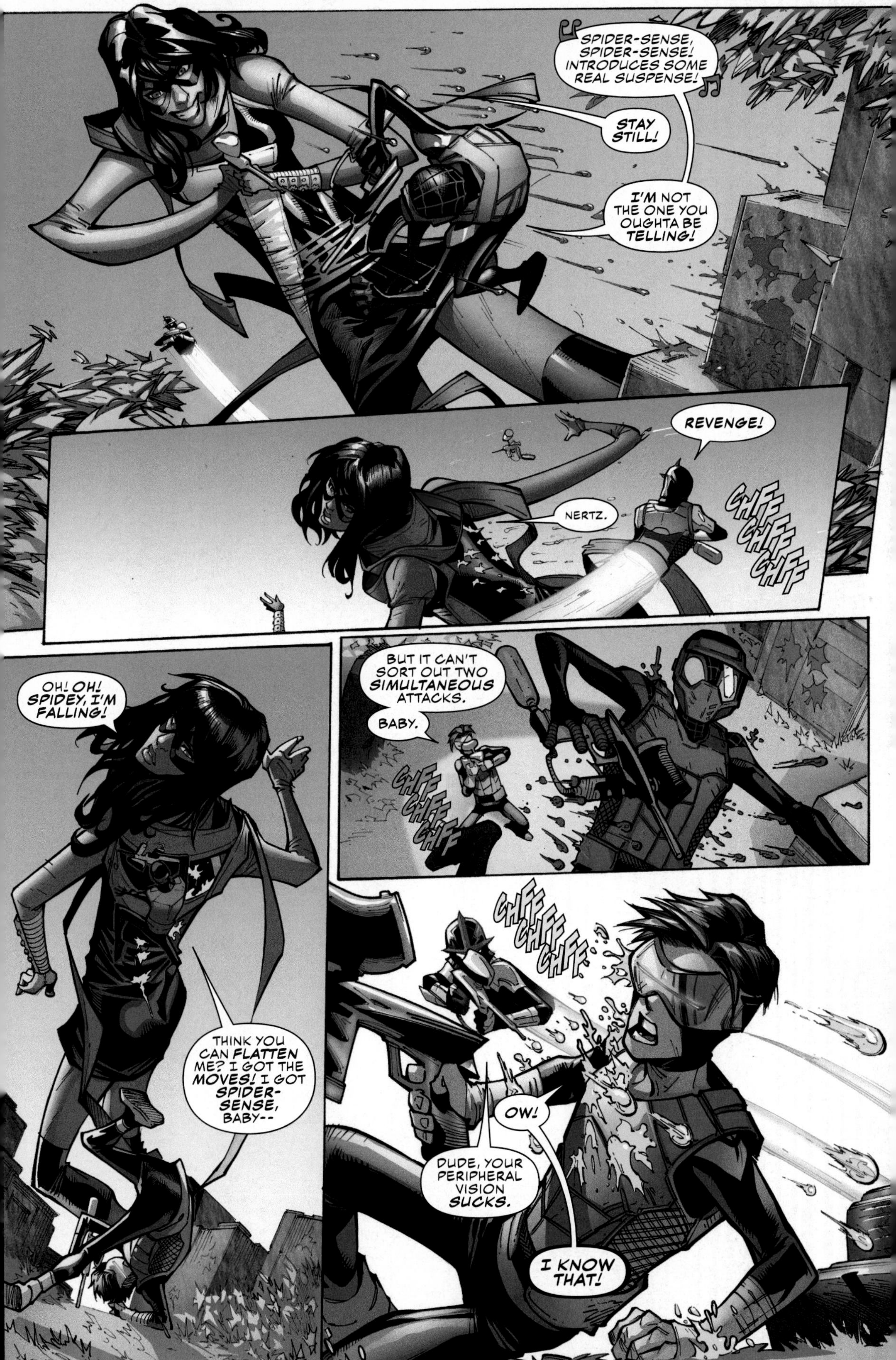
SPIDER-SENSE, SPIDER-SENSE! INTRODUCES SOME REAL SUSPENSE!
STAY STILL!
I'M NOT THE ONE YOU OUGHTA BE TELLING!
REVENGE!
NERTZ.
CHFF CHFF CHFF
OH! OH! SPIDEY, I'M FALLING!
BUT IT CAN'T SORT OUT TWO SIMULTANEOUS ATTACKS.
BABY.
CHFF CHFF CHFF
CHFF CHFF CHFF
THINK YOU CAN FLATTEN ME? I GOT THE MOVES! I GOT SPIDER-SENSE, BABY--
OW!
DUDE, YOUR PERIPHERAL VISION SUCKS.
I KNOW THAT!

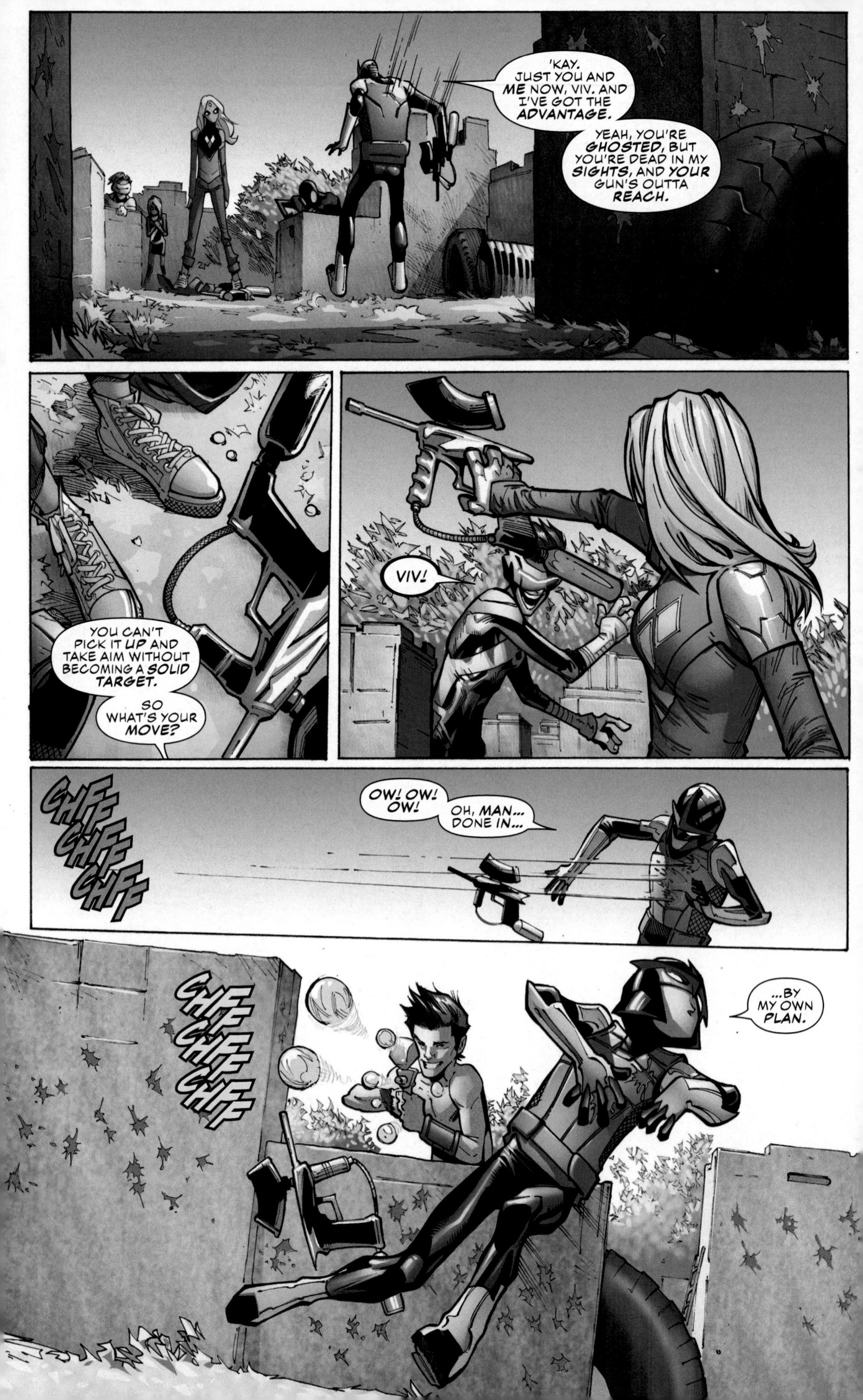
'KAY. JUST YOU AND ME NOW, VIV. AND I'VE GOT THE ADVANTAGE.
YEAH, YOU'RE GHOSTED, BUT YOU'RE DEAD IN MY SIGHTS, AND YOUR GUN'S OUTTA REACH.
YOU CAN'T PICK IT UP AND TAKE AIM WITHOUT BECOMING A SOLID TARGET.
SO WHAT'S YOUR MOVE?
VIV!
CHFF CHFF CHFF
OW! OW! OW!
OH, MAN... DONE IN...
CHFF CHFF CHFF
...BY MY OWN PLAN.

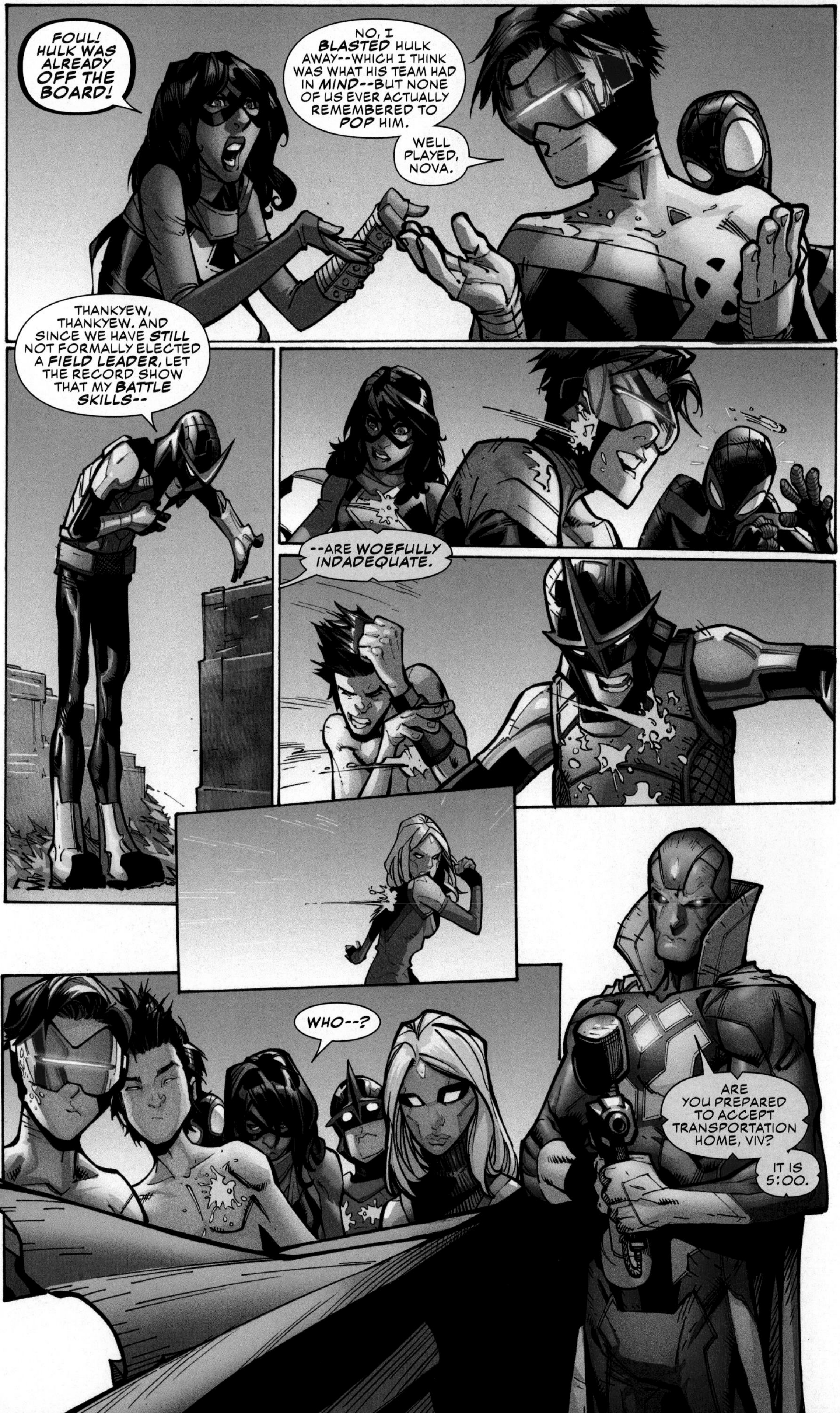

FOUL! HULK WAS ALREADY OFF THE BOARD!
NO, I BLASTED HULK AWAY--WHICH I THINK WAS WHAT HIS TEAM HAD IN MIND--BUT NONE OF US EVER ACTUALLY REMEMBERED TO POP HIM.
WELL PLAYED, NOVA.
THANKYEW, THANKYEW. AND SINCE WE HAVE STILL NOT FORMALLY ELECTED A FIELD LEADER, LET THE RECORD SHOW THAT MY BATTLE SKILLS--
--ARE WOEFULLY INDADEQUATE.
WHO--?
ARE YOU PREPARED TO ACCEPT TRANSPORTATION HOME, VIV?
IT IS 5:00.

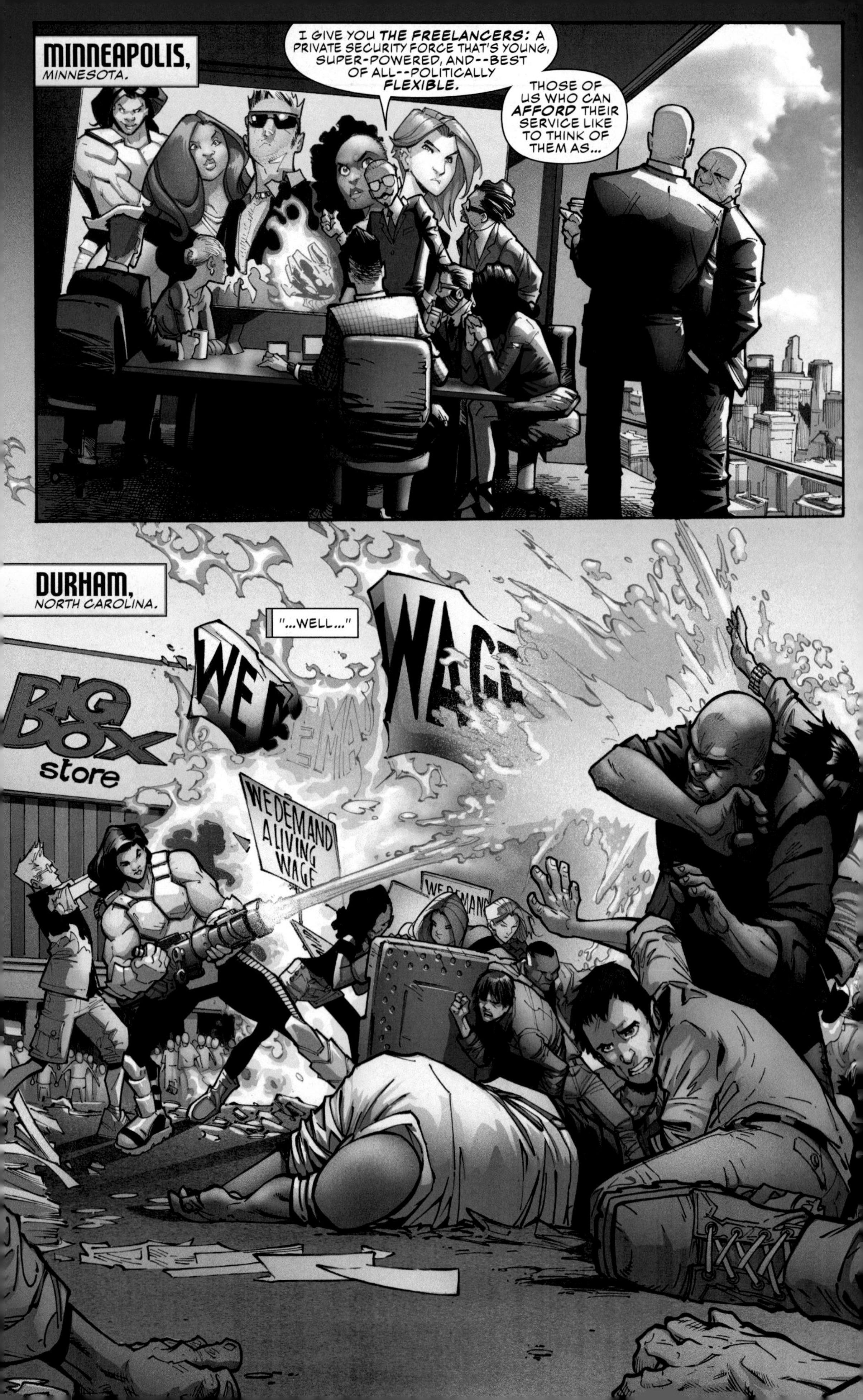
MINNEAPOLIS, MINNESOTA.
I GIVE YOU THE FREELANCERS: A PRIVATE SECURITY FORCE THAT'S YOUNG, SUPER-POWERED, AND--BEST OF ALL--POLITICALLY FLEXIBLE.
THOSE OF US WHO CAN AFFORD THEIR SERVICE LIKE TO THINK OF THEM AS...
DURHAM, NORTH CAROLINA.
"...WELL..."
BIG BOX store
WE DEMAND A LIVING WAGE

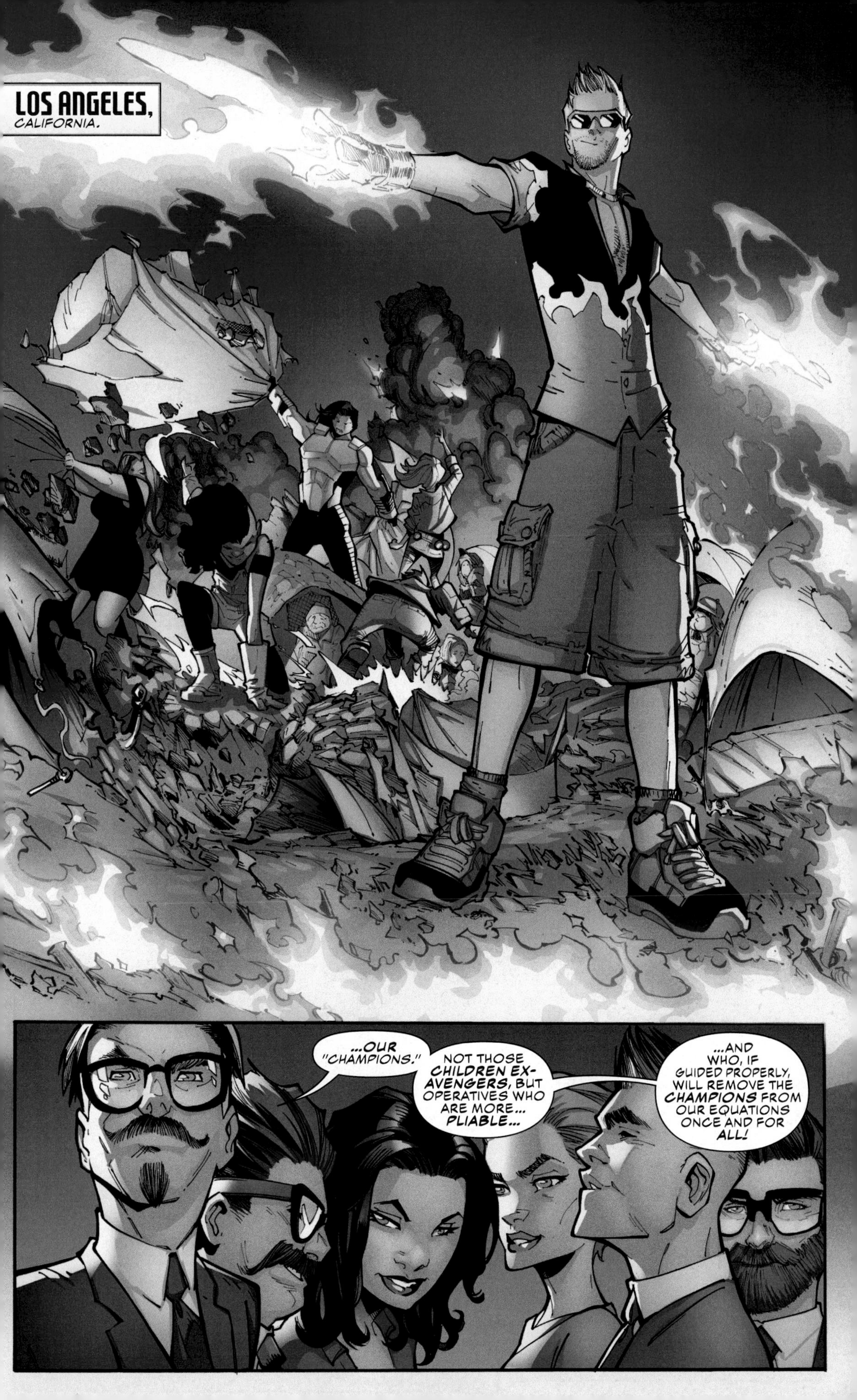
LOS ANGELES, CALIFORNIA.
...OUR "CHAMPIONS."
NOT THOSE CHILDREN EX-AVENGERS, BUT OPERATIVES WHO ARE MORE... PLIABLE...
...AND WHO, IF GUIDED PROPERLY, WILL REMOVE THE CHAMPIONS FROM OUR EQUATIONS ONCE AND FOR ALL!

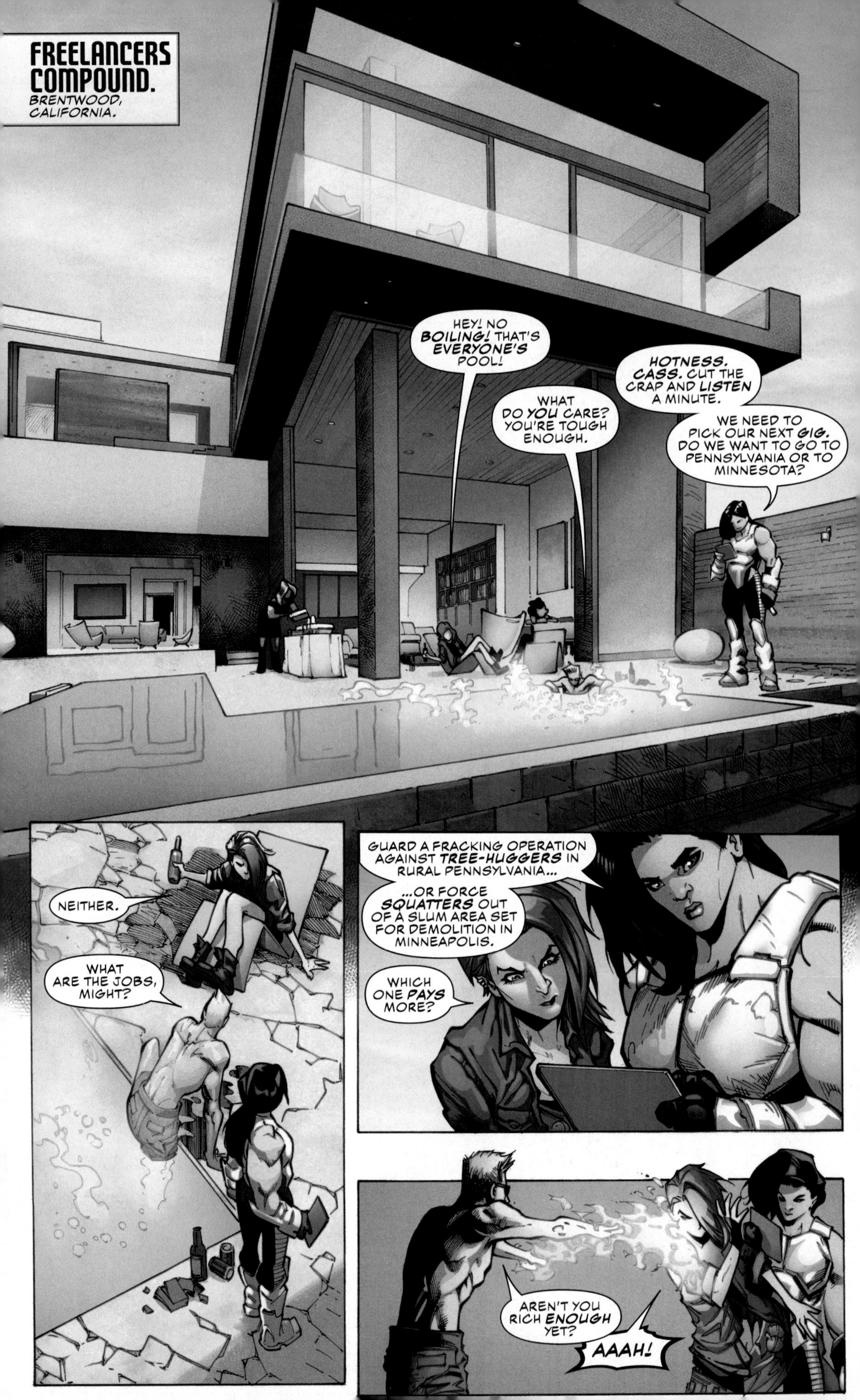
FREELANCERS COMPOUND.
BRENTWOOD, CALIFORNIA.
HEY! NO BOILING! THAT'S EVERYONE'S POOL!
WHAT DO YOU CARE? YOU'RE TOUGH ENOUGH.
HOTNESS. CASS. CUT THE CRAP AND LISTEN A MINUTE.
WE NEED TO PICK OUR NEXT GIG. DO WE WANT TO GO TO PENNSYLVANIA OR TO MINNESOTA?
NEITHER.
WHAT ARE THE JOBS, MIGHT?
GUARD A FRACKING OPERATION AGAINST TREE-HUGGERS IN RURAL PENNSYLVANIA...
...OR FORCE SQUATTERS OUT OF A SLUM AREA SET FOR DEMOLITION IN MINNEAPOLIS.
WHICH ONE PAYS MORE?
AREN'T YOU RICH ENOUGH YET?
AAAH!

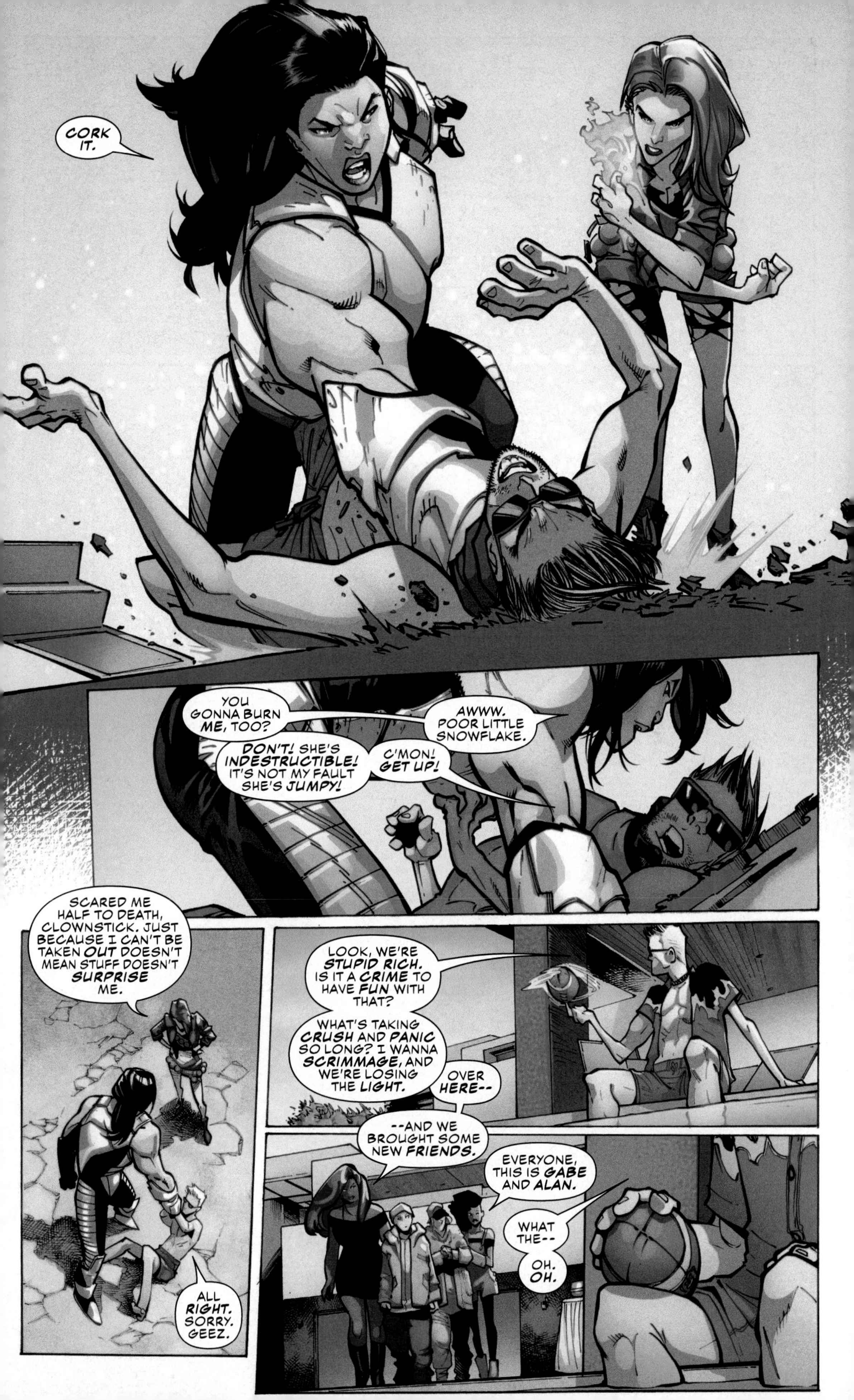
CORK IT.
YOU GONNA BURN ME, TOO?
AWWW. POOR LITTLE SNOWFLAKE.
DON'T! SHE'S INDESTRUCTIBLE! IT'S NOT MY FAULT SHE'S JUMPY!
C'MON! GET UP!
SCARED ME HALF TO DEATH, CLOWNSTICK. JUST BECAUSE I CAN'T BE TAKEN OUT DOESN'T MEAN STUFF DOESN'T SURPRISE ME.
ALL RIGHT. SORRY. GEEZ.
LOOK, WE'RE STUPID RICH. IS IT A CRIME TO HAVE FUN WITH THAT?
WHAT'S TAKING CRUSH AND PANIC SO LONG? I WANNA SCRIMMAGE, AND WE'RE LOSING THE LIGHT.
OVER HERE--
--AND WE BROUGHT SOME NEW FRIENDS.
EVERYONE, THIS IS GABE AND ALAN.
WHAT THE--
OH. OH.

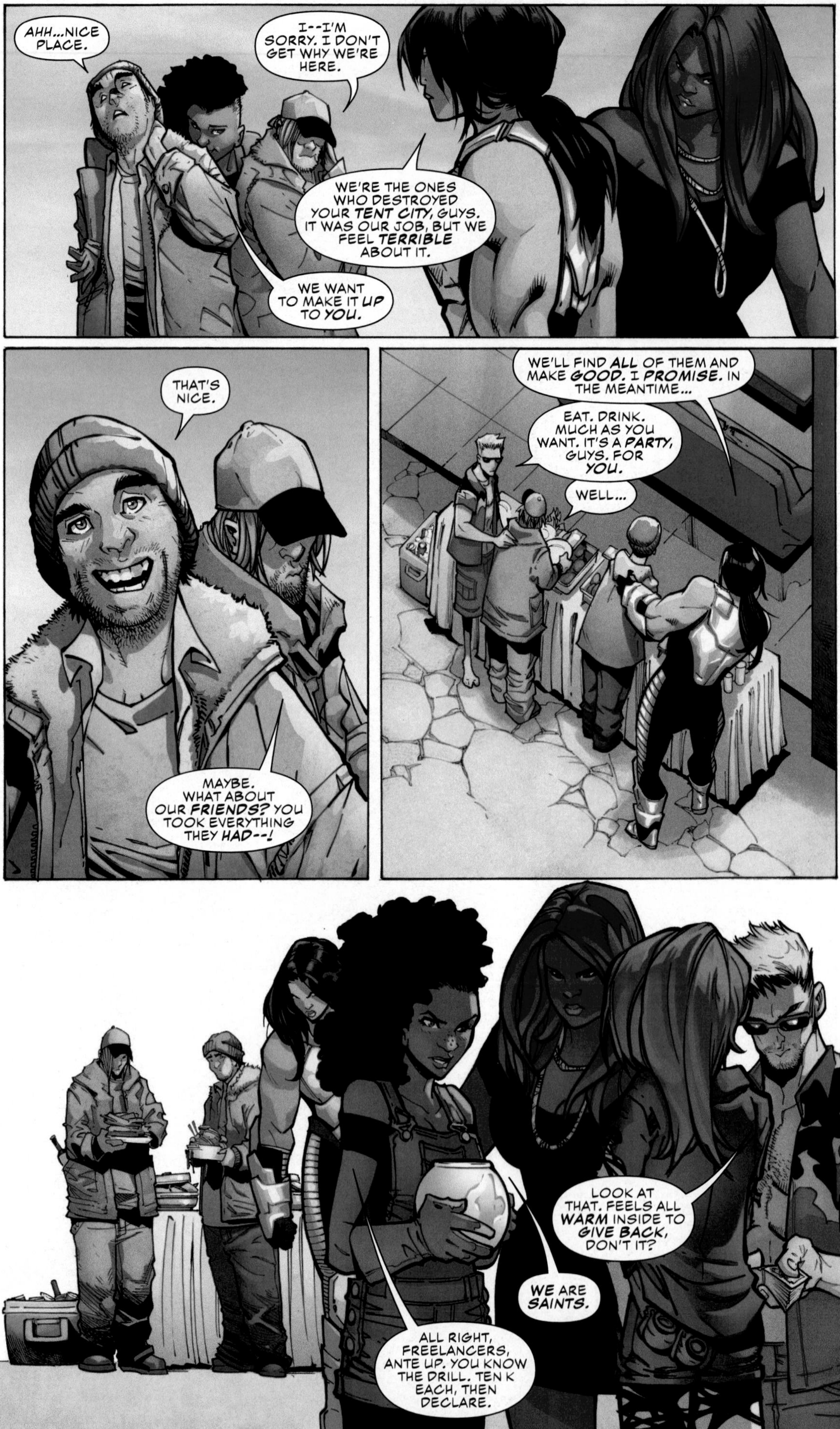
AHH...NICE PLACE.
I--I'M SORRY. I DON'T GET WHY WE'RE HERE.
WE'RE THE ONES WHO DESTROYED YOUR TENT CITY, GUYS. IT WAS OUR JOB, BUT WE FEEL TERRIBLE ABOUT IT.
WE WANT TO MAKE IT UP TO YOU.
THAT'S NICE.
MAYBE. WHAT ABOUT OUR FRIENDS? YOU TOOK EVERYTHING THEY HAD--!
WE'LL FIND ALL OF THEM AND MAKE GOOD. I PROMISE. IN THE MEANTIME...
EAT. DRINK. MUCH AS YOU WANT. IT'S A PARTY, GUYS. FOR YOU.
WELL...
LOOK AT THAT. FEELS ALL WARM INSIDE TO GIVE BACK, DON'T IT?
WE ARE SAINTS.
ALL RIGHT, FREELANCERS, ANTE UP. YOU KNOW THE DRILL. TEN K EACH, THEN DECLARE.

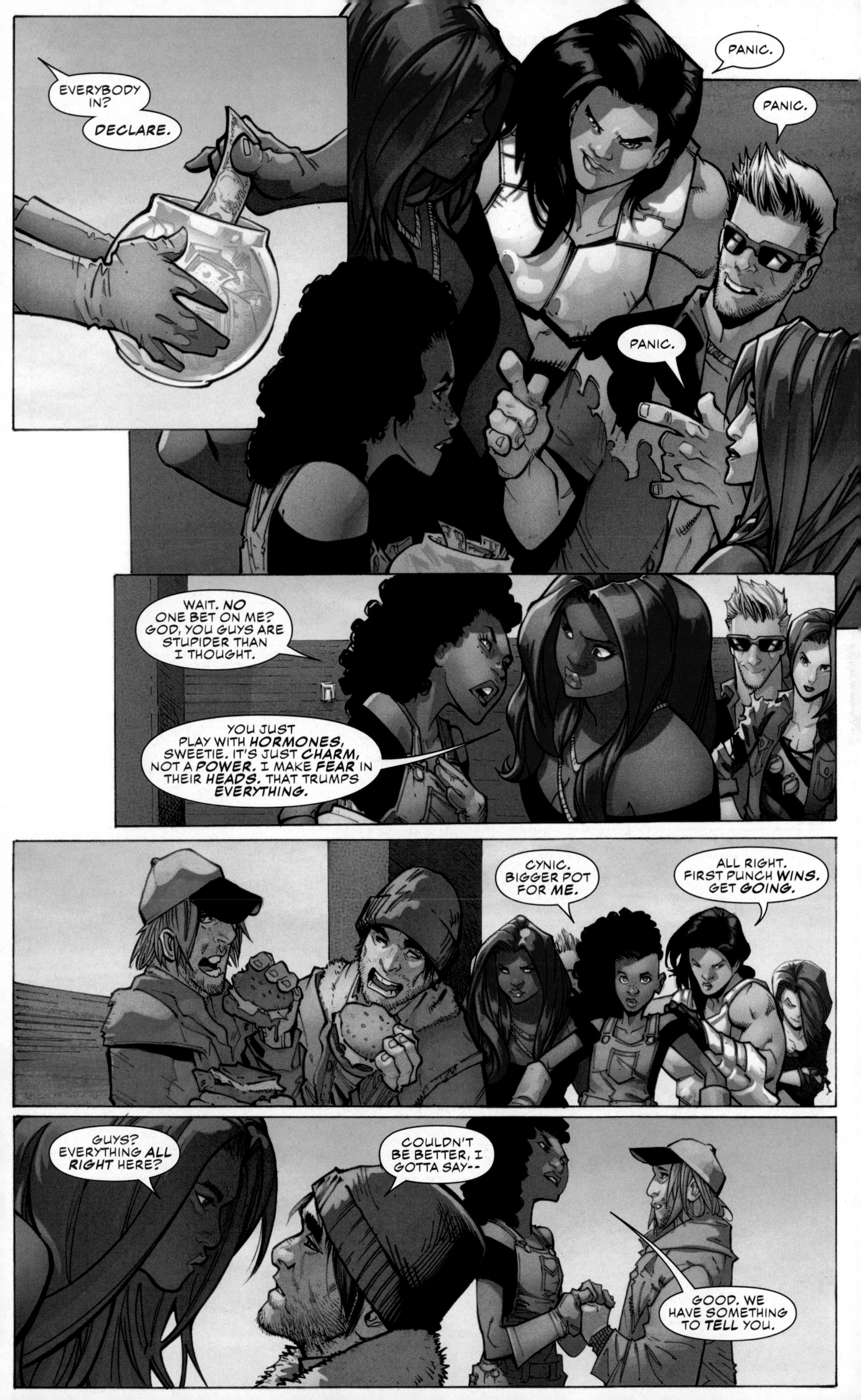
EVERYBODY IN?
DECLARE.
PANIC.
PANIC.
PANIC.
WAIT. NO ONE BET ON ME? GOD, YOU GUYS ARE STUPIDER THAN I THOUGHT.
YOU JUST PLAY WITH HORMONES, SWEETIE. IT'S JUST CHARM, NOT A POWER. I MAKE FEAR IN THEIR HEADS. THAT TRUMPS EVERYTHING.
CYNIC. BIGGER POT FOR ME.
ALL RIGHT. FIRST PUNCH WINS. GET GOING.
GUYS? EVERYTHING ALL RIGHT HERE?
COULDN'T BE BETTER, I GOTTA SAY--
GOOD. WE HAVE SOMETHING TO TELL YOU.

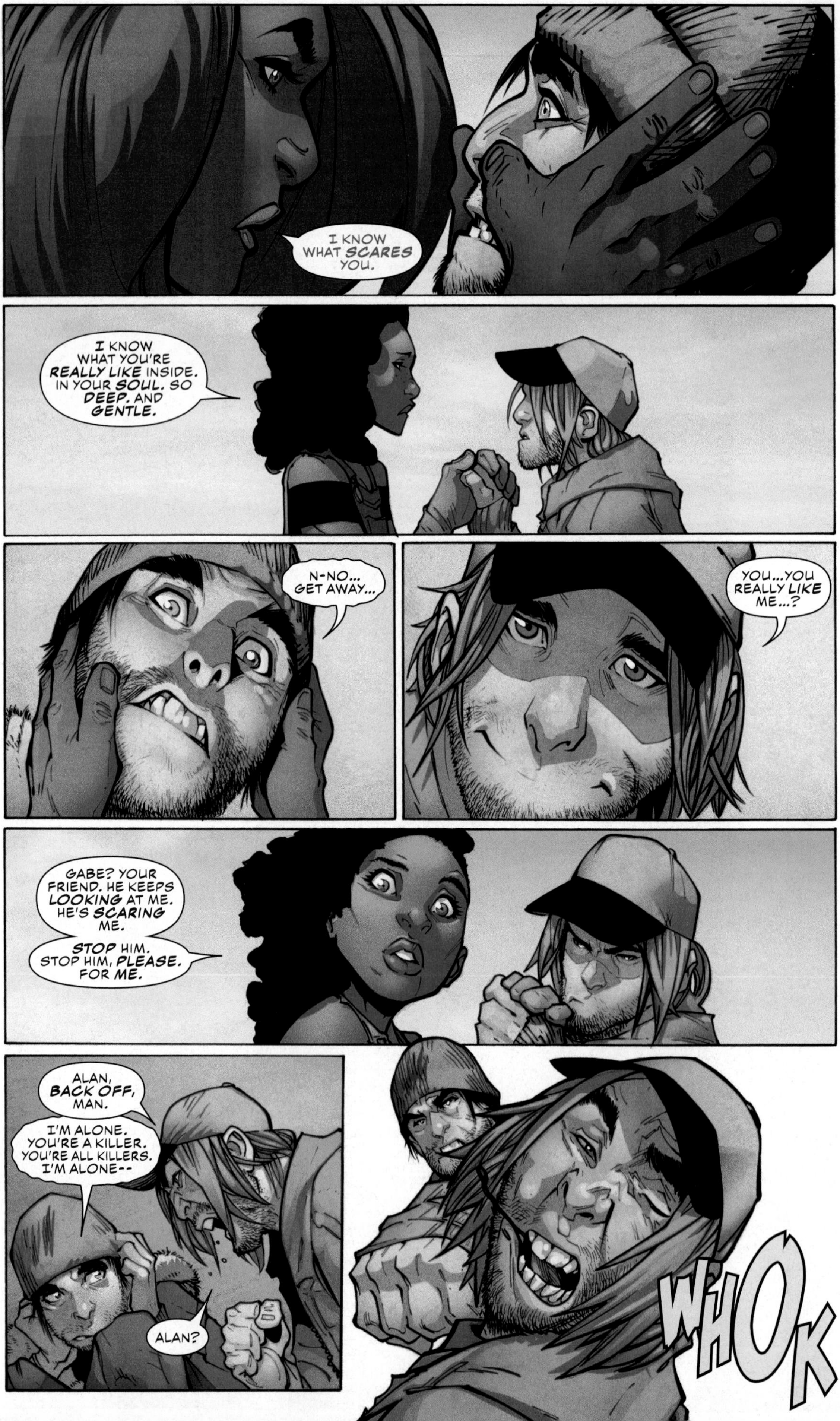
I KNOW WHAT SCARES YOU.
I KNOW WHAT YOU'RE REALLY LIKE INSIDE. IN YOUR SOUL. SO DEEP. AND GENTLE.
N-NO... GET AWAY...
YOU...YOU REALLY LIKE ME...?
GABE? YOUR FRIEND. HE KEEPS LOOKING AT ME. HE'S SCARING ME.
STOP HIM. STOP HIM, PLEASE. FOR ME.
ALAN, BACK OFF, MAN.
I'M ALONE. YOU'RE A KILLER. YOU'RE ALL KILLERS. I'M ALONE--
ALAN?
WHOK

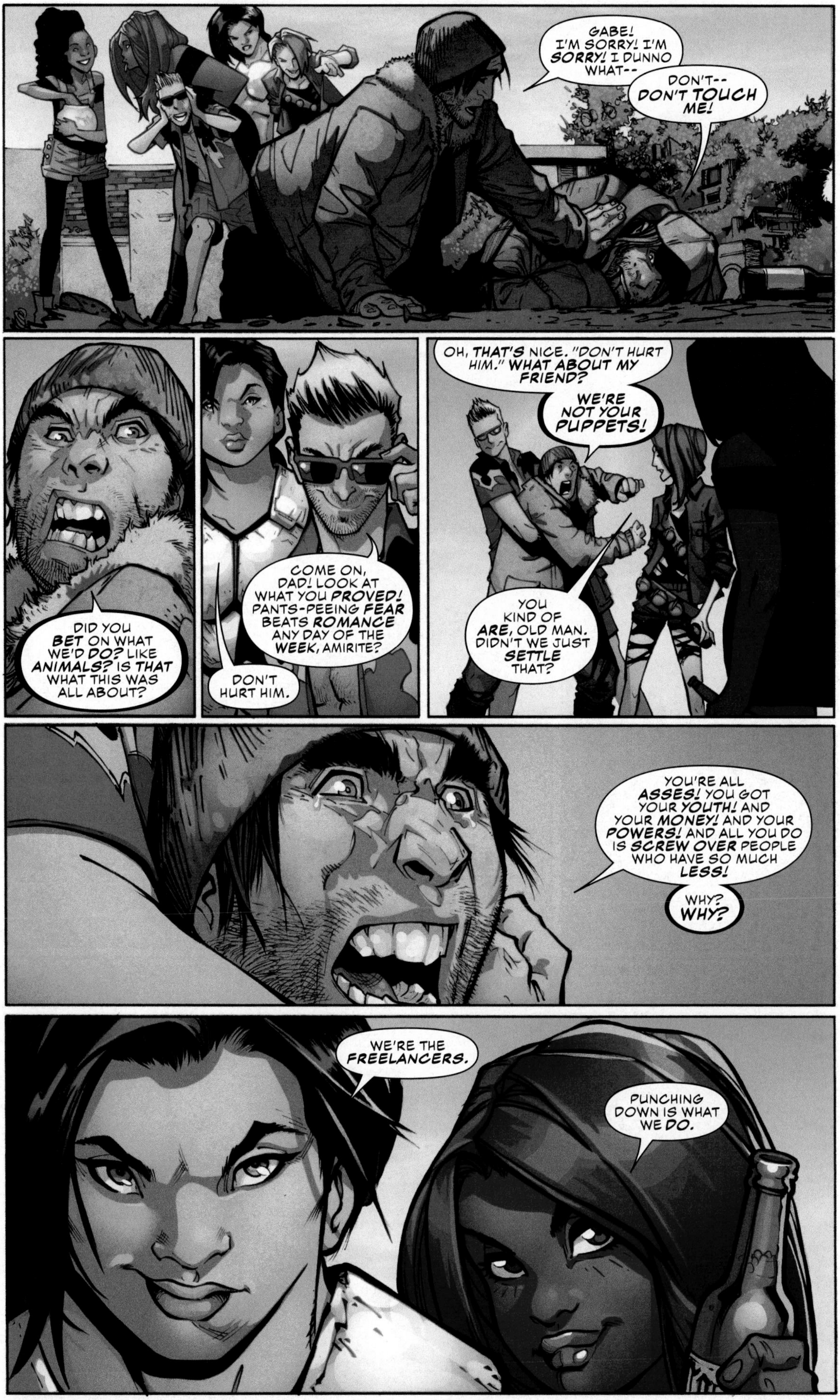
GABE! I'M SORRY! I'M SORRY! I DUNNO WHAT--
DON'T-- DON'T TOUCH ME!
DID YOU BET ON WHAT WE'D DO? LIKE ANIMALS? IS THAT WHAT THIS WAS ALL ABOUT?
COME ON, DAD! LOOK AT WHAT YOU PROVED! PANTS-PEEING FEAR BEATS ROMANCE ANY DAY OF THE WEEK, AMIRITE?
DON'T HURT HIM.
OH, THAT'S NICE. "DON'T HURT HIM." WHAT ABOUT MY FRIEND?
WE'RE NOT YOUR PUPPETS!
YOU KIND OF ARE, OLD MAN. DIDN'T WE JUST SETTLE THAT?
YOU'RE ALL ASSES! YOU GOT YOUR YOUTH! AND YOUR MONEY! AND YOUR POWERS! AND ALL YOU DO IS SCREW OVER PEOPLE WHO HAVE SO MUCH LESS!
WHY? WHY?
WE'RE THE FREELANCERS.
PUNCHING DOWN IS WHAT WE DO.

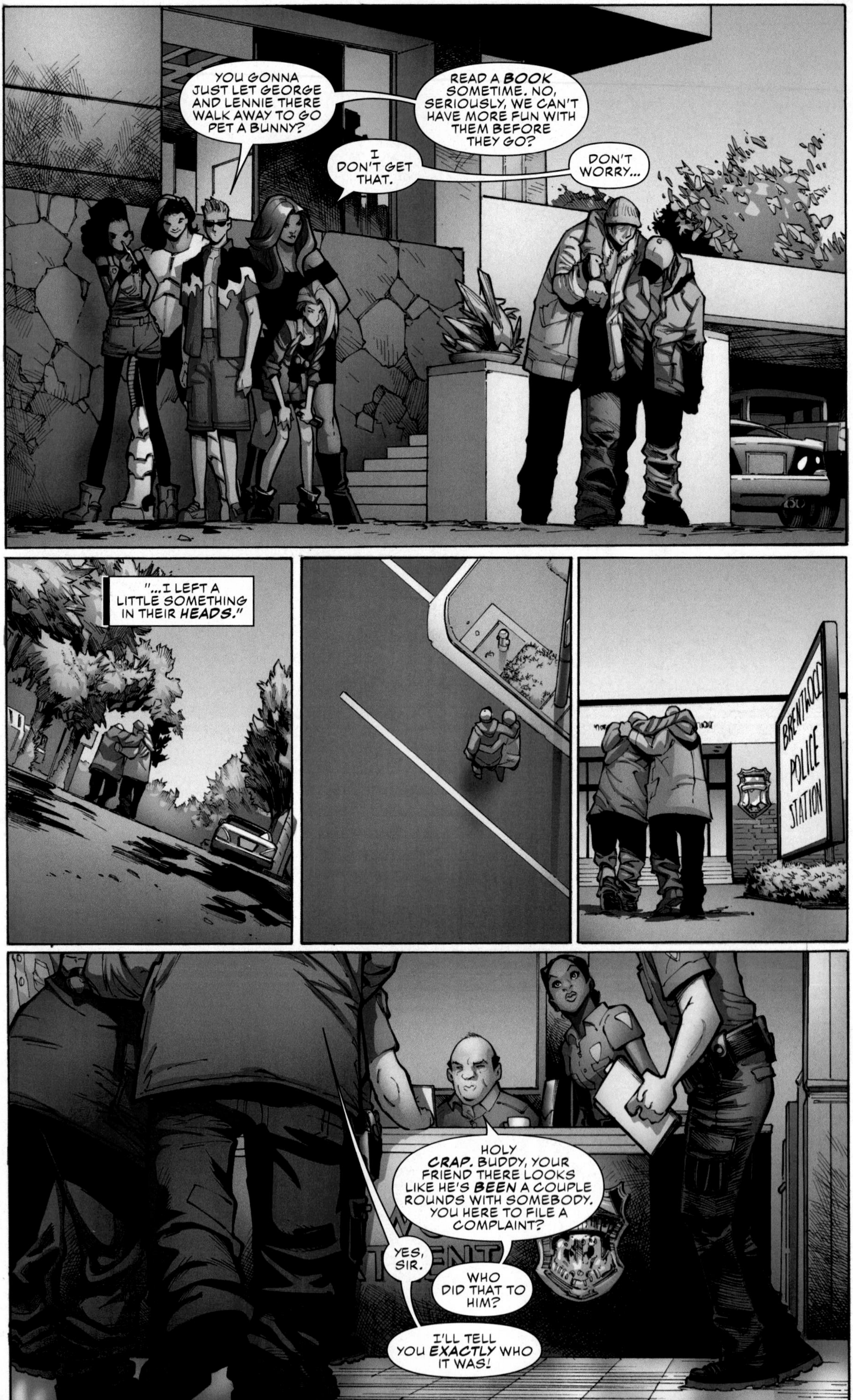

YOU GONNA JUST LET GEORGE AND LENNIE THERE WALK AWAY TO GO PET A BUNNY?
READ A BOOK SOMETIME. NO, SERIOUSLY, WE CAN'T HAVE MORE FUN WITH THEM BEFORE THEY GO?
I DON'T GET THAT.
DON'T WORRY...
"...I LEFT A LITTLE SOMETHING IN THEIR HEADS."
BRENTWOOD POLICE STATION
HOLY CRAP. BUDDY, YOUR FRIEND THERE LOOKS LIKE HE'S BEEN A COUPLE ROUNDS WITH SOMEBODY. YOU HERE TO FILE A COMPLAINT?
YES, SIR.
WHO DID THAT TO HIM?
I'LL TELL YOU EXACTLY WHO IT WAS!

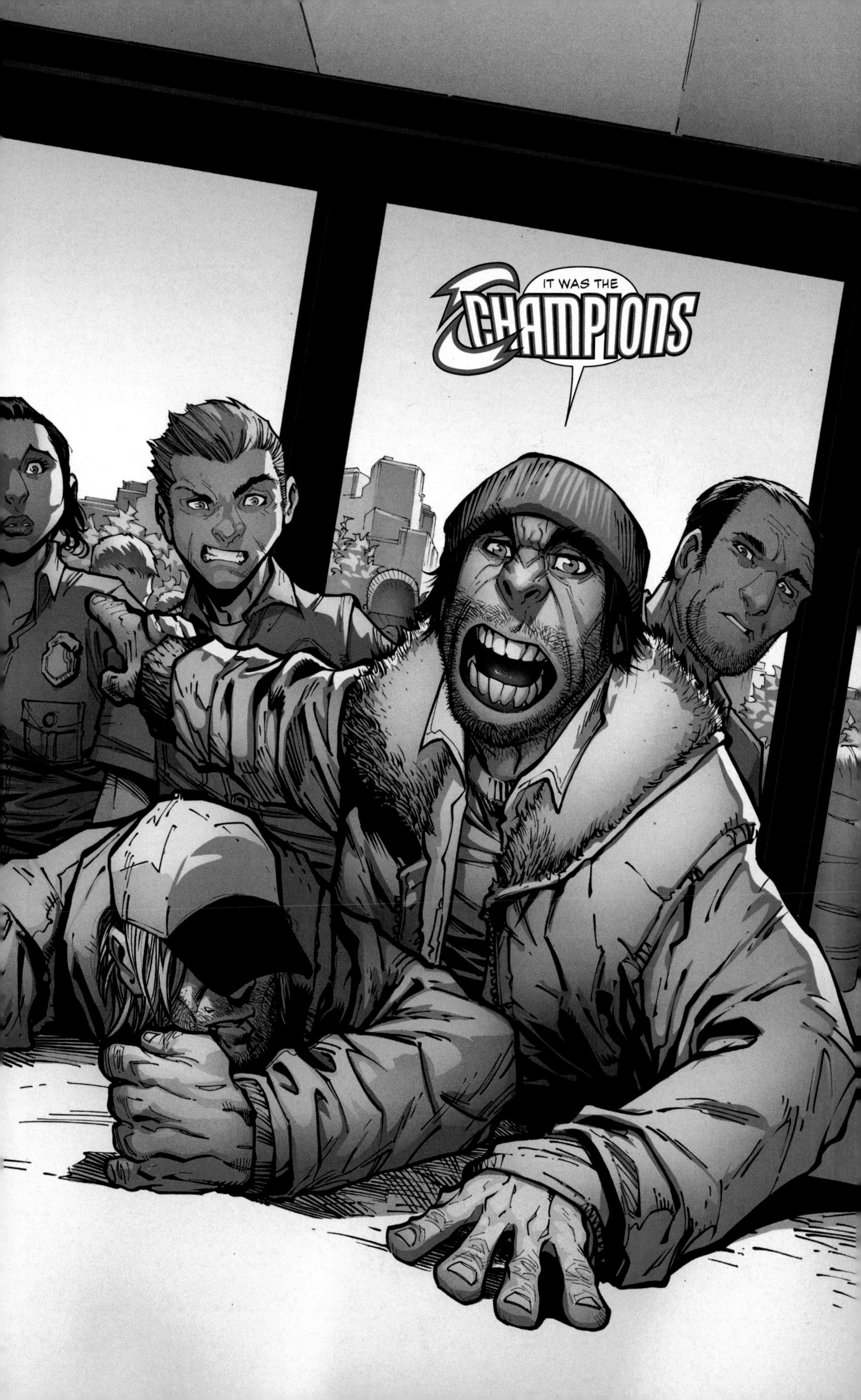
IT WAS THE CHAMPIONS

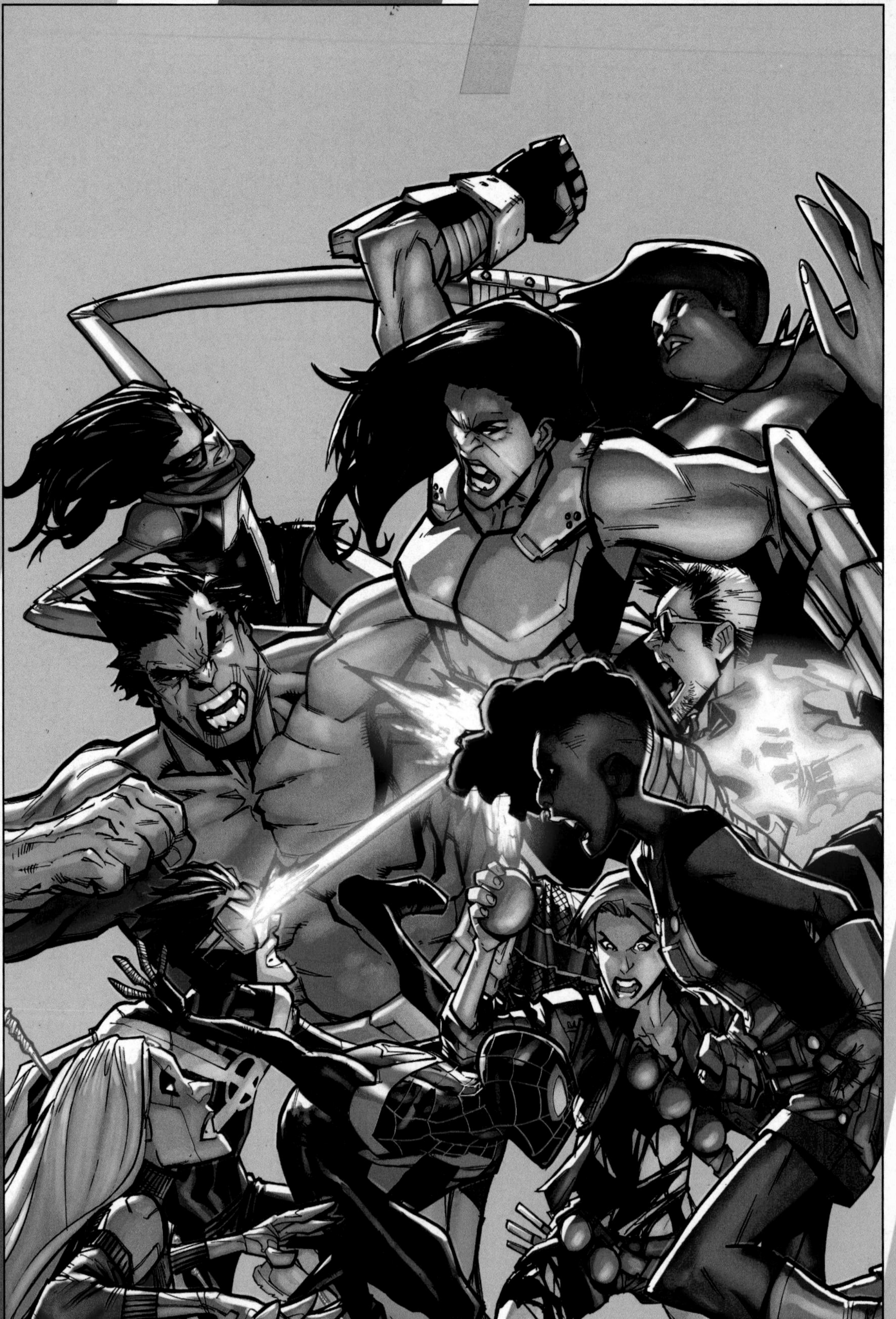
RAMOS 16
delgado

7

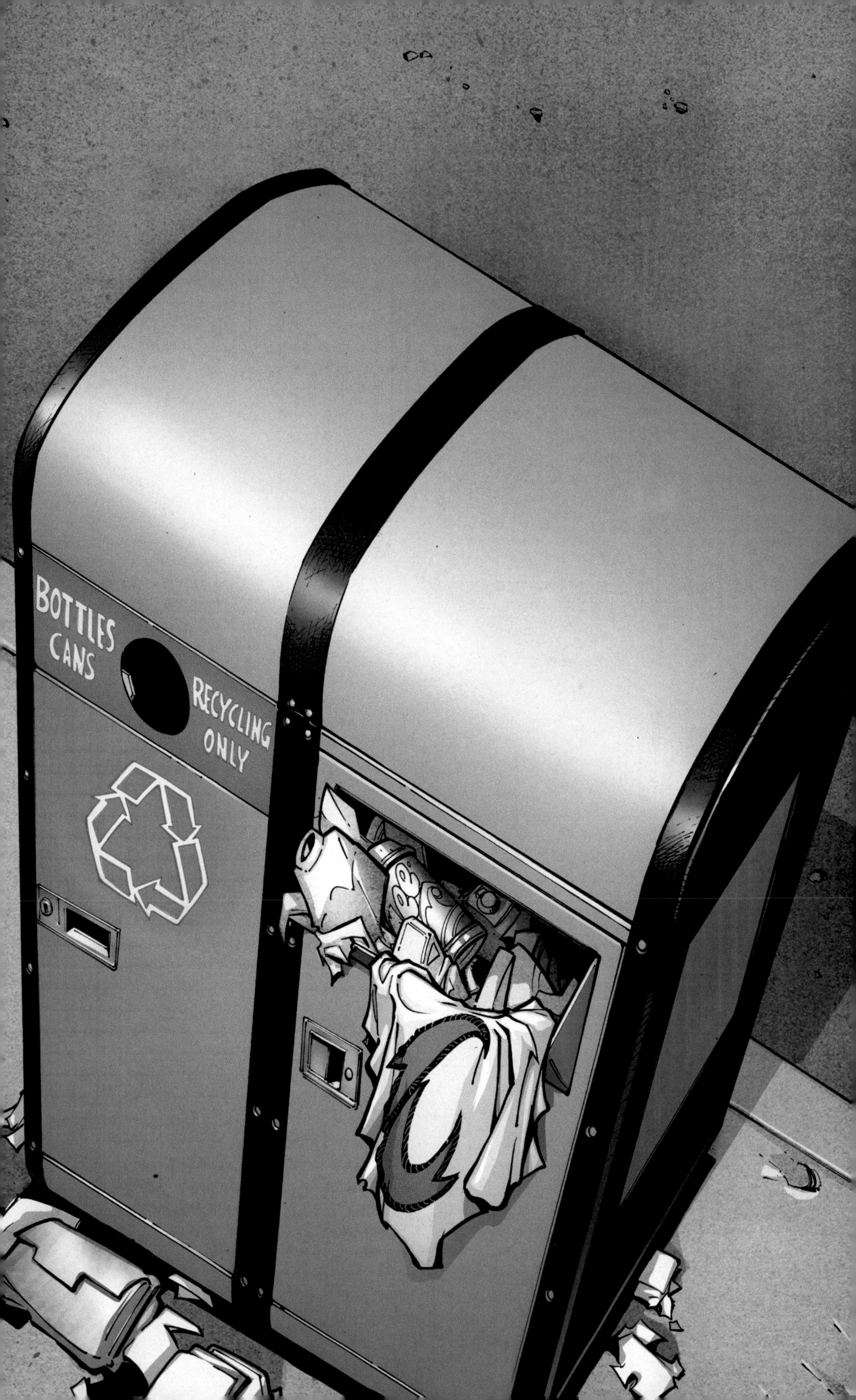
BOTTLES
CANS
RECYCLING
ONLY

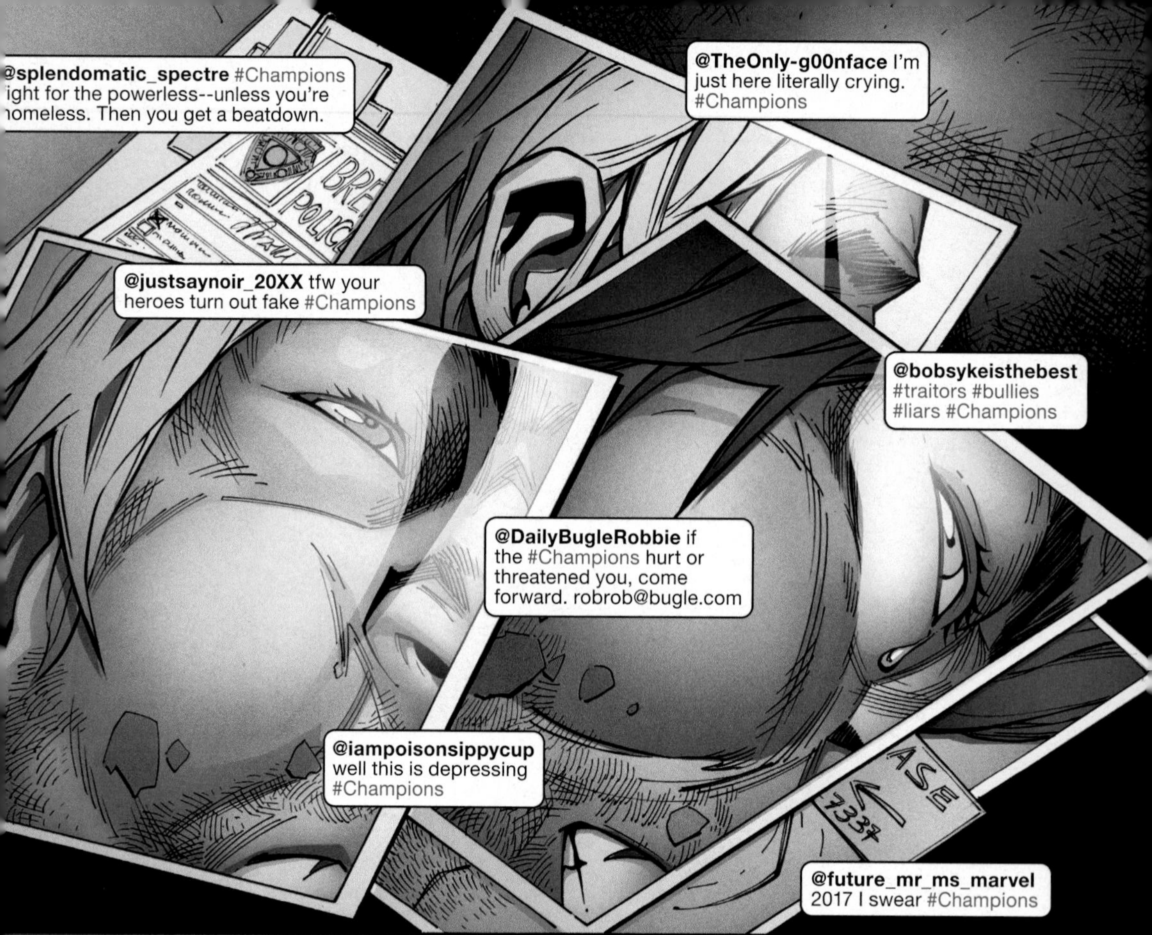
@splendomatic_spectre #Champions ight for the powerless--unless you're iomeless. Then you get a beatdown.
@TheOnly-g00nface I'm just here literally crying. #Champions
BRE POLICE
@justsaynoir_20XX tfw your heroes turn out fake #Champions
@bobsykeisthebest #traitors #bullies #liars #Champions
@DailyBugleRobbie if the #Champions hurt or threatened you, come forward. robrob@bugle.com
@iampoisonsippycup well this is depressing #Champions
ASE
7337
@future_mr_ms_marvel 2017 I swear #Champions

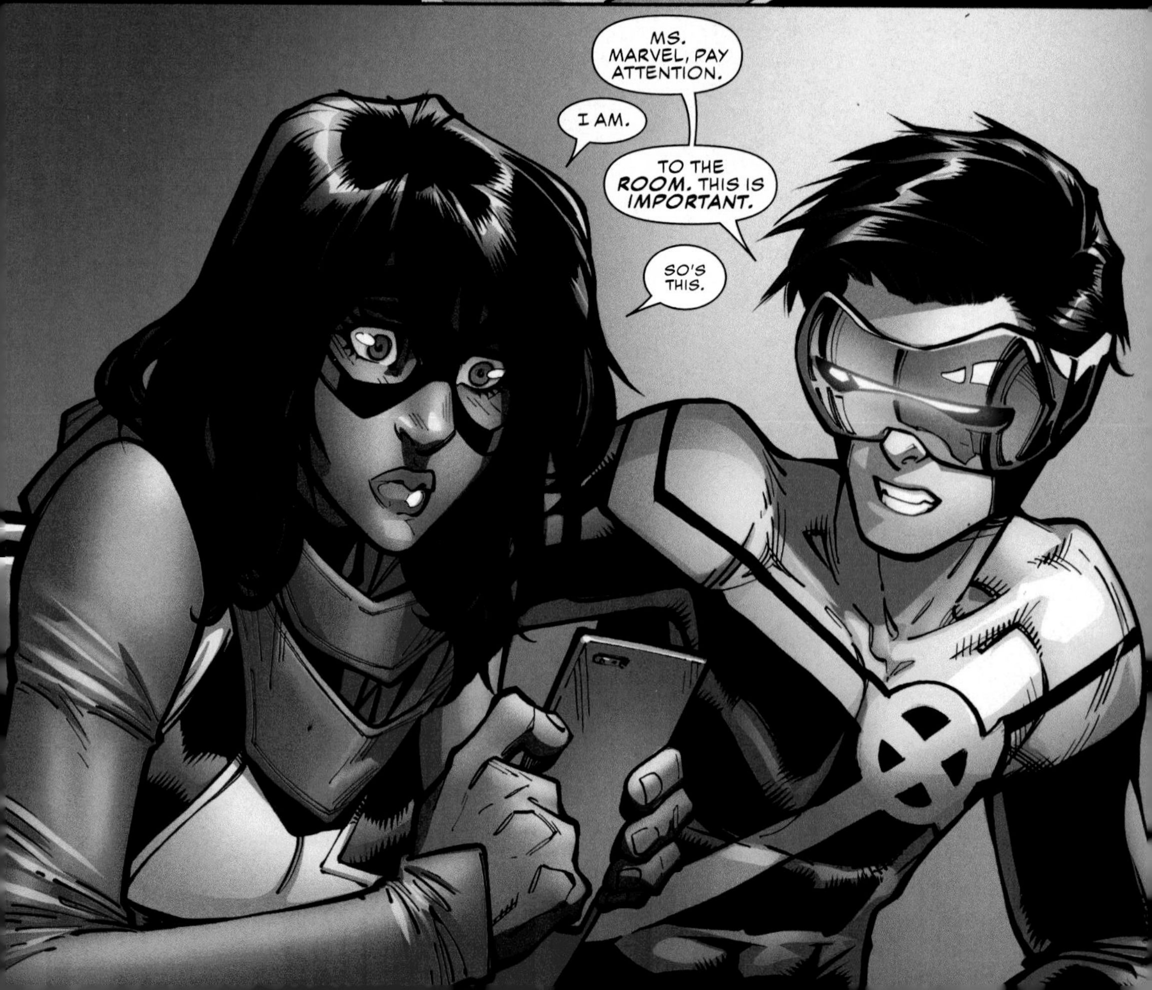
MS. MARVEL, PAY ATTENTION.
I AM.
TO THE ROOM. THIS IS IMPORTANT.
SO'S THIS.

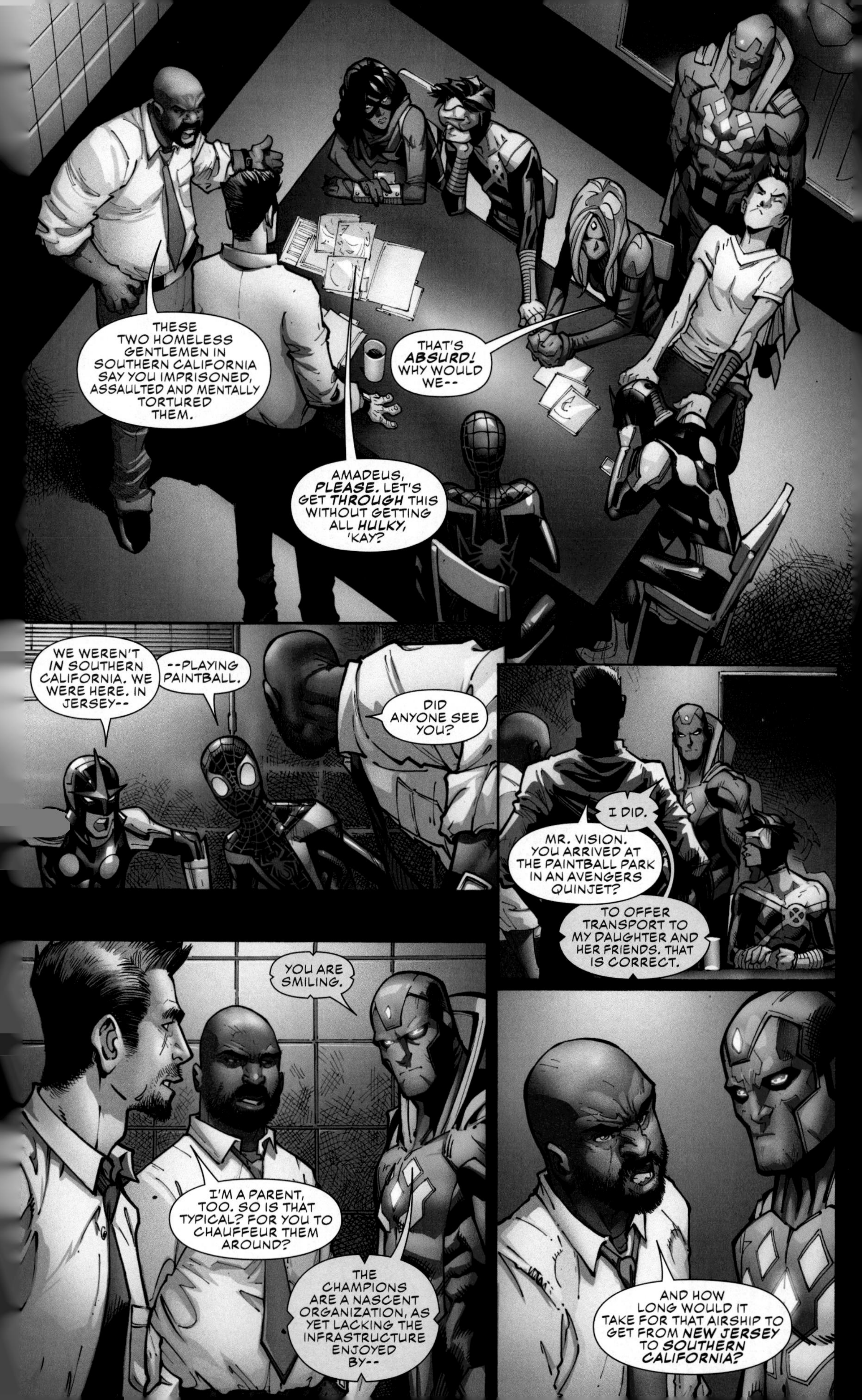
THESE TWO HOMELESS GENTLEMEN IN SOUTHERN CALIFORNIA SAY YOU IMPRISONED, ASSAULTED AND MENTALLY TORTURED THEM.
THAT'S **ABSURD!** WHY WOULD WE--
AMADEUS, **PLEASE.** LET'S GET **THROUGH** THIS WITHOUT GETTING ALL **HULKY,** 'KAY?
WE WEREN'T **IN** SOUTHERN CALIFORNIA. WE WERE HERE. IN JERSEY--
--PLAYING PAINTBALL.
DID ANYONE SEE YOU?
I DID.
MR. VISION. YOU ARRIVED AT THE PAINTBALL PARK IN AN AVENGERS QUINJET?
TO OFFER TRANSPORT TO MY DAUGHTER AND HER FRIENDS. THAT IS CORRECT.
YOU ARE SMILING.
I'M A PARENT, TOO. SO IS THAT TYPICAL? FOR YOU TO CHAUFFEUR THEM AROUND?
THE CHAMPIONS ARE A NASCENT ORGANIZATION, AS YET LACKING THE INFRASTRUCTURE ENJOYED BY--
AND HOW LONG WOULD IT TAKE FOR THAT AIRSHIP TO GET FROM **NEW JERSEY** TO **SOUTHERN CALIFORNIA?**

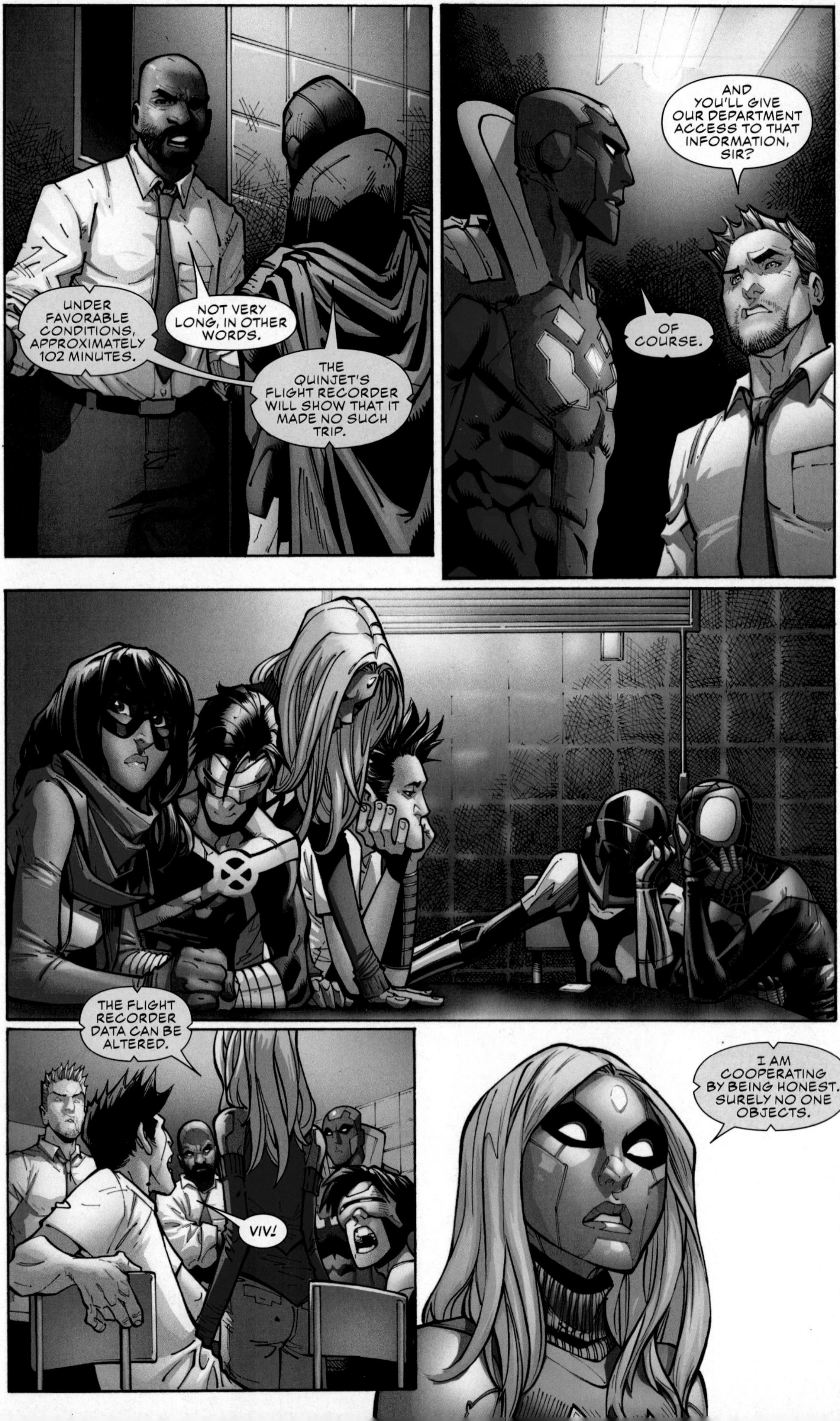
UNDER FAVORABLE CONDITIONS, APPROXIMATELY 102 MINUTES.
NOT VERY LONG, IN OTHER WORDS.
THE QUINJET'S FLIGHT RECORDER WILL SHOW THAT IT MADE NO SUCH TRIP.
AND YOU'LL GIVE OUR DEPARTMENT ACCESS TO THAT INFORMATION, SIR?
OF COURSE.
THE FLIGHT RECORDER DATA CAN BE ALTERED.
VIV!
I AM COOPERATING BY BEING HONEST. SURELY NO ONE OBJECTS.

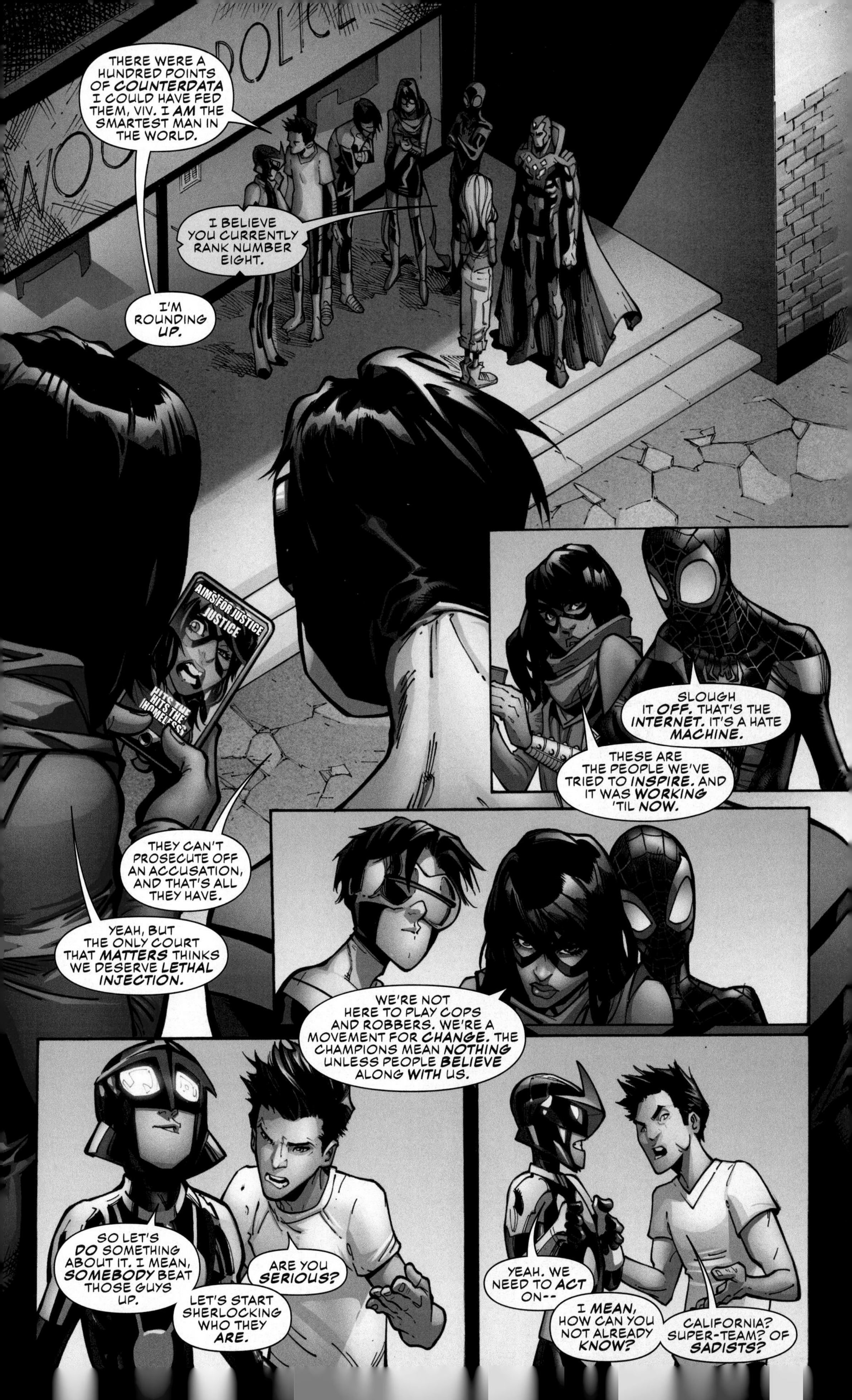
THERE WERE A HUNDRED POINTS OF COUNTERDATA I COULD HAVE FED THEM, VIV. I AM THE SMARTEST MAN IN THE WORLD.
I BELIEVE YOU CURRENTLY RANK NUMBER EIGHT.
I'M ROUNDING UP.
AIMS FOR JUSTICE
SLOUGH IT OFF. THAT'S THE INTERNET. IT'S A HATE MACHINE.
THESE ARE THE PEOPLE WE'VE TRIED TO INSPIRE. AND IT WAS WORKING 'TIL NOW.
THEY CAN'T PROSECUTE OFF AN ACCUSATION, AND THAT'S ALL THEY HAVE.
YEAH, BUT THE ONLY COURT THAT MATTERS THINKS WE DESERVE LETHAL INJECTION.
WE'RE NOT HERE TO PLAY COPS AND ROBBERS. WE'RE A MOVEMENT FOR CHANGE. THE CHAMPIONS MEAN NOTHING UNLESS PEOPLE BELIEVE ALONG WITH US.
SO LET'S DO SOMETHING ABOUT IT. I MEAN, SOMEBODY BEAT THOSE GUYS UP.
LET'S START SHERLOCKING WHO THEY ARE.
ARE YOU SERIOUS?
YEAH. WE NEED TO ACT ON--
I MEAN, HOW CAN YOU NOT ALREADY KNOW?
CALIFORNIA? SUPER-TEAM? OF SADISTS?

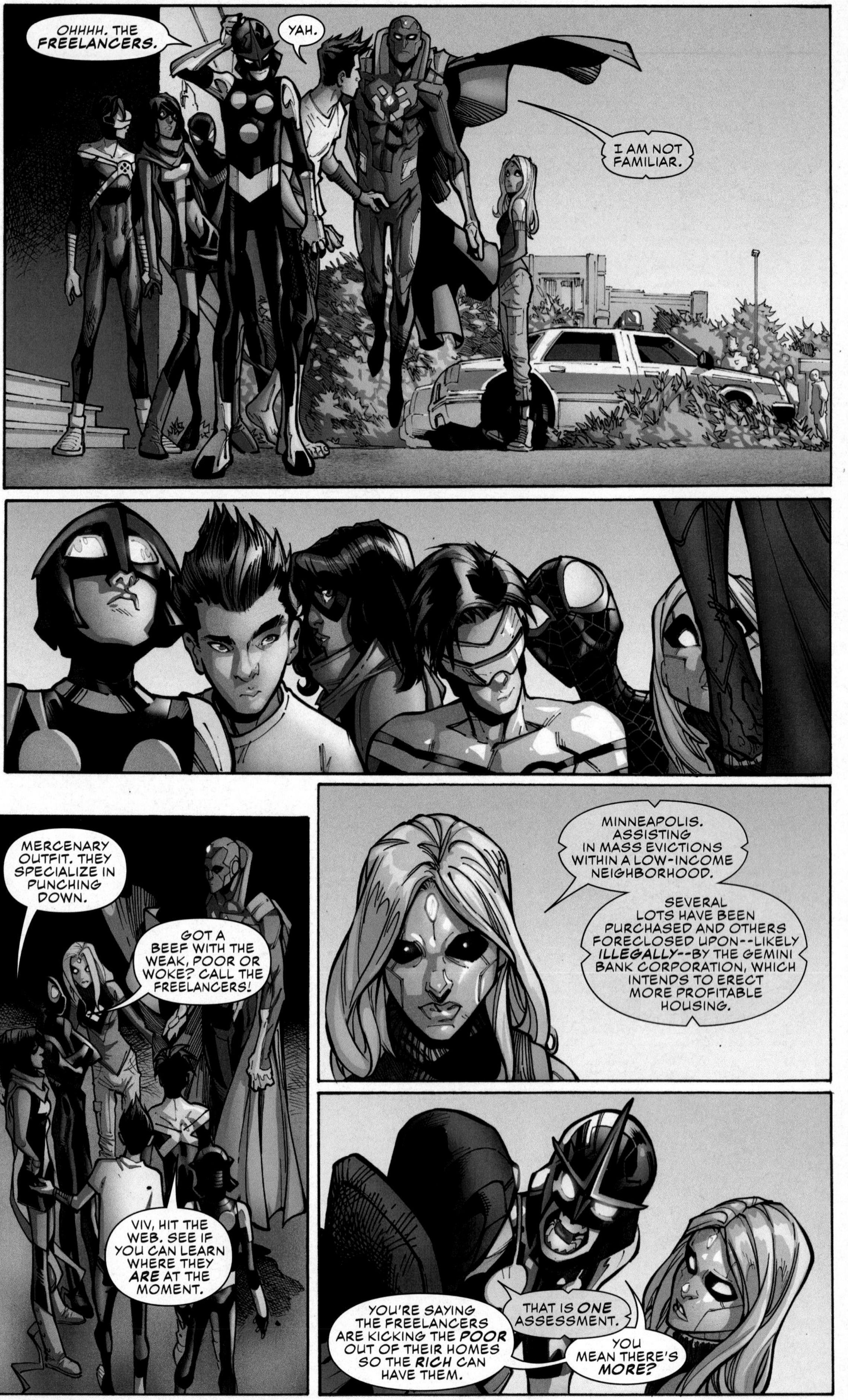
OHHHH. THE FREELANCERS.
YAH.
I AM NOT FAMILIAR.
MERCENARY OUTFIT. THEY SPECIALIZE IN PUNCHING DOWN.
GOT A BEEF WITH THE WEAK, POOR OR WOKE? CALL THE FREELANCERS!
VIV, HIT THE WEB. SEE IF YOU CAN LEARN WHERE THEY ARE AT THE MOMENT.
MINNEAPOLIS. ASSISTING IN MASS EVICTIONS WITHIN A LOW-INCOME NEIGHBORHOOD.
SEVERAL LOTS HAVE BEEN PURCHASED AND OTHERS FORECLOSED UPON--LIKELY ILLEGALLY--BY THE GEMINI BANK CORPORATION, WHICH INTENDS TO ERECT MORE PROFITABLE HOUSING.
YOU'RE SAYING THE FREELANCERS ARE KICKING THE POOR OUT OF THEIR HOMES SO THE RICH CAN HAVE THEM.
THAT IS ONE ASSESSMENT.
YOU MEAN THERE'S MORE?

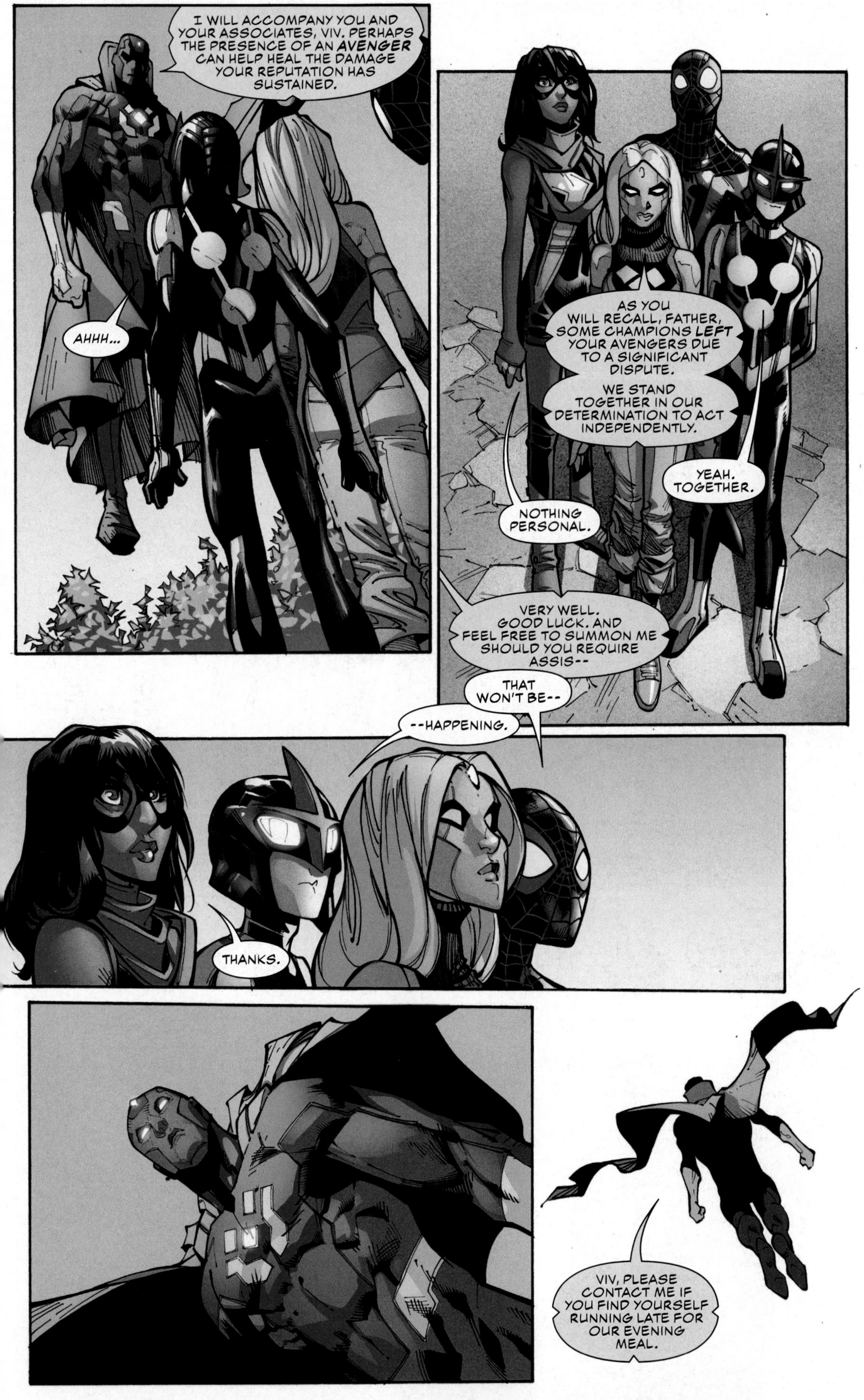
I WILL ACCOMPANY YOU AND YOUR ASSOCIATES, VIV. PERHAPS THE PRESENCE OF AN **AVENGER** CAN HELP HEAL THE DAMAGE YOUR REPUTATION HAS SUSTAINED.
AHHH...
AS YOU WILL RECALL, FATHER, SOME CHAMPIONS **LEFT** YOUR AVENGERS DUE TO A SIGNIFICANT DISPUTE.
WE STAND TOGETHER IN OUR DETERMINATION TO ACT INDEPENDENTLY.
NOTHING PERSONAL.
YEAH. TOGETHER.
VERY WELL. GOOD LUCK. AND FEEL FREE TO SUMMON ME SHOULD YOU REQUIRE ASSIS--
THAT WON'T BE--
--HAPPENING.
THANKS.
VIV, PLEASE CONTACT ME IF YOU FIND YOURSELF RUNNING LATE FOR OUR EVENING MEAL.

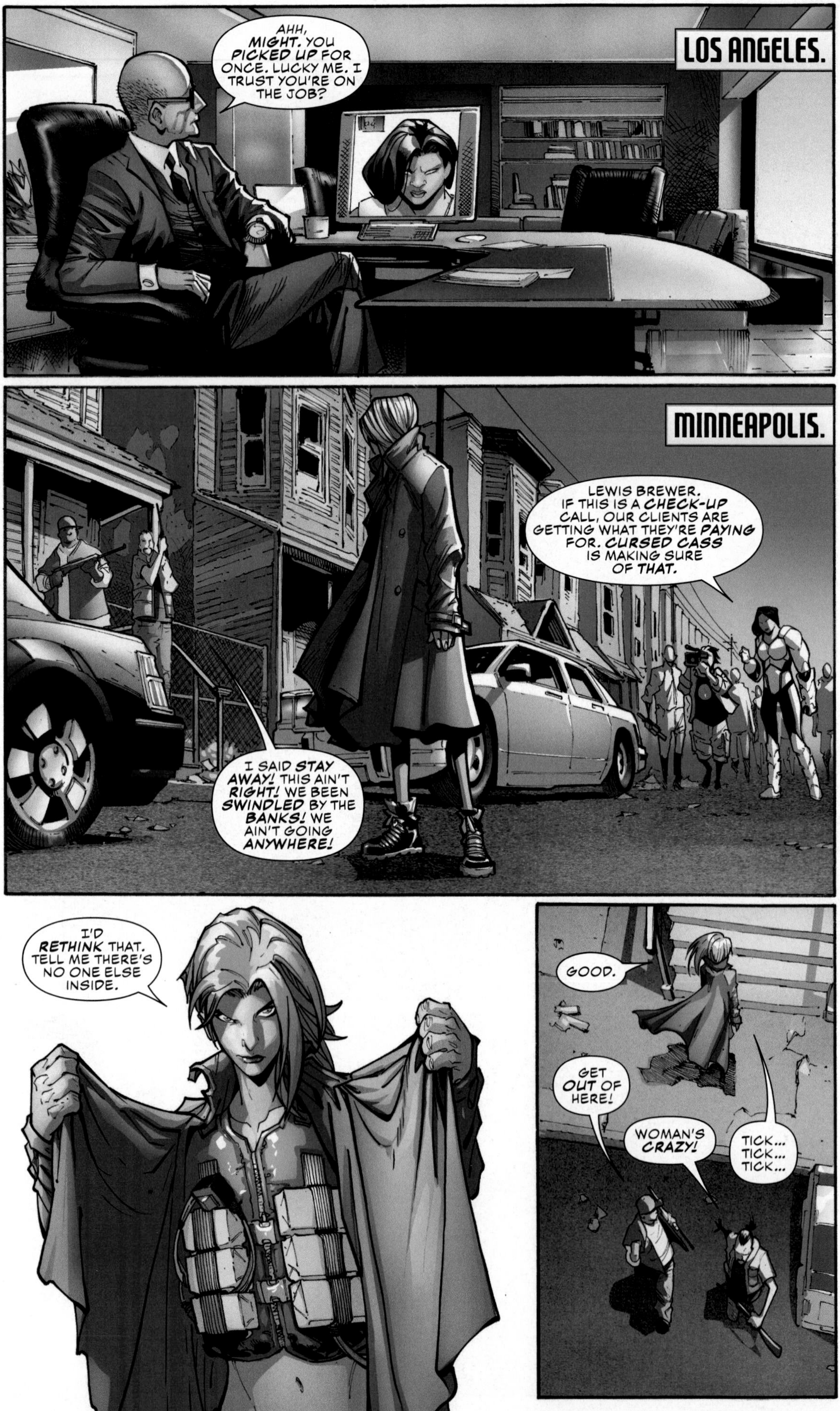
LOS ANGELES.
AHH, MIGHT. YOU PICKED UP FOR ONCE. LUCKY ME. I TRUST YOU'RE ON THE JOB?
MINNEAPOLIS.
LEWIS BREWER. IF THIS IS A CHECK-UP CALL, OUR CLIENTS ARE GETTING WHAT THEY'RE PAYING FOR. CURSED CASS IS MAKING SURE OF THAT.
I SAID STAY AWAY! THIS AIN'T RIGHT! WE BEEN SWINDLED BY THE BANKS! WE AIN'T GOING ANYWHERE!
I'D RETHINK THAT. TELL ME THERE'S NO ONE ELSE INSIDE.
GOOD.
GET OUT OF HERE!
WOMAN'S CRAZY!
TICK... TICK... TICK...

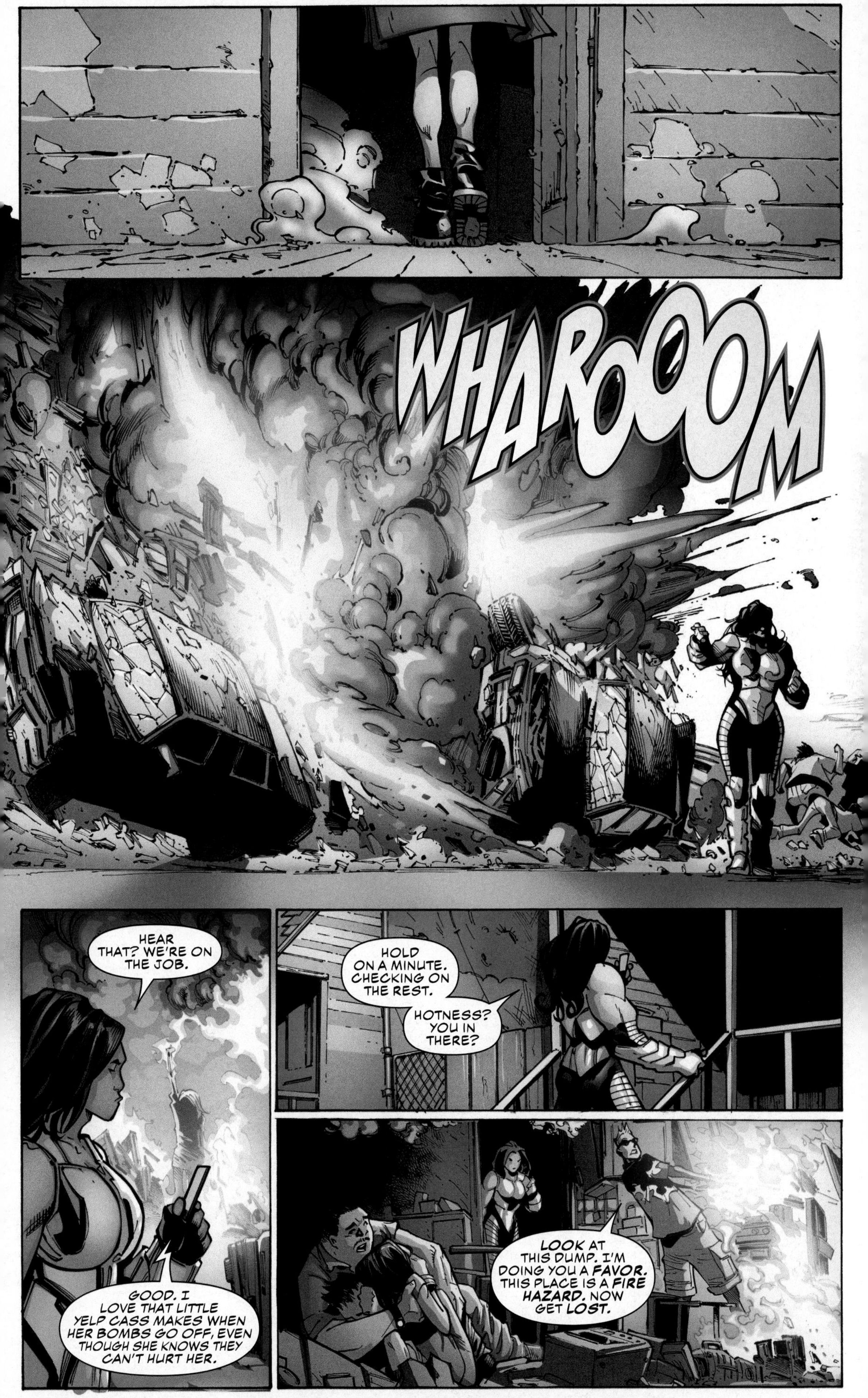
WHAROOOM
HEAR THAT? WE'RE ON THE JOB.
GOOD. I LOVE THAT LITTLE YELP CASS MAKES WHEN HER BOMBS GO OFF, EVEN THOUGH SHE KNOWS THEY CAN'T HURT HER.
HOLD ON A MINUTE. CHECKING ON THE REST.
HOTNESS? YOU IN THERE?
LOOK AT THIS DUMP. I'M DOING YOU A FAVOR. THIS PLACE IS A FIRE HAZARD. NOW GET LOST.

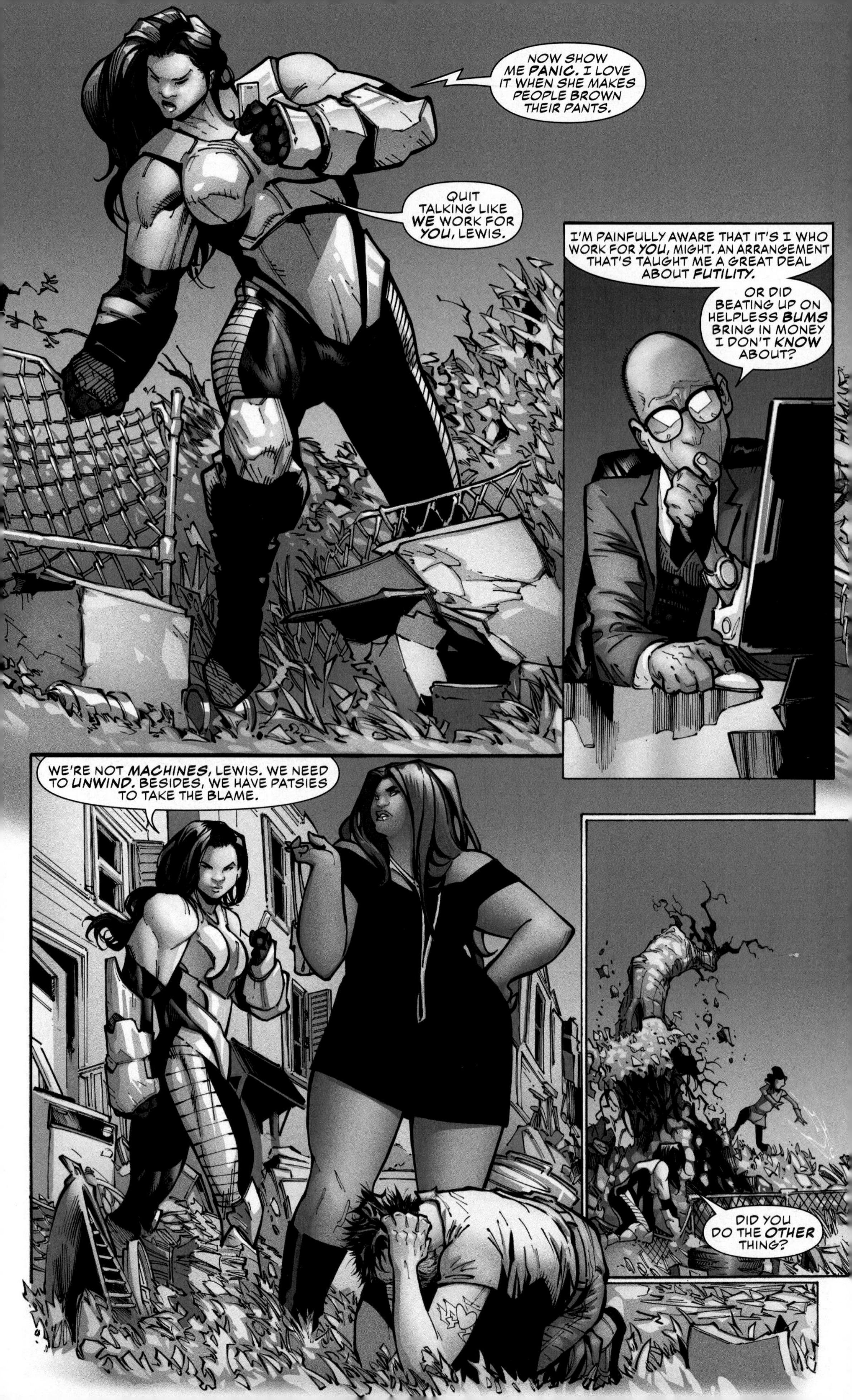
NOW SHOW ME PANIC. I LOVE IT WHEN SHE MAKES PEOPLE BROWN THEIR PANTS.
QUIT TALKING LIKE WE WORK FOR YOU, LEWIS.
I'M PAINFULLY AWARE THAT IT'S I WHO WORK FOR YOU, MIGHT. AN ARRANGEMENT THAT'S TAUGHT ME A GREAT DEAL ABOUT FUTILITY.
OR DID BEATING UP ON HELPLESS BUMS BRING IN MONEY I DON'T KNOW ABOUT?
WE'RE NOT MACHINES, LEWIS. WE NEED TO UNWIND. BESIDES, WE HAVE PATSIES TO TAKE THE BLAME.
DID YOU DO THE OTHER THING?

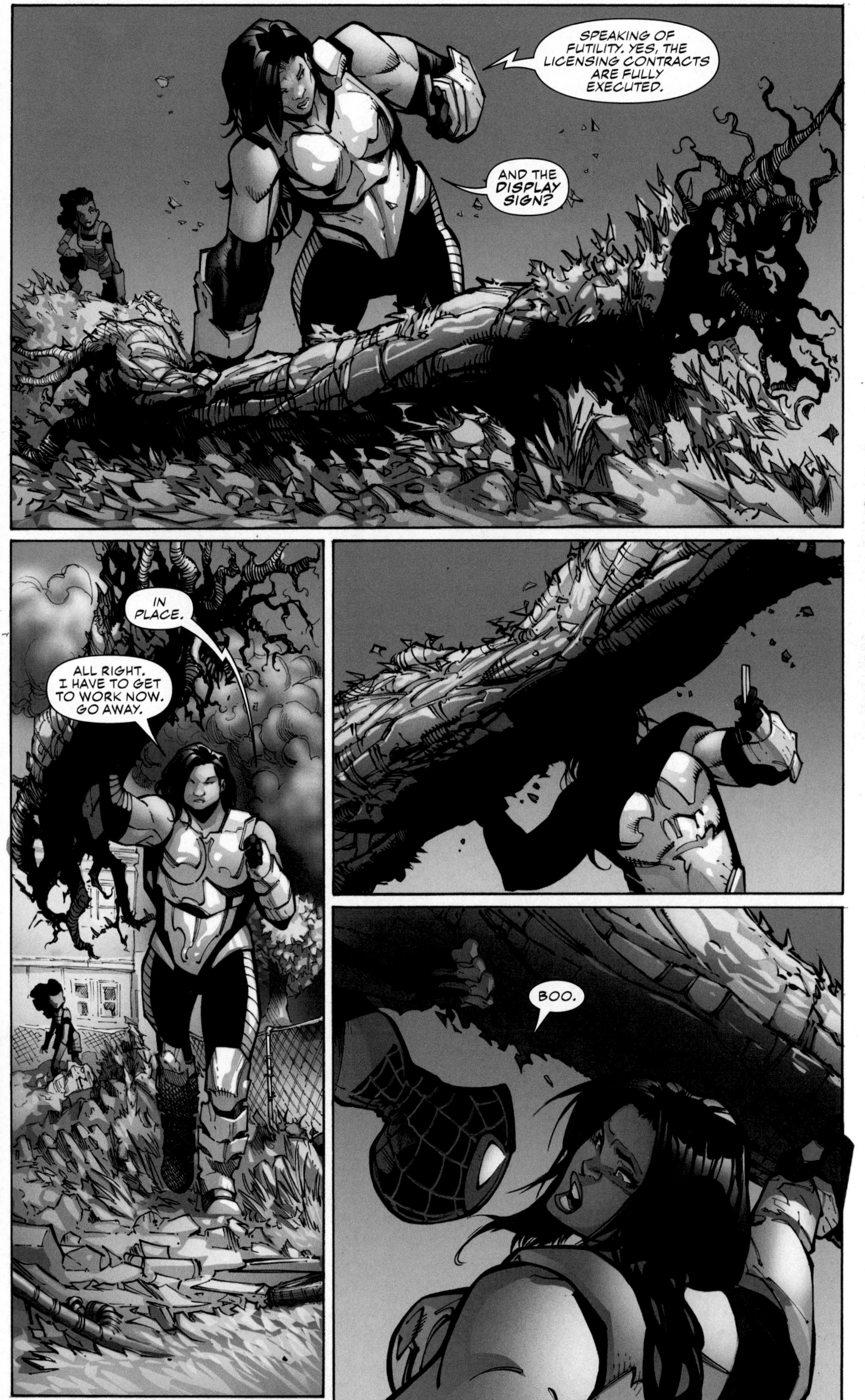
SPEAKING OF FUTILITY. YES, THE LICENSING CONTRACTS ARE FULLY EXECUTED.
AND THE DISPLAY SIGN?
IN PLACE.
ALL RIGHT. I HAVE TO GET TO WORK NOW. GO AWAY.
BOO.

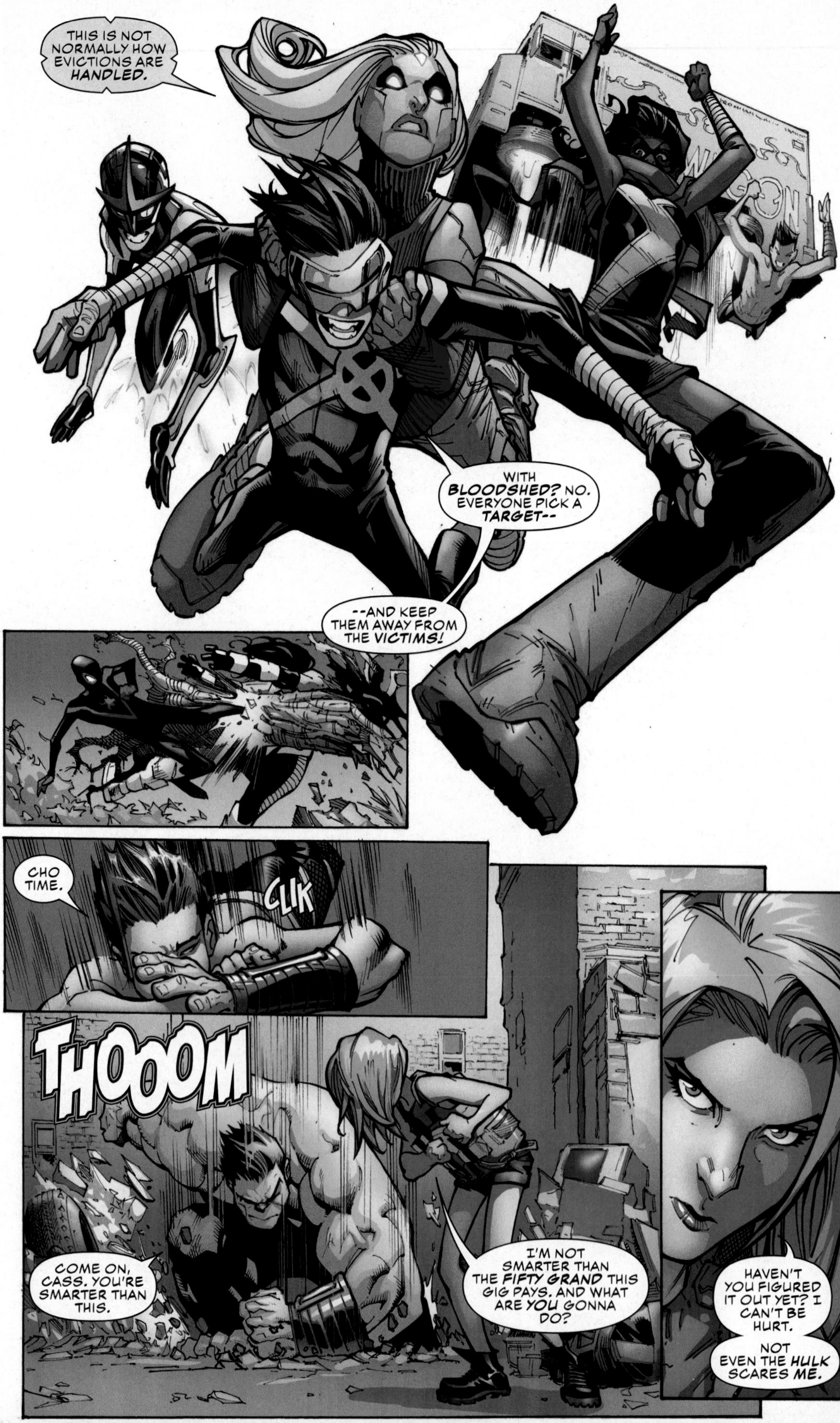
THIS IS NOT NORMALLY HOW EVICTIONS ARE HANDLED.
WITH BLOODSHED? NO. EVERYONE PICK A TARGET--
--AND KEEP THEM AWAY FROM THE VICTIMS!
CHO TIME.
CLIK
THOOOM
COME ON, CASS. YOU'RE SMARTER THAN THIS.
I'M NOT SMARTER THAN THE FIFTY GRAND THIS GIG PAYS. AND WHAT ARE YOU GONNA DO?
HAVEN'T YOU FIGURED IT OUT YET? I CAN'T BE HURT.
NOT EVEN THE HULK SCARES ME.

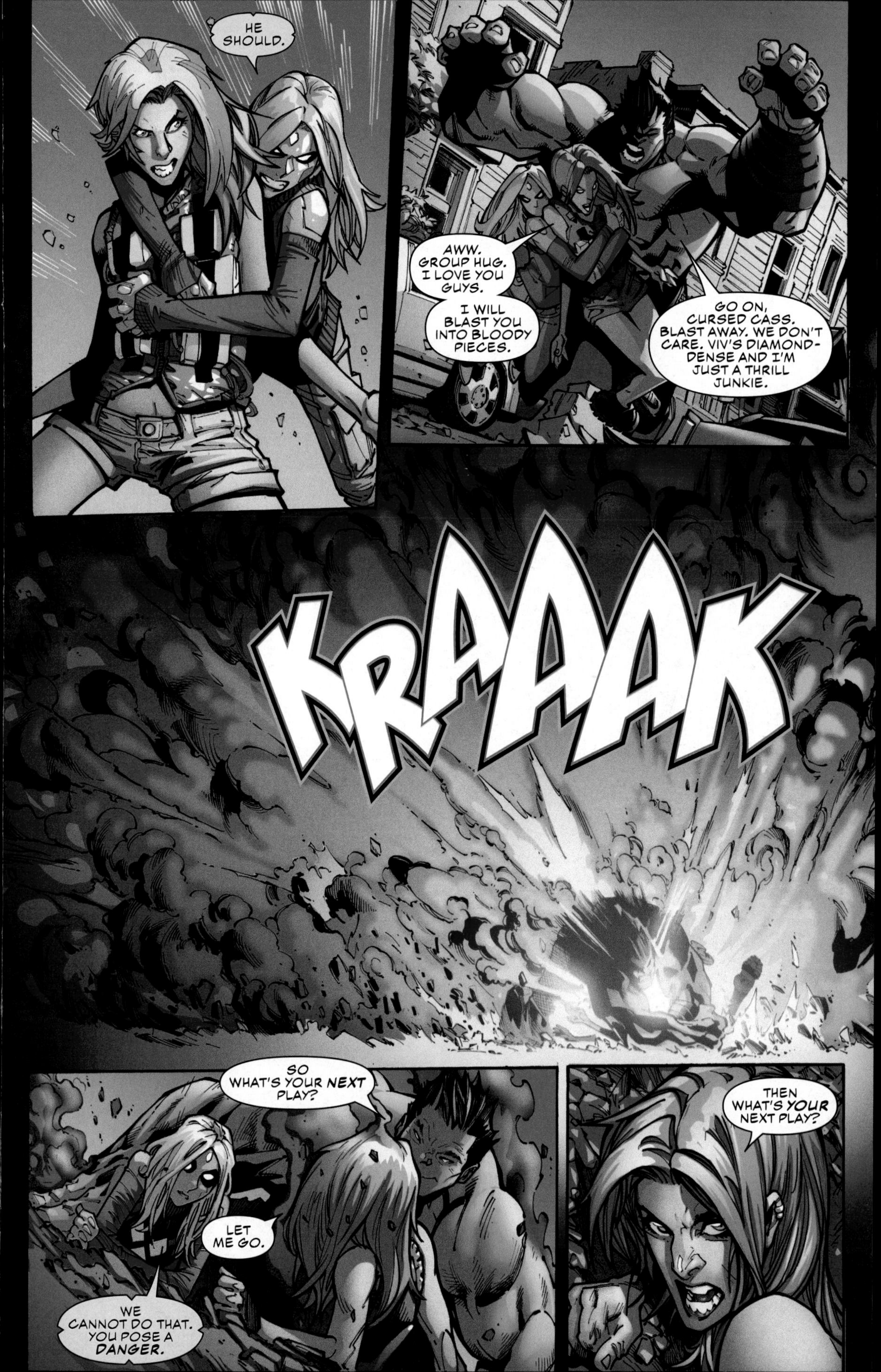

HE SHOULD.
AWW. GROUP HUG. I LOVE YOU GUYS.
I WILL BLAST YOU INTO BLOODY PIECES.
GO ON, CURSED CASS. BLAST AWAY. WE DON'T CARE. VIV'S DIAMOND-DENSE AND I'M JUST A THRILL JUNKIE.
KRAAAK
SO WHAT'S YOUR NEXT PLAY?
LET ME GO.
WE CANNOT DO THAT. YOU POSE A DANGER.
THEN WHAT'S YOUR NEXT PLAY?

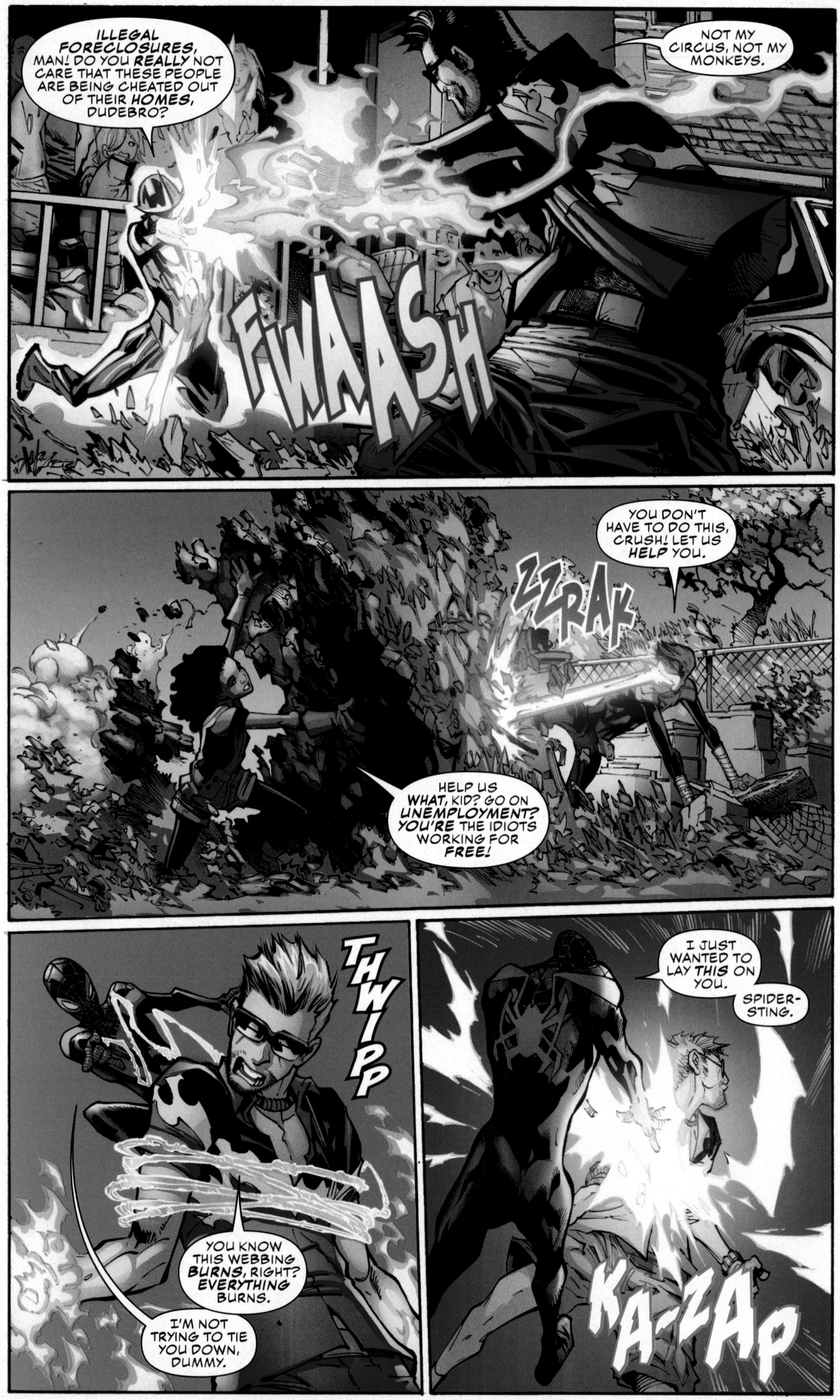
ILLEGAL FORECLOSURES, MAN! DO YOU REALLY NOT CARE THAT THESE PEOPLE ARE BEING CHEATED OUT OF THEIR HOMES, DUDEBRO?
NOT MY CIRCUS, NOT MY MONKEYS.
FWAASH
YOU DON'T HAVE TO DO THIS, CRUSH! LET US HELP YOU.
ZZRAK
HELP US WHAT, KID? GO ON UNEMPLOYMENT? YOU'RE THE IDIOTS WORKING FOR FREE!
THWIPP
YOU KNOW THIS WEBBING BURNS, RIGHT? EVERYTHING BURNS.
I'M NOT TRYING TO TIE YOU DOWN, DUMMY.
I JUST WANTED TO LAY THIS ON YOU.
SPIDER-STING.
KA-ZAP

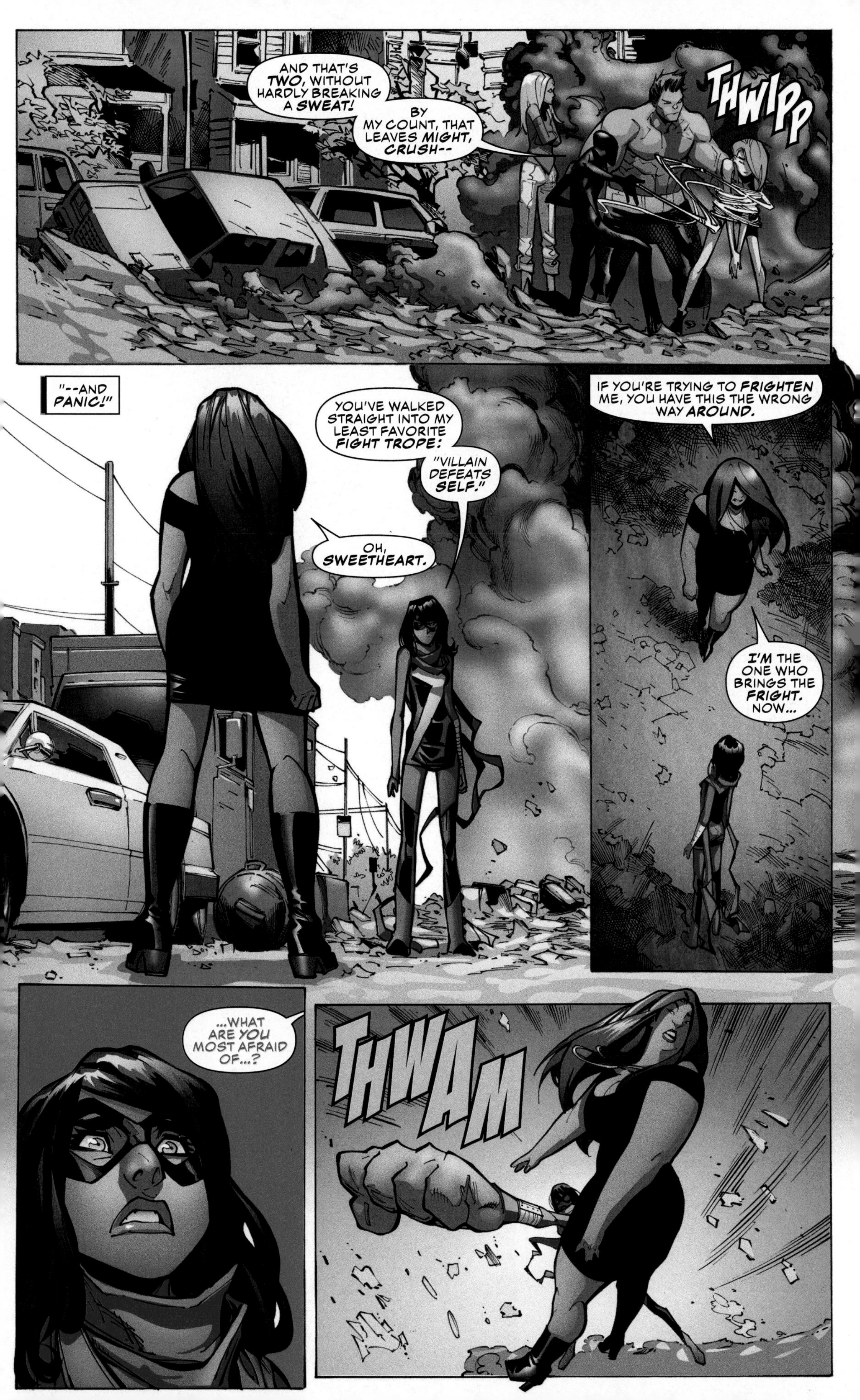

AND THAT'S TWO, WITHOUT HARDLY BREAKING A SWEAT!
BY MY COUNT, THAT LEAVES MIGHT, CRUSH--
THWIPP
"--AND PANIC!"
YOU'VE WALKED STRAIGHT INTO MY LEAST FAVORITE FIGHT TROPE:
"VILLAIN DEFEATS SELF."
OH, SWEETHEART.
IF YOU'RE TRYING TO FRIGHTEN ME, YOU HAVE THIS THE WRONG WAY AROUND.
I'M THE ONE WHO BRINGS THE FRIGHT. NOW...
...WHAT ARE YOU MOST AFRAID OF...?
THWAM

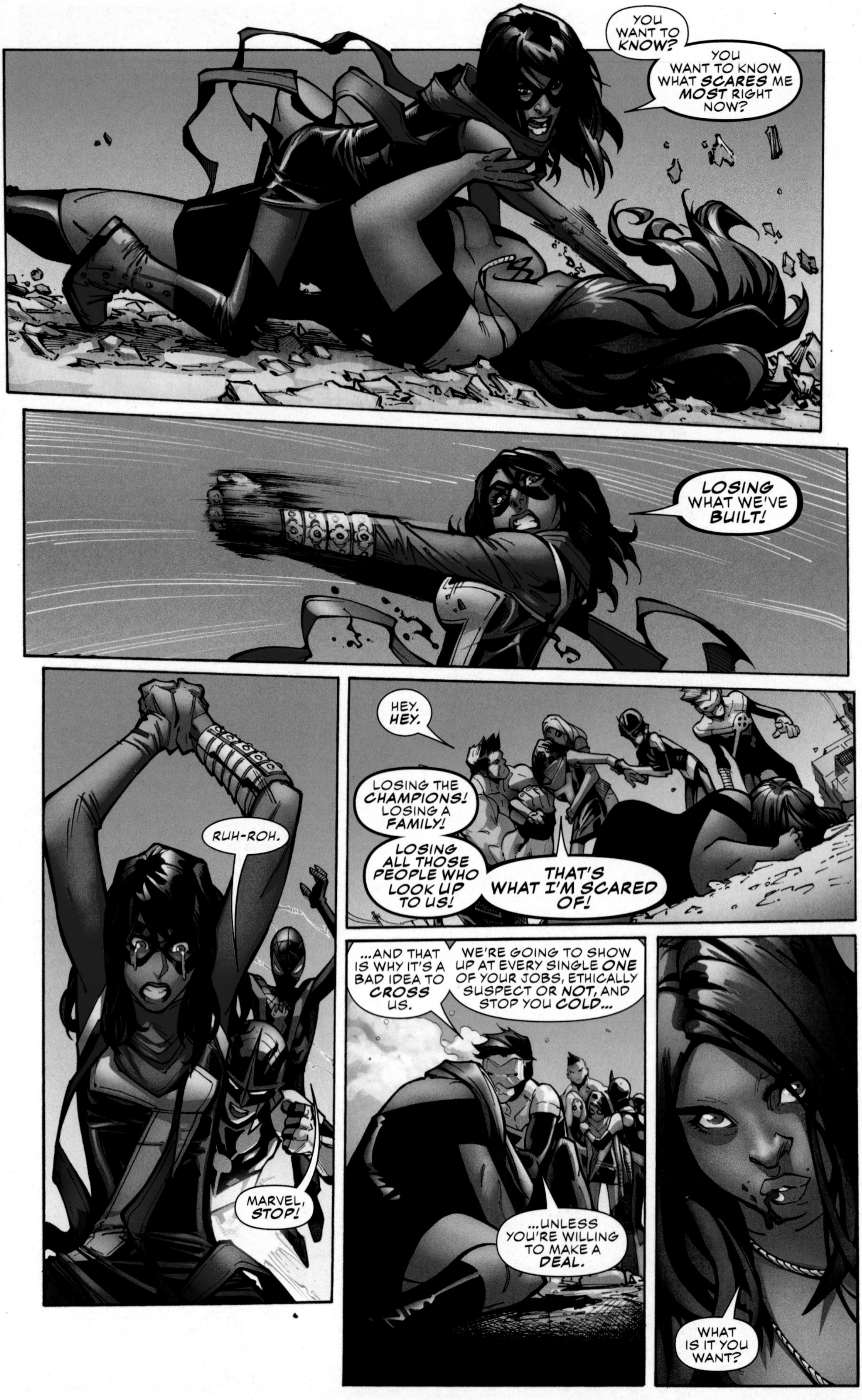

YOU WANT TO KNOW?
YOU WANT TO KNOW WHAT SCARES ME MOST RIGHT NOW?
LOSING WHAT WE'VE BUILT!
RUH-ROH.
MARVEL, STOP!
HEY. HEY.
LOSING THE CHAMPIONS! LOSING A FAMILY!
LOSING ALL THOSE PEOPLE WHO LOOK UP TO US!
THAT'S WHAT I'M SCARED OF!
...AND THAT IS WHY IT'S A BAD IDEA TO CROSS US.
WE'RE GOING TO SHOW UP AT EVERY SINGLE ONE OF YOUR JOBS, ETHICALLY SUSPECT OR NOT, AND STOP YOU COLD...
...UNLESS YOU'RE WILLING TO MAKE A DEAL.
WHAT IS IT YOU WANT?

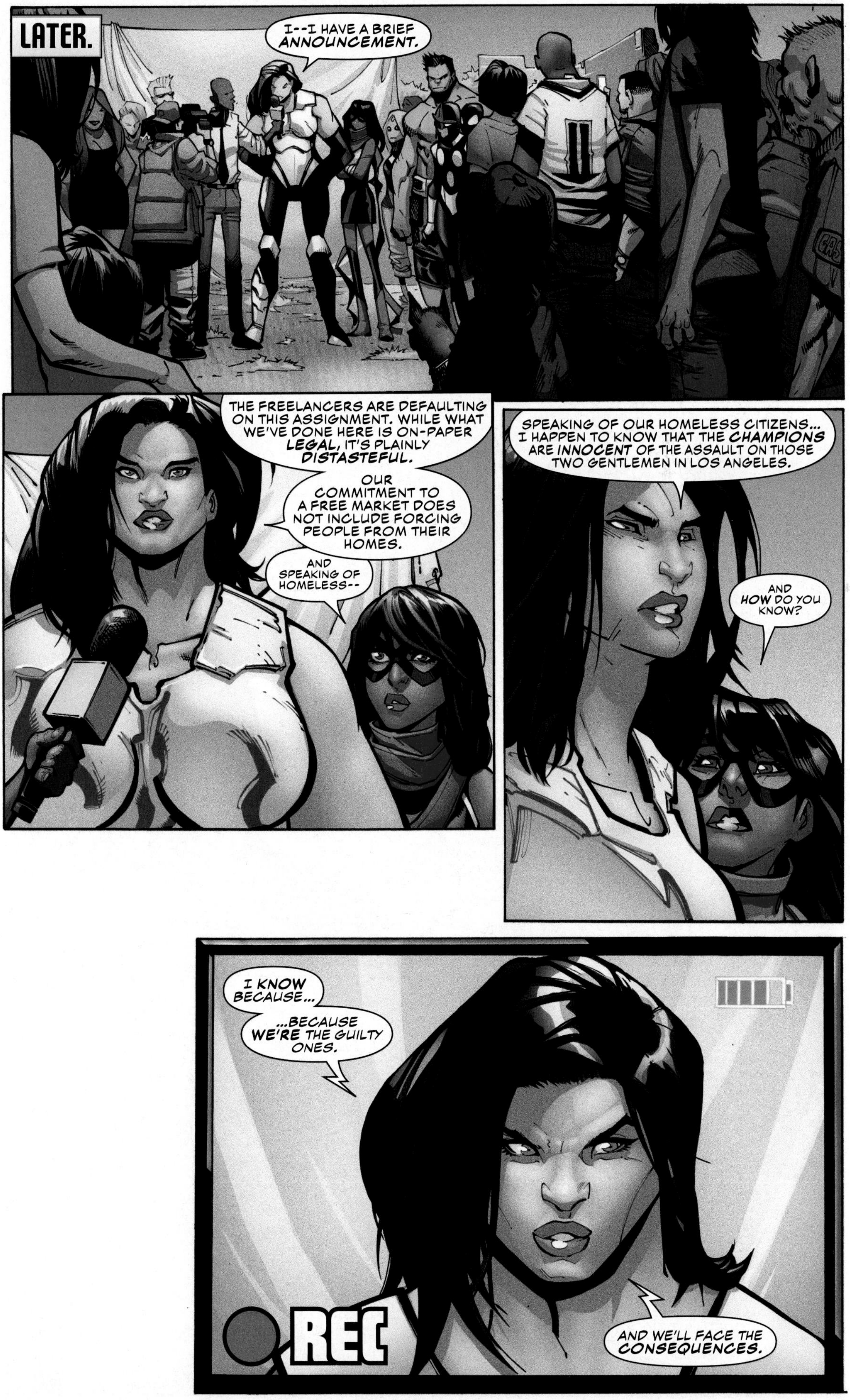
LATER.
I--I HAVE A BRIEF ANNOUNCEMENT.
THE FREELANCERS ARE DEFAULTING ON THIS ASSIGNMENT. WHILE WHAT WE'VE DONE HERE IS ON-PAPER LEGAL, IT'S PLAINLY DISTASTEFUL.
OUR COMMITMENT TO A FREE MARKET DOES NOT INCLUDE FORCING PEOPLE FROM THEIR HOMES.
AND SPEAKING OF HOMELESS--
SPEAKING OF OUR HOMELESS CITIZENS... I HAPPEN TO KNOW THAT THE CHAMPIONS ARE INNOCENT OF THE ASSAULT ON THOSE TWO GENTLEMEN IN LOS ANGELES.
AND HOW DO YOU KNOW?
I KNOW BECAUSE...
...BECAUSE WE'RE THE GUILTY ONES.
REC
AND WE'LL FACE THE CONSEQUENCES.

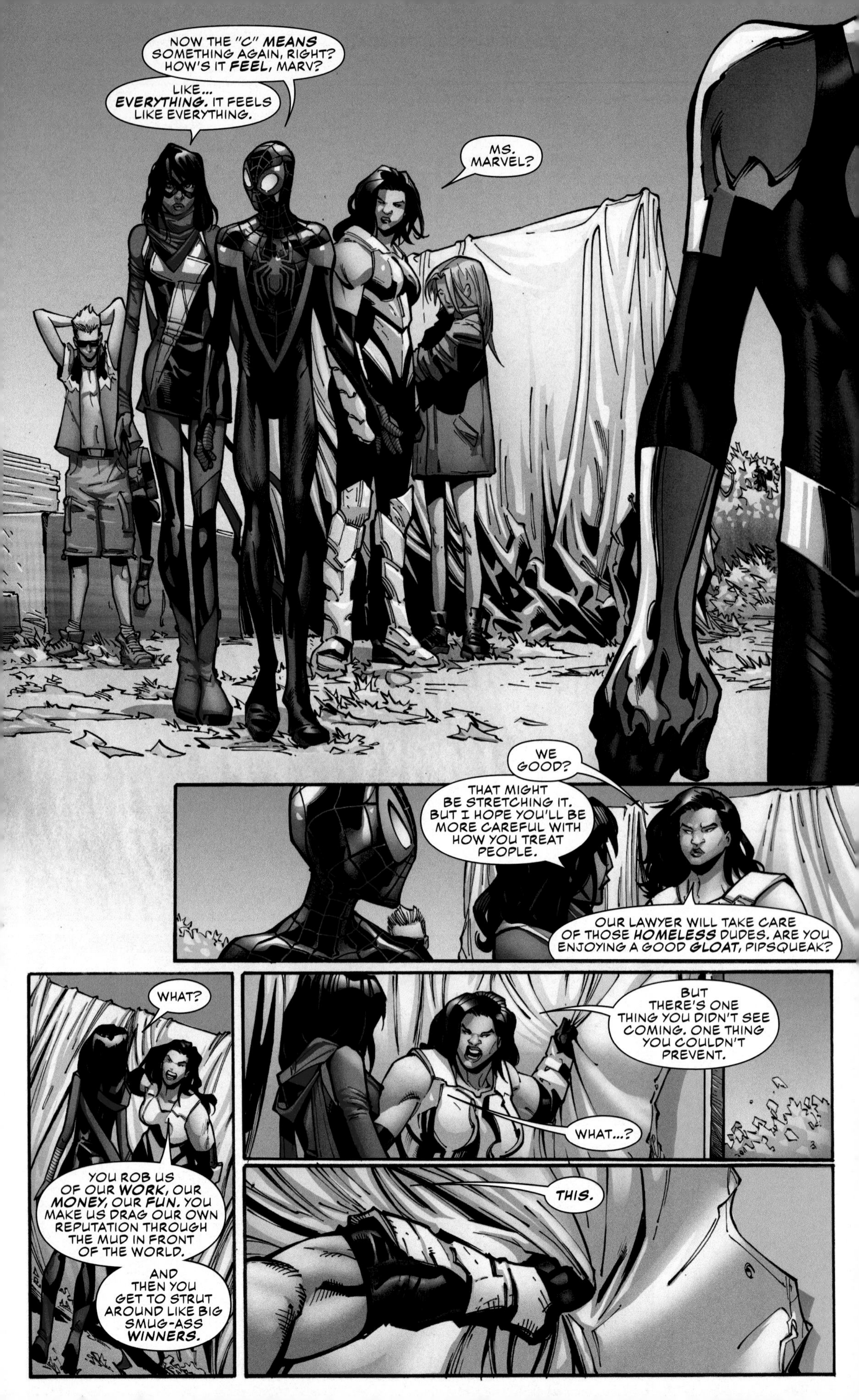

NOW THE "C" MEANS SOMETHING AGAIN, RIGHT? HOW'S IT FEEL, MARV?
LIKE... EVERYTHING. IT FEELS LIKE EVERYTHING.
MS. MARVEL?
WE GOOD?
THAT MIGHT BE STRETCHING IT. BUT I HOPE YOU'LL BE MORE CAREFUL WITH HOW YOU TREAT PEOPLE.
OUR LAWYER WILL TAKE CARE OF THOSE HOMELESS DUDES. ARE YOU ENJOYING A GOOD GLOAT, PIPSQUEAK?
WHAT?
YOU ROB US OF OUR WORK, OUR MONEY, OUR FUN. YOU MAKE US DRAG OUR OWN REPUTATION THROUGH THE MUD IN FRONT OF THE WORLD.
AND THEN YOU GET TO STRUT AROUND LIKE BIG SMUG-ASS WINNERS.
BUT THERE'S ONE THING YOU DIDN'T SEE COMING. ONE THING YOU COULDN'T PREVENT.
WHAT...?
THIS.

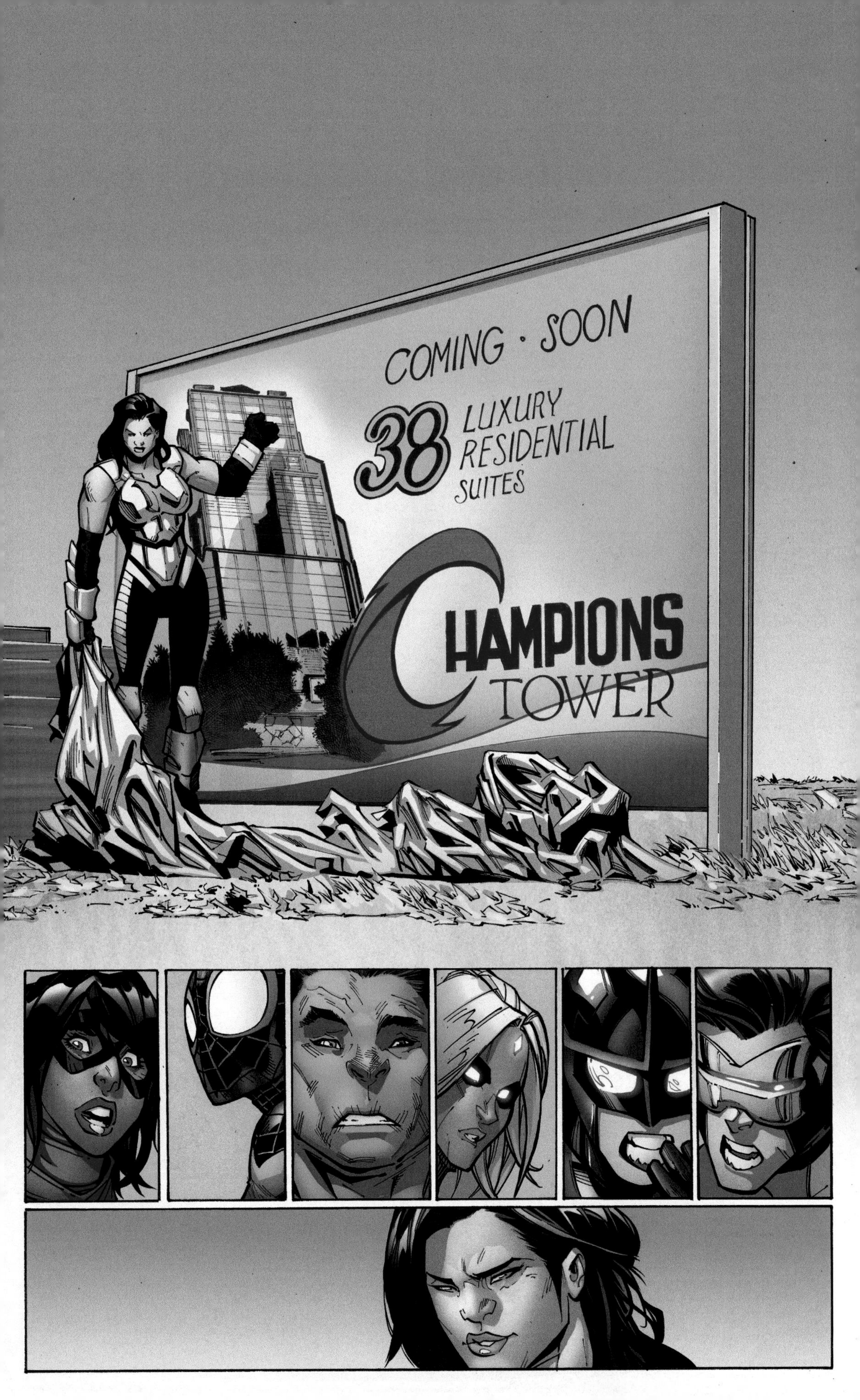
COMING · SOON
38 LUXURY RESIDENTIAL SUITES
CHAMPIONS TOWER

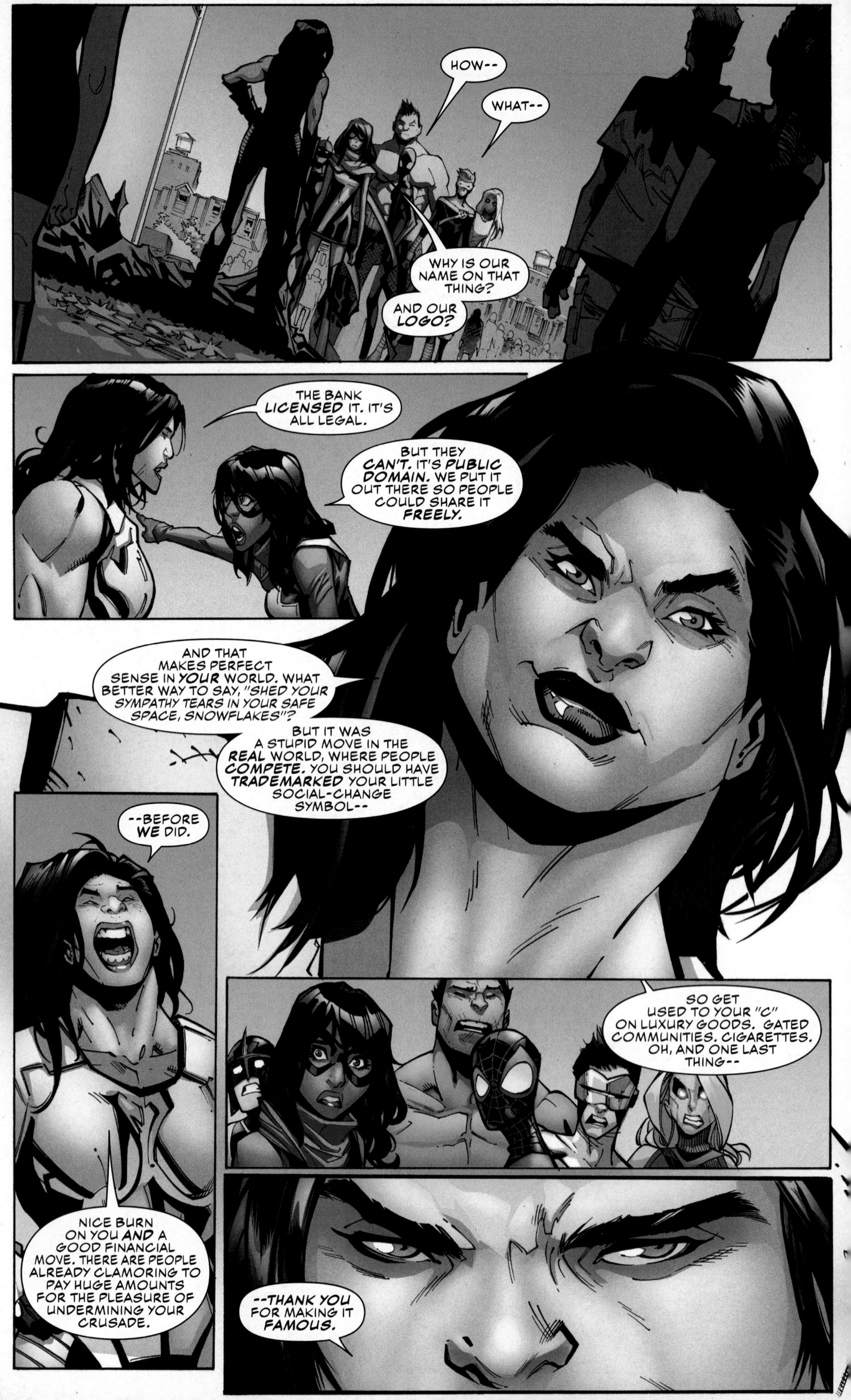
HOW--
WHAT--
WHY IS OUR NAME ON THAT THING?
AND OUR LOGO?
THE BANK LICENSED IT. IT'S ALL LEGAL.
BUT THEY CAN'T. IT'S PUBLIC DOMAIN. WE PUT IT OUT THERE SO PEOPLE COULD SHARE IT FREELY.
AND THAT MAKES PERFECT SENSE IN YOUR WORLD. WHAT BETTER WAY TO SAY, "SHED YOUR SYMPATHY TEARS IN YOUR SAFE SPACE, SNOWFLAKES"?
BUT IT WAS A STUPID MOVE IN THE REAL WORLD, WHERE PEOPLE COMPETE. YOU SHOULD HAVE TRADEMARKED YOUR LITTLE SOCIAL-CHANGE SYMBOL--
--BEFORE WE DID.
NICE BURN ON YOU AND A GOOD FINANCIAL MOVE. THERE ARE PEOPLE ALREADY CLAMORING TO PAY HUGE AMOUNTS FOR THE PLEASURE OF UNDERMINING YOUR CRUSADE.
SO GET USED TO YOUR "C" ON LUXURY GOODS. GATED COMMUNITIES. CIGARETTES. OH, AND ONE LAST THING--
--THANK YOU FOR MAKING IT FAMOUS.

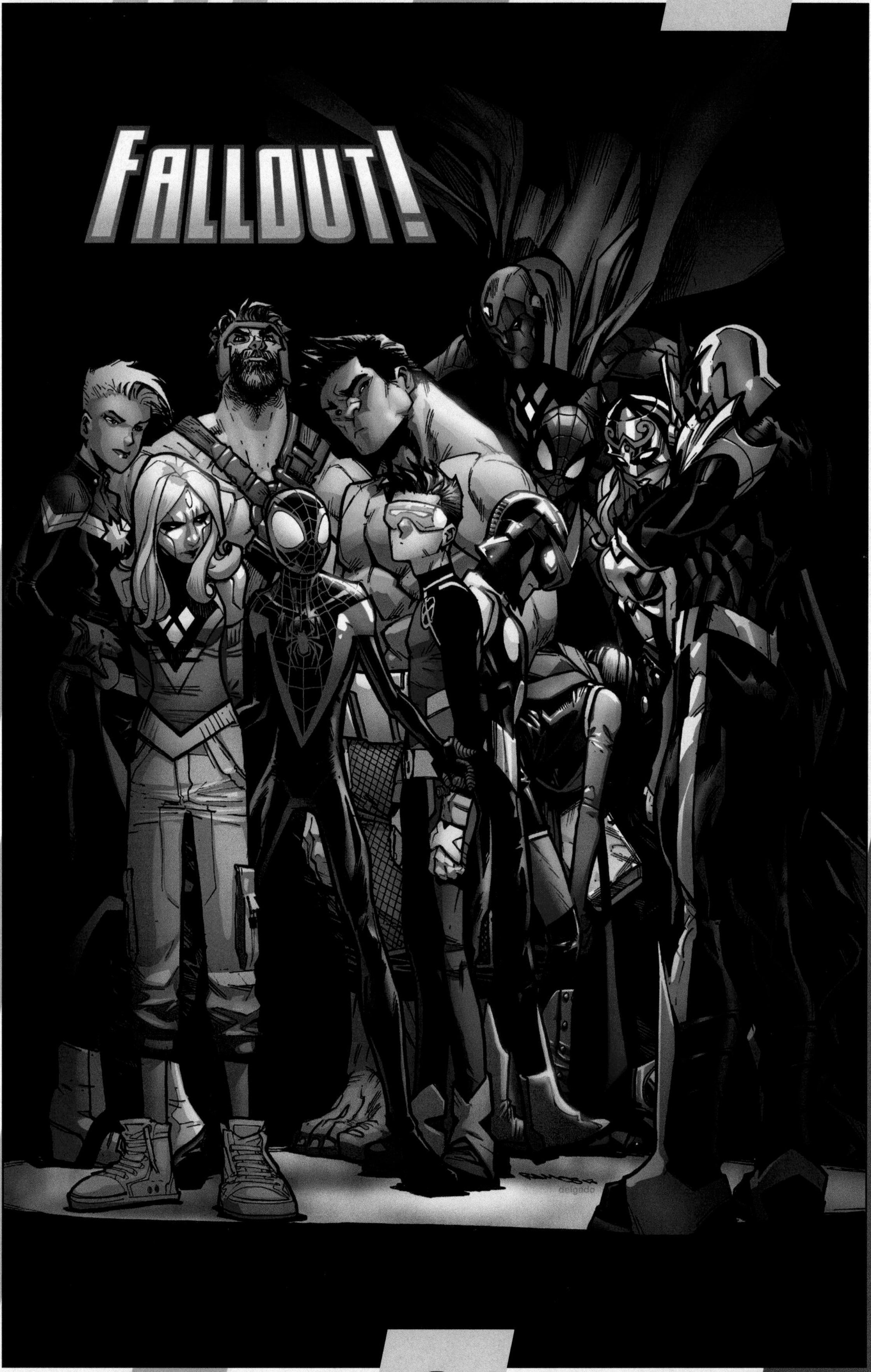
FALLOUT!

8

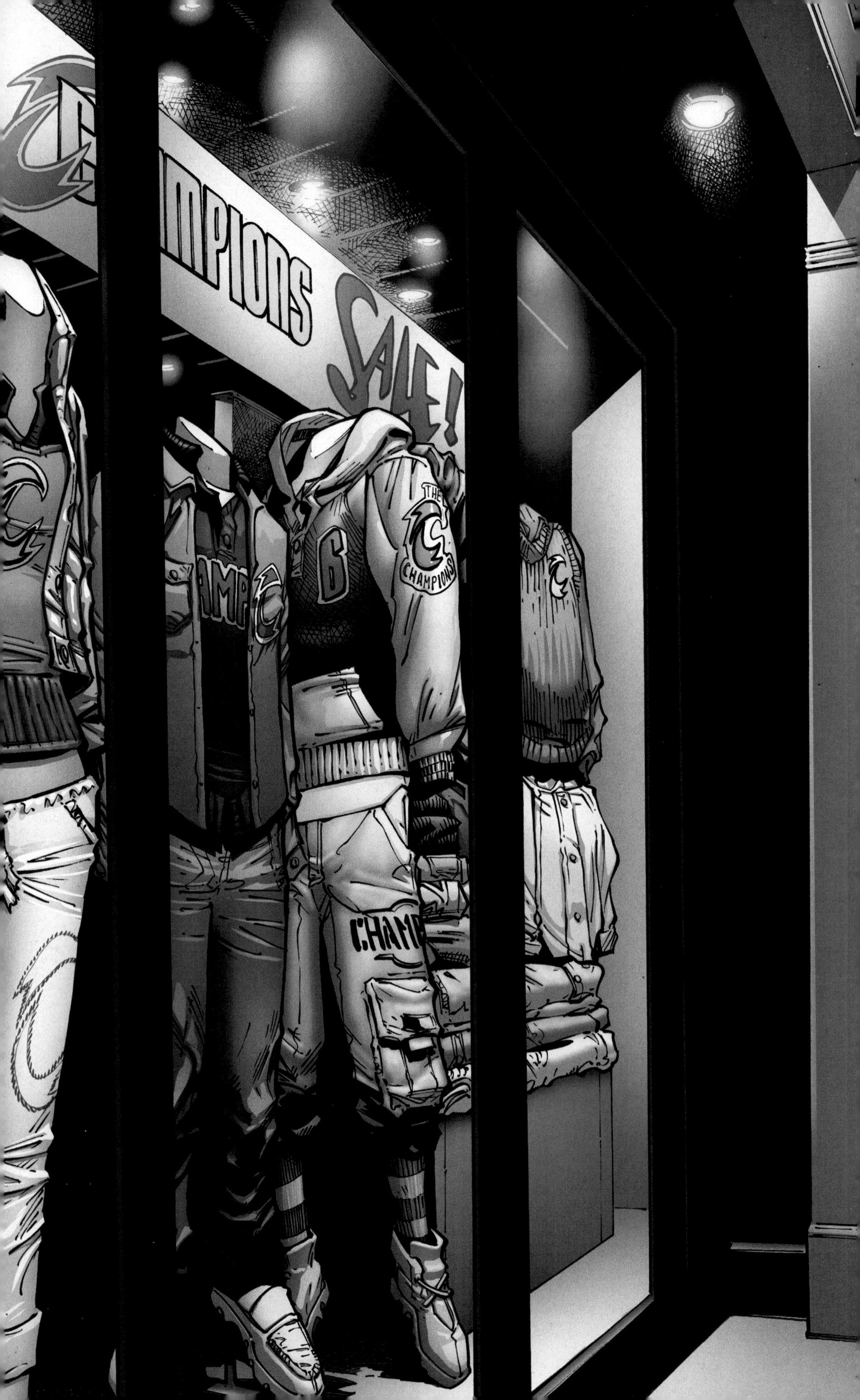
SALE!
THE CHAMPIONS
6
CHAMP

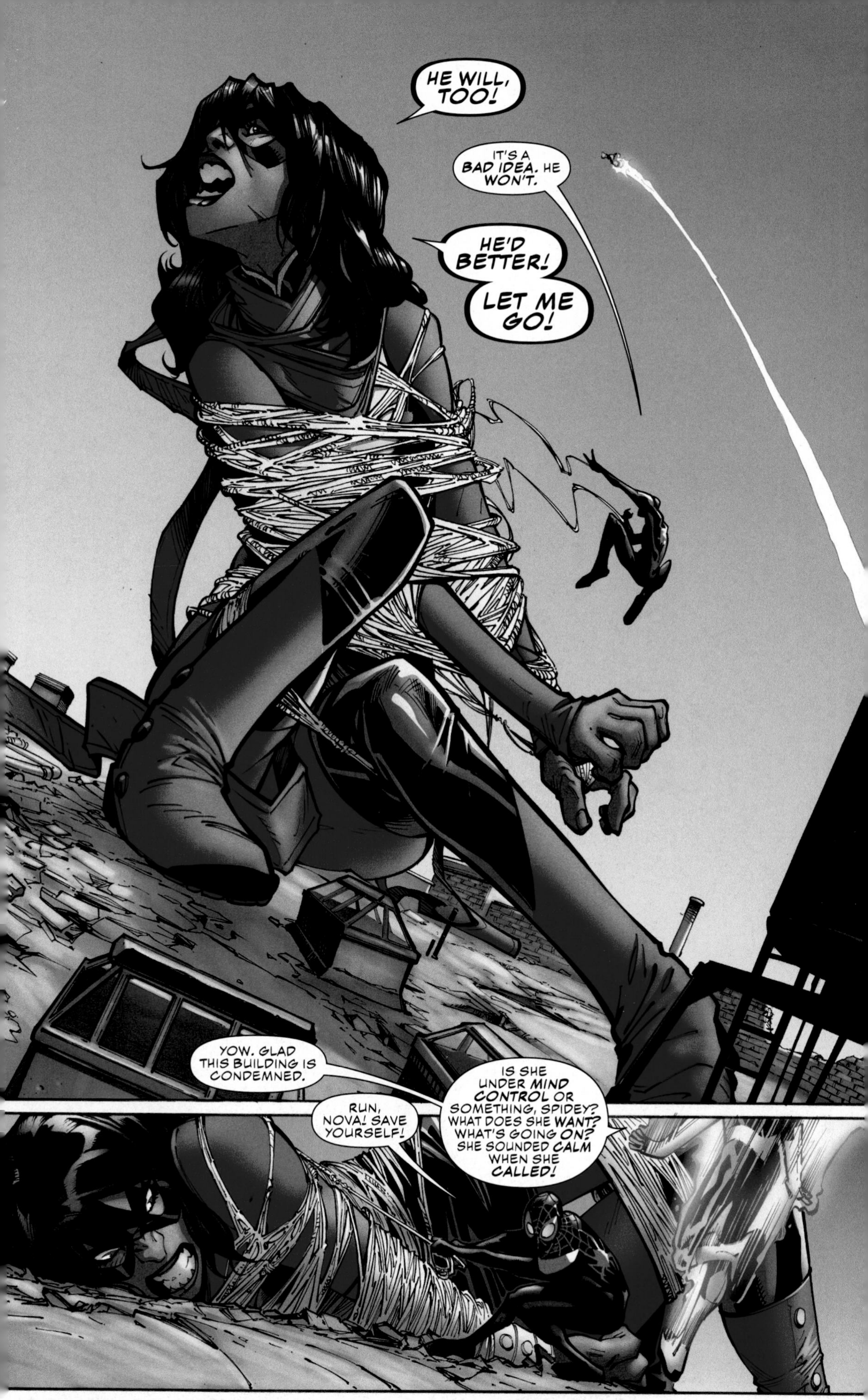
HE WILL, TOO!
IT'S A BAD IDEA. HE WON'T.
HE'D BETTER!
LET ME GO!
YOW. GLAD THIS BUILDING IS CONDEMNED.
RUN, NOVA! SAVE YOURSELF!
IS SHE UNDER MIND CONTROL OR SOMETHING, SPIDEY? WHAT DOES SHE WANT? WHAT'S GOING ON? SHE SOUNDED CALM WHEN SHE CALLED!

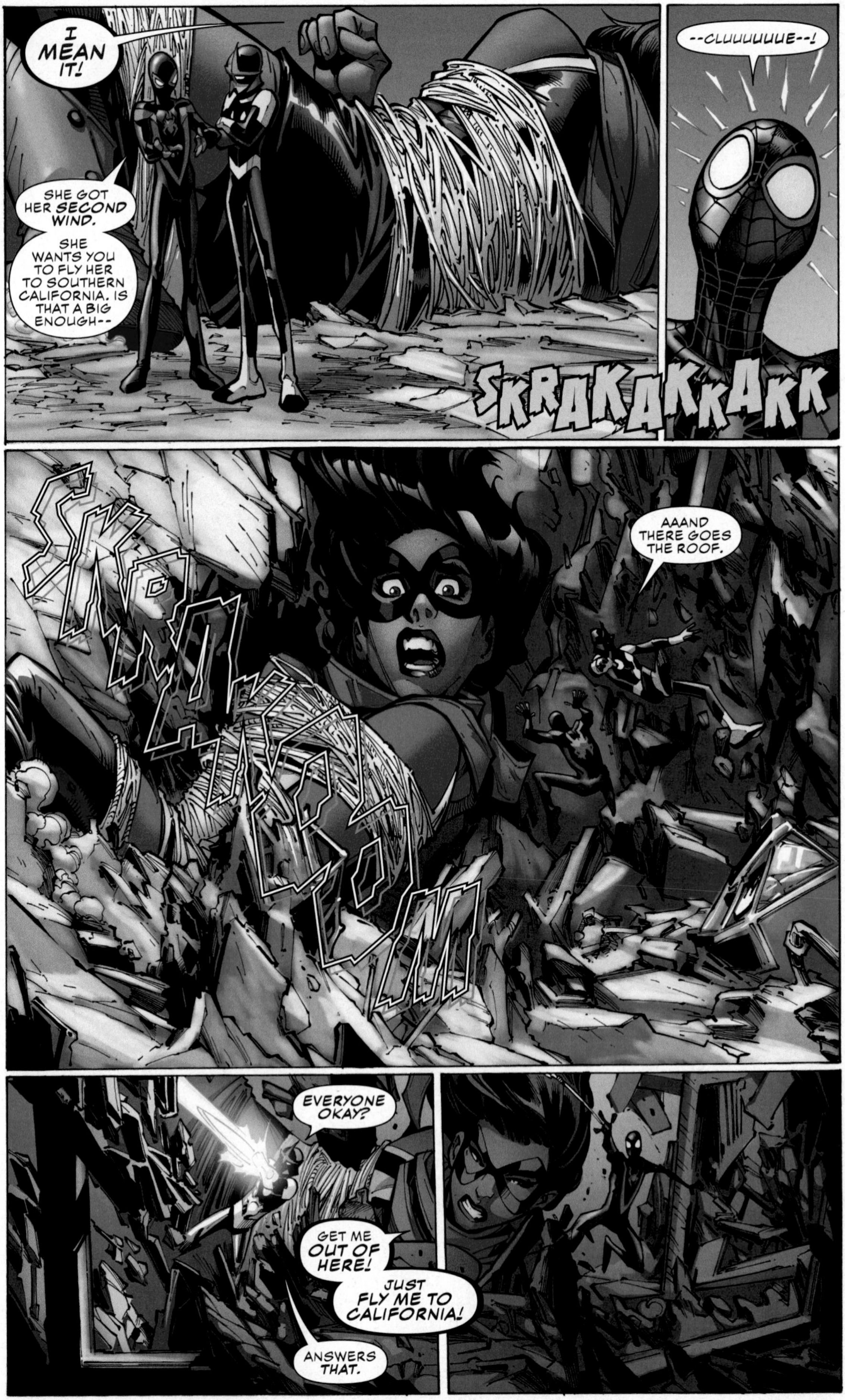
I MEAN IT!
SHE GOT HER SECOND WIND.
SHE WANTS YOU TO FLY HER TO SOUTHERN CALIFORNIA. IS THAT A BIG ENOUGH--
--CLUUUUUUE--!
SKRAKAKKKAKK
AAAND THERE GOES THE ROOF.
EVERYONE OKAY?
GET ME OUT OF HERE!
JUST FLY ME TO CALIFORNIA!
ANSWERS THAT.

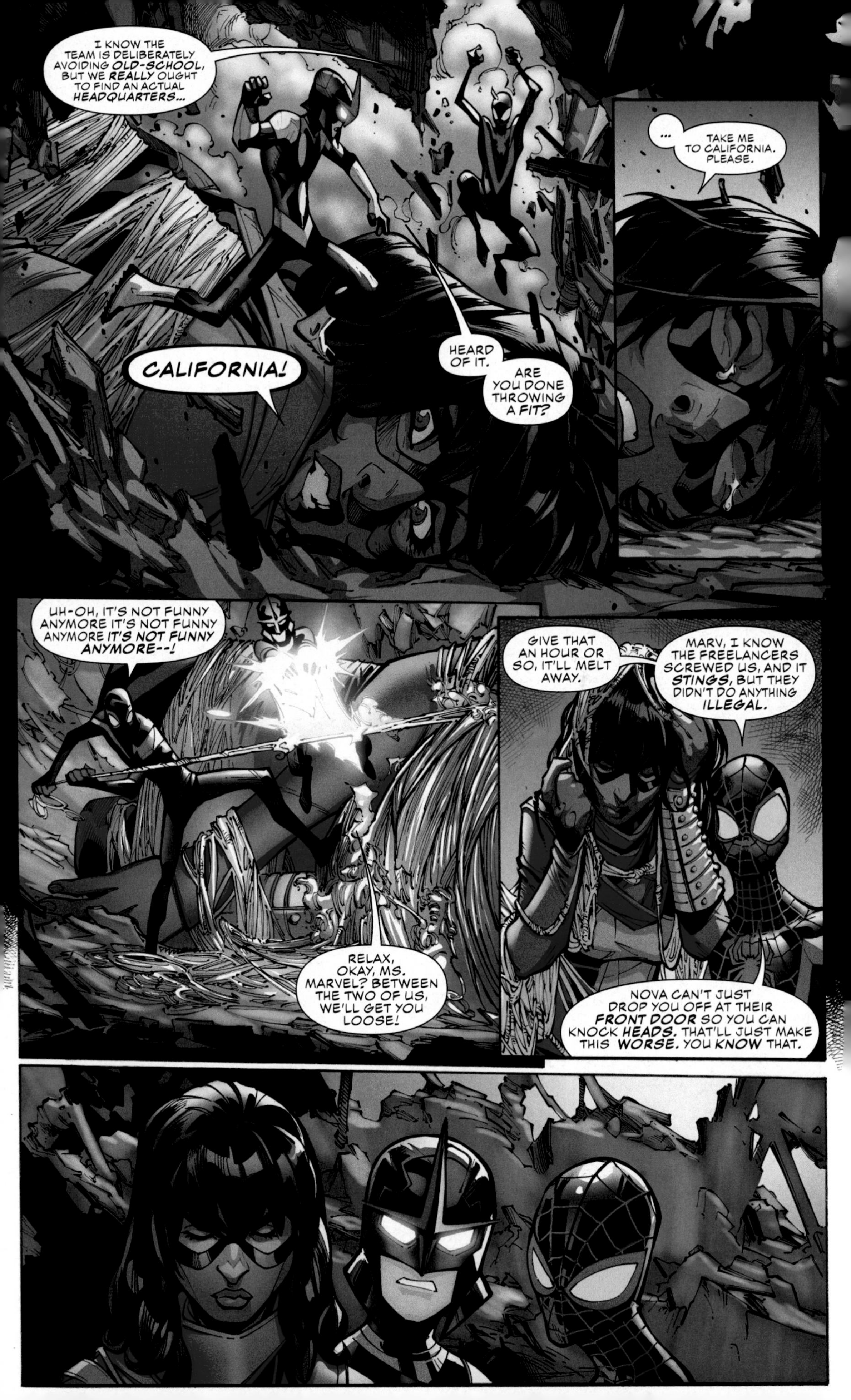

I KNOW THE TEAM IS DELIBERATELY AVOIDING OLD-SCHOOL, BUT WE REALLY OUGHT TO FIND AN ACTUAL HEADQUARTERS...
CALIFORNIA!
HEARD OF IT.
ARE YOU DONE THROWING A FIT?
...
TAKE ME TO CALIFORNIA. PLEASE.
UH-OH, IT'S NOT FUNNY ANYMORE IT'S NOT FUNNY ANYMORE IT'S NOT FUNNY ANYMORE--!
RELAX, OKAY, MS. MARVEL? BETWEEN THE TWO OF US, WE'LL GET YOU LOOSE!
GIVE THAT AN HOUR OR SO, IT'LL MELT AWAY.
MARV, I KNOW THE FREELANCERS SCREWED US, AND IT STINGS, BUT THEY DIDN'T DO ANYTHING ILLEGAL.
NOVA CAN'T JUST DROP YOU OFF AT THEIR FRONT DOOR SO YOU CAN KNOCK HEADS. THAT'LL JUST MAKE THIS WORSE. YOU KNOW THAT.

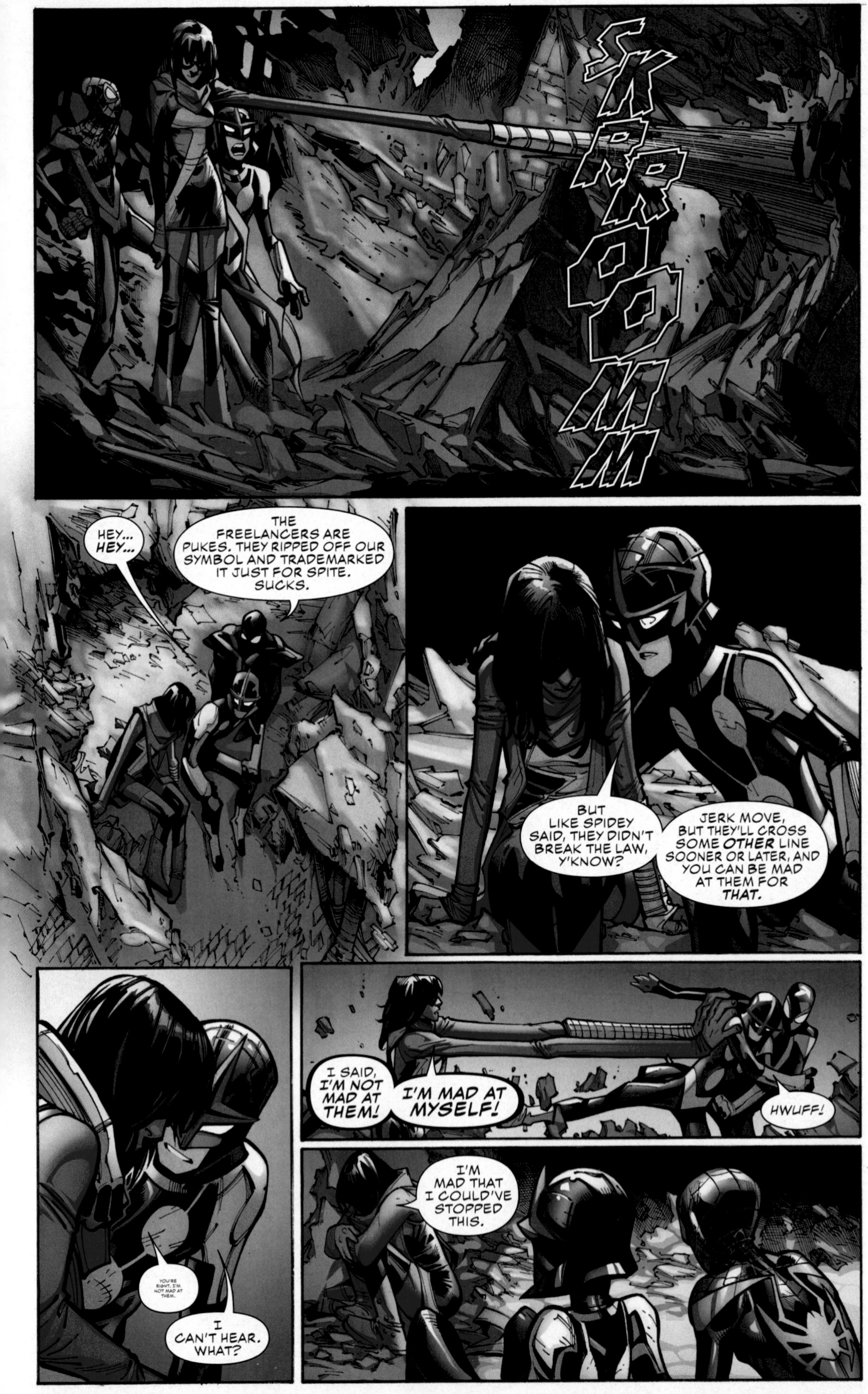
SKRROOMMM
HEY... HEY...
THE FREELANCERS ARE PUKES. THEY RIPPED OFF OUR SYMBOL AND TRADEMARKED IT JUST FOR SPITE. SUCKS.
BUT LIKE SPIDEY SAID, THEY DIDN'T BREAK THE LAW, Y'KNOW?
JERK MOVE, BUT THEY'LL CROSS SOME OTHER LINE SOONER OR LATER, AND YOU CAN BE MAD AT THEM FOR THAT.
YOU'RE RIGHT. I'M NOT MAD AT THEM.
I CAN'T HEAR. WHAT?
I SAID, I'M NOT MAD AT THEM!
I'M MAD AT MYSELF!
HWUFF!
I'M MAD THAT I COULD'VE STOPPED THIS.

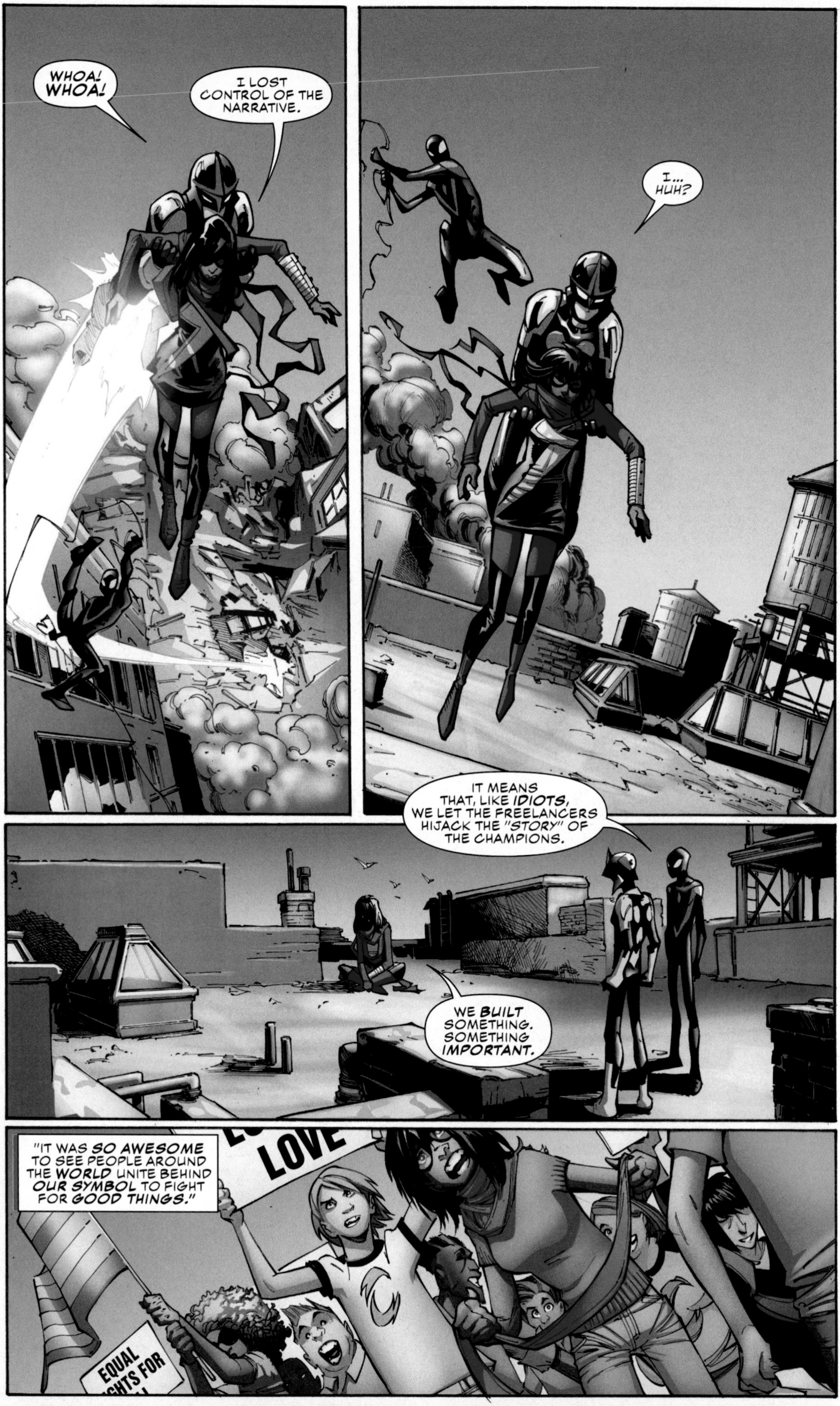
WHOA! WHOA!
I LOST CONTROL OF THE NARRATIVE.
I... HUH?
IT MEANS THAT, LIKE IDIOTS, WE LET THE FREELANCERS HIJACK THE "STORY" OF THE CHAMPIONS.
WE BUILT SOMETHING. SOMETHING IMPORTANT.
"IT WAS SO AWESOME TO SEE PEOPLE AROUND THE WORLD UNITE BEHIND OUR SYMBOL TO FIGHT FOR GOOD THINGS."
LOVE
EQUAL

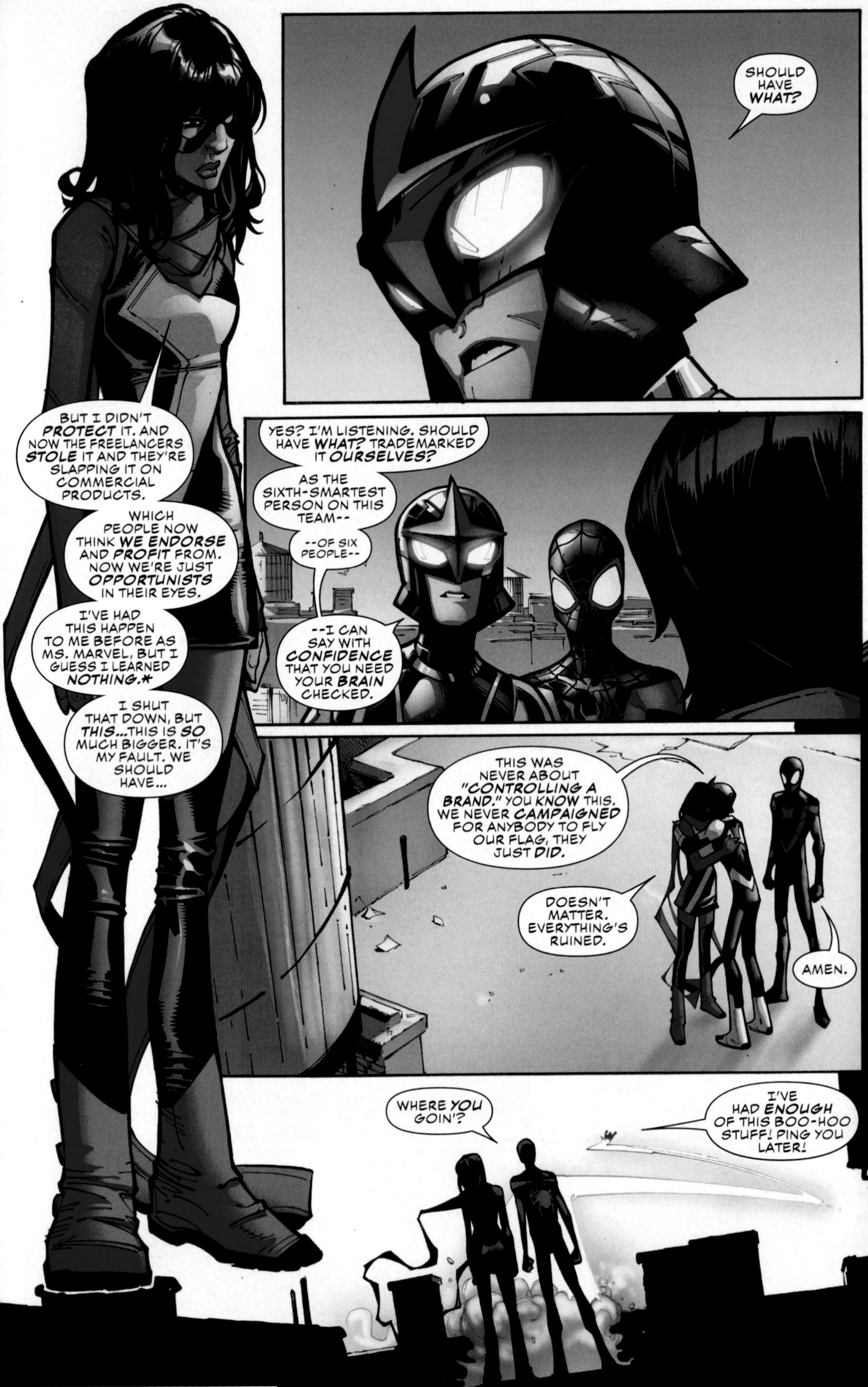
SHOULD HAVE WHAT?
BUT I DIDN'T PROTECT IT. AND NOW THE FREELANCERS STOLE IT AND THEY'RE SLAPPING IT ON COMMERCIAL PRODUCTS.
WHICH PEOPLE NOW THINK WE ENDORSE AND PROFIT FROM. NOW WE'RE JUST OPPORTUNISTS IN THEIR EYES.
I'VE HAD THIS HAPPEN TO ME BEFORE AS MS. MARVEL, BUT I GUESS I LEARNED NOTHING.*
I SHUT THAT DOWN, BUT THIS...THIS IS SO MUCH BIGGER. IT'S MY FAULT. WE SHOULD HAVE...
YES? I'M LISTENING. SHOULD HAVE WHAT? TRADEMARKED IT OURSELVES?
AS THE SIXTH-SMARTEST PERSON ON THIS TEAM--
--OF SIX PEOPLE--
--I CAN SAY WITH CONFIDENCE THAT YOU NEED YOUR BRAIN CHECKED.
THIS WAS NEVER ABOUT "CONTROLLING A BRAND." YOU KNOW THIS. WE NEVER CAMPAIGNED FOR ANYBODY TO FLY OUR FLAG, THEY JUST DID.
DOESN'T MATTER. EVERYTHING'S RUINED.
AMEN.
WHERE YOU GOIN'?
I'VE HAD ENOUGH OF THIS BOO-HOO STUFF! PING YOU LATER!

*SEE MS. MARVEL (2016) # 1-3. -TOM.

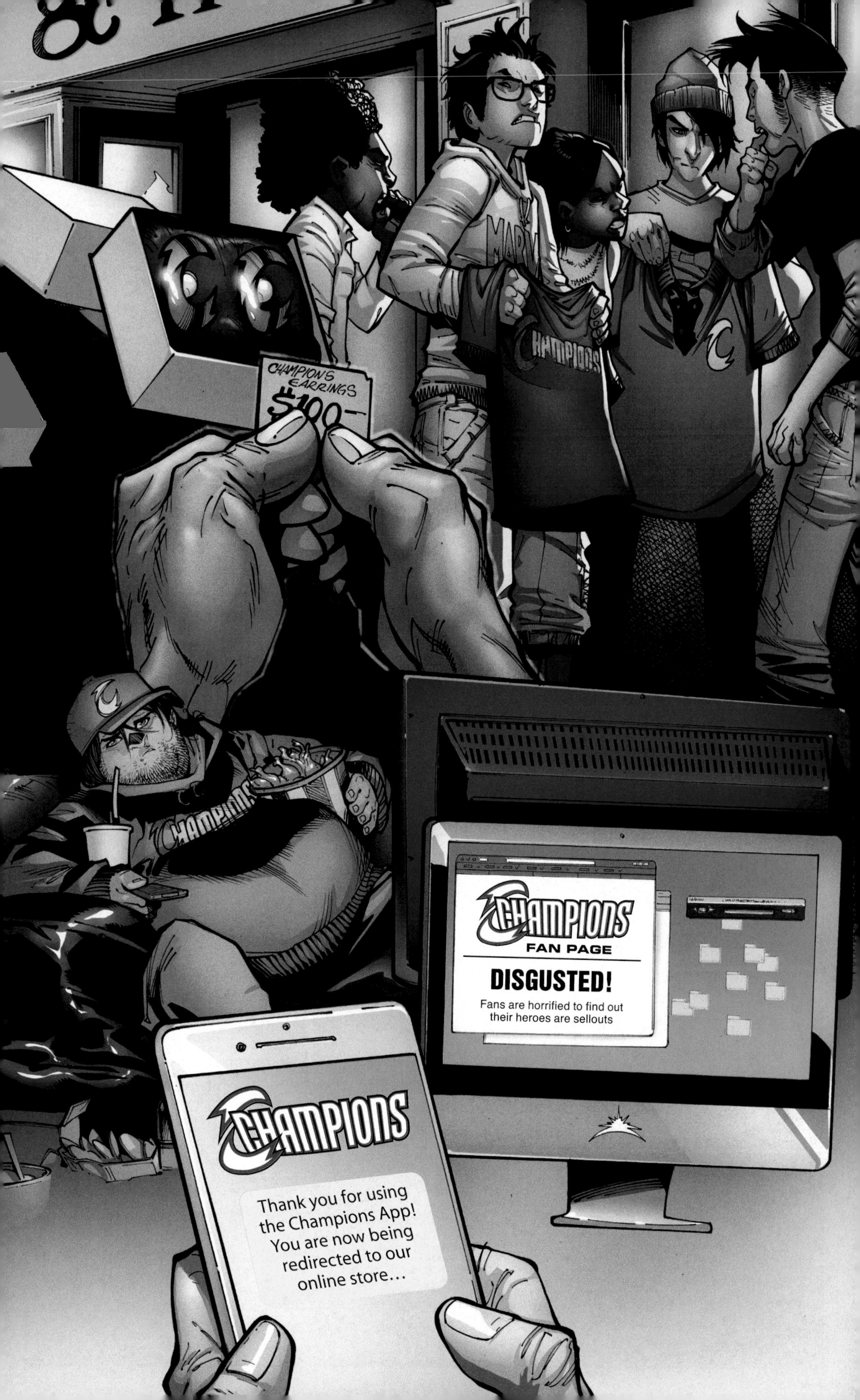

CHAMPIONS EARRINGS $100.-
CHAMPIONS
CHAMPIONS FAN PAGE
DISGUSTED!
Fans are horrified to find out their heroes are sellouts
CHAMPIONS
Thank you for using the Champions App! You are now being redirected to our online store...

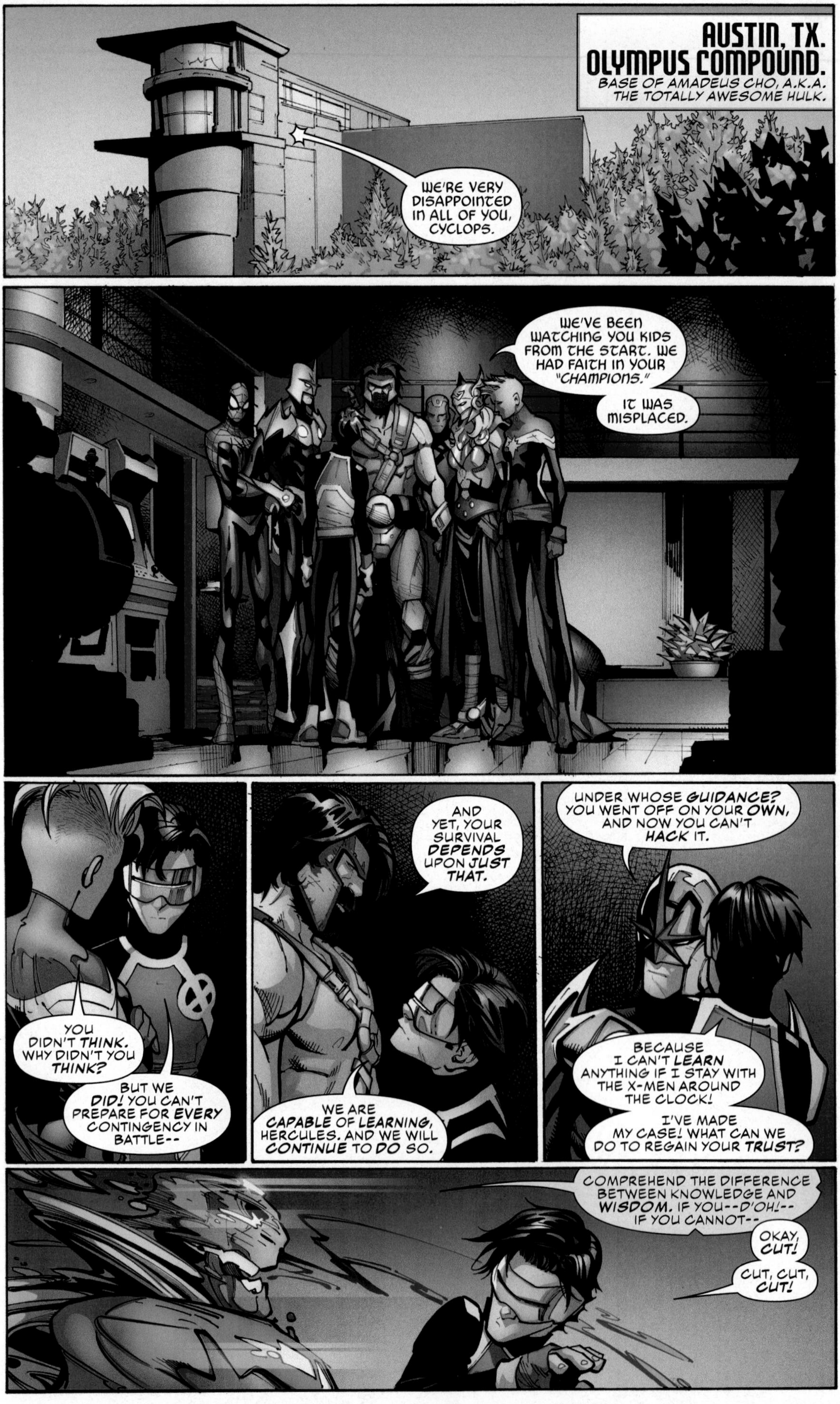
AUSTIN, TX.
OLYMPUS COMPOUND.
BASE OF AMADEUS CHO, A.K.A. THE TOTALLY AWESOME HULK.
WE'RE VERY DISAPPOINTED IN ALL OF YOU, CYCLOPS.
WE'VE BEEN WATCHING YOU KIDS FROM THE START. WE HAD FAITH IN YOUR "CHAMPIONS."
IT WAS MISPLACED.
YOU DIDN'T THINK. WHY DIDN'T YOU THINK?
BUT WE DID! YOU CAN'T PREPARE FOR EVERY CONTINGENCY IN BATTLE--
AND YET, YOUR SURVIVAL DEPENDS UPON JUST THAT.
WE ARE CAPABLE OF LEARNING, HERCULES. AND WE WILL CONTINUE TO DO SO.
UNDER WHOSE GUIDANCE? YOU WENT OFF ON YOUR OWN, AND NOW YOU CAN'T HACK IT.
BECAUSE I CAN'T LEARN ANYTHING IF I STAY WITH THE X-MEN AROUND THE CLOCK!
I'VE MADE MY CASE! WHAT CAN WE DO TO REGAIN YOUR TRUST?
COMPREHEND THE DIFFERENCE BETWEEN KNOWLEDGE AND WISDOM. IF YOU--D'OH!-- IF YOU CANNOT--
OKAY, CUT!
CUT, CUT, CUT!

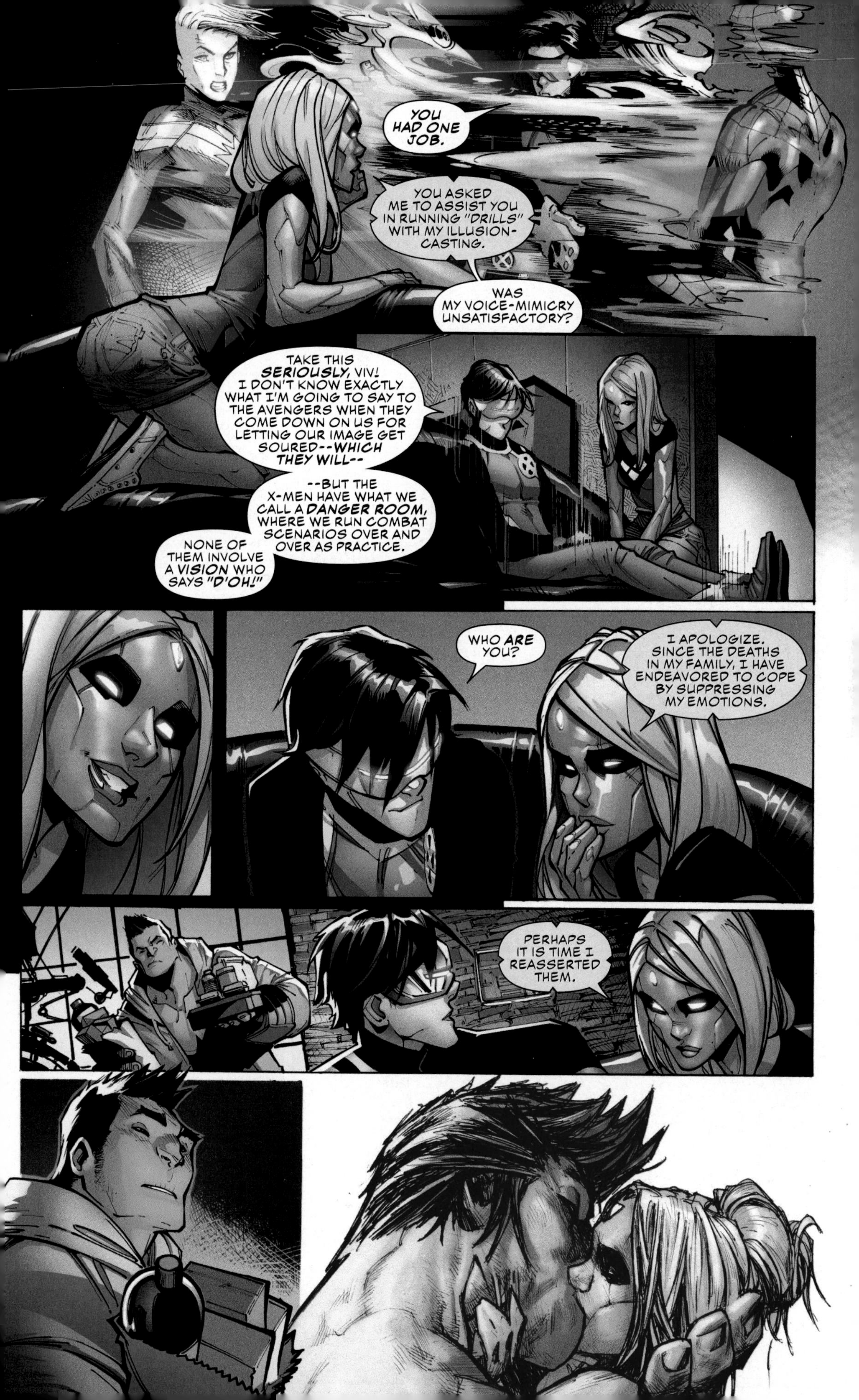
YOU HAD ONE JOB.
YOU ASKED ME TO ASSIST YOU IN RUNNING "DRILLS" WITH MY ILLUSION-CASTING.
WAS MY VOICE-MIMICRY UNSATISFACTORY?
TAKE THIS SERIOUSLY, VIV! I DON'T KNOW EXACTLY WHAT I'M GOING TO SAY TO THE AVENGERS WHEN THEY COME DOWN ON US FOR LETTING OUR IMAGE GET SOURED--WHICH THEY WILL--
--BUT THE X-MEN HAVE WHAT WE CALL A DANGER ROOM, WHERE WE RUN COMBAT SCENARIOS OVER AND OVER AS PRACTICE.
NONE OF THEM INVOLVE A VISION WHO SAYS "D'OH!"
WHO ARE YOU?
I APOLOGIZE. SINCE THE DEATHS IN MY FAMILY, I HAVE ENDEAVORED TO COPE BY SUPPRESSING MY EMOTIONS.
PERHAPS IT IS TIME I REASSERTED THEM.

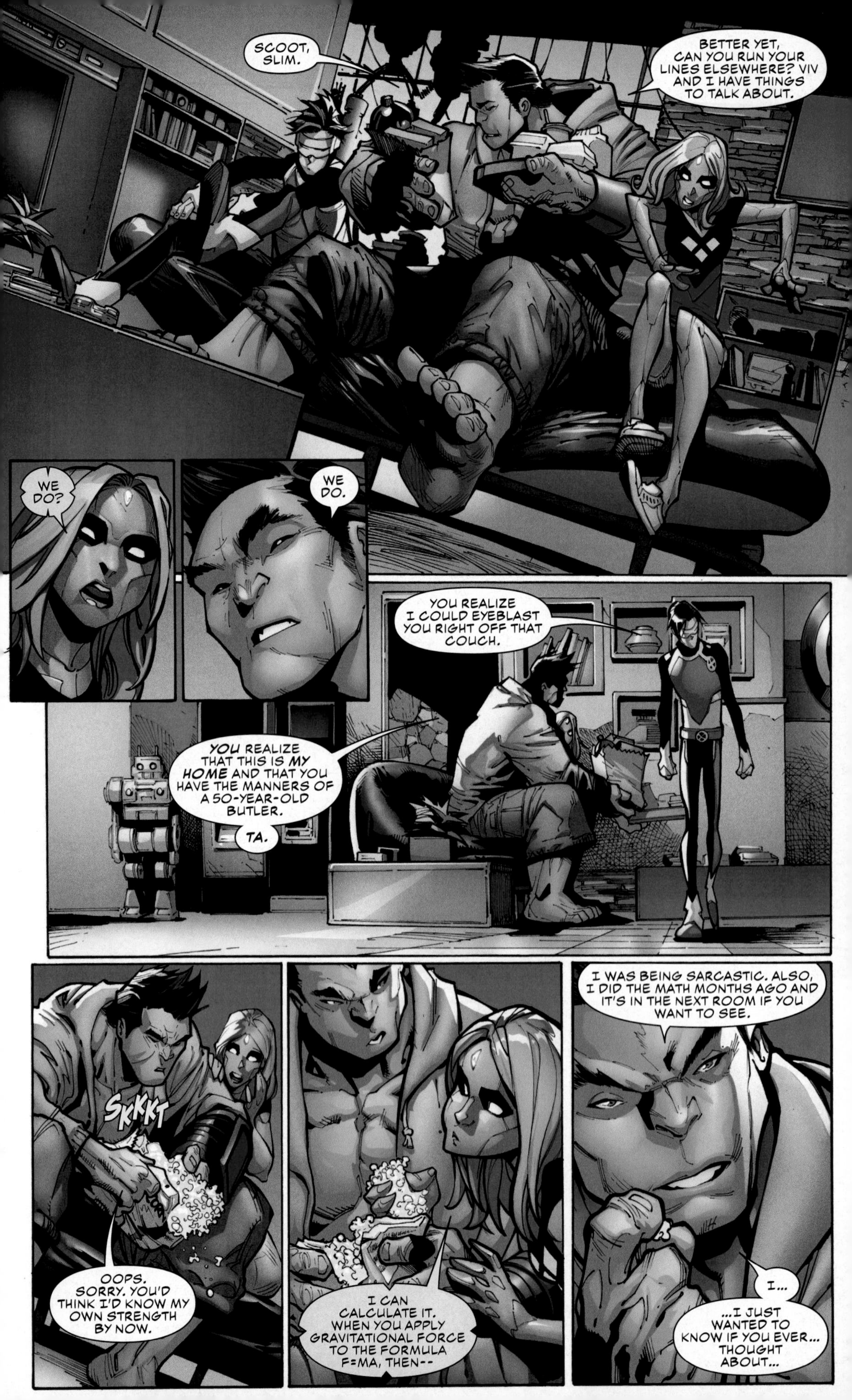
SCOOT, SLIM.
BETTER YET, CAN YOU RUN YOUR LINES ELSEWHERE? VIV AND I HAVE THINGS TO TALK ABOUT.
WE DO?
WE DO.
YOU REALIZE I COULD EYEBLAST YOU RIGHT OFF THAT COUCH.
YOU REALIZE THAT THIS IS MY HOME AND THAT YOU HAVE THE MANNERS OF A 50-YEAR-OLD BUTLER.
TA.
SKKKT
OOPS. SORRY. YOU'D THINK I'D KNOW MY OWN STRENGTH BY NOW.
I CAN CALCULATE IT. WHEN YOU APPLY GRAVITATIONAL FORCE TO THE FORMULA F=MA, THEN--
I WAS BEING SARCASTIC. ALSO, I DID THE MATH MONTHS AGO AND IT'S IN THE NEXT ROOM IF YOU WANT TO SEE.
I...
...I JUST WANTED TO KNOW IF YOU EVER... THOUGHT ABOUT...

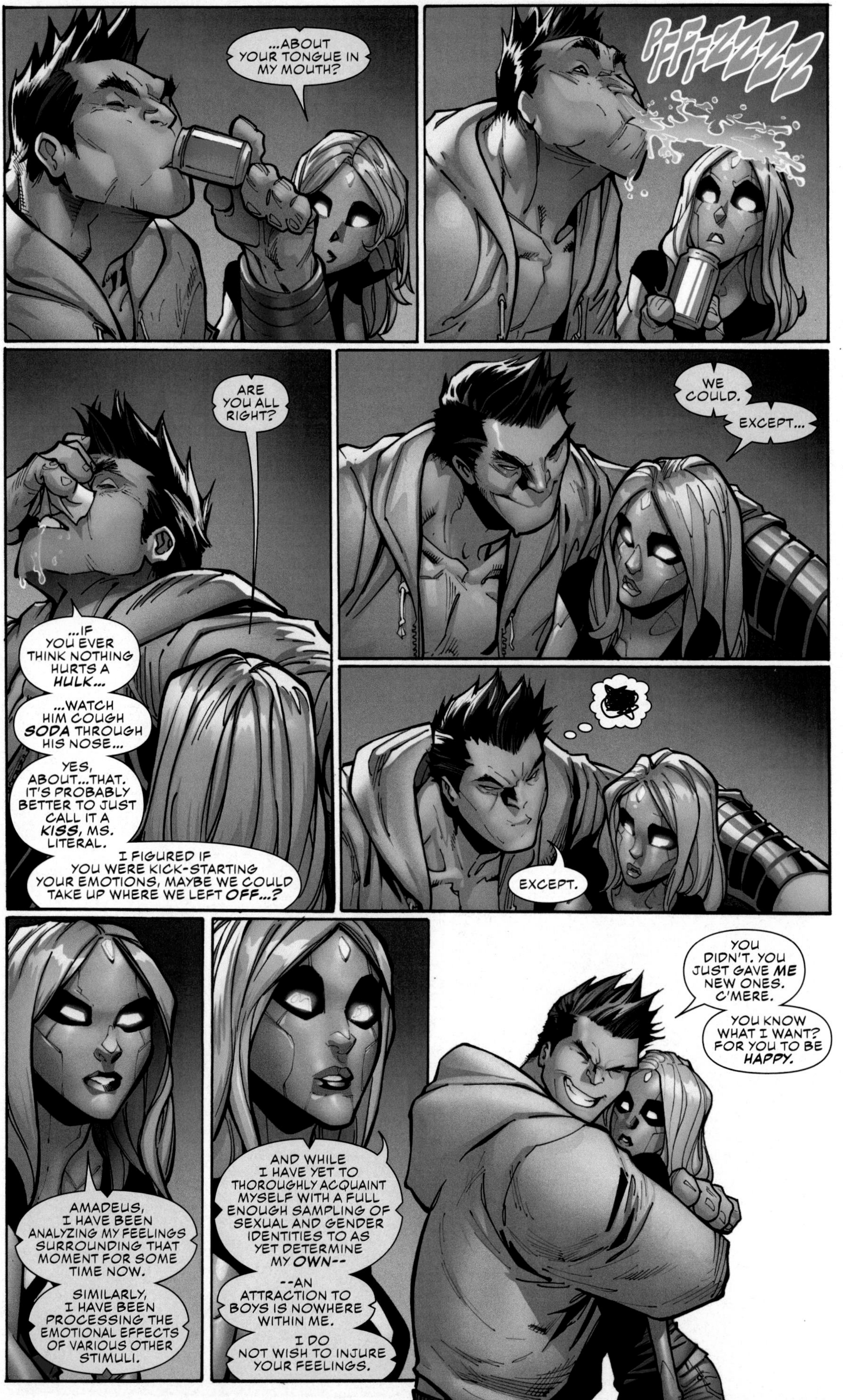
...ABOUT YOUR TONGUE IN MY MOUTH?
PFFFZZZZZ
ARE YOU ALL RIGHT?
...IF YOU EVER THINK NOTHING HURTS A HULK...
...WATCH HIM COUGH SODA THROUGH HIS NOSE...
YES, ABOUT...THAT. IT'S PROBABLY BETTER TO JUST CALL IT A KISS, MS. LITERAL.
I FIGURED IF YOU WERE KICK-STARTING YOUR EMOTIONS, MAYBE WE COULD TAKE UP WHERE WE LEFT OFF...?
WE COULD.
EXCEPT...
EXCEPT.
AMADEUS, I HAVE BEEN ANALYZING MY FEELINGS SURROUNDING THAT MOMENT FOR SOME TIME NOW.
SIMILARLY, I HAVE BEEN PROCESSING THE EMOTIONAL EFFECTS OF VARIOUS OTHER STIMULI.
AND WHILE I HAVE YET TO THOROUGHLY ACQUAINT MYSELF WITH A FULL ENOUGH SAMPLING OF SEXUAL AND GENDER IDENTITIES TO AS YET DETERMINE MY OWN--
--AN ATTRACTION TO BOYS IS NOWHERE WITHIN ME.
I DO NOT WISH TO INJURE YOUR FEELINGS.
YOU DIDN'T. YOU JUST GAVE ME NEW ONES. C'MERE.
YOU KNOW WHAT I WANT? FOR YOU TO BE HAPPY.

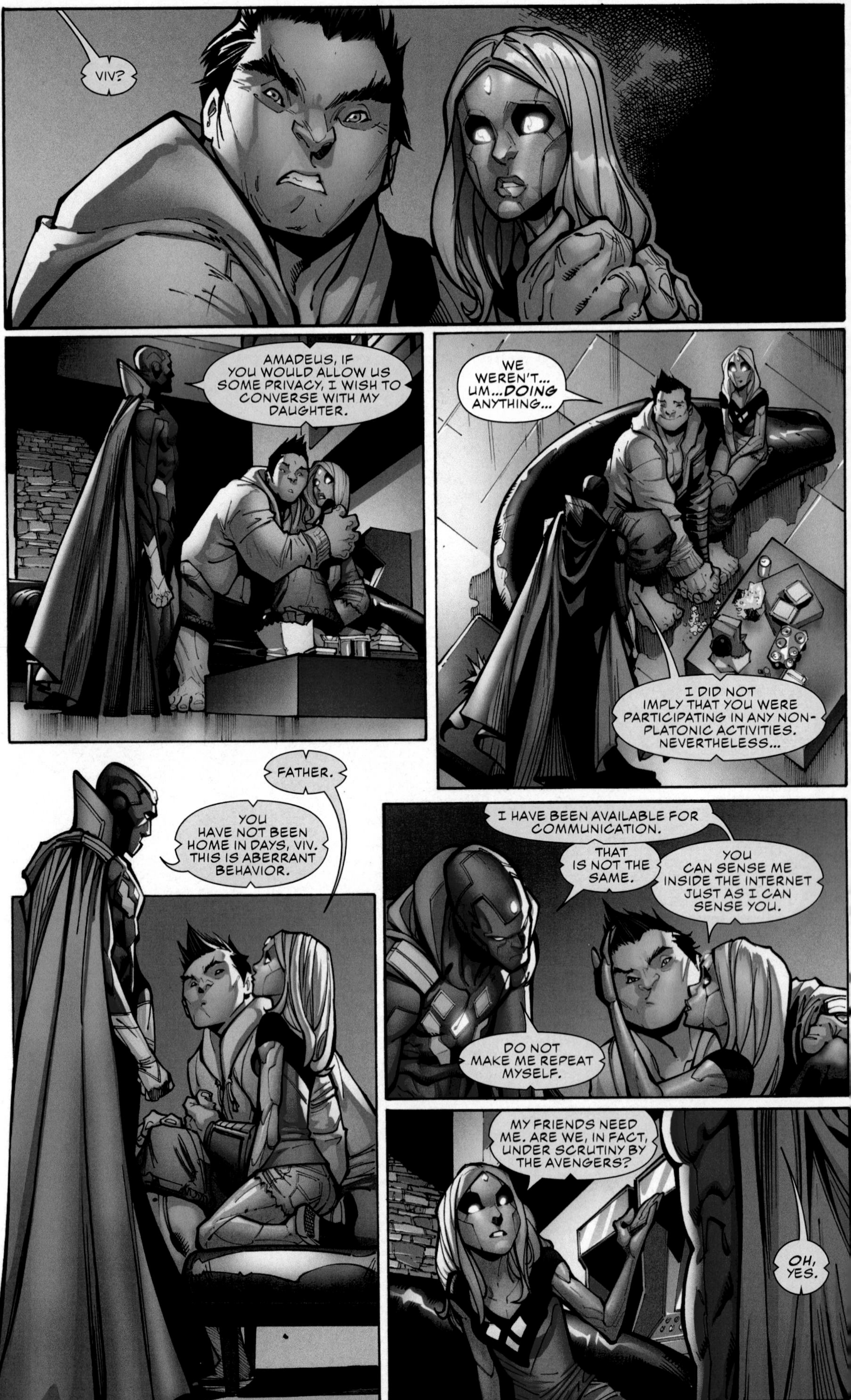
VIV?
AMADEUS, IF YOU WOULD ALLOW US SOME PRIVACY, I WISH TO CONVERSE WITH MY DAUGHTER.
WE WEREN'T... UM...DOING ANYTHING...
I DID NOT IMPLY THAT YOU WERE PARTICIPATING IN ANY NON-PLATONIC ACTIVITIES. NEVERTHELESS...
FATHER.
YOU HAVE NOT BEEN HOME IN DAYS, VIV. THIS IS ABERRANT BEHAVIOR.
I HAVE BEEN AVAILABLE FOR COMMUNICATION.
THAT IS NOT THE SAME.
YOU CAN SENSE ME INSIDE THE INTERNET JUST AS I CAN SENSE YOU.
DO NOT MAKE ME REPEAT MYSELF.
MY FRIENDS NEED ME. ARE WE, IN FACT, UNDER SCRUTINY BY THE AVENGERS?
OH, YES.

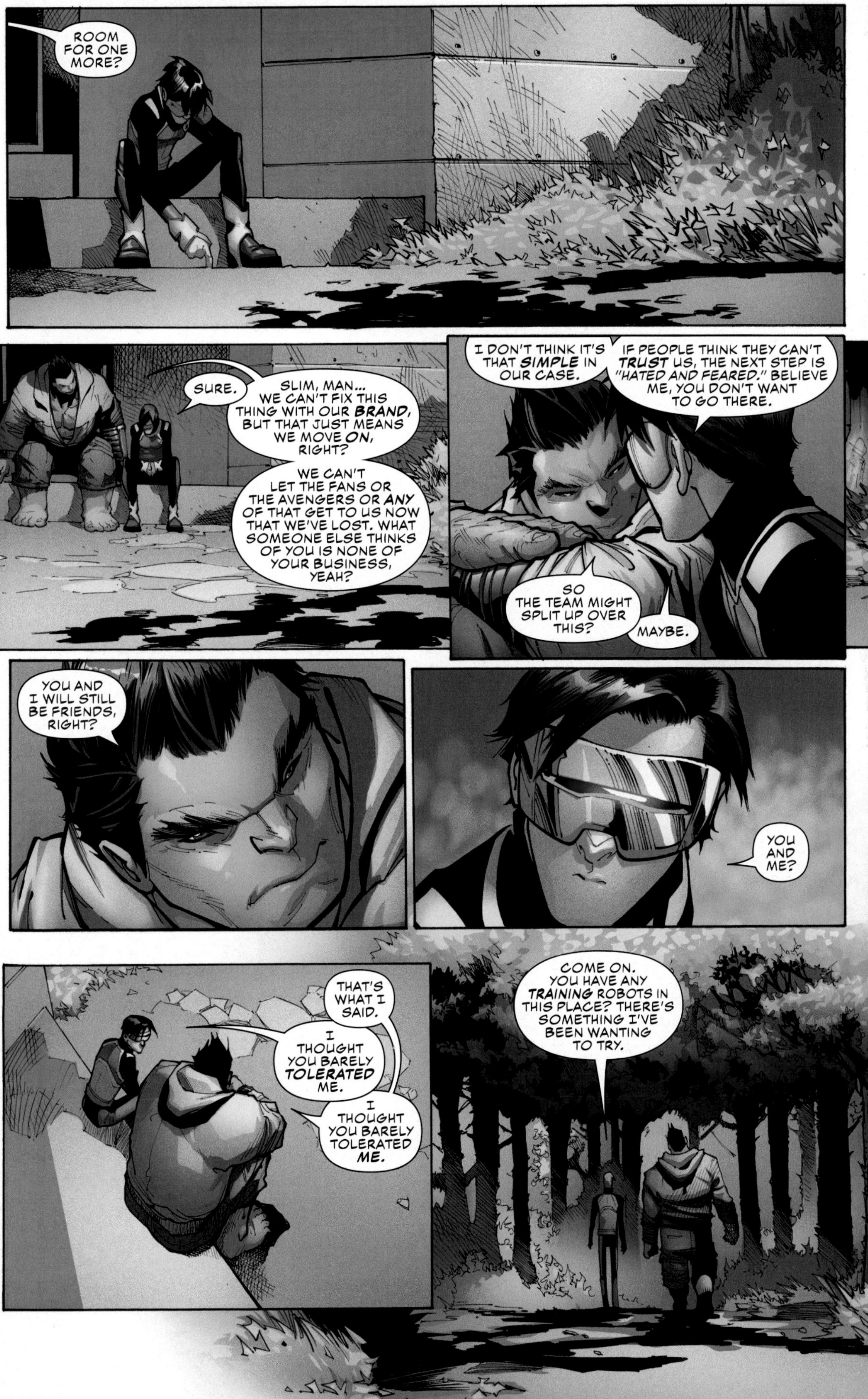
ROOM FOR ONE MORE?
SURE.
SLIM, MAN... WE CAN'T FIX THIS THING WITH OUR BRAND, BUT THAT JUST MEANS WE MOVE ON, RIGHT?
WE CAN'T LET THE FANS OR THE AVENGERS OR ANY OF THAT GET TO US NOW THAT WE'VE LOST. WHAT SOMEONE ELSE THINKS OF YOU IS NONE OF YOUR BUSINESS, YEAH?
I DON'T THINK IT'S THAT SIMPLE IN OUR CASE.
IF PEOPLE THINK THEY CAN'T TRUST US, THE NEXT STEP IS "HATED AND FEARED." BELIEVE ME, YOU DON'T WANT TO GO THERE.
SO THE TEAM MIGHT SPLIT UP OVER THIS?
MAYBE.
YOU AND I WILL STILL BE FRIENDS, RIGHT?
YOU AND ME?
THAT'S WHAT I SAID.
I THOUGHT YOU BARELY TOLERATED ME.
I THOUGHT YOU BARELY TOLERATED ME.
COME ON. YOU HAVE ANY TRAINING ROBOTS IN THIS PLACE? THERE'S SOMETHING I'VE BEEN WANTING TO TRY.

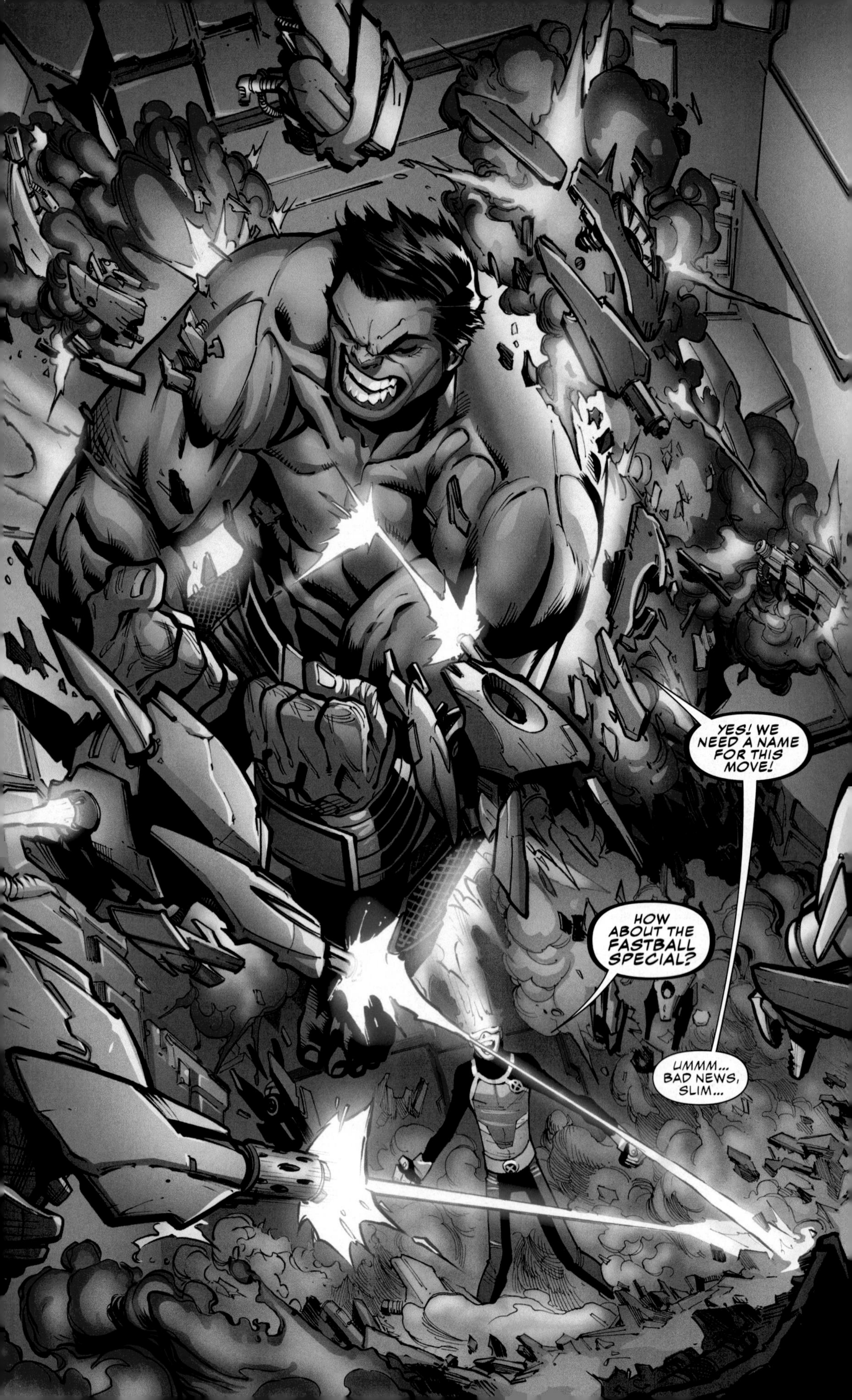
YES! WE NEED A NAME FOR THIS MOVE!
HOW ABOUT THE FASTBALL SPECIAL?
UMMM... BAD NEWS, SLIM...

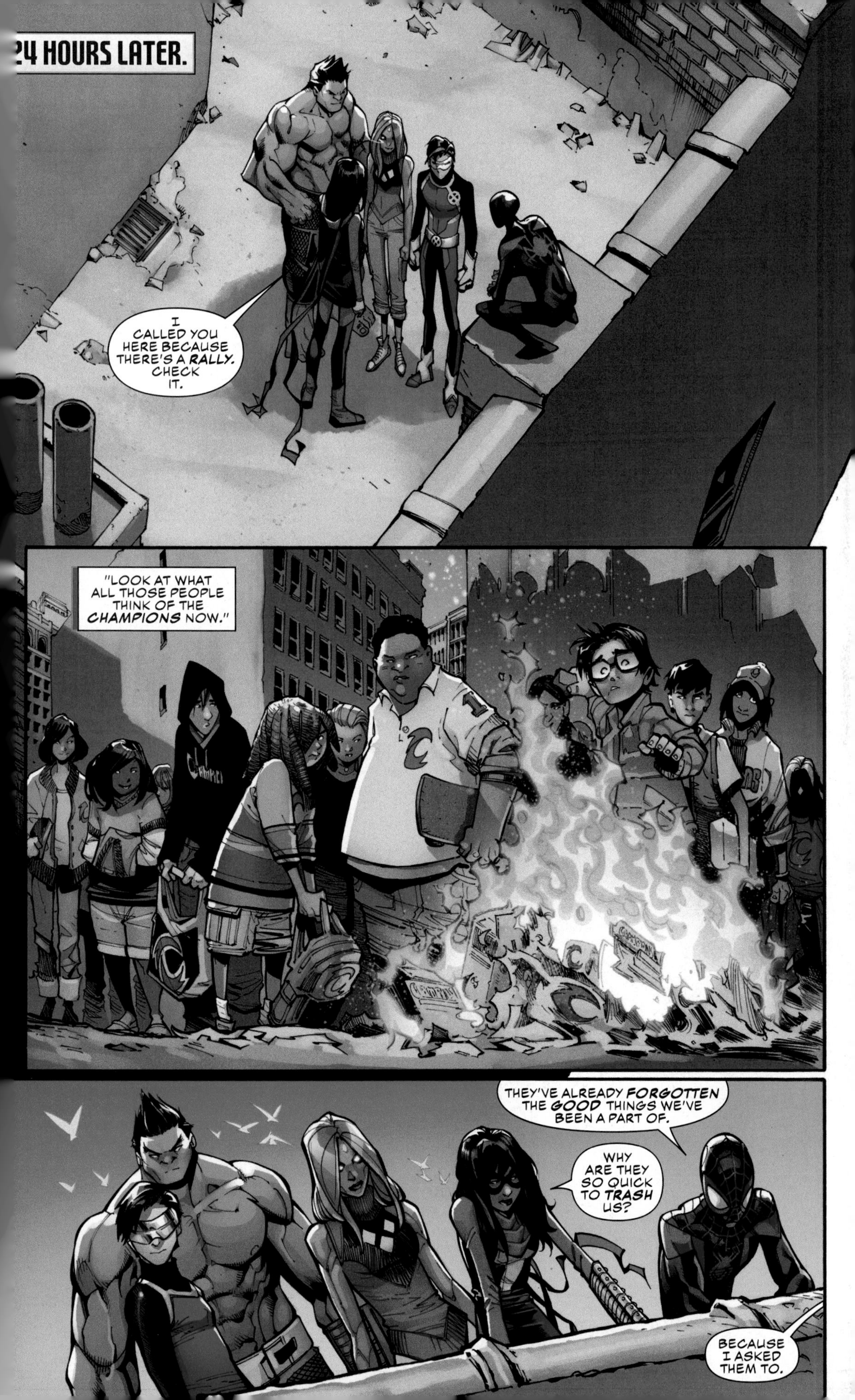
24 HOURS LATER.
I CALLED YOU HERE BECAUSE THERE'S A RALLY. CHECK IT.
"LOOK AT WHAT ALL THOSE PEOPLE THINK OF THE CHAMPIONS NOW."
THEY'VE ALREADY FORGOTTEN THE GOOD THINGS WE'VE BEEN A PART OF.
WHY ARE THEY SO QUICK TO TRASH US?
BECAUSE I ASKED THEM TO.

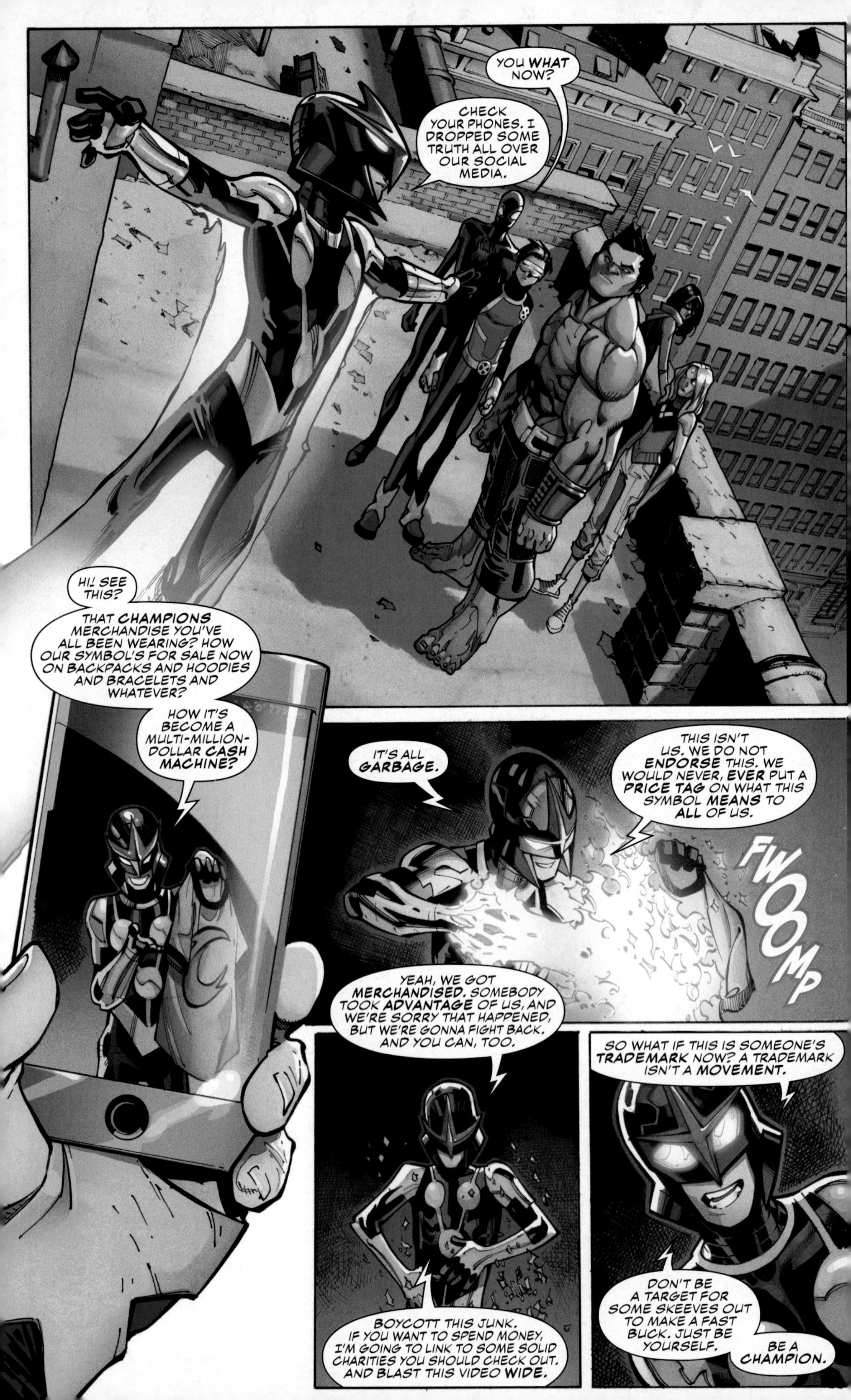
YOU WHAT NOW?
CHECK YOUR PHONES. I DROPPED SOME TRUTH ALL OVER OUR SOCIAL MEDIA.
HI! SEE THIS?
THAT CHAMPIONS MERCHANDISE YOU'VE ALL BEEN WEARING? HOW OUR SYMBOL'S FOR SALE NOW ON BACKPACKS AND HOODIES AND BRACELETS AND WHATEVER?
HOW IT'S BECOME A MULTI-MILLION-DOLLAR CASH MACHINE?
IT'S ALL GARBAGE.
THIS ISN'T US. WE DO NOT ENDORSE THIS. WE WOULD NEVER, EVER PUT A PRICE TAG ON WHAT THIS SYMBOL MEANS TO ALL OF US.
FWOOMP
YEAH, WE GOT MERCHANDISED. SOMEBODY TOOK ADVANTAGE OF US, AND WE'RE SORRY THAT HAPPENED, BUT WE'RE GONNA FIGHT BACK. AND YOU CAN, TOO.
BOYCOTT THIS JUNK. IF YOU WANT TO SPEND MONEY, I'M GOING TO LINK TO SOME SOLID CHARITIES YOU SHOULD CHECK OUT. AND BLAST THIS VIDEO WIDE.
SO WHAT IF THIS IS SOMEONE'S TRADEMARK NOW? A TRADEMARK ISN'T A MOVEMENT.
DON'T BE A TARGET FOR SOME SKEEVES OUT TO MAKE A FAST BUCK. JUST BE YOURSELF.
BE A CHAMPION.

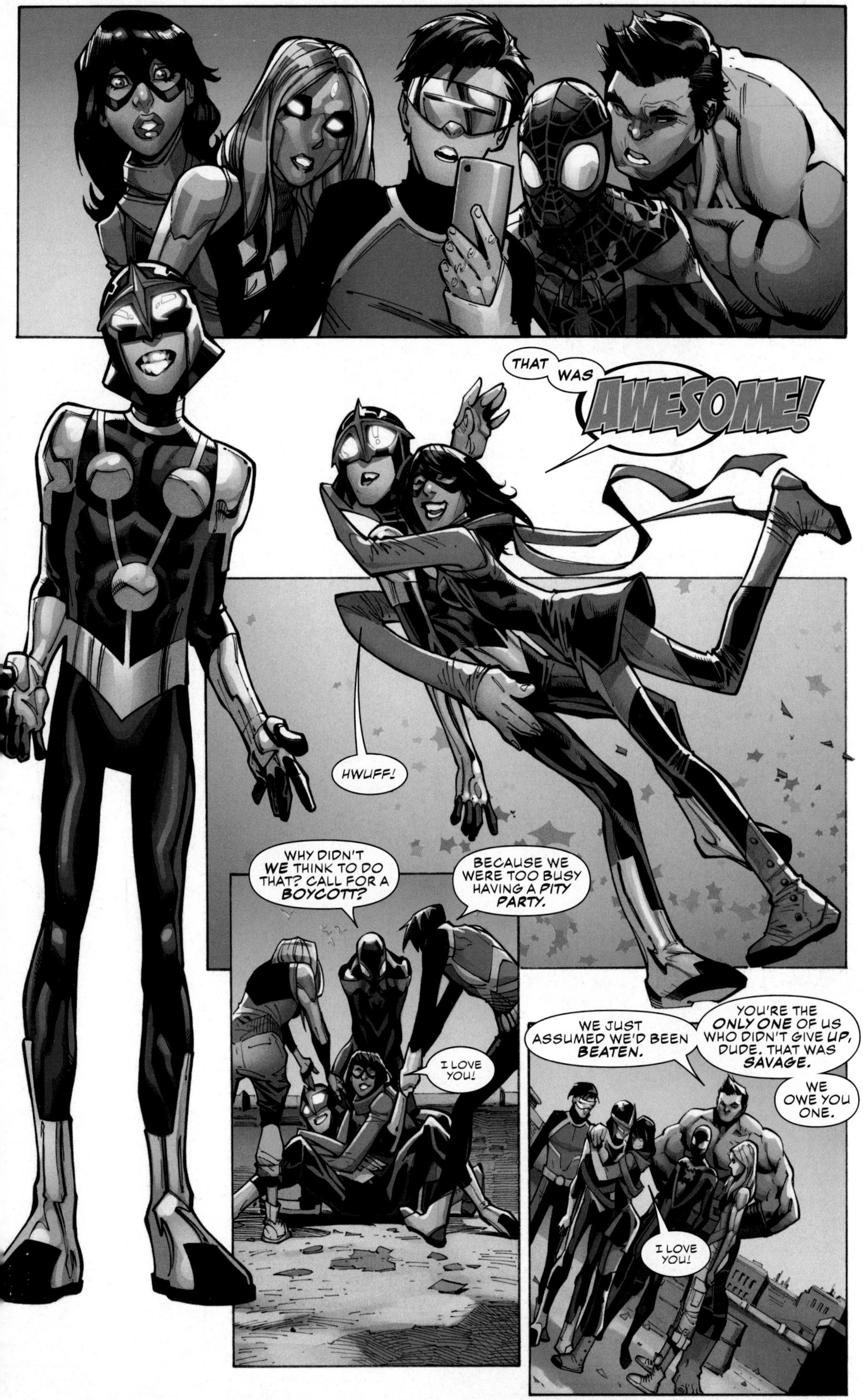
THAT WAS AWESOME!
HWUFF!
WHY DIDN'T WE THINK TO DO THAT? CALL FOR A BOYCOTT?
BECAUSE WE WERE TOO BUSY HAVING A PITY PARTY.
I LOVE YOU!
WE JUST ASSUMED WE'D BEEN BEATEN.
YOU'RE THE ONLY ONE OF US WHO DIDN'T GIVE UP, DUDE. THAT WAS SAVAGE.
WE OWE YOU ONE.
I LOVE YOU!

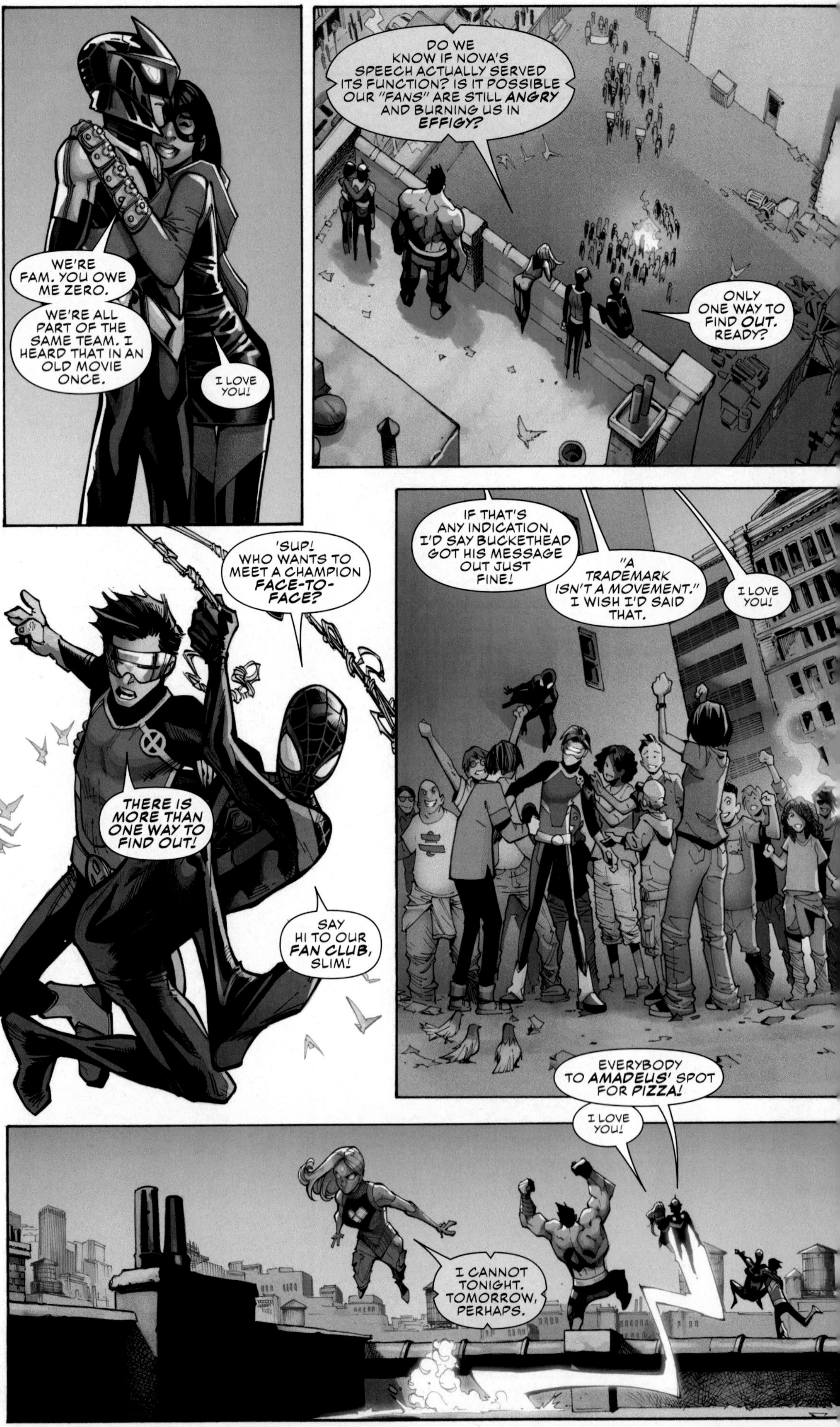
WE'RE FAM. YOU OWE ME ZERO.
WE'RE ALL PART OF THE SAME TEAM. I HEARD THAT IN AN OLD MOVIE ONCE.
I LOVE YOU!
DO WE KNOW IF NOVA'S SPEECH ACTUALLY SERVED ITS FUNCTION? IS IT POSSIBLE OUR "FANS" ARE STILL ANGRY AND BURNING US IN EFFIGY?
ONLY ONE WAY TO FIND OUT. READY?
'SUP! WHO WANTS TO MEET A CHAMPION FACE-TO-FACE?
THERE IS MORE THAN ONE WAY TO FIND OUT!
SAY HI TO OUR FAN CLUB, SLIM!
IF THAT'S ANY INDICATION, I'D SAY BUCKETHEAD GOT HIS MESSAGE OUT JUST FINE!
"A TRADEMARK ISN'T A MOVEMENT." I WISH I'D SAID THAT.
I LOVE YOU!
EVERYBODY TO AMADEUS' SPOT FOR PIZZA!
I LOVE YOU!
I CANNOT TONIGHT. TOMORROW, PERHAPS.

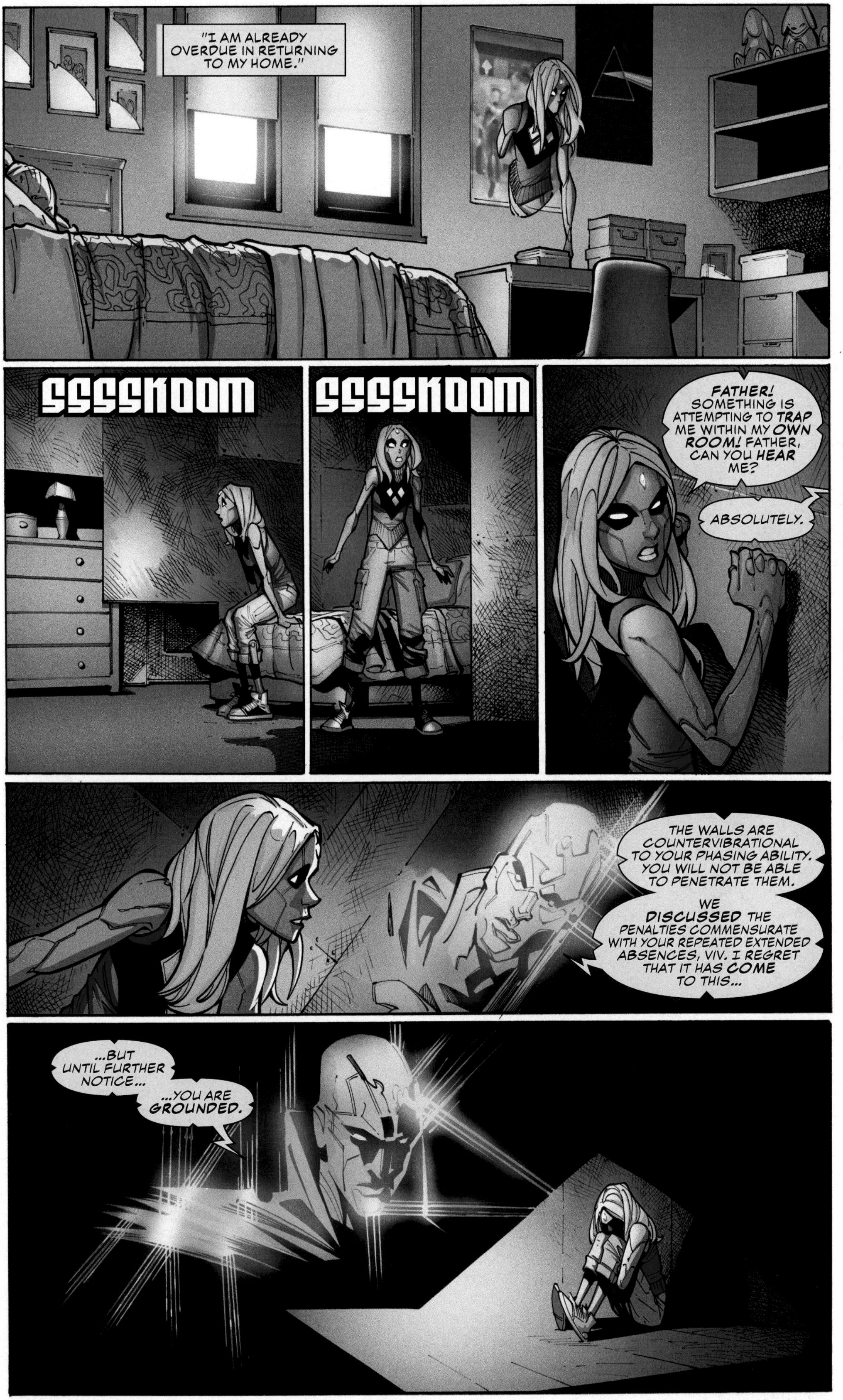
"I AM ALREADY OVERDUE IN RETURNING TO MY HOME."
SSSSKOOM
SSSSKOOM
FATHER! SOMETHING IS ATTEMPTING TO TRAP ME WITHIN MY OWN ROOM! FATHER, CAN YOU HEAR ME?
ABSOLUTELY.
THE WALLS ARE COUNTERVIBRATIONAL TO YOUR PHASING ABILITY. YOU WILL NOT BE ABLE TO PENETRATE THEM.
WE DISCUSSED THE PENALTIES COMMENSURATE WITH YOUR REPEATED EXTENDED ABSENCES, VIV. I REGRET THAT IT HAS COME TO THIS...
...BUT UNTIL FURTHER NOTICE...
...YOU ARE GROUNDED.

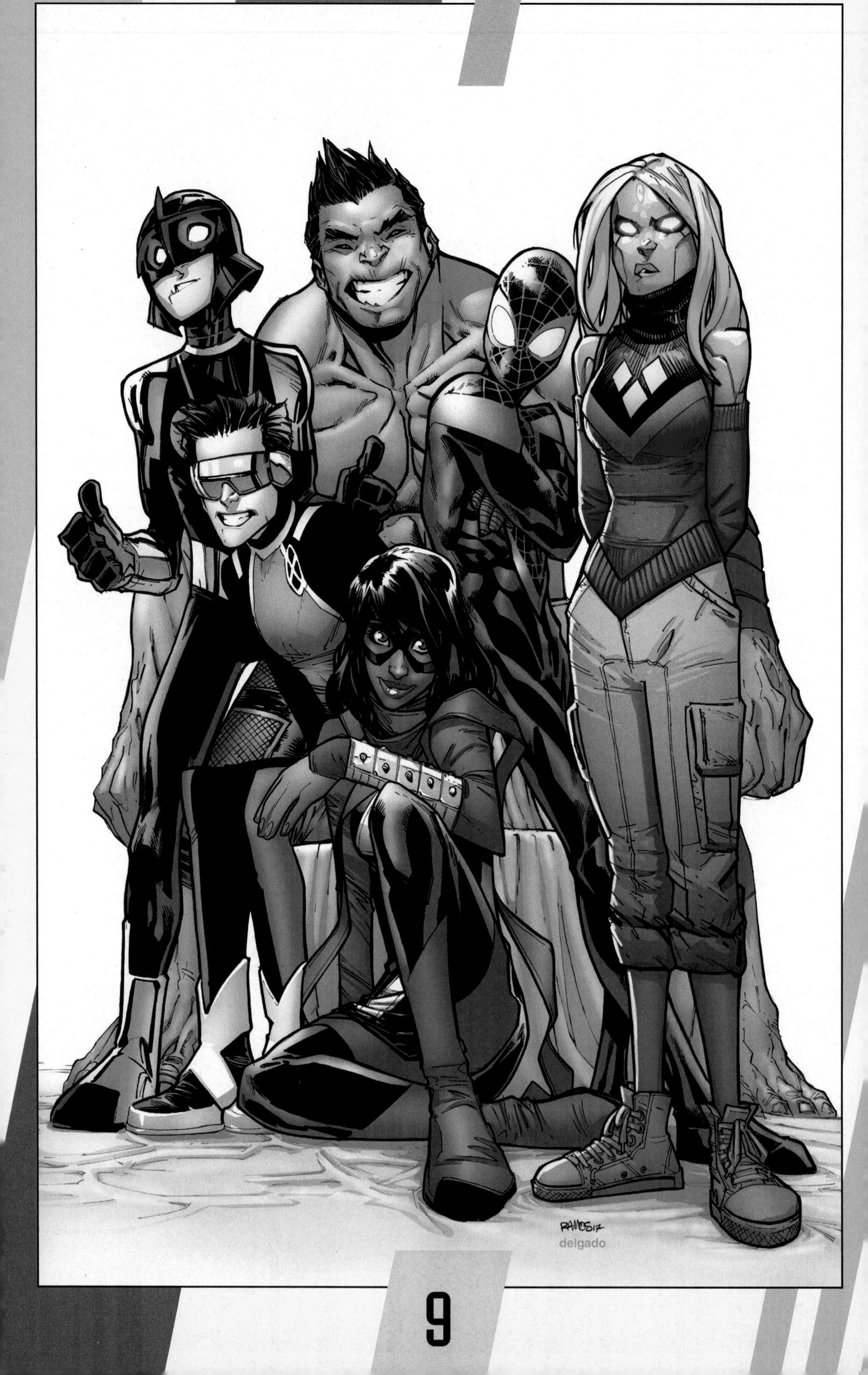
RAMOS17
delgado

9

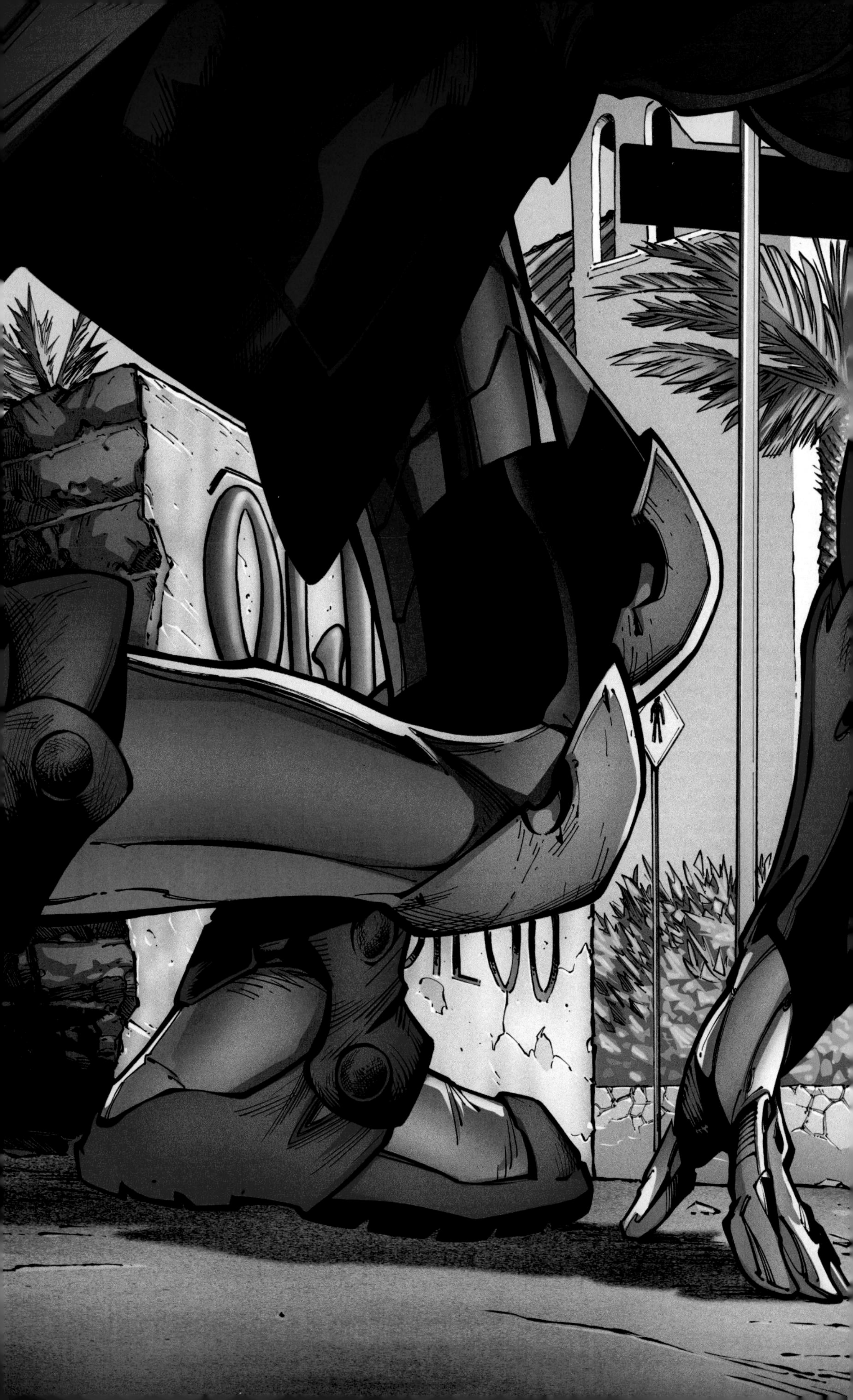

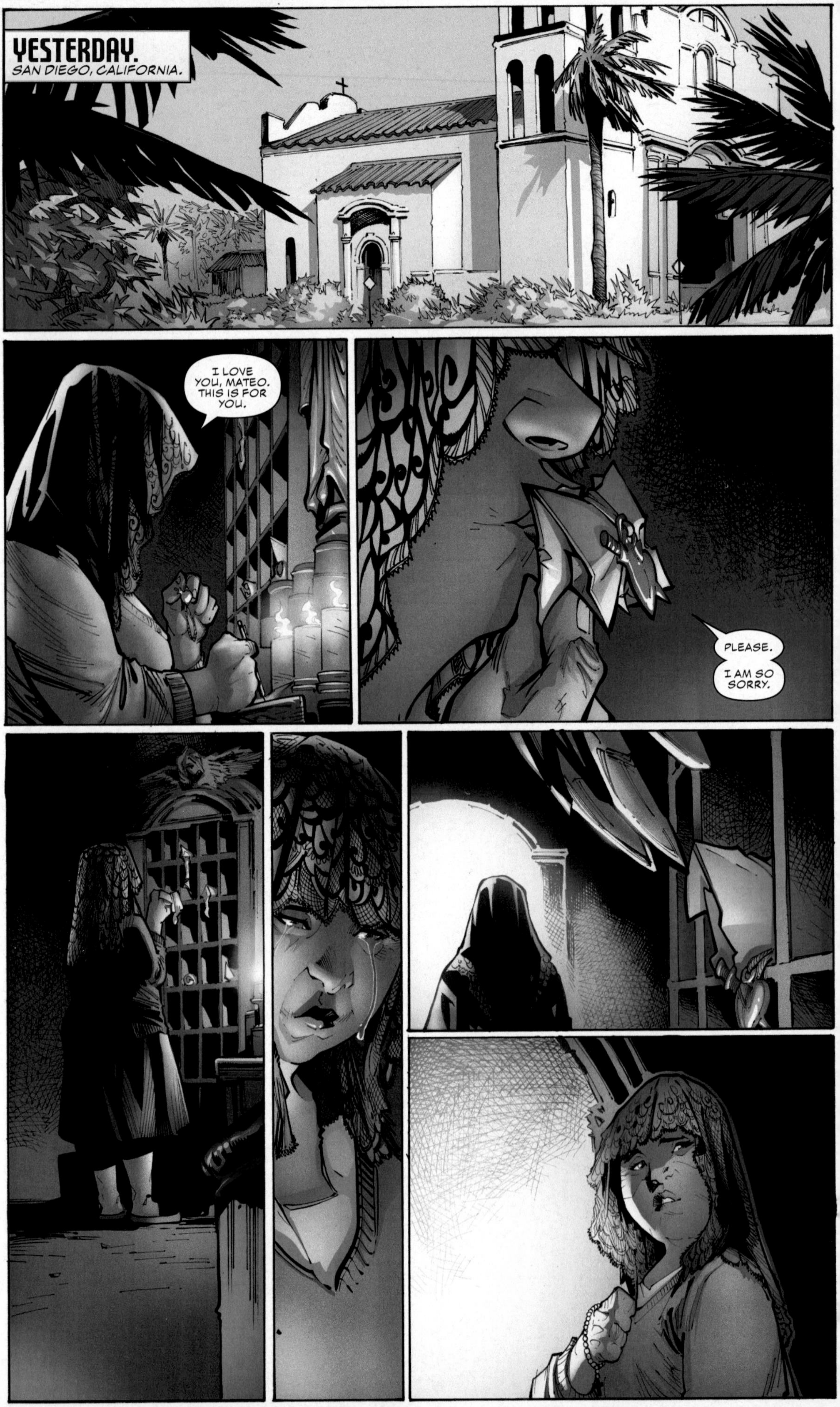
YESTERDAY.
SAN DIEGO, CALIFORNIA.
I LOVE YOU, MATEO. THIS IS FOR YOU.
PLEASE.
I AM SO SORRY.

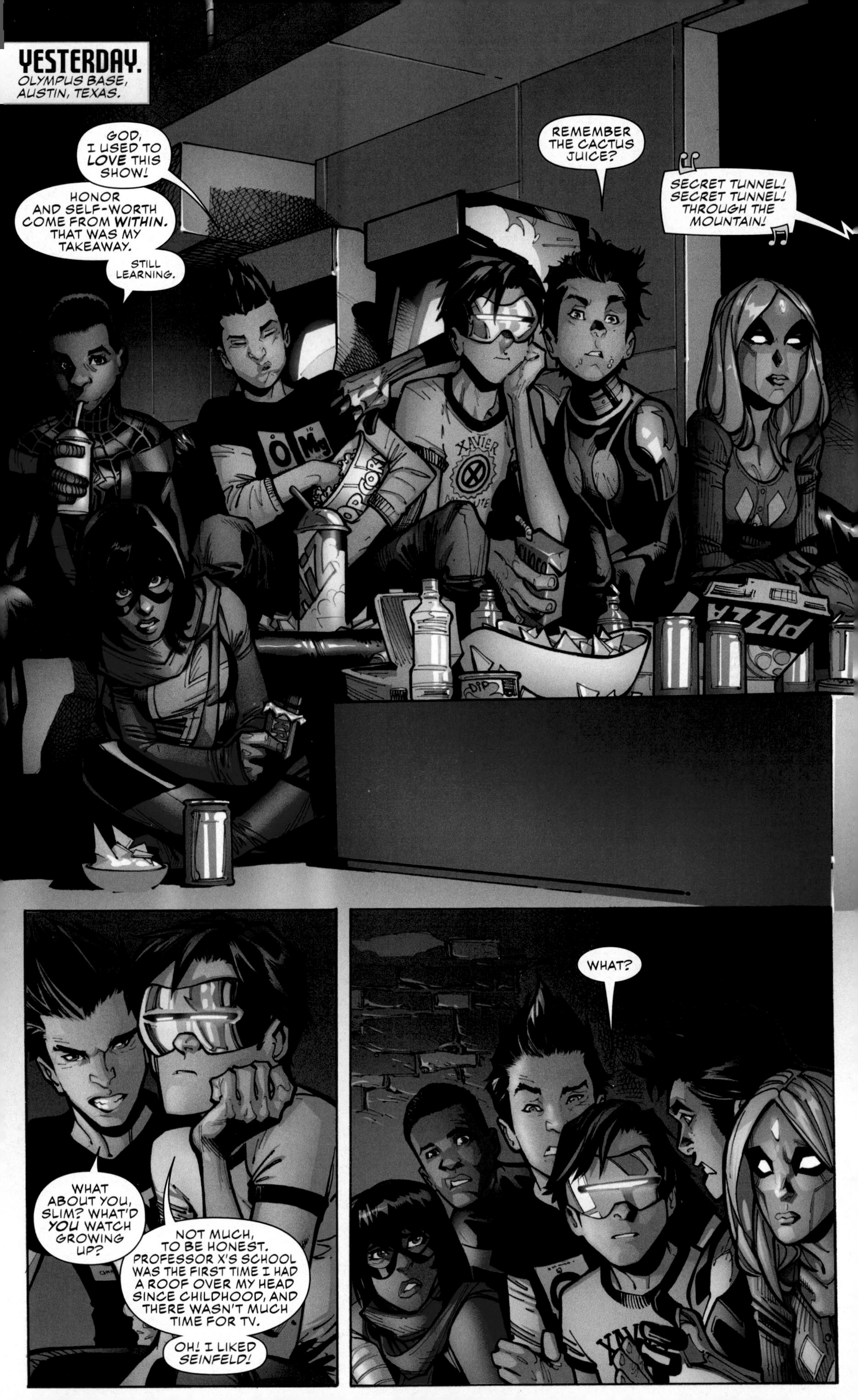
YESTERDAY.
OLYMPUS BASE, AUSTIN, TEXAS.
GOD, I USED TO LOVE THIS SHOW!
HONOR AND SELF-WORTH COME FROM WITHIN. THAT WAS MY TAKEAWAY.
STILL LEARNING.
REMEMBER THE CACTUS JUICE?
SECRET TUNNEL! SECRET TUNNEL! THROUGH THE MOUNTAIN!
WHAT ABOUT YOU, SLIM? WHAT'D YOU WATCH GROWING UP?
NOT MUCH, TO BE HONEST. PROFESSOR X'S SCHOOL WAS THE FIRST TIME I HAD A ROOF OVER MY HEAD SINCE CHILDHOOD, AND THERE WASN'T MUCH TIME FOR TV.
OH! I LIKED SEINFELD!
WHAT?

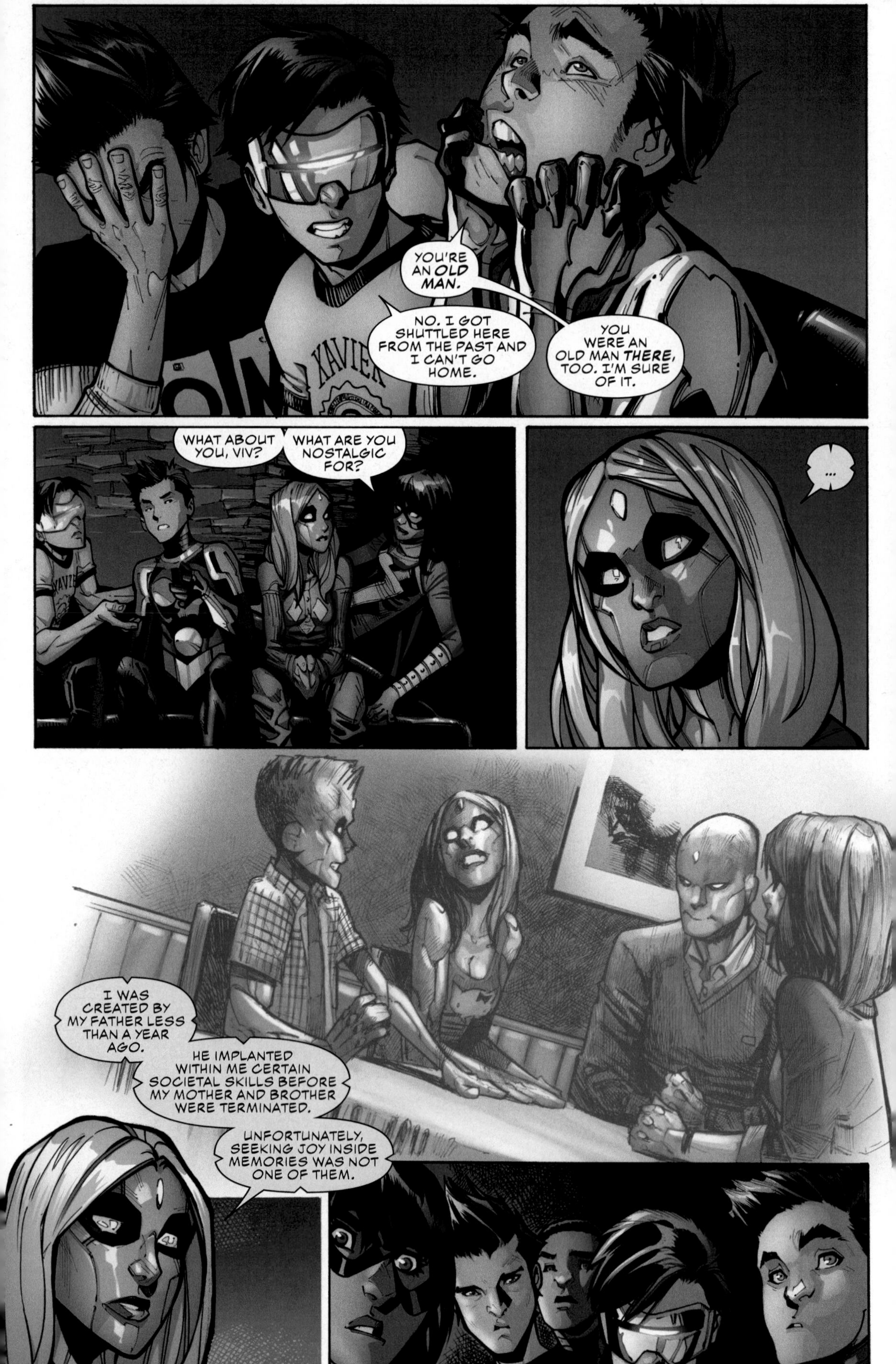
YOU'RE AN OLD MAN.
NO. I GOT SHUTTLED HERE FROM THE PAST AND I CAN'T GO HOME.
YOU WERE AN OLD MAN THERE, TOO. I'M SURE OF IT.
XAVIER
WHAT ABOUT YOU, VIV?
WHAT ARE YOU NOSTALGIC FOR?
...
I WAS CREATED BY MY FATHER LESS THAN A YEAR AGO.
HE IMPLANTED WITHIN ME CERTAIN SOCIETAL SKILLS BEFORE MY MOTHER AND BROTHER WERE TERMINATED.
UNFORTUNATELY, SEEKING JOY INSIDE MEMORIES WAS NOT ONE OF THEM.

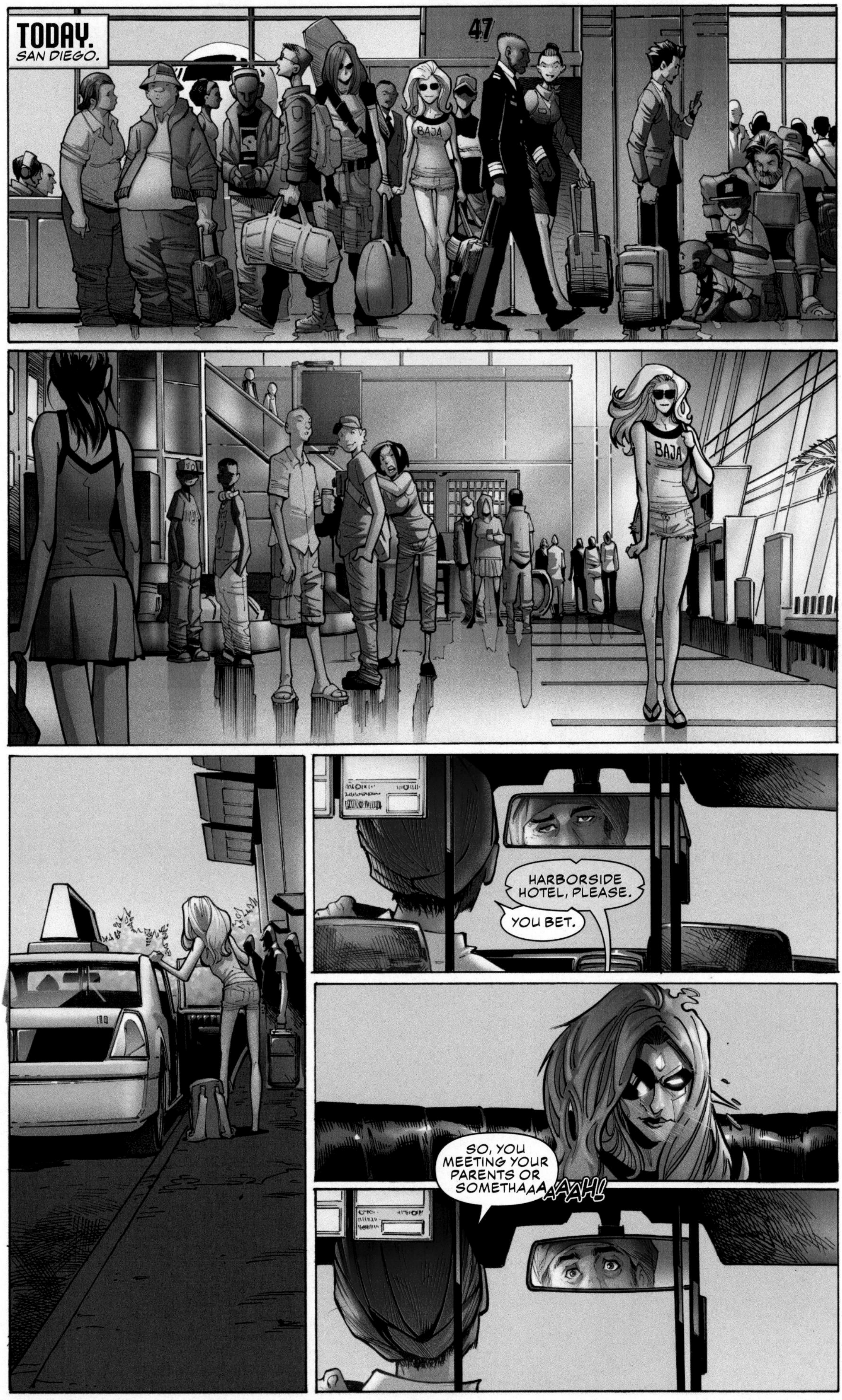
TODAY.
SAN DIEGO.
BAJA
BAJA
HARBORSIDE HOTEL, PLEASE.
YOU BET.
SO, YOU MEETING YOUR PARENTS OR SOMETHAAAAAH!

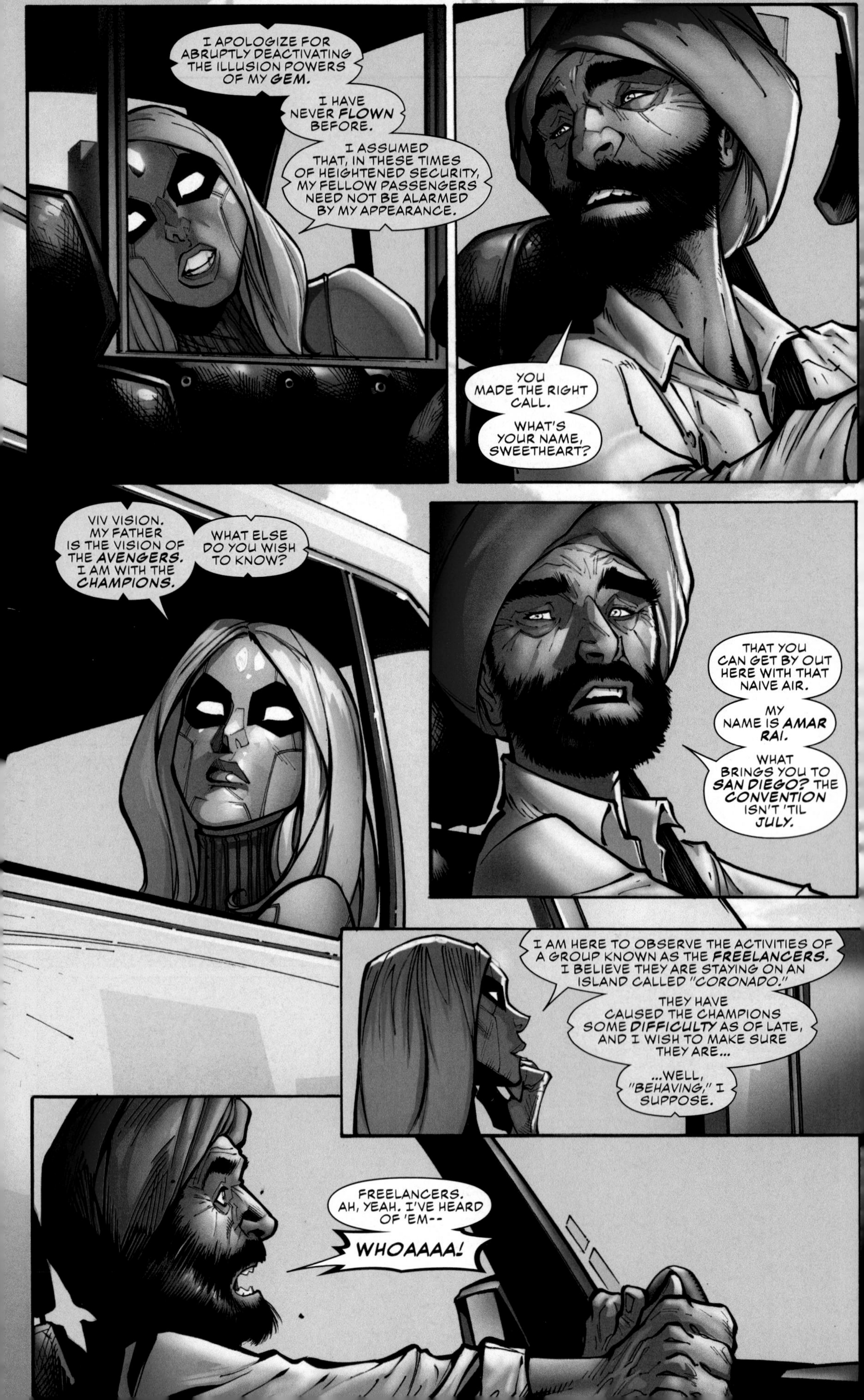
I APOLOGIZE FOR ABRUPTLY DEACTIVATING THE ILLUSION POWERS OF MY GEM.
I HAVE NEVER FLOWN BEFORE.
I ASSUMED THAT, IN THESE TIMES OF HEIGHTENED SECURITY, MY FELLOW PASSENGERS NEED NOT BE ALARMED BY MY APPEARANCE.
YOU MADE THE RIGHT CALL.
WHAT'S YOUR NAME, SWEETHEART?
VIV VISION. MY FATHER IS THE VISION OF THE AVENGERS. I AM WITH THE CHAMPIONS.
WHAT ELSE DO YOU WISH TO KNOW?
THAT YOU CAN GET BY OUT HERE WITH THAT NAIVE AIR.
MY NAME IS AMAR RAI.
WHAT BRINGS YOU TO SAN DIEGO? THE CONVENTION ISN'T 'TIL JULY.
I AM HERE TO OBSERVE THE ACTIVITIES OF A GROUP KNOWN AS THE FREELANCERS. I BELIEVE THEY ARE STAYING ON AN ISLAND CALLED "CORONADO."
THEY HAVE CAUSED THE CHAMPIONS SOME DIFFICULTY AS OF LATE, AND I WISH TO MAKE SURE THEY ARE...
...WELL, "BEHAVING," I SUPPOSE.
FREELANCERS. AH, YEAH. I'VE HEARD OF 'EM--
WHOAAAA!

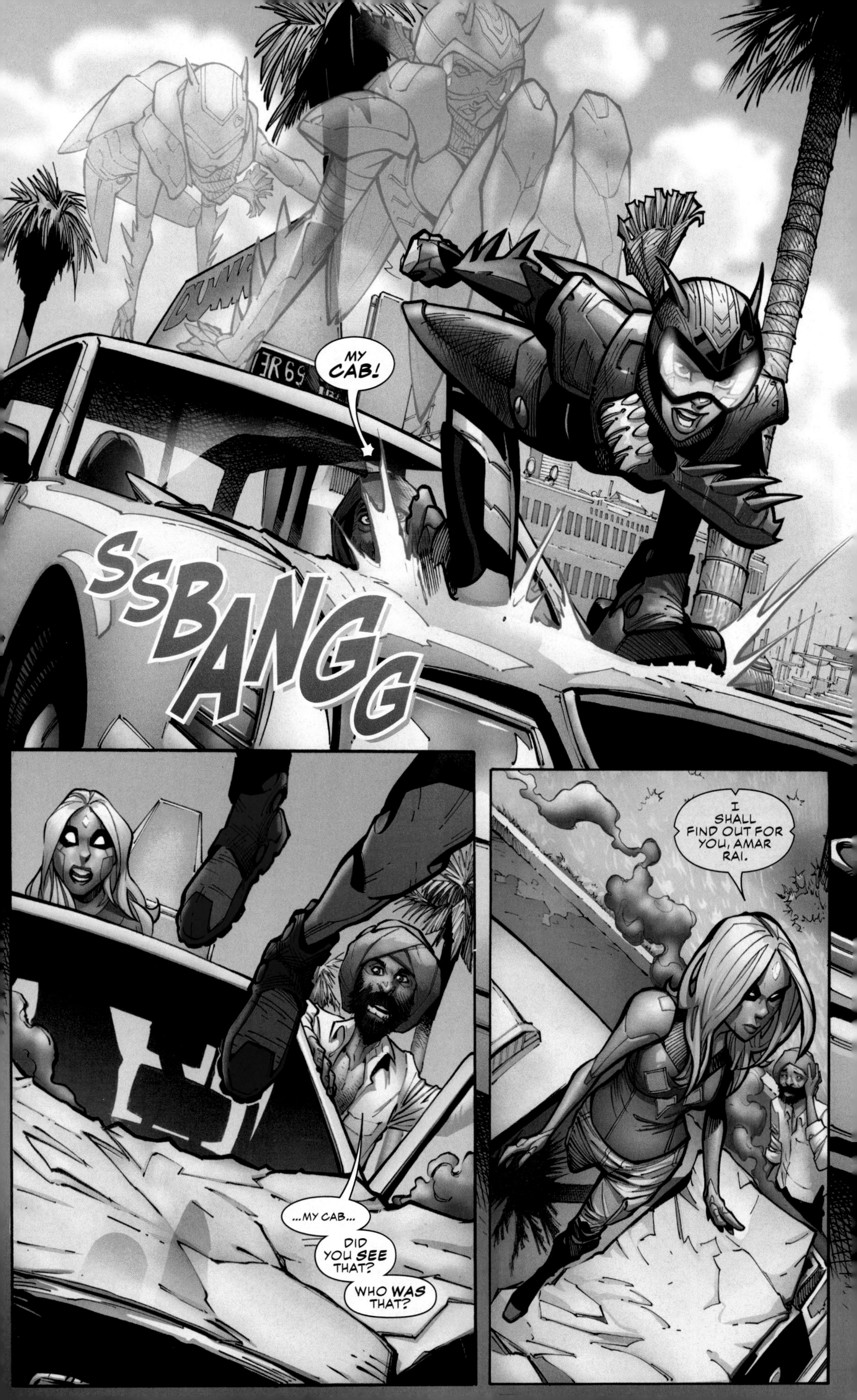
MY CAB!
SSBANGG
...MY CAB...
DID YOU SEE THAT?
WHO WAS THAT?
I SHALL FIND OUT FOR YOU, AMAR RAI.

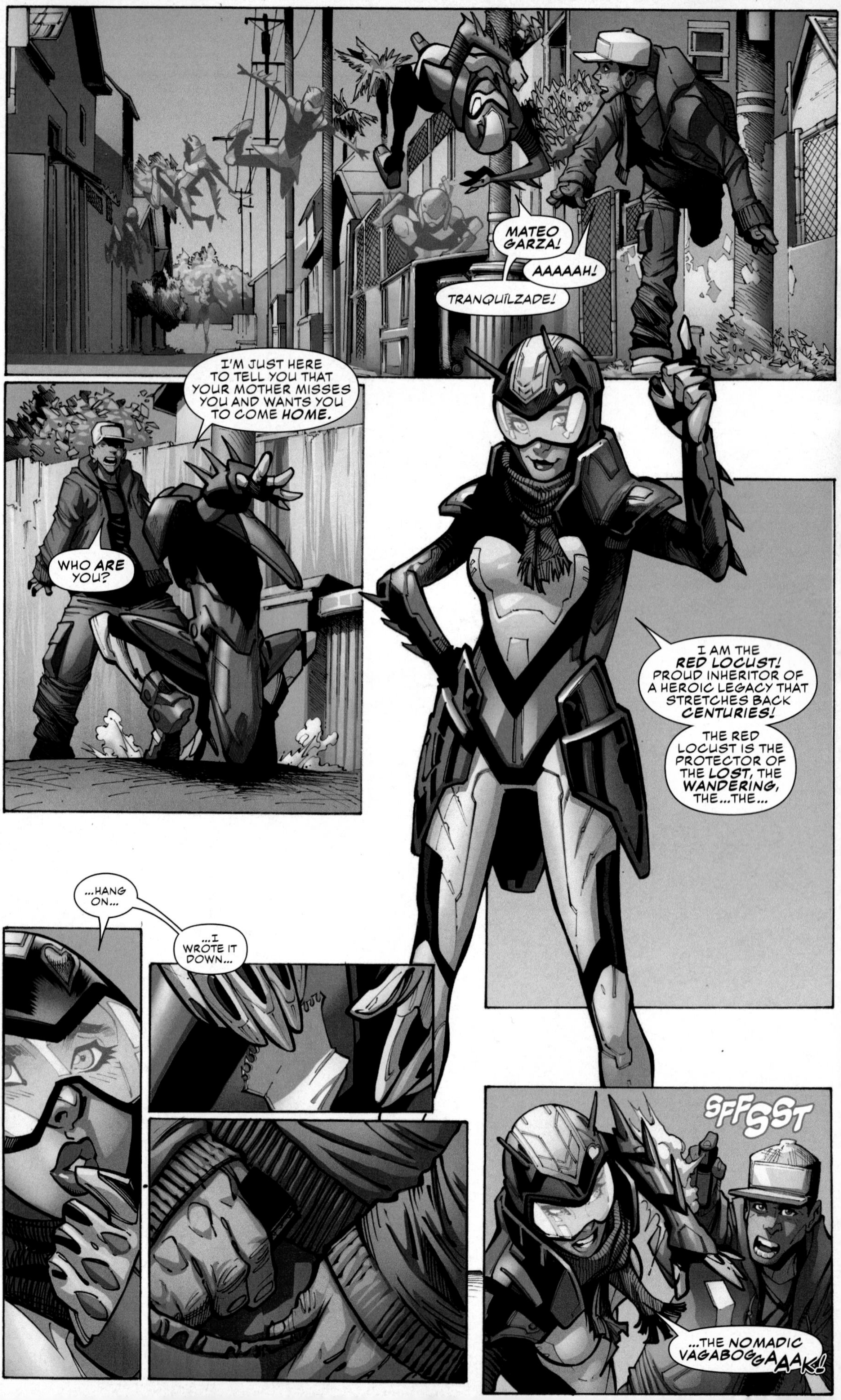
MATEO GARZA!
AAAAAH!
TRANQUILZADE!
I'M JUST HERE TO TELL YOU THAT YOUR MOTHER MISSES YOU AND WANTS YOU TO COME HOME.
WHO ARE YOU?
I AM THE RED LOCUST! PROUD INHERITOR OF A HEROIC LEGACY THAT STRETCHES BACK CENTURIES!
THE RED LOCUST IS THE PROTECTOR OF THE LOST, THE WANDERING, THE...THE...
...HANG ON...
...I WROTE IT DOWN...
SFFSST
...THE NOMADIC VAGABOGGAAAK!

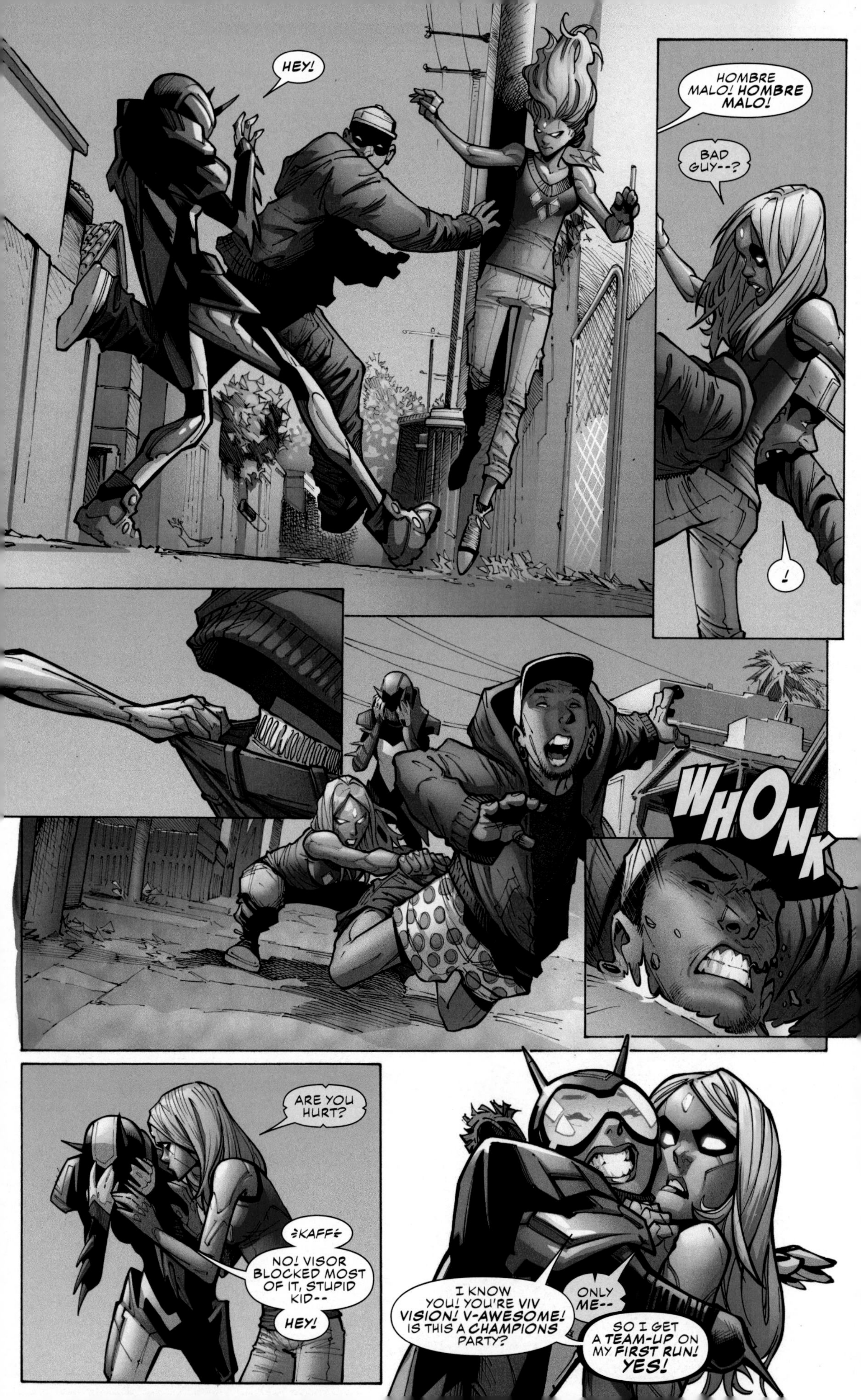
HEY!
HOMBRE MALO! HOMBRE MALO!
BAD GUY--?
!
WHONK
ARE YOU HURT?
KAFF
NO! VISOR BLOCKED MOST OF IT, STUPID KID--
HEY!
I KNOW YOU! YOU'RE VIV VISION! V-AWESOME! IS THIS A CHAMPIONS PARTY?
ONLY ME--
SO I GET A TEAM-UP ON MY FIRST RUN! YES!

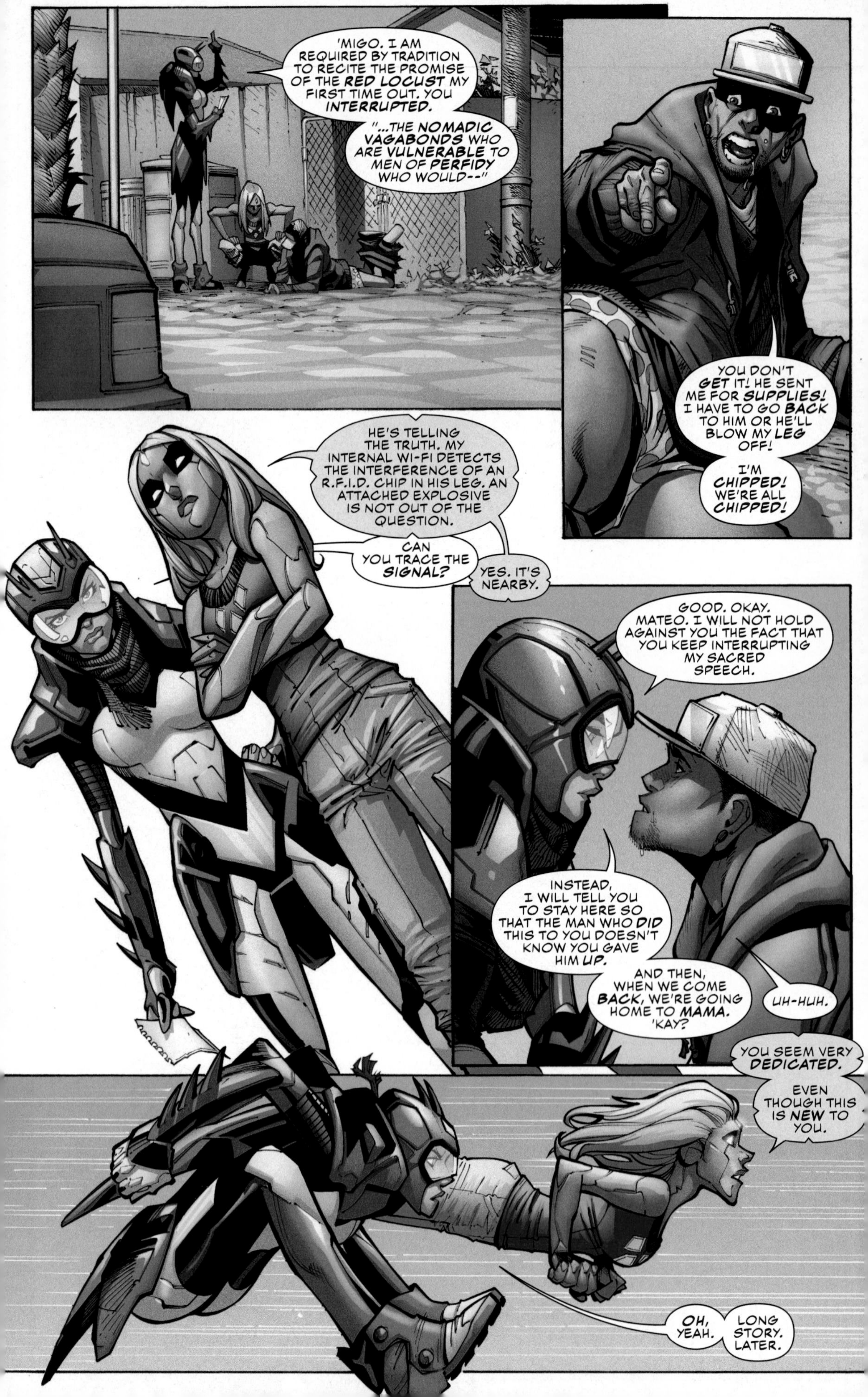
'MIGO. I AM REQUIRED BY TRADITION TO RECITE THE PROMISE OF THE RED LOCUST MY FIRST TIME OUT. YOU INTERRUPTED.
"...THE NOMADIC VAGABONDS WHO ARE VULNERABLE TO MEN OF PERFIDY WHO WOULD--"
YOU DON'T GET IT! HE SENT ME FOR SUPPLIES! I HAVE TO GO BACK TO HIM OR HE'LL BLOW MY LEG OFF!
I'M CHIPPED! WE'RE ALL CHIPPED!
HE'S TELLING THE TRUTH. MY INTERNAL WI-FI DETECTS THE INTERFERENCE OF AN R.F.I.D. CHIP IN HIS LEG. AN ATTACHED EXPLOSIVE IS NOT OUT OF THE QUESTION.
CAN YOU TRACE THE SIGNAL?
YES. IT'S NEARBY.
GOOD. OKAY. MATEO. I WILL NOT HOLD AGAINST YOU THE FACT THAT YOU KEEP INTERRUPTING MY SACRED SPEECH.
INSTEAD, I WILL TELL YOU TO STAY HERE SO THAT THE MAN WHO DID THIS TO YOU DOESN'T KNOW YOU GAVE HIM UP.
AND THEN, WHEN WE COME BACK, WE'RE GOING HOME TO MAMA. 'KAY?
UH-HUH.
YOU SEEM VERY DEDICATED.
EVEN THOUGH THIS IS NEW TO YOU.
OH, YEAH.
LONG STORY. LATER.

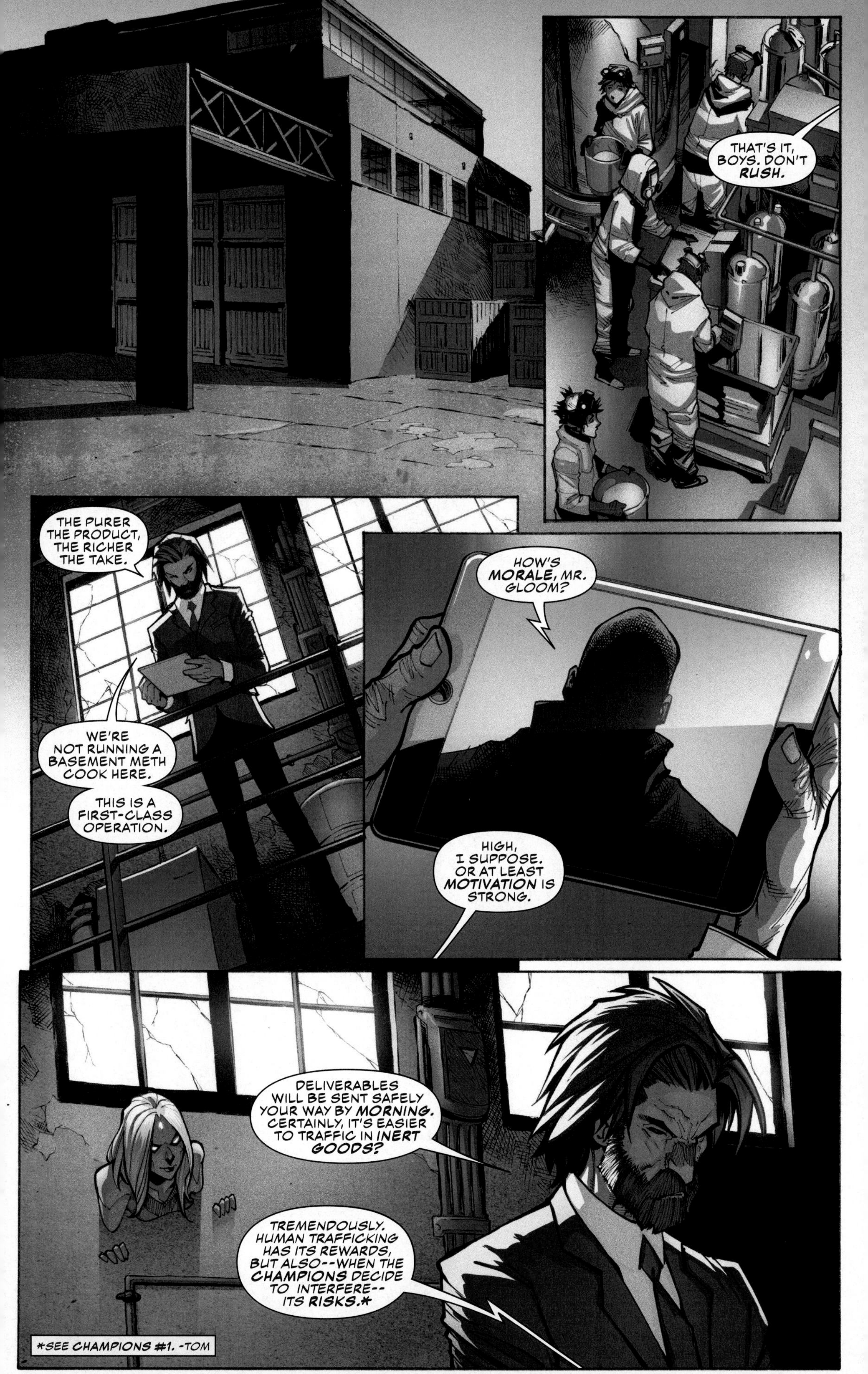
THAT'S IT, BOYS. DON'T RUSH.
THE PURER THE PRODUCT, THE RICHER THE TAKE.
WE'RE NOT RUNNING A BASEMENT METH COOK HERE.
THIS IS A FIRST-CLASS OPERATION.
HOW'S MORALE, MR. GLOOM?
HIGH, I SUPPOSE. OR AT LEAST MOTIVATION IS STRONG.
DELIVERABLES WILL BE SENT SAFELY YOUR WAY BY MORNING. CERTAINLY, IT'S EASIER TO TRAFFIC IN INERT GOODS?
TREMENDOUSLY. HUMAN TRAFFICKING HAS ITS REWARDS, BUT ALSO--WHEN THE CHAMPIONS DECIDE TO INTERFERE--ITS RISKS.*
*SEE CHAMPIONS #1. -TOM

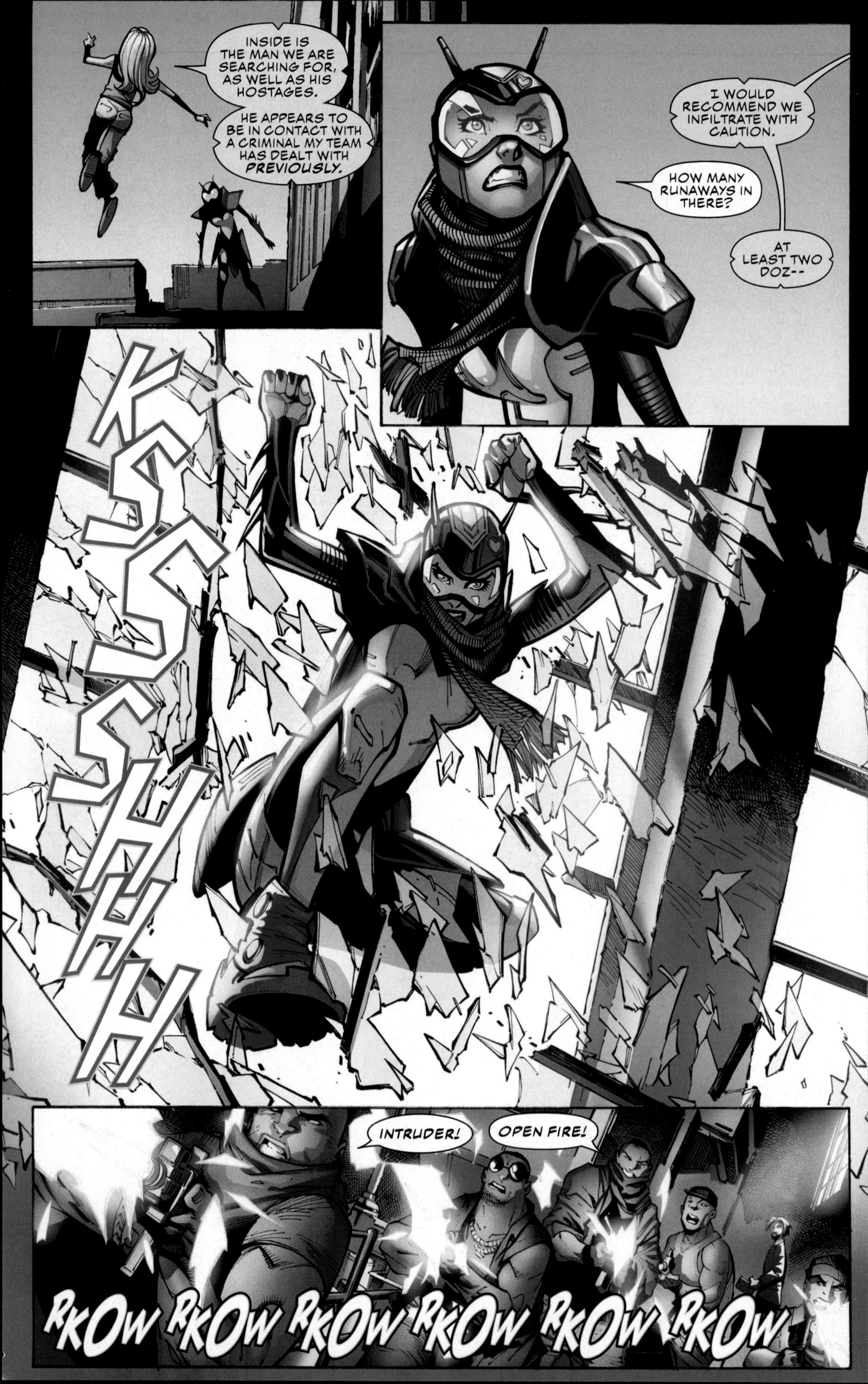
INSIDE IS THE MAN WE ARE SEARCHING FOR, AS WELL AS HIS HOSTAGES.
HE APPEARS TO BE IN CONTACT WITH A CRIMINAL MY TEAM HAS DEALT WITH *PREVIOUSLY*.
I WOULD RECOMMEND WE INFILTRATE WITH CAUTION.
HOW MANY RUNAWAYS IN THERE?
AT LEAST TWO DOZ--
KSSSHHHH
INTRUDER!
OPEN FIRE!
RKOW RKOW RKOW RKOW RKOW RKOW

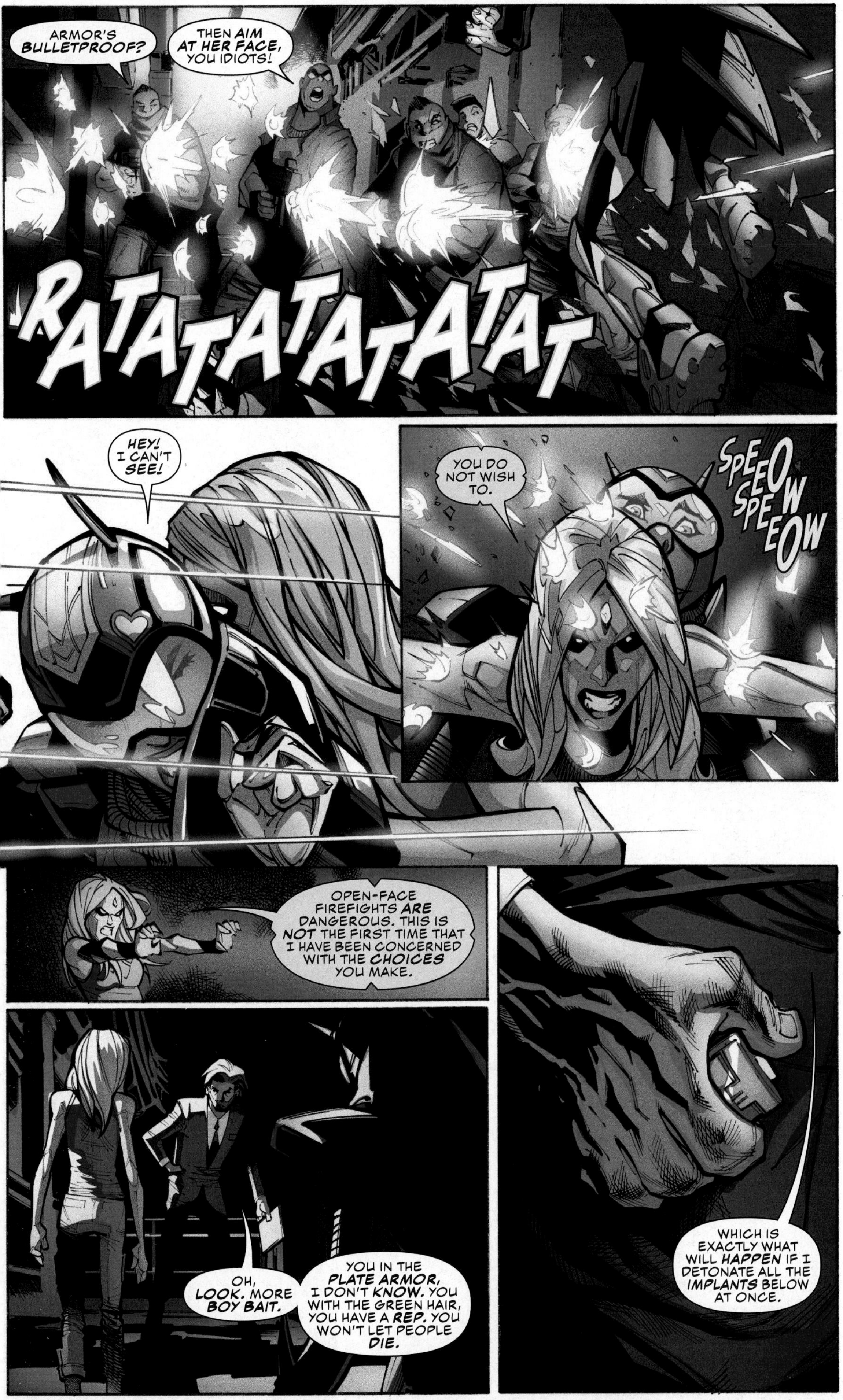
ARMOR'S BULLETPROOF?
THEN AIM AT HER FACE, YOU IDIOTS!
RATATATATATATAT
HEY! I CAN'T SEE!
YOU DO NOT WISH TO.
SPEEOW SPEEOW
OPEN-FACE FIREFIGHTS ARE DANGEROUS. THIS IS NOT THE FIRST TIME THAT I HAVE BEEN CONCERNED WITH THE CHOICES YOU MAKE.
OH, LOOK. MORE BOY BAIT.
YOU IN THE PLATE ARMOR, I DON'T KNOW. YOU WITH THE GREEN HAIR, YOU HAVE A REP. YOU WON'T LET PEOPLE DIE.
WHICH IS EXACTLY WHAT WILL HAPPEN IF I DETONATE ALL THE IMPLANTS BELOW AT ONCE.

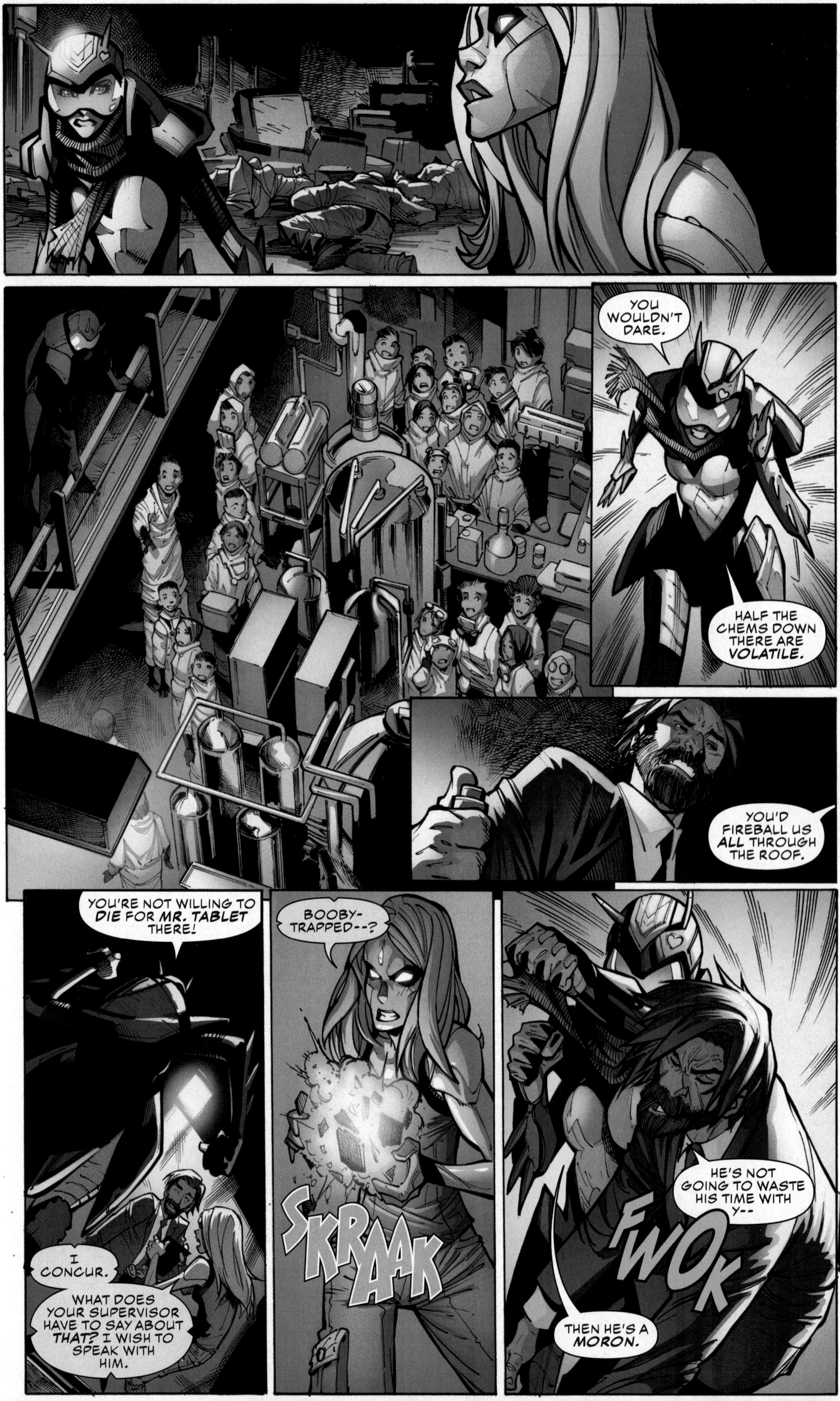
YOU WOULDN'T DARE.
HALF THE CHEMS DOWN THERE ARE VOLATILE.
YOU'D FIREBALL US ALL THROUGH THE ROOF.
YOU'RE NOT WILLING TO DIE FOR MR. TABLET THERE!
I CONCUR.
WHAT DOES YOUR SUPERVISOR HAVE TO SAY ABOUT THAT? I WISH TO SPEAK WITH HIM.
BOOBY-TRAPPED--?
SKRAAAK
HE'S NOT GOING TO WASTE HIS TIME WITH Y--
FWOK
THEN HE'S A MORON.

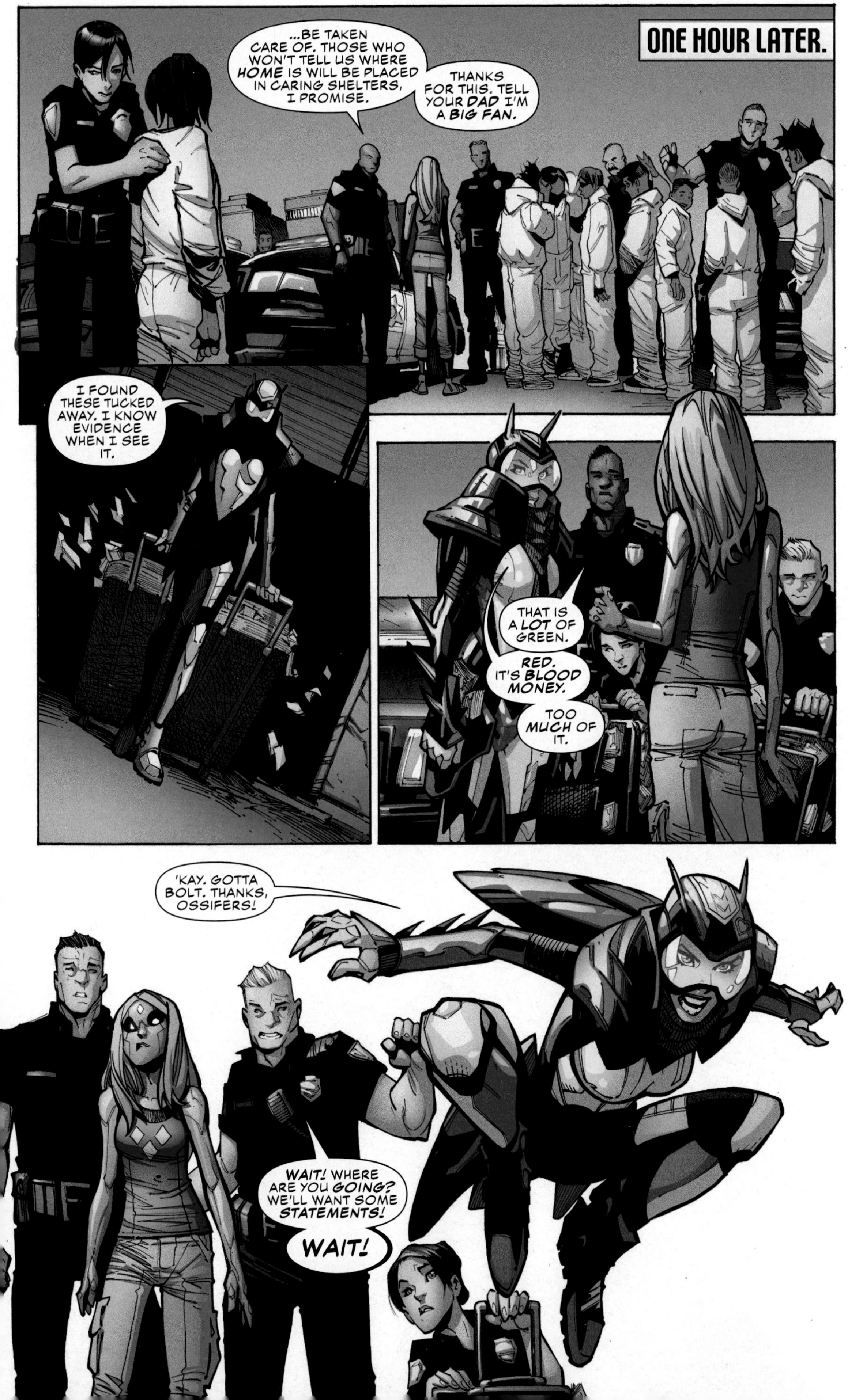
ONE HOUR LATER.
...BE TAKEN CARE OF. THOSE WHO WON'T TELL US WHERE HOME IS WILL BE PLACED IN CARING SHELTERS, I PROMISE.
THANKS FOR THIS. TELL YOUR DAD I'M A BIG FAN.
I FOUND THESE TUCKED AWAY. I KNOW EVIDENCE WHEN I SEE IT.
THAT IS A LOT OF GREEN.
RED. IT'S BLOOD MONEY.
TOO MUCH OF IT.
'KAY. GOTTA BOLT. THANKS, OSSIFERS!
WAIT! WHERE ARE YOU GOING? WE'LL WANT SOME STATEMENTS!
WAIT!

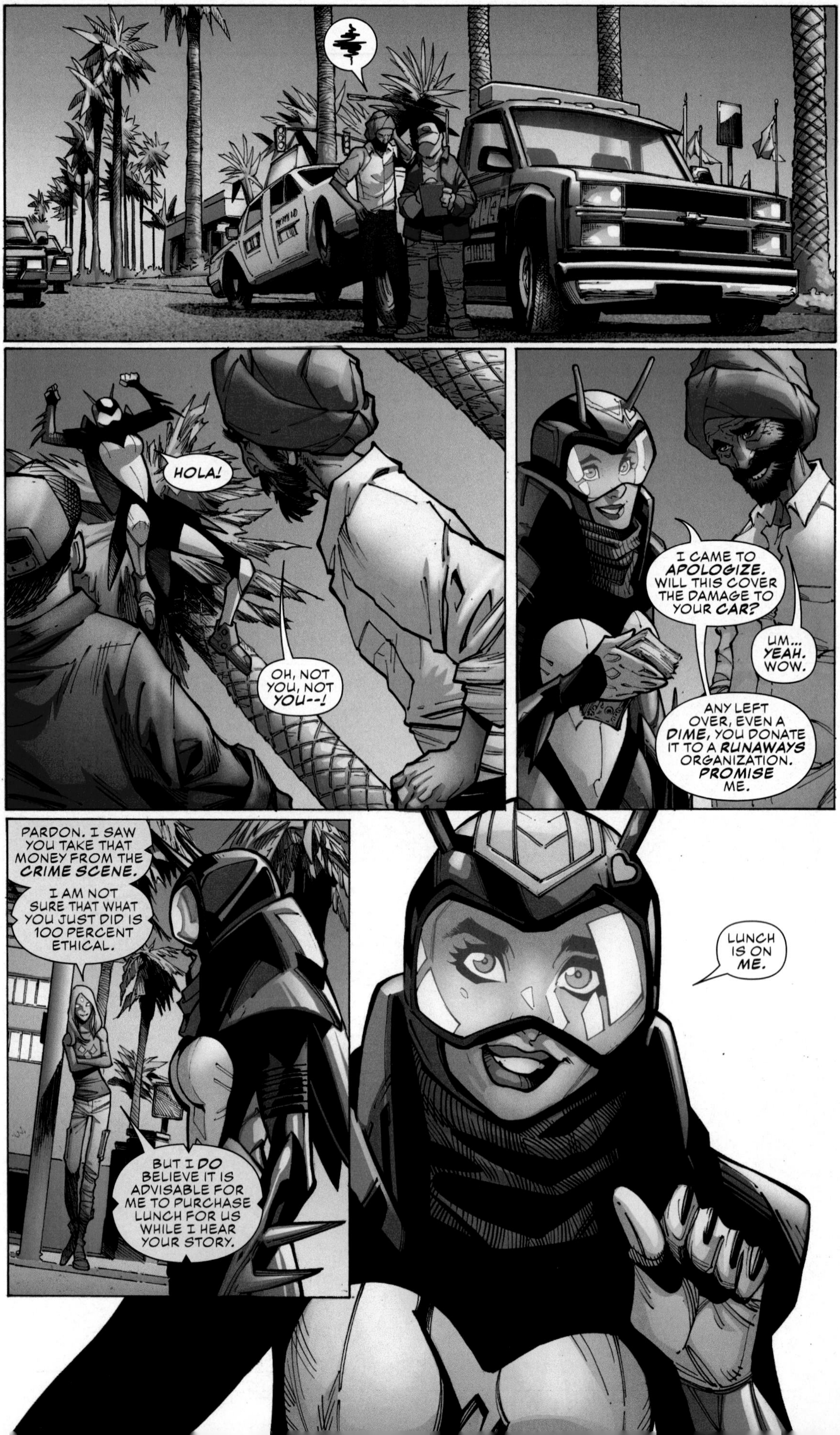
HOLA!
OH, NOT YOU, NOT YOU--!
I CAME TO APOLOGIZE. WILL THIS COVER THE DAMAGE TO YOUR CAR?
UM... YEAH. WOW.
ANY LEFT OVER, EVEN A DIME, YOU DONATE IT TO A RUNAWAYS ORGANIZATION. PROMISE ME.
PARDON. I SAW YOU TAKE THAT MONEY FROM THE CRIME SCENE.
I AM NOT SURE THAT WHAT YOU JUST DID IS 100 PERCENT ETHICAL.
BUT I DO BELIEVE IT IS ADVISABLE FOR ME TO PURCHASE LUNCH FOR US WHILE I HEAR YOUR STORY.
LUNCH IS ON ME.

WHO IS THE RED LOCUST?

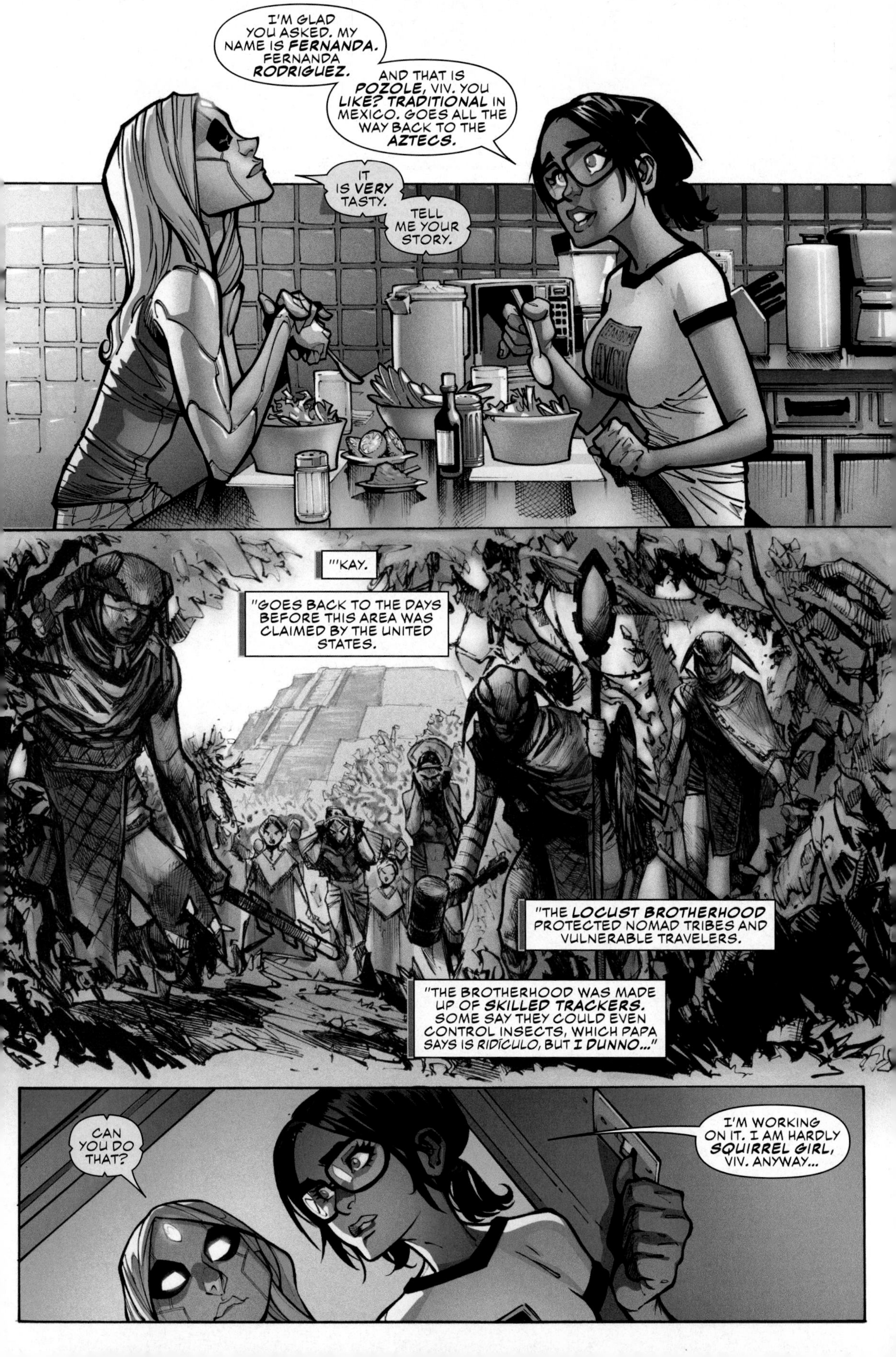

I'M GLAD YOU ASKED. MY NAME IS FERNANDA. FERNANDA RODRIGUEZ.
AND THAT IS POZOLE, VIV. YOU LIKE? TRADITIONAL IN MEXICO. GOES ALL THE WAY BACK TO THE AZTECS.
IT IS VERY TASTY.
TELL ME YOUR STORY.
"'KAY.
"GOES BACK TO THE DAYS BEFORE THIS AREA WAS CLAIMED BY THE UNITED STATES.
"THE LOCUST BROTHERHOOD PROTECTED NOMAD TRIBES AND VULNERABLE TRAVELERS.
"THE BROTHERHOOD WAS MADE UP OF SKILLED TRACKERS. SOME SAY THEY COULD EVEN CONTROL INSECTS, WHICH PAPA SAYS IS RIDÍCULO, BUT I DUNNO..."
CAN YOU DO THAT?
I'M WORKING ON IT. I AM HARDLY SQUIRREL GIRL, VIV. ANYWAY...

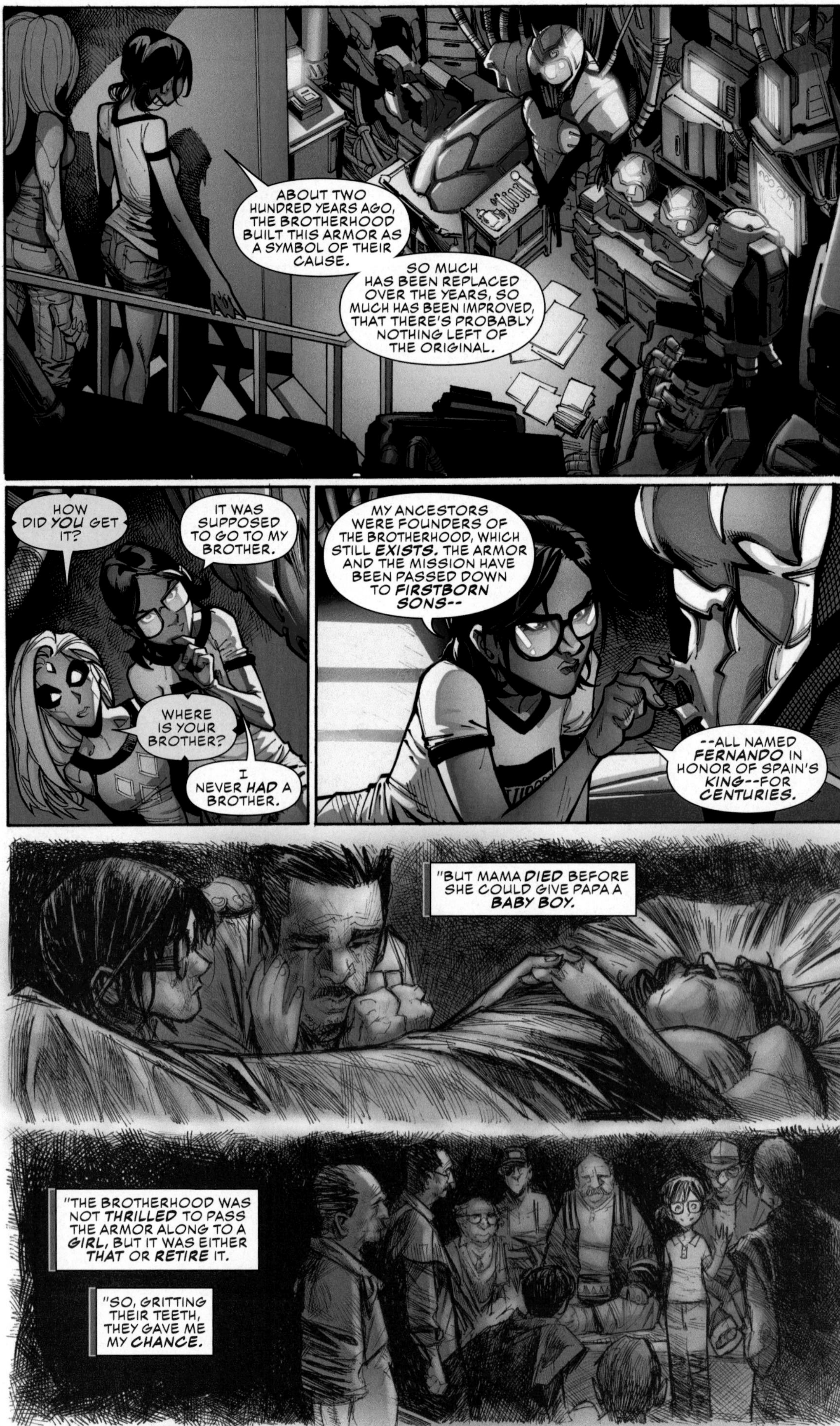
ABOUT TWO HUNDRED YEARS AGO, THE BROTHERHOOD BUILT THIS ARMOR AS A SYMBOL OF THEIR CAUSE.
SO MUCH HAS BEEN REPLACED OVER THE YEARS, SO MUCH HAS BEEN IMPROVED, THAT THERE'S PROBABLY NOTHING LEFT OF THE ORIGINAL.
HOW DID *YOU* GET IT?
IT WAS SUPPOSED TO GO TO MY BROTHER.
WHERE IS YOUR BROTHER?
I NEVER *HAD* A BROTHER.
MY ANCESTORS WERE FOUNDERS OF THE BROTHERHOOD, WHICH STILL *EXISTS.* THE ARMOR AND THE MISSION HAVE BEEN PASSED DOWN TO *FIRSTBORN SONS--*
--ALL NAMED *FERNANDO* IN HONOR OF SPAIN'S *KING*--FOR *CENTURIES.*
"BUT MAMA *DIED* BEFORE SHE COULD GIVE PAPA A *BABY BOY.*
"THE BROTHERHOOD WAS NOT *THRILLED* TO PASS THE ARMOR ALONG TO A *GIRL,* BUT IT WAS EITHER *THAT* OR *RETIRE* IT.
"SO, GRITTING THEIR TEETH, THEY GAVE ME MY *CHANCE.*

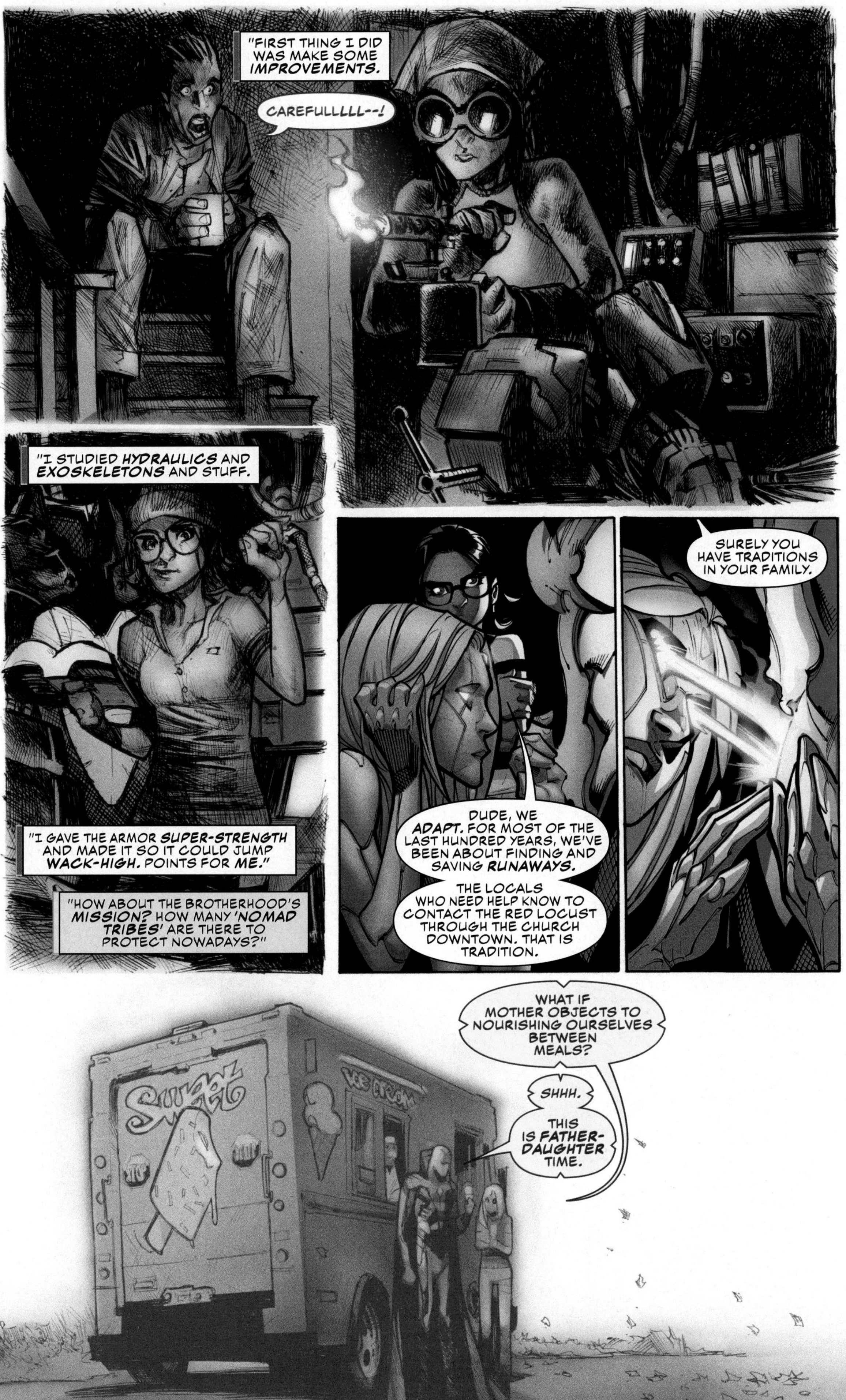
"FIRST THING I DID WAS MAKE SOME IMPROVEMENTS.
CAREFULLLLLL--!
"I STUDIED HYDRAULICS AND EXOSKELETONS AND STUFF.
"I GAVE THE ARMOR SUPER-STRENGTH AND MADE IT SO IT COULD JUMP WACK-HIGH. POINTS FOR ME."
"HOW ABOUT THE BROTHERHOOD'S MISSION? HOW MANY 'NOMAD TRIBES' ARE THERE TO PROTECT NOWADAYS?"
DUDE, WE ADAPT. FOR MOST OF THE LAST HUNDRED YEARS, WE'VE BEEN ABOUT FINDING AND SAVING RUNAWAYS.
THE LOCALS WHO NEED HELP KNOW TO CONTACT THE RED LOCUST THROUGH THE CHURCH DOWNTOWN. THAT IS TRADITION.
SURELY YOU HAVE TRADITIONS IN YOUR FAMILY.
WHAT IF MOTHER OBJECTS TO NOURISHING OURSELVES BETWEEN MEALS?
SHHH.
THIS IS FATHER-DAUGHTER TIME.

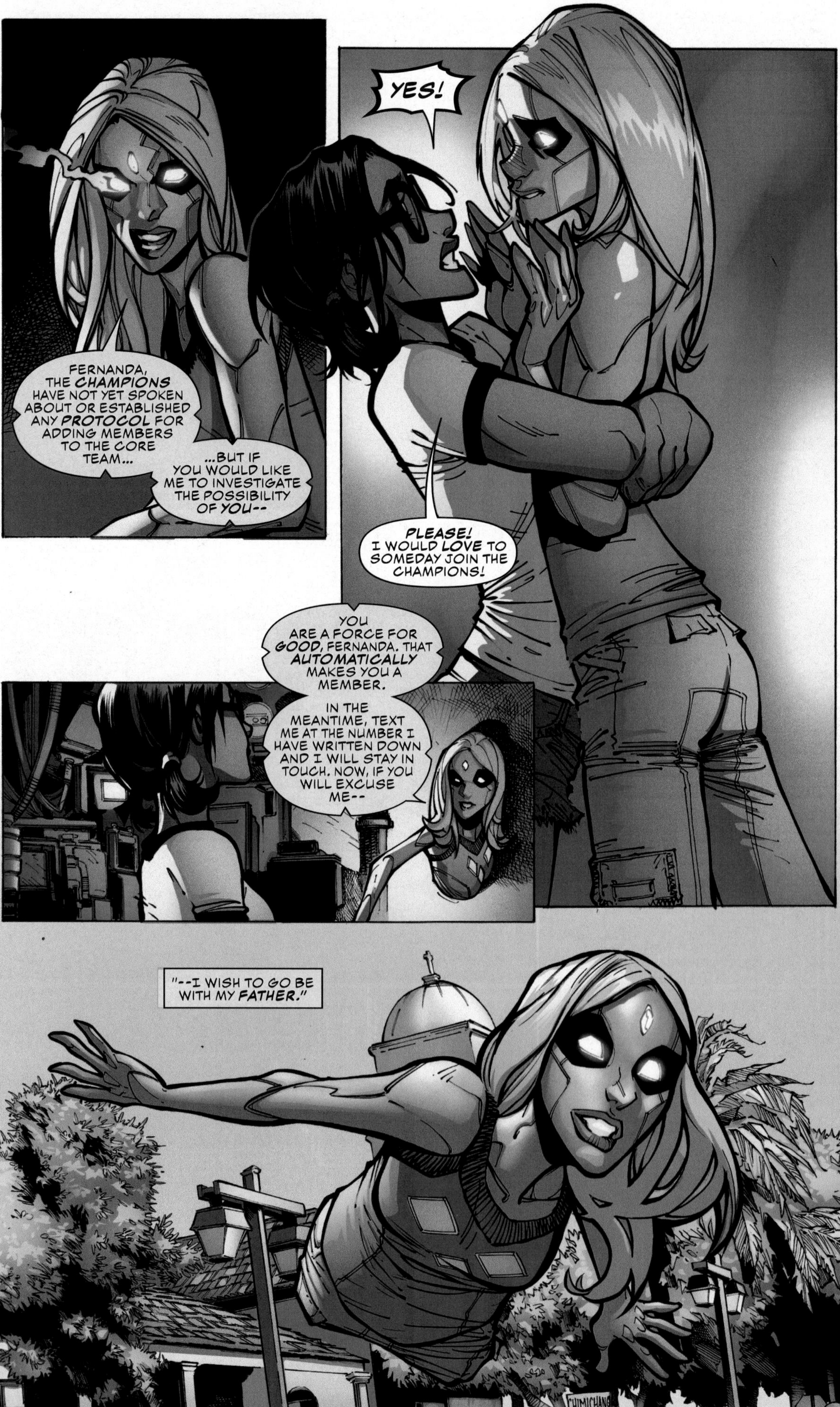
FERNANDA, THE CHAMPIONS HAVE NOT YET SPOKEN ABOUT OR ESTABLISHED ANY PROTOCOL FOR ADDING MEMBERS TO THE CORE TEAM...
...BUT IF YOU WOULD LIKE ME TO INVESTIGATE THE POSSIBILITY OF YOU--
YES!
PLEASE! I WOULD LOVE TO SOMEDAY JOIN THE CHAMPIONS!
YOU ARE A FORCE FOR GOOD, FERNANDA. THAT AUTOMATICALLY MAKES YOU A MEMBER.
IN THE MEANTIME, TEXT ME AT THE NUMBER I HAVE WRITTEN DOWN AND I WILL STAY IN TOUCH. NOW, IF YOU WILL EXCUSE ME--
"--I WISH TO GO BE WITH MY FATHER."

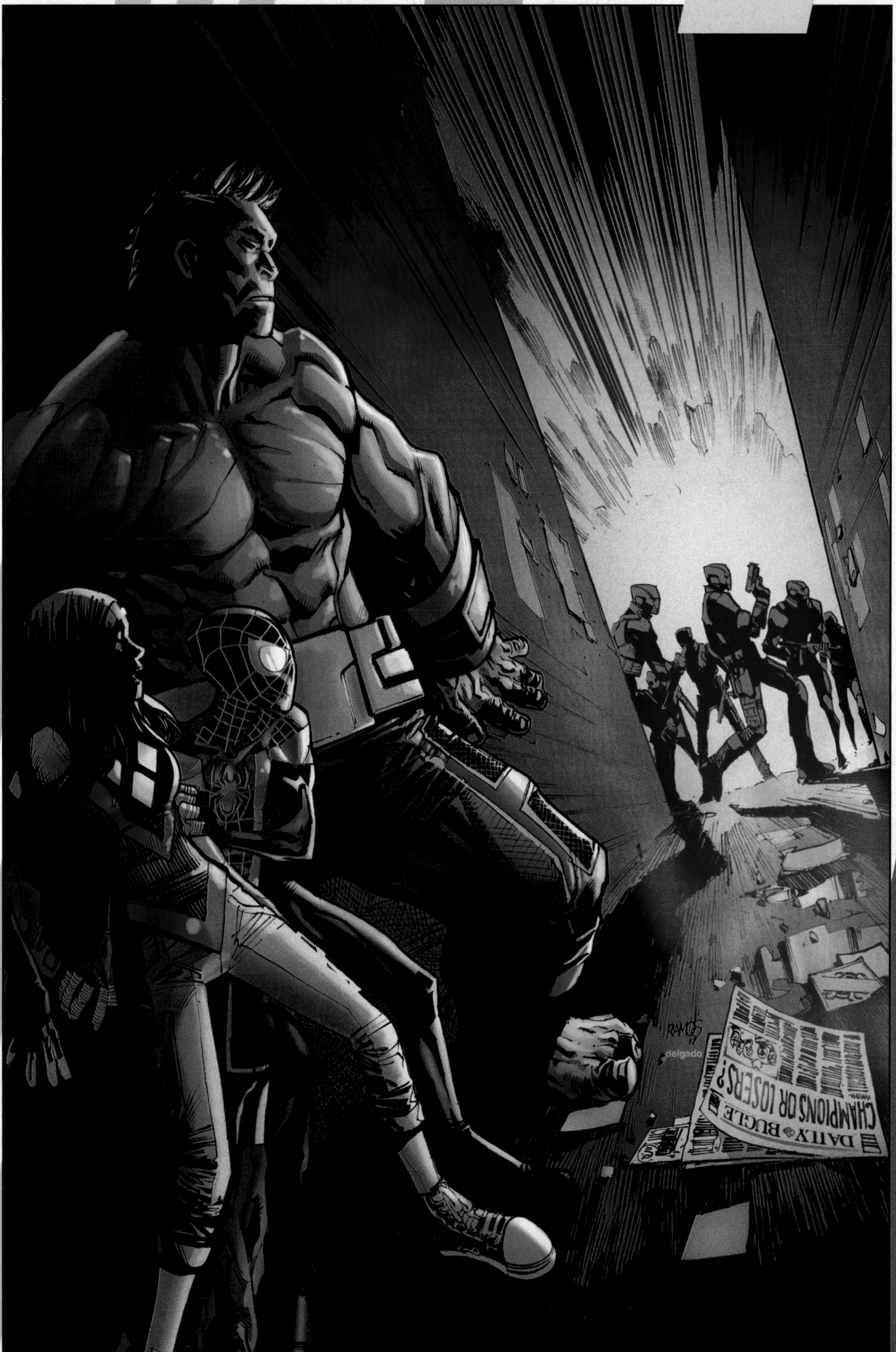
DAILY BUGLE
CHAMPIONS OR LOSERS?

10

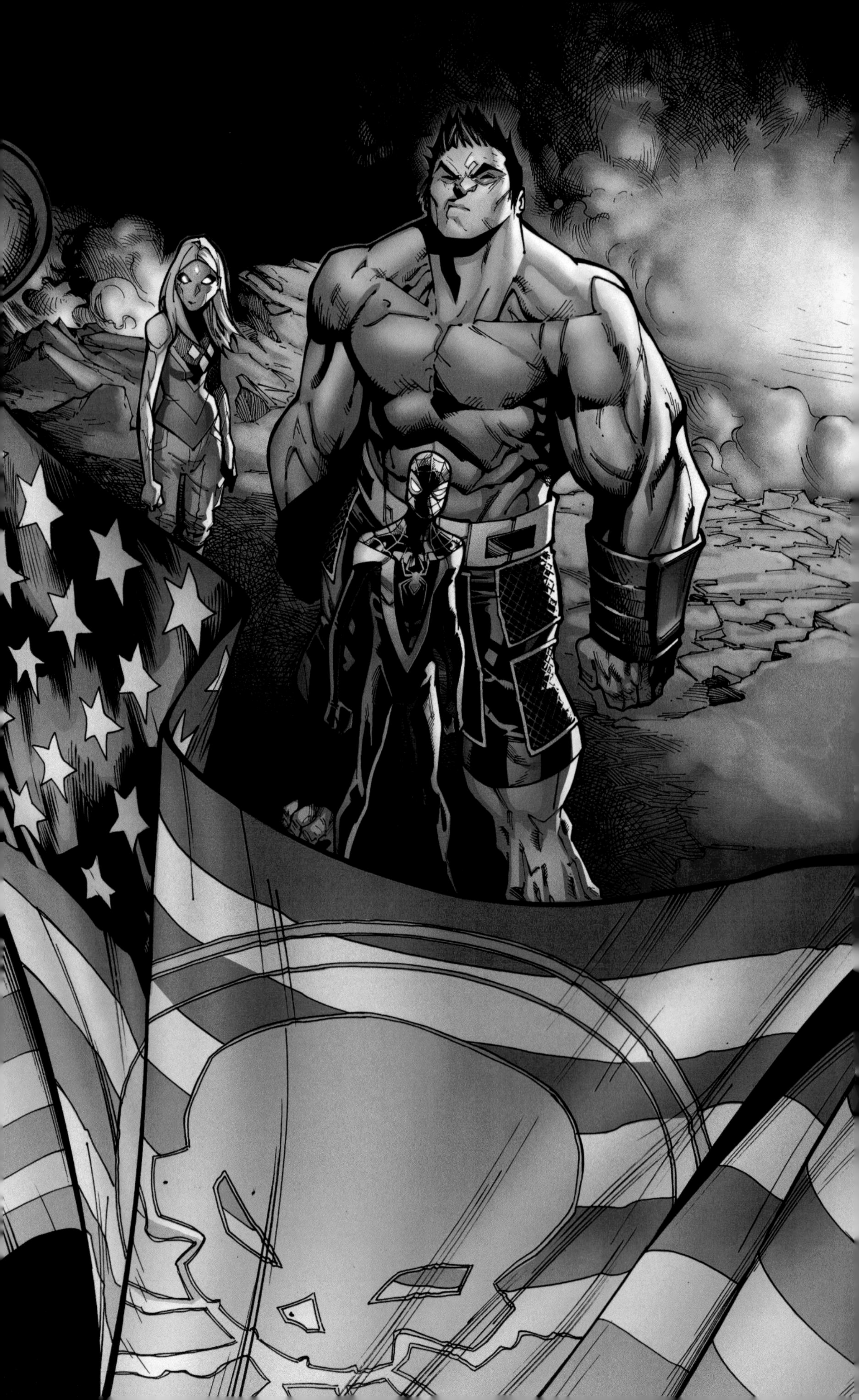

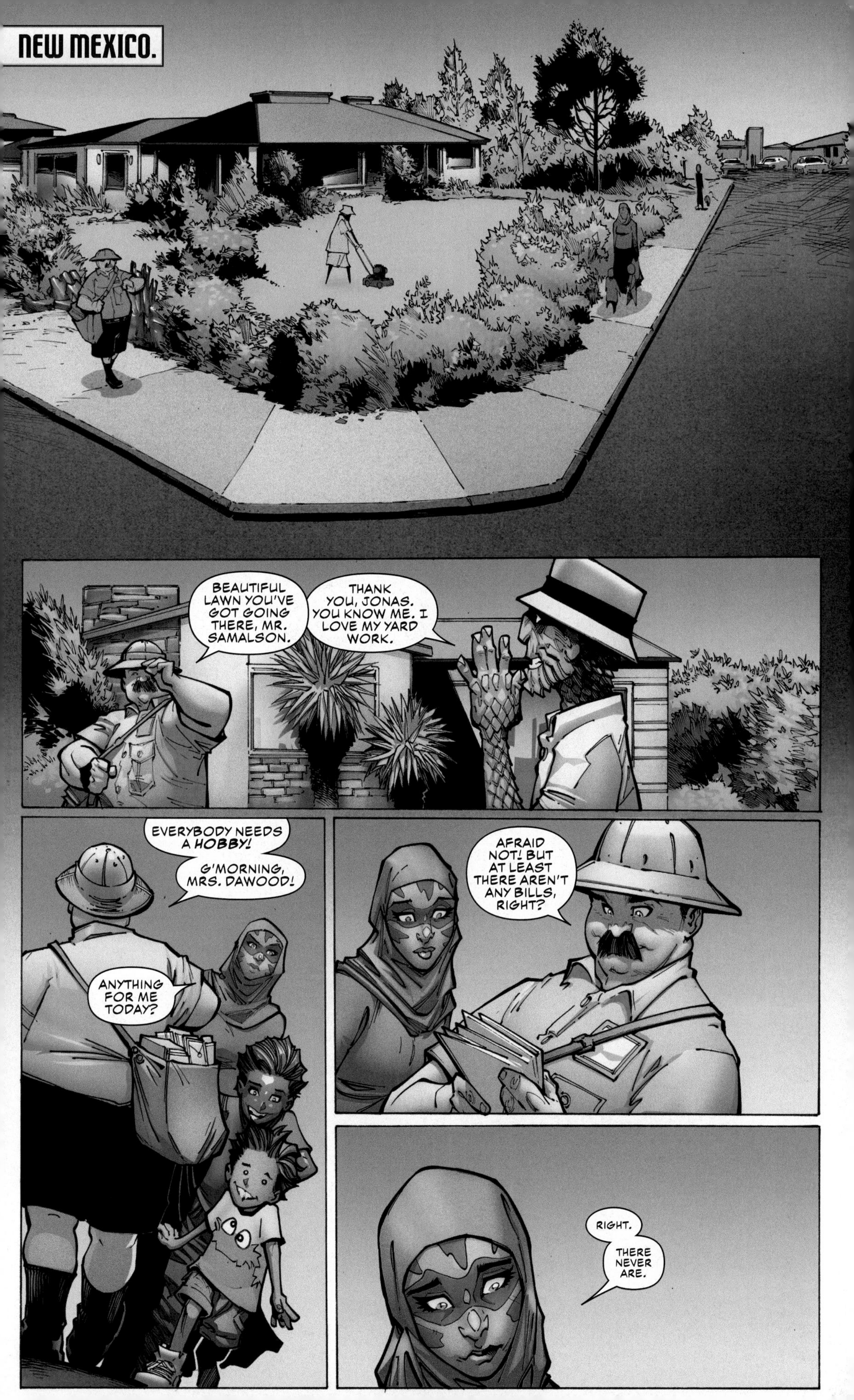
NEW MEXICO.
BEAUTIFUL LAWN YOU'VE GOT GOING THERE, MR. SAMALSON.
THANK YOU, JONAS. YOU KNOW ME. I LOVE MY YARD WORK.
EVERYBODY NEEDS A HOBBY!
G'MORNING, MRS. DAWOOD!
ANYTHING FOR ME TODAY?
AFRAID NOT! BUT AT LEAST THERE AREN'T ANY BILLS, RIGHT?
RIGHT.
THERE NEVER ARE.

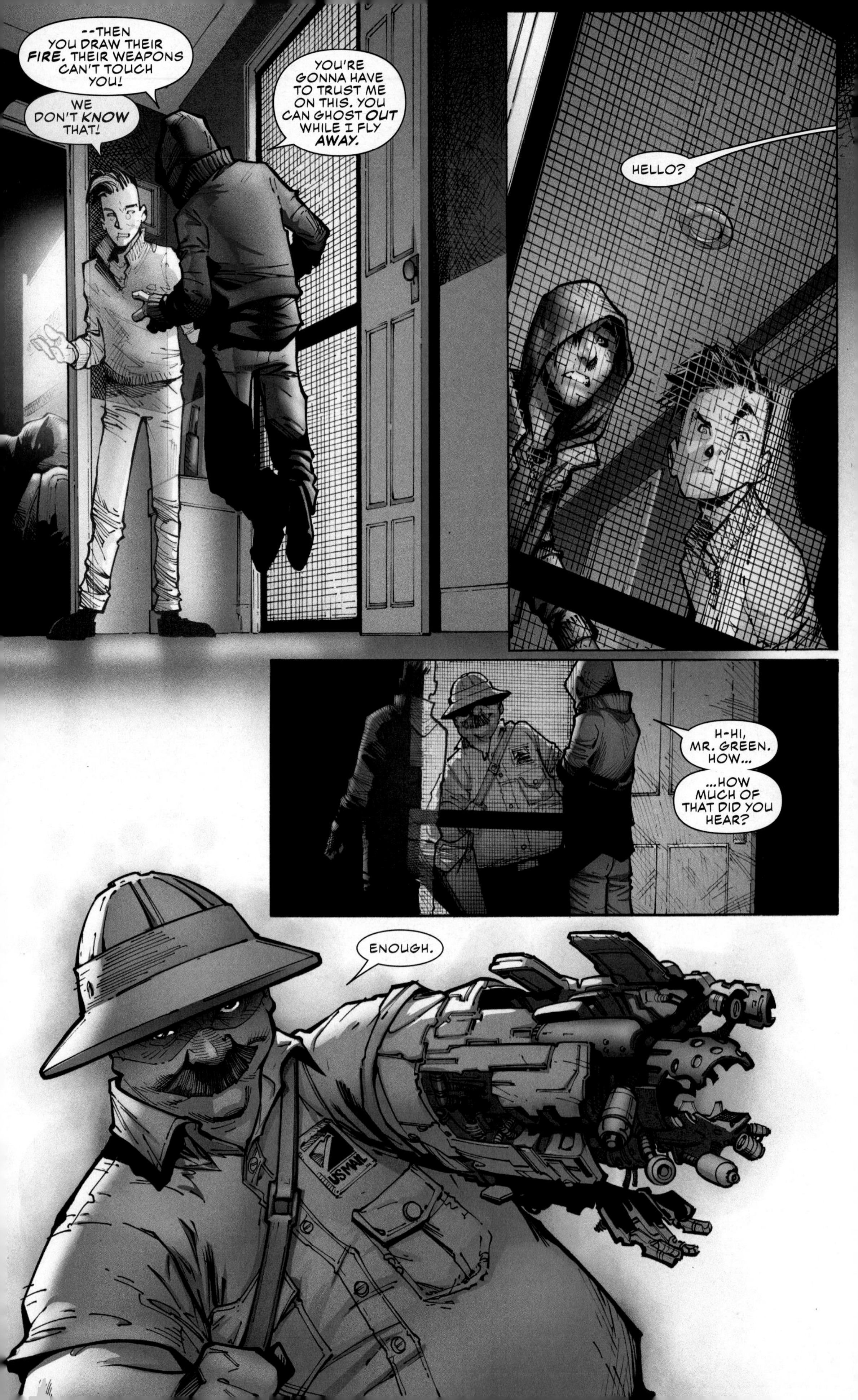
--THEN YOU DRAW THEIR FIRE. THEIR WEAPONS CAN'T TOUCH YOU!
WE DON'T KNOW THAT!
YOU'RE GONNA HAVE TO TRUST ME ON THIS. YOU CAN GHOST OUT WHILE I FLY AWAY.
HELLO?
H-HI, MR. GREEN. HOW...
...HOW MUCH OF THAT DID YOU HEAR?
ENOUGH.
US MAIL

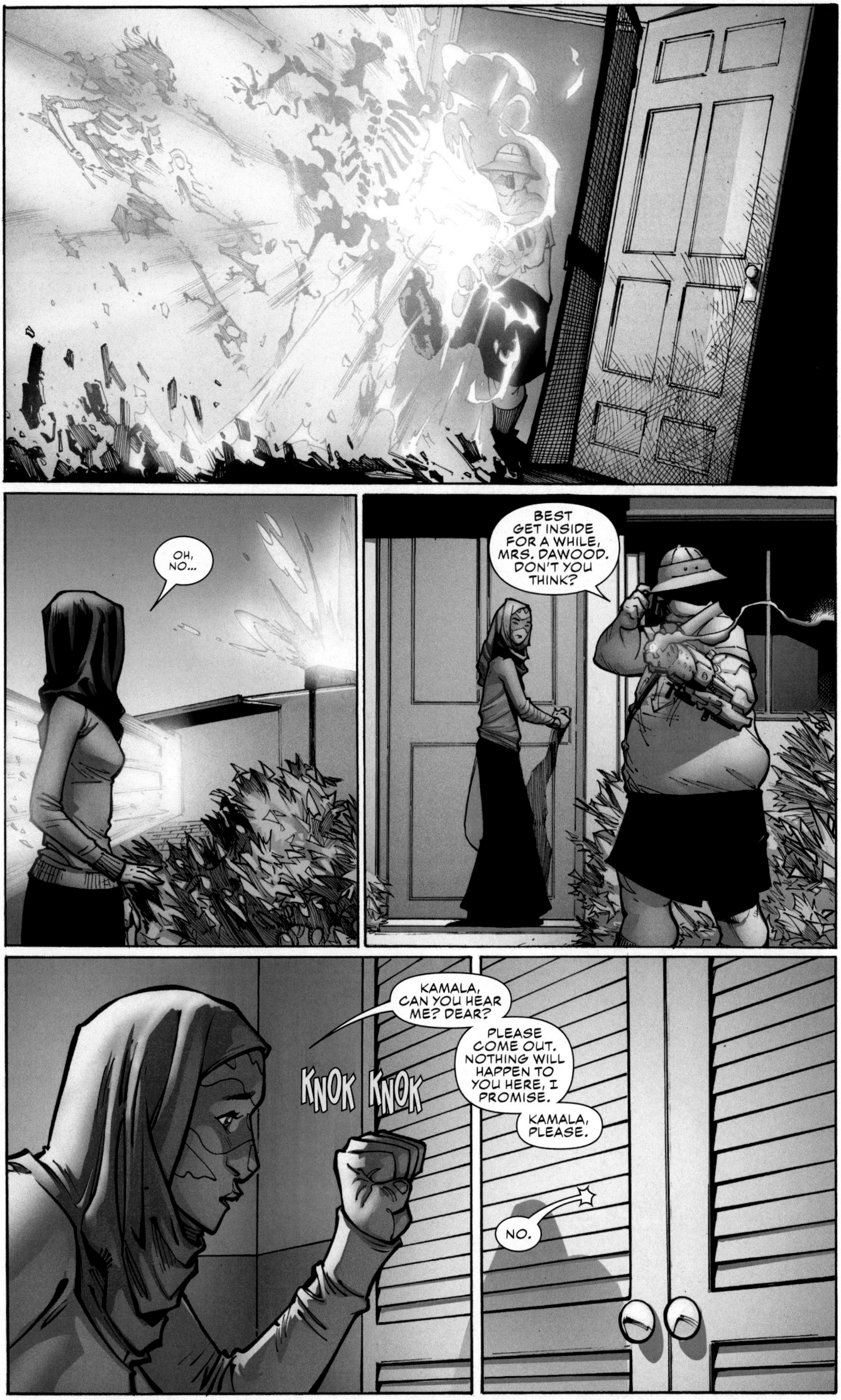
OH, NO...
BEST GET INSIDE FOR A WHILE, MRS. DAWOOD. DON'T YOU THINK?
KAMALA, CAN YOU HEAR ME? DEAR?
PLEASE COME OUT. NOTHING WILL HAPPEN TO YOU HERE, I PROMISE.
KAMALA, PLEASE.
KNOK KNOK
NO.

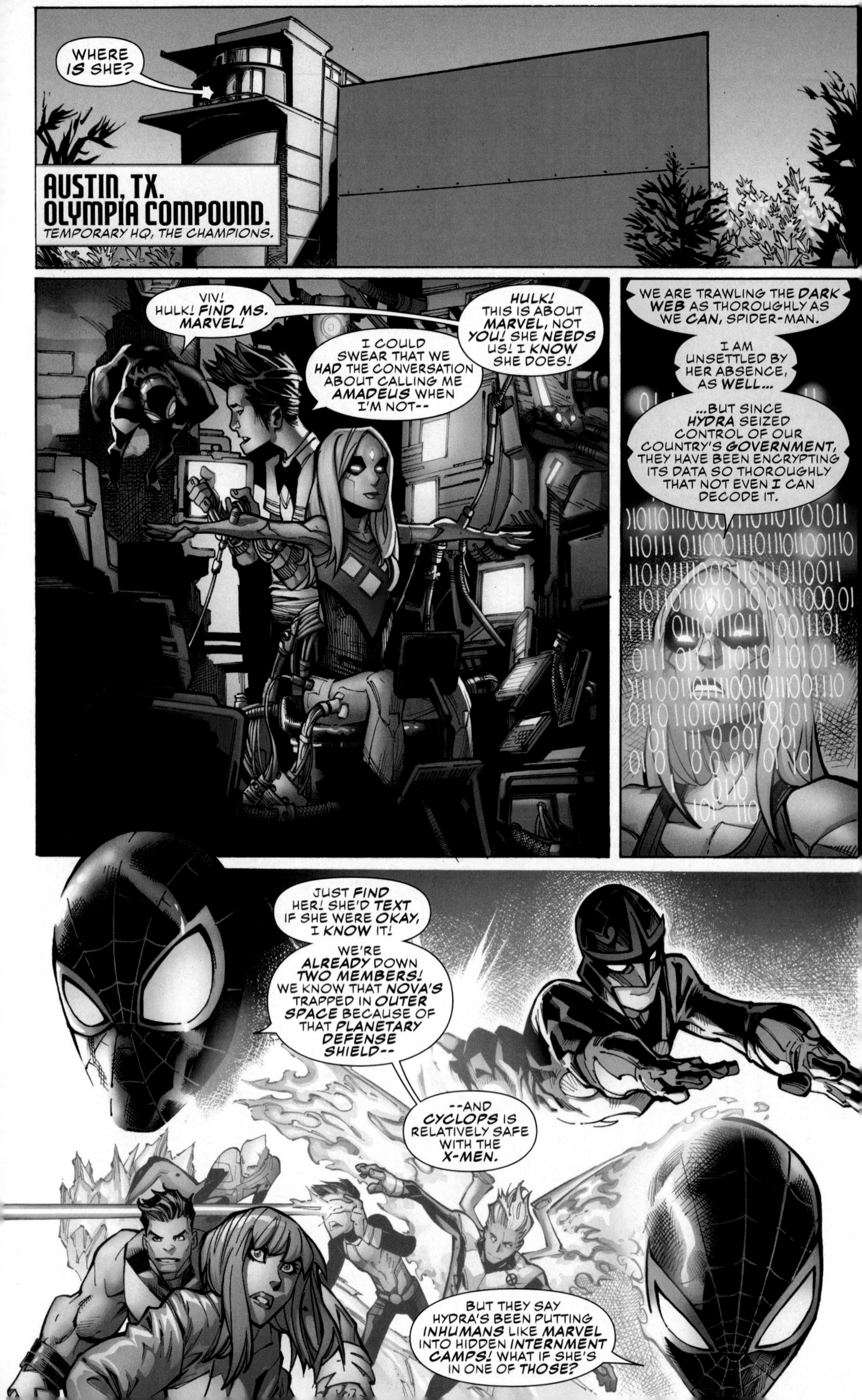

WHERE IS SHE?
AUSTIN, TX. OLYMPIA COMPOUND.
TEMPORARY HQ, THE CHAMPIONS.
VIV! HULK! FIND MS. MARVEL!
I COULD SWEAR THAT WE HAD THE CONVERSATION ABOUT CALLING ME AMADEUS WHEN I'M NOT--
HULK! THIS IS ABOUT MARVEL, NOT YOU! SHE NEEDS US! I KNOW SHE DOES!
WE ARE TRAWLING THE DARK WEB AS THOROUGHLY AS WE CAN, SPIDER-MAN.
I AM UNSETTLED BY HER ABSENCE, AS WELL...
...BUT SINCE HYDRA SEIZED CONTROL OF OUR COUNTRY'S GOVERNMENT, THEY HAVE BEEN ENCRYPTING ITS DATA SO THOROUGHLY THAT NOT EVEN I CAN DECODE IT.
JUST FIND HER! SHE'D TEXT IF SHE WERE OKAY, I KNOW IT!
WE'RE ALREADY DOWN TWO MEMBERS! WE KNOW THAT NOVA'S TRAPPED IN OUTER SPACE BECAUSE OF THAT PLANETARY DEFENSE SHIELD--
--AND CYCLOPS IS RELATIVELY SAFE WITH THE X-MEN.
BUT THEY SAY HYDRA'S BEEN PUTTING INHUMANS LIKE MARVEL INTO HIDDEN INTERNMENT CAMPS! WHAT IF SHE'S IN ONE OF THOSE?

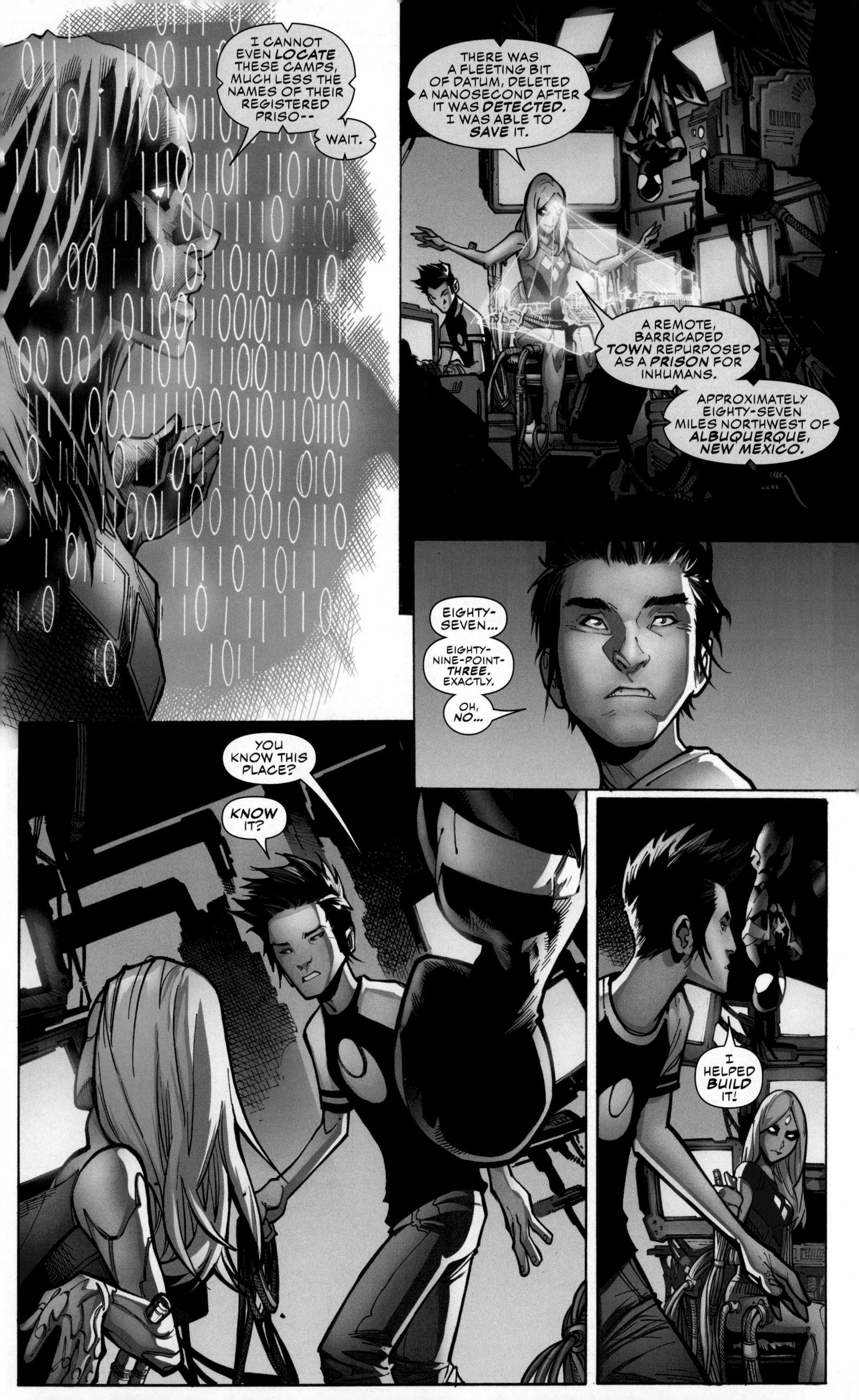
I CANNOT EVEN LOCATE THESE CAMPS, MUCH LESS THE NAMES OF THEIR REGISTERED PRISO--
WAIT.
THERE WAS A FLEETING BIT OF DATUM, DELETED A NANOSECOND AFTER IT WAS DETECTED. I WAS ABLE TO SAVE IT.
A REMOTE, BARRICADED TOWN REPURPOSED AS A PRISON FOR INHUMANS.
APPROXIMATELY EIGHTY-SEVEN MILES NORTHWEST OF ALBUQUERQUE, NEW MEXICO.
EIGHTY-SEVEN...
EIGHTY-NINE-POINT-THREE. EXACTLY.
OH, NO...
YOU KNOW THIS PLACE?
KNOW IT?
I HELPED BUILD IT!

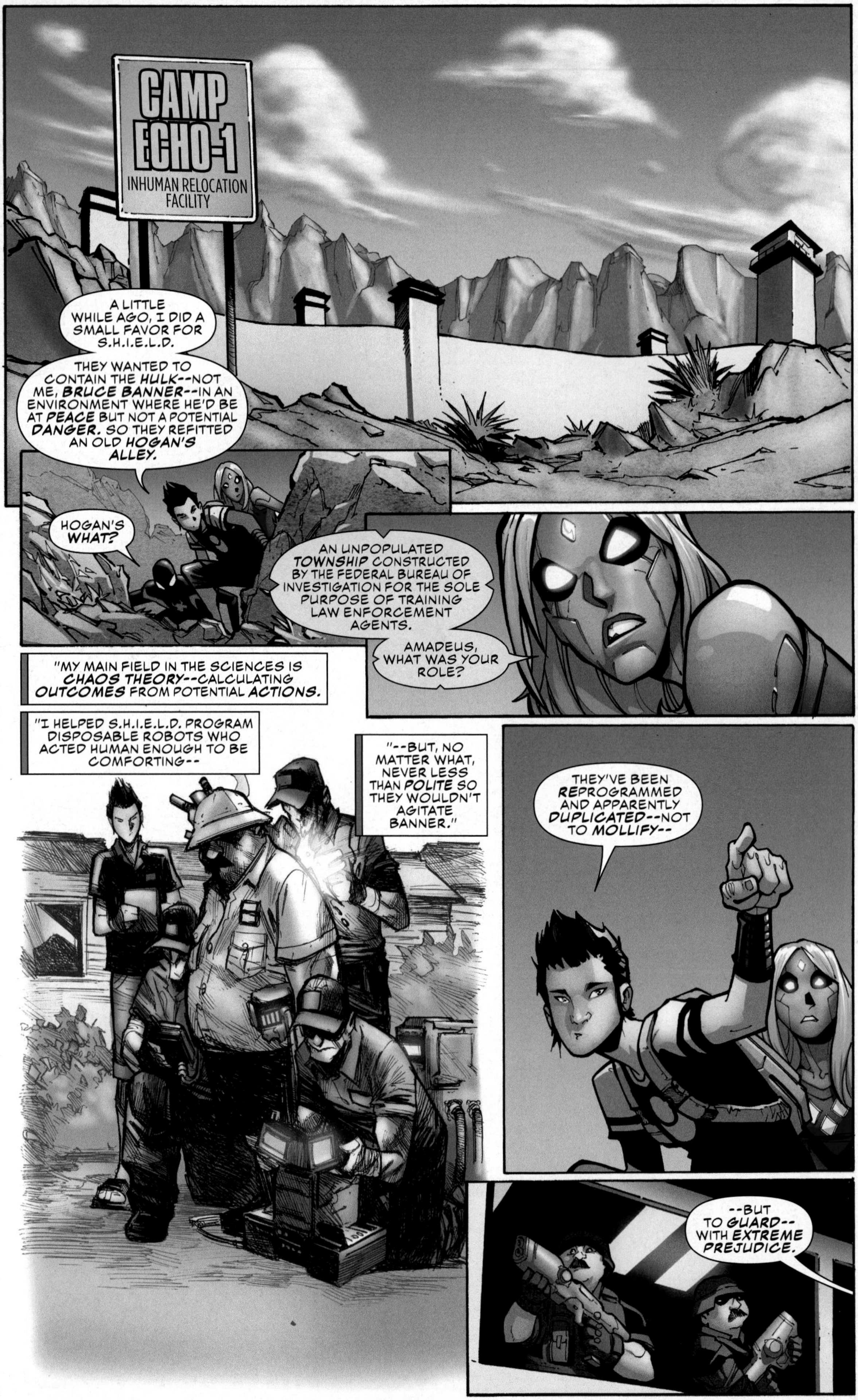
CAMP ECHO-1
INHUMAN RELOCATION FACILITY
A LITTLE WHILE AGO, I DID A SMALL FAVOR FOR S.H.I.E.L.D.
THEY WANTED TO CONTAIN THE HULK--NOT ME, BRUCE BANNER--IN AN ENVIRONMENT WHERE HE'D BE AT PEACE BUT NOT A POTENTIAL DANGER. SO THEY REFITTED AN OLD HOGAN'S ALLEY.
HOGAN'S WHAT?
AN UNPOPULATED TOWNSHIP CONSTRUCTED BY THE FEDERAL BUREAU OF INVESTIGATION FOR THE SOLE PURPOSE OF TRAINING LAW ENFORCEMENT AGENTS.
AMADEUS, WHAT WAS YOUR ROLE?
"MY MAIN FIELD IN THE SCIENCES IS CHAOS THEORY--CALCULATING OUTCOMES FROM POTENTIAL ACTIONS.
"I HELPED S.H.I.E.L.D. PROGRAM DISPOSABLE ROBOTS WHO ACTED HUMAN ENOUGH TO BE COMFORTING--
"--BUT, NO MATTER WHAT, NEVER LESS THAN POLITE SO THEY WOULDN'T AGITATE BANNER."
THEY'VE BEEN REPROGRAMMED AND APPARENTLY DUPLICATED--NOT TO MOLLIFY--
--BUT TO GUARD--WITH EXTREME PREJUDICE.

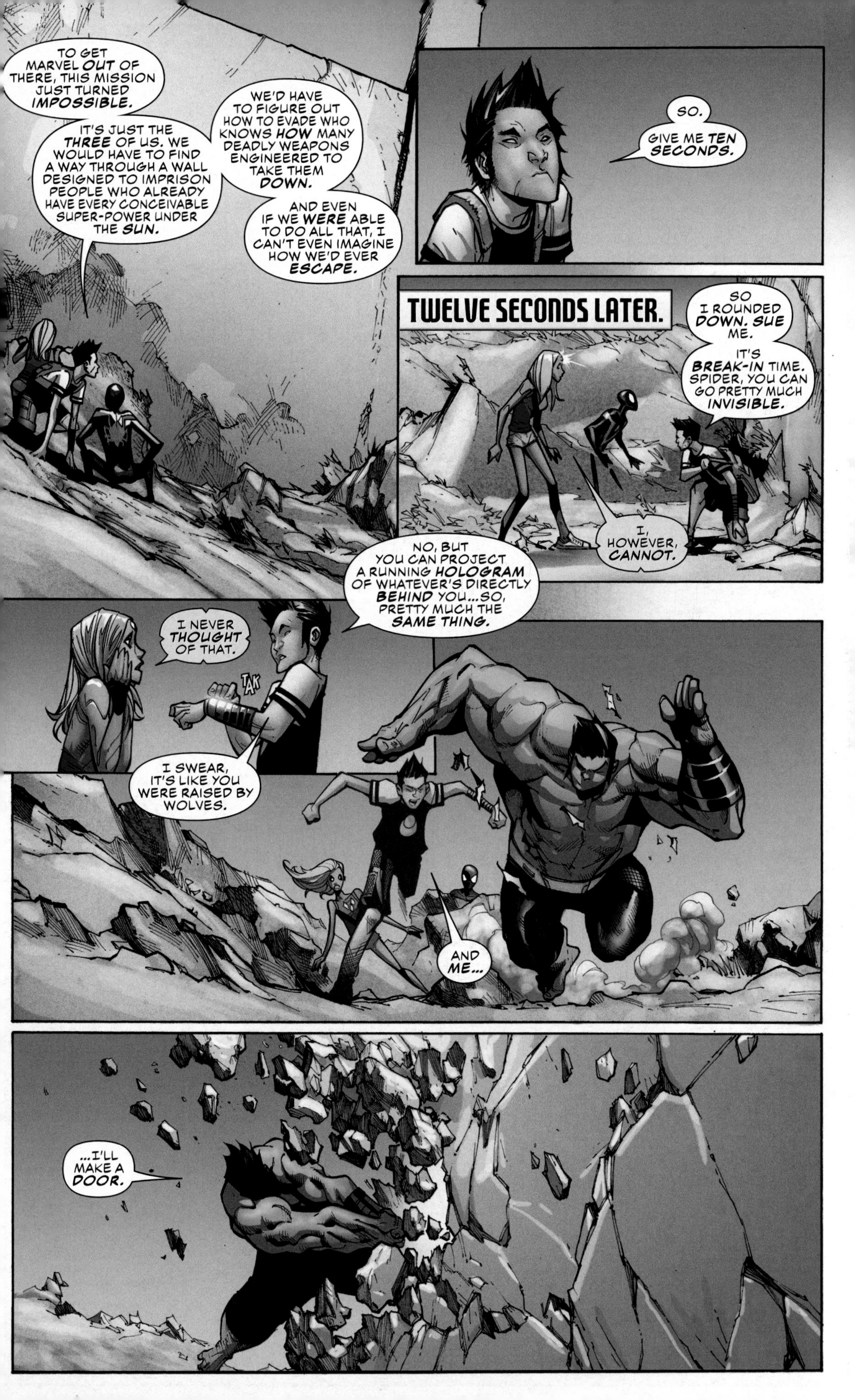
TO GET MARVEL OUT OF THERE, THIS MISSION JUST TURNED IMPOSSIBLE.
IT'S JUST THE THREE OF US. WE WOULD HAVE TO FIND A WAY THROUGH A WALL DESIGNED TO IMPRISON PEOPLE WHO ALREADY HAVE EVERY CONCEIVABLE SUPER-POWER UNDER THE SUN.
WE'D HAVE TO FIGURE OUT HOW TO EVADE WHO KNOWS HOW MANY DEADLY WEAPONS ENGINEERED TO TAKE THEM DOWN.
AND EVEN IF WE WERE ABLE TO DO ALL THAT, I CAN'T EVEN IMAGINE HOW WE'D EVER ESCAPE.
SO.
GIVE ME TEN SECONDS.
TWELVE SECONDS LATER.
SO I ROUNDED DOWN. SUE ME.
IT'S BREAK-IN TIME. SPIDER, YOU CAN GO PRETTY MUCH INVISIBLE.
I, HOWEVER, CANNOT.
NO, BUT YOU CAN PROJECT A RUNNING HOLOGRAM OF WHATEVER'S DIRECTLY BEHIND YOU...SO, PRETTY MUCH THE SAME THING.
I NEVER THOUGHT OF THAT.
TAK
I SWEAR, IT'S LIKE YOU WERE RAISED BY WOLVES.
AND ME...
...I'LL MAKE A DOOR.

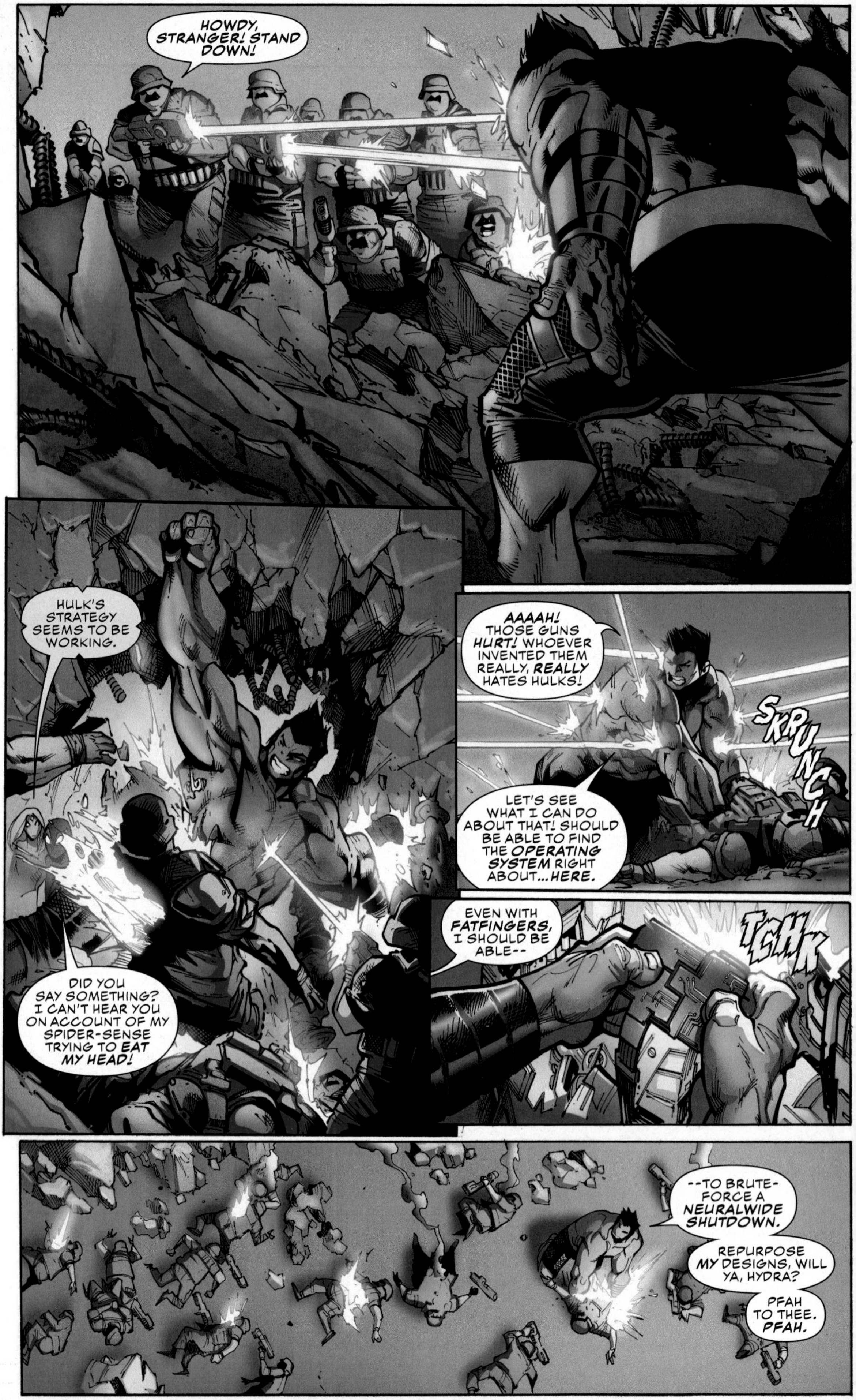
HOWDY, STRANGER! STAND DOWN!
HULK'S STRATEGY SEEMS TO BE WORKING.
DID YOU SAY SOMETHING? I CAN'T HEAR YOU ON ACCOUNT OF MY SPIDER-SENSE TRYING TO EAT MY HEAD!
AAAAH! THOSE GUNS HURT! WHOEVER INVENTED THEM REALLY, REALLY HATES HULKS!
SKRUNCH
LET'S SEE WHAT I CAN DO ABOUT THAT! SHOULD BE ABLE TO FIND THE OPERATING SYSTEM RIGHT ABOUT... HERE.
EVEN WITH FATFINGERS, I SHOULD BE ABLE--
TCHK
--TO BRUTE-FORCE A NEURALWIDE SHUTDOWN.
REPURPOSE MY DESIGNS, WILL YA, HYDRA?
PFAH TO THEE. PFAH.

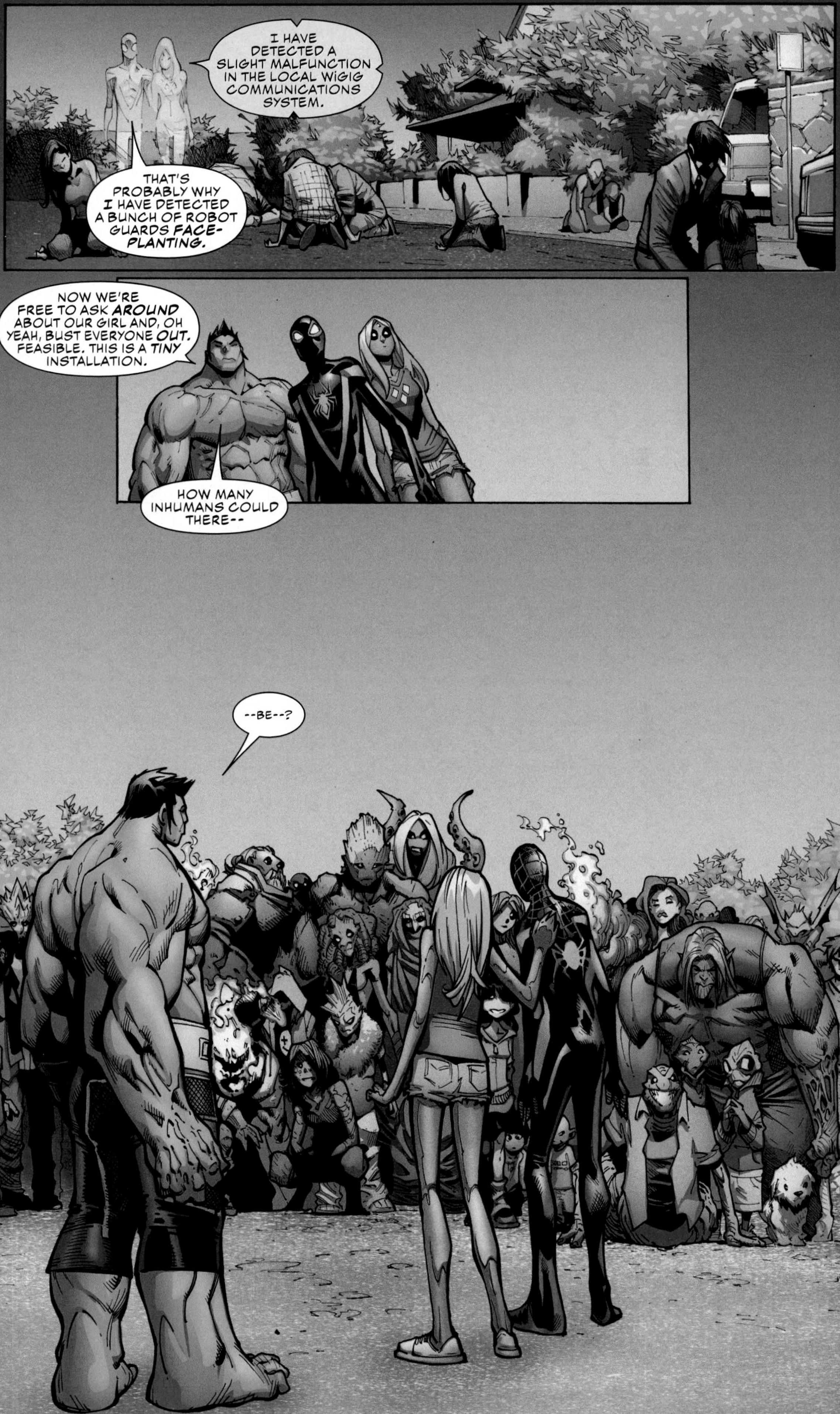
I HAVE DETECTED A SLIGHT MALFUNCTION IN THE LOCAL WiGIG COMMUNICATIONS SYSTEM.
THAT'S PROBABLY WHY I HAVE DETECTED A BUNCH OF ROBOT GUARDS FACE-PLANTING.
NOW WE'RE FREE TO ASK AROUND ABOUT OUR GIRL AND, OH YEAH, BUST EVERYONE OUT. FEASIBLE. THIS IS A TINY INSTALLATION.
HOW MANY INHUMANS COULD THERE--
--BE--?

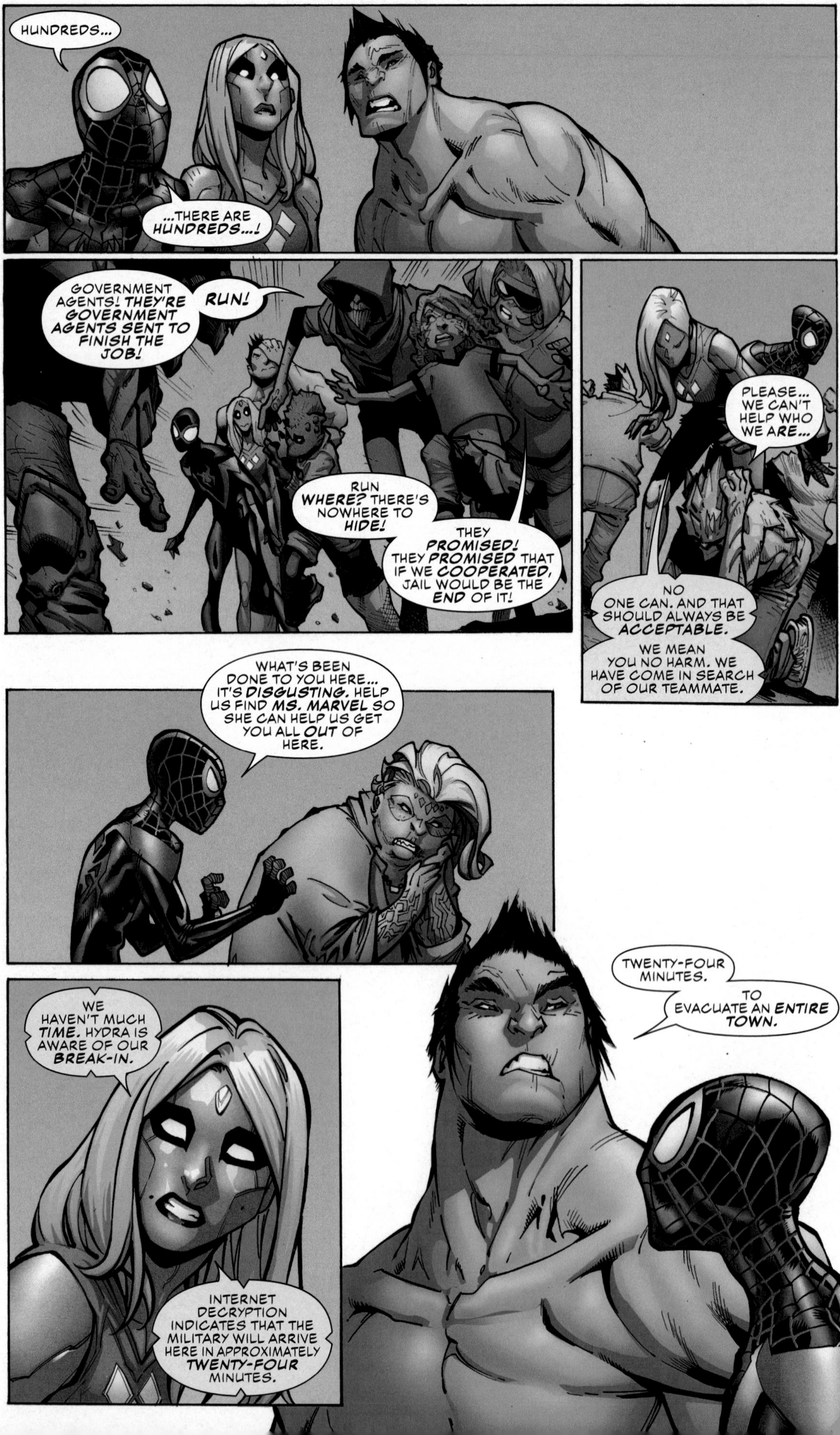
HUNDREDS...
...THERE ARE HUNDREDS...!
GOVERNMENT AGENTS! THEY'RE GOVERNMENT AGENTS SENT TO FINISH THE JOB!
RUN!
RUN WHERE? THERE'S NOWHERE TO HIDE!
THEY PROMISED! THEY PROMISED THAT IF WE COOPERATED, JAIL WOULD BE THE END OF IT!
PLEASE... WE CAN'T HELP WHO WE ARE...
NO ONE CAN. AND THAT SHOULD ALWAYS BE ACCEPTABLE.
WE MEAN YOU NO HARM. WE HAVE COME IN SEARCH OF OUR TEAMMATE.
WHAT'S BEEN DONE TO YOU HERE... IT'S DISGUSTING. HELP US FIND MS. MARVEL SO SHE CAN HELP US GET YOU ALL OUT OF HERE.
WE HAVEN'T MUCH TIME. HYDRA IS AWARE OF OUR BREAK-IN.
INTERNET DECRYPTION INDICATES THAT THE MILITARY WILL ARRIVE HERE IN APPROXIMATELY TWENTY-FOUR MINUTES.
TWENTY-FOUR MINUTES.
TO EVACUATE AN ENTIRE TOWN.

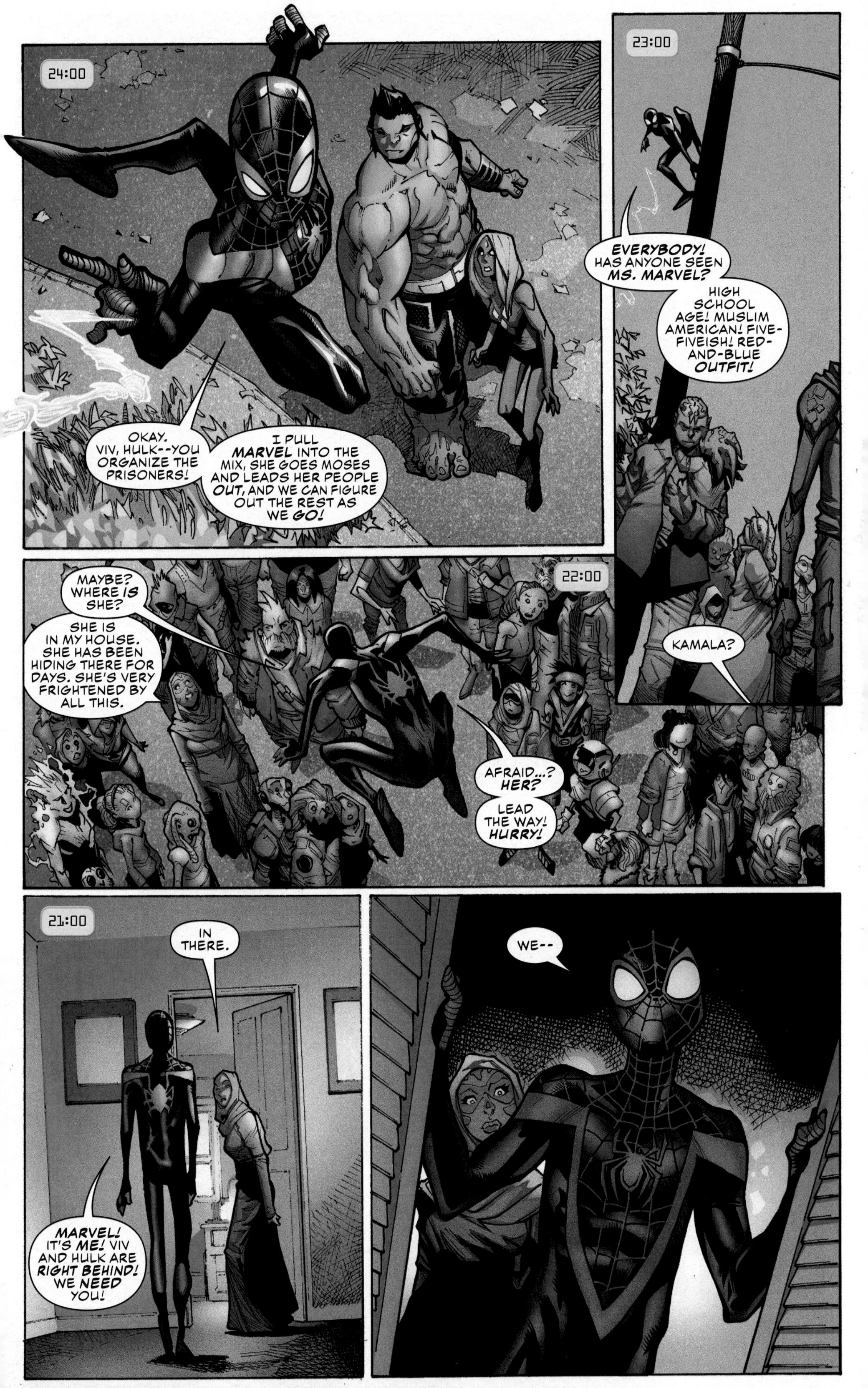
24:00
OKAY. VIV, HULK--YOU ORGANIZE THE PRISONERS!
I PULL MARVEL INTO THE MIX, SHE GOES MOSES AND LEADS HER PEOPLE OUT, AND WE CAN FIGURE OUT THE REST AS WE GO!
23:00
EVERYBODY! HAS ANYONE SEEN MS. MARVEL?
HIGH SCHOOL AGE! MUSLIM AMERICAN! FIVE-FIVEISH! RED-AND-BLUE OUTFIT!
KAMALA?
22:00
MAYBE? WHERE IS SHE?
SHE IS IN MY HOUSE. SHE HAS BEEN HIDING THERE FOR DAYS. SHE'S VERY FRIGHTENED BY ALL THIS.
AFRAID...? HER?
LEAD THE WAY! HURRY!
21:00
IN THERE.
MARVEL! IT'S ME! VIV AND HULK ARE RIGHT BEHIND! WE NEED YOU!
WE--

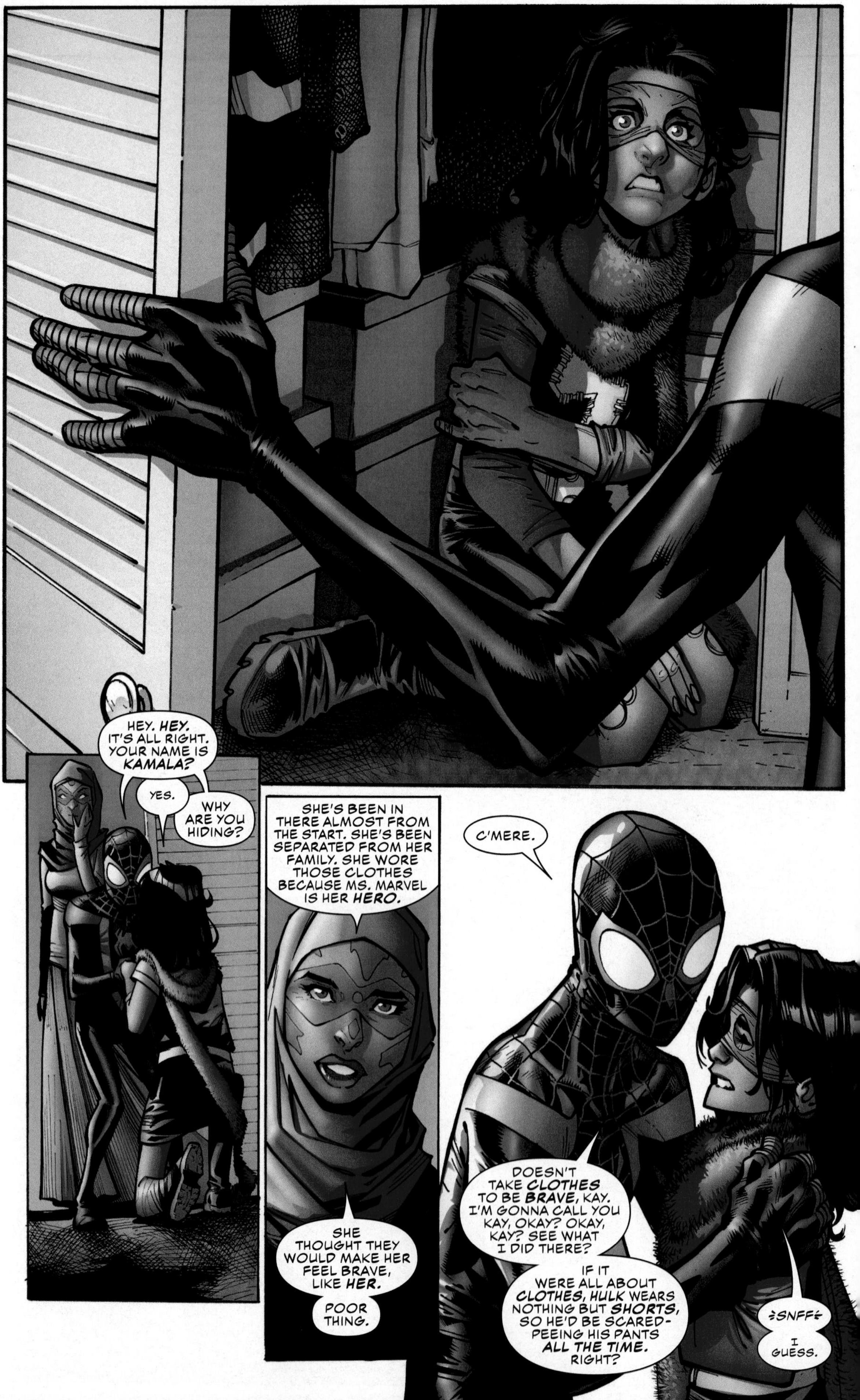
HEY. HEY. IT'S ALL RIGHT. YOUR NAME IS KAMALA?
YES.
WHY ARE YOU HIDING?
SHE'S BEEN IN THERE ALMOST FROM THE START. SHE'S BEEN SEPARATED FROM HER FAMILY. SHE WORE THOSE CLOTHES BECAUSE MS. MARVEL IS HER HERO.
SHE THOUGHT THEY WOULD MAKE HER FEEL BRAVE, LIKE HER.
POOR THING.
C'MERE.
DOESN'T TAKE CLOTHES TO BE BRAVE, KAY. I'M GONNA CALL YOU KAY, OKAY? OKAY, KAY? SEE WHAT I DID THERE?
IF IT WERE ALL ABOUT CLOTHES, HULK WEARS NOTHING BUT SHORTS, SO HE'D BE SCARED-PEEING HIS PANTS ALL THE TIME. RIGHT?
SNFF
I GUESS.

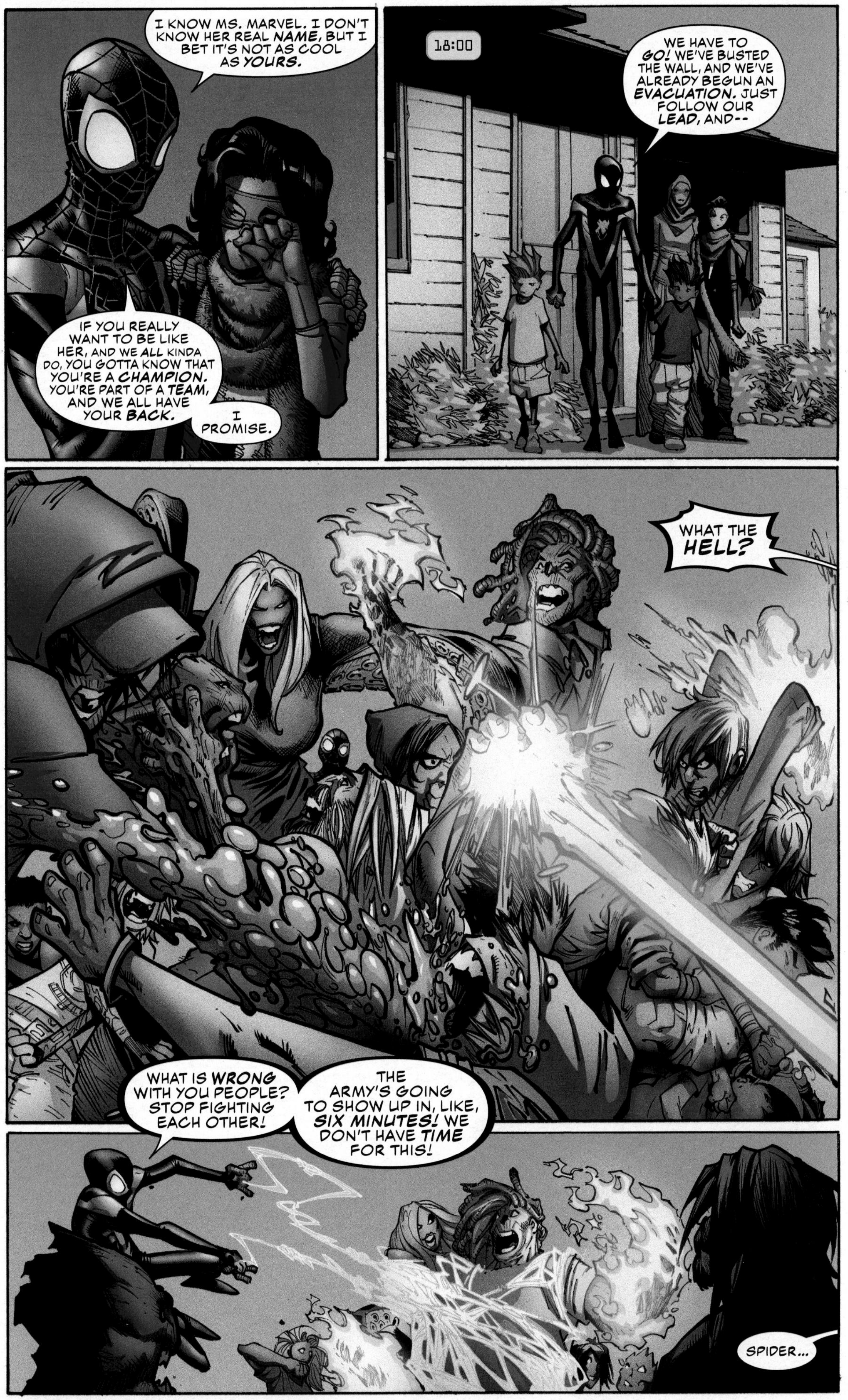
I KNOW MS. MARVEL. I DON'T KNOW HER REAL NAME, BUT I BET IT'S NOT AS COOL AS YOURS.
IF YOU REALLY WANT TO BE LIKE HER, AND WE ALL KINDA DO, YOU GOTTA KNOW THAT YOU'RE A CHAMPION. YOU'RE PART OF A TEAM, AND WE ALL HAVE YOUR BACK.
I PROMISE.
18:00
WE HAVE TO GO! WE'VE BUSTED THE WALL, AND WE'VE ALREADY BEGUN AN EVACUATION. JUST FOLLOW OUR LEAD, AND--
WHAT THE HELL?
WHAT IS WRONG WITH YOU PEOPLE? STOP FIGHTING EACH OTHER!
THE ARMY'S GOING TO SHOW UP IN, LIKE, SIX MINUTES! WE DON'T HAVE TIME FOR THIS!
SPIDER...

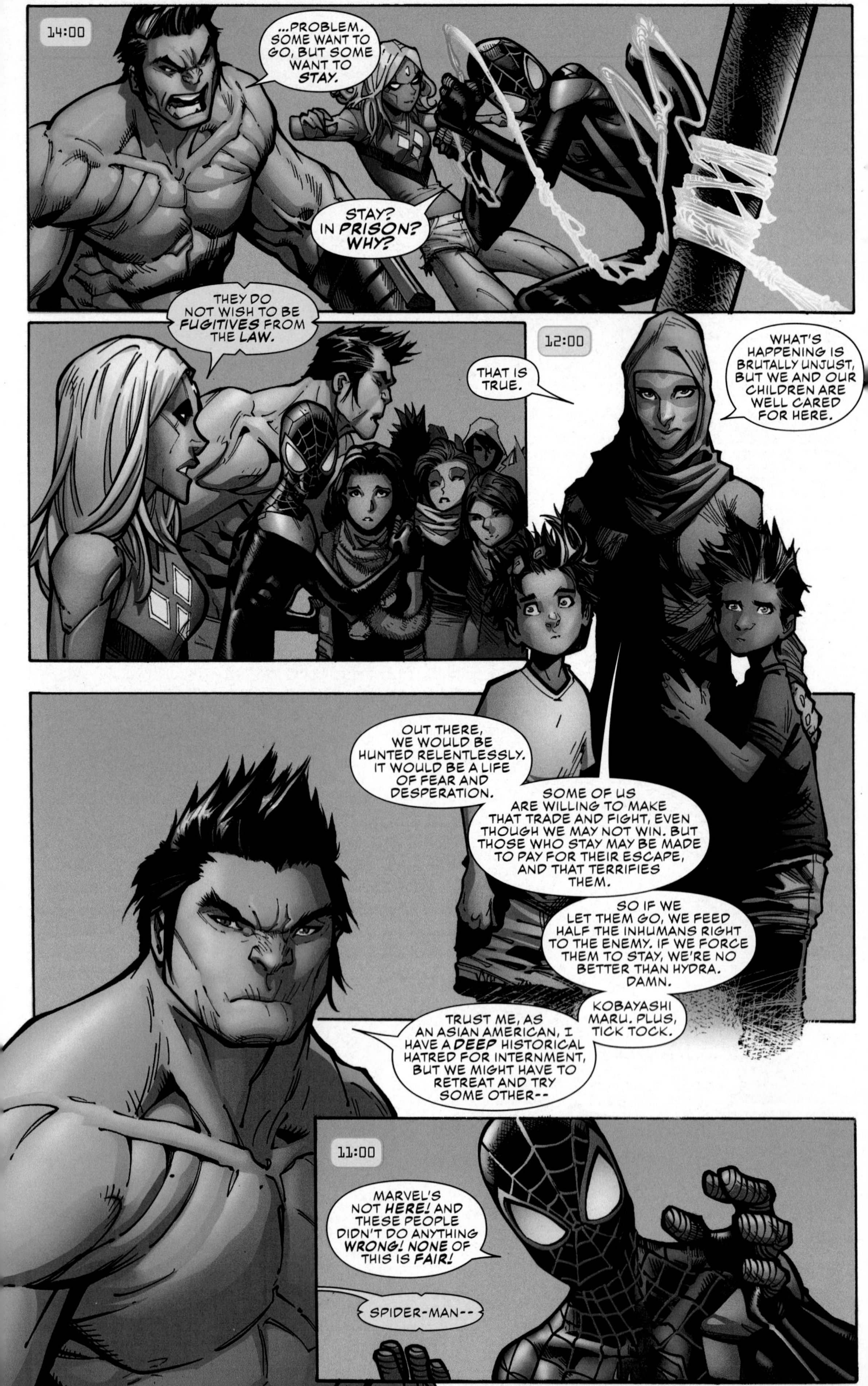
14:00
...PROBLEM. SOME WANT TO GO, BUT SOME WANT TO STAY.
STAY? IN PRISON? WHY?
THEY DO NOT WISH TO BE FUGITIVES FROM THE LAW.
12:00
THAT IS TRUE.
WHAT'S HAPPENING IS BRUTALLY UNJUST, BUT WE AND OUR CHILDREN ARE WELL CARED FOR HERE.
OUT THERE, WE WOULD BE HUNTED RELENTLESSLY. IT WOULD BE A LIFE OF FEAR AND DESPERATION.
SOME OF US ARE WILLING TO MAKE THAT TRADE AND FIGHT, EVEN THOUGH WE MAY NOT WIN. BUT THOSE WHO STAY MAY BE MADE TO PAY FOR THEIR ESCAPE, AND THAT TERRIFIES THEM.
SO IF WE LET THEM GO, WE FEED HALF THE INHUMANS RIGHT TO THE ENEMY. IF WE FORCE THEM TO STAY, WE'RE NO BETTER THAN HYDRA. DAMN.
KOBAYASHI MARU. PLUS, TICK TOCK.
TRUST ME, AS AN ASIAN AMERICAN, I HAVE A DEEP HISTORICAL HATRED FOR INTERNMENT, BUT WE MIGHT HAVE TO RETREAT AND TRY SOME OTHER--
11:00
MARVEL'S NOT HERE! AND THESE PEOPLE DIDN'T DO ANYTHING WRONG! NONE OF THIS IS FAIR!
SPIDER-MAN--

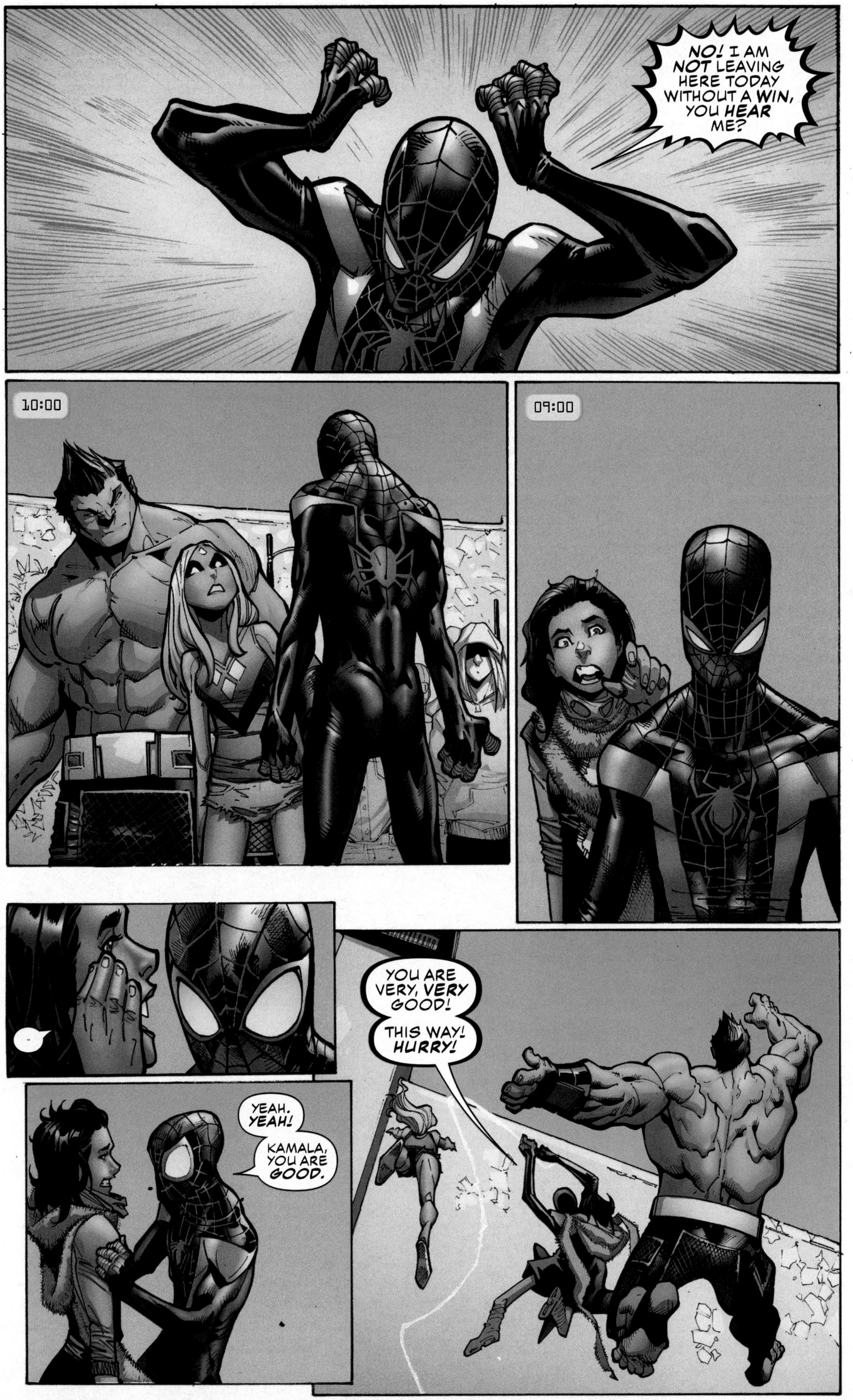
NO! I AM NOT LEAVING HERE TODAY WITHOUT A WIN, YOU HEAR ME?
10:00
09:00
YOU ARE VERY, VERY GOOD!
THIS WAY! HURRY!
YEAH. YEAH!
KAMALA, YOU ARE GOOD.

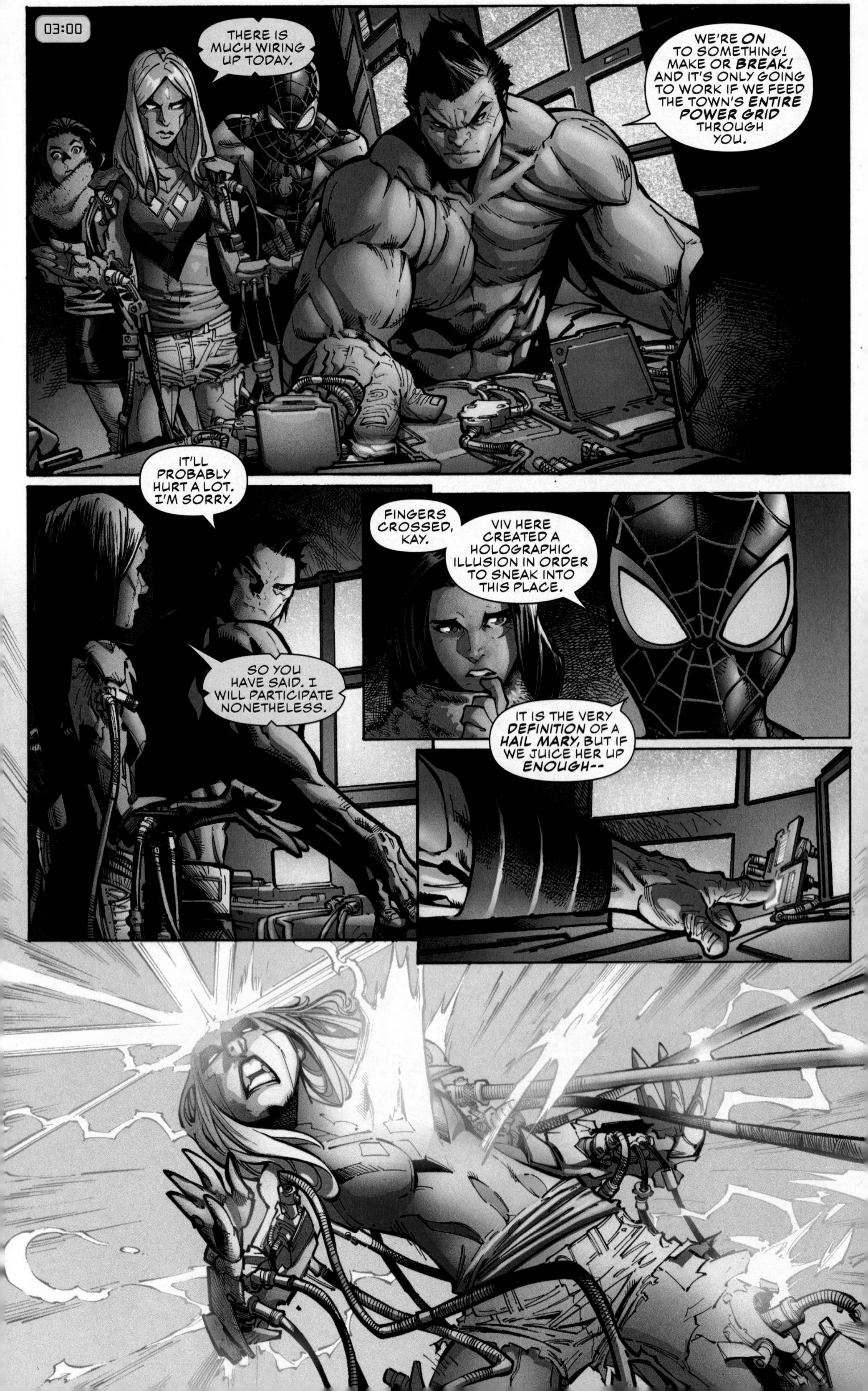
03:00
THERE IS MUCH WIRING UP TODAY.
WE'RE ON TO SOMETHING! MAKE OR BREAK! AND IT'S ONLY GOING TO WORK IF WE FEED THE TOWN'S ENTIRE POWER GRID THROUGH YOU.
IT'LL PROBABLY HURT A LOT. I'M SORRY.
SO YOU HAVE SAID. I WILL PARTICIPATE NONETHELESS.
FINGERS CROSSED, KAY.
VIV HERE CREATED A HOLOGRAPHIC ILLUSION IN ORDER TO SNEAK INTO THIS PLACE.
IT IS THE VERY DEFINITION OF A HAIL MARY, BUT IF WE JUICE HER UP ENOUGH--

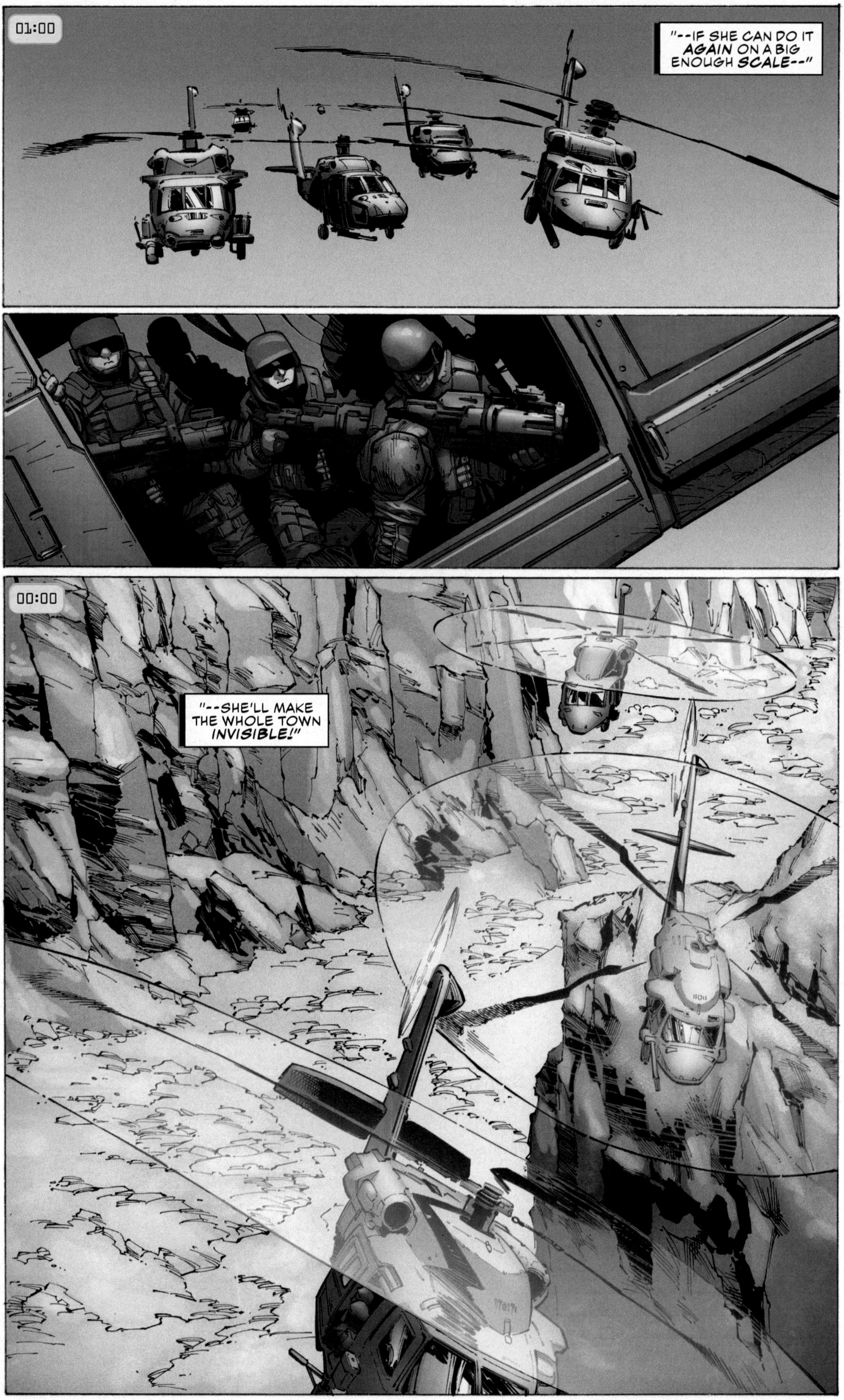
01:00
"--IF SHE CAN DO IT AGAIN ON A BIG ENOUGH SCALE--"
00:00
"--SHE'LL MAKE THE WHOLE TOWN INVISIBLE!"

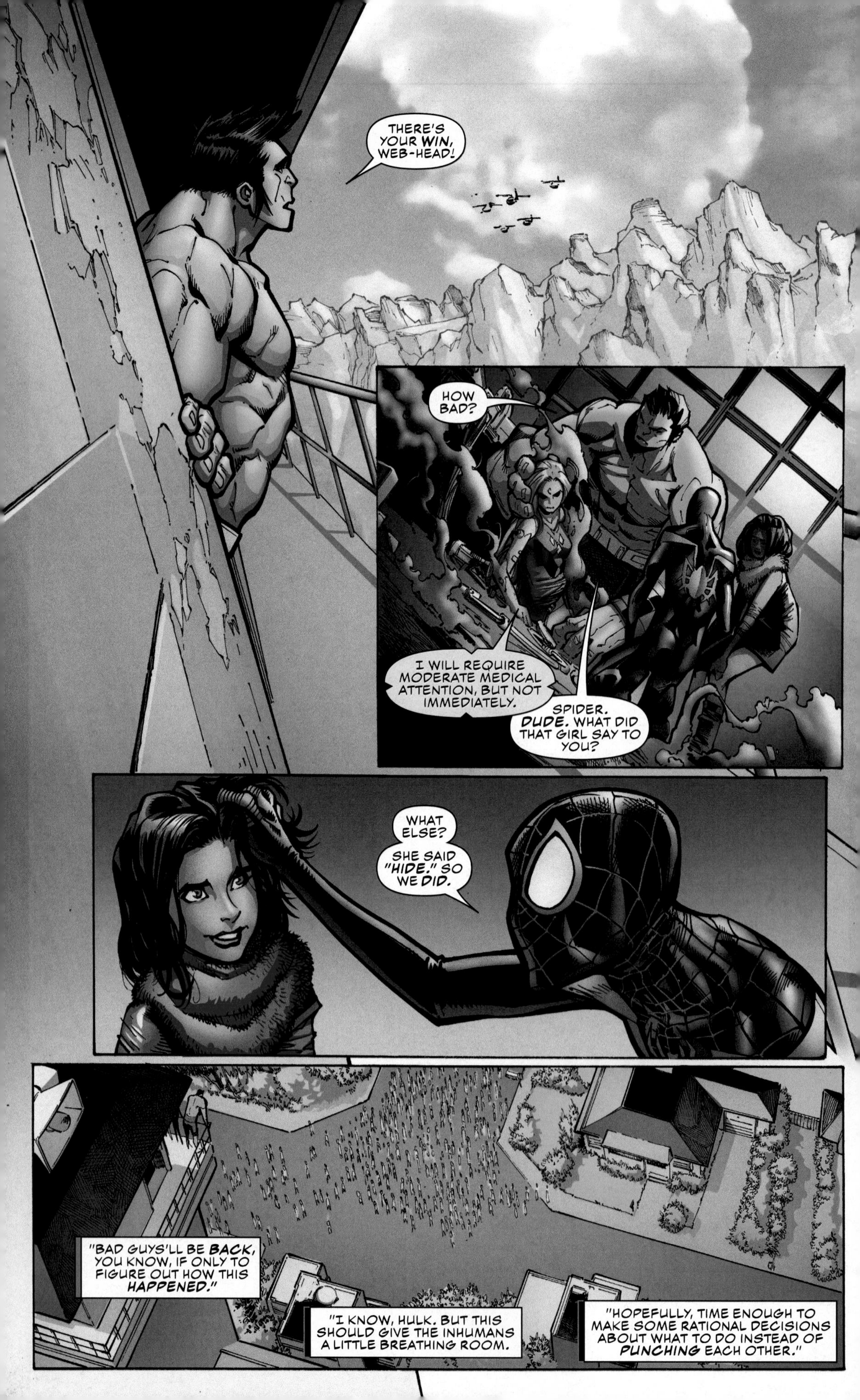
THERE'S YOUR WIN, WEB-HEAD!
HOW BAD?
I WILL REQUIRE MODERATE MEDICAL ATTENTION, BUT NOT IMMEDIATELY.
SPIDER. DUDE. WHAT DID THAT GIRL SAY TO YOU?
WHAT ELSE?
SHE SAID "HIDE." SO WE DID.
"BAD GUYS'LL BE BACK, YOU KNOW, IF ONLY TO FIGURE OUT HOW THIS HAPPENED."
"I KNOW, HULK. BUT THIS SHOULD GIVE THE INHUMANS A LITTLE BREATHING ROOM.
"HOPEFULLY, TIME ENOUGH TO MAKE SOME RATIONAL DECISIONS ABOUT WHAT TO DO INSTEAD OF PUNCHING EACH OTHER."

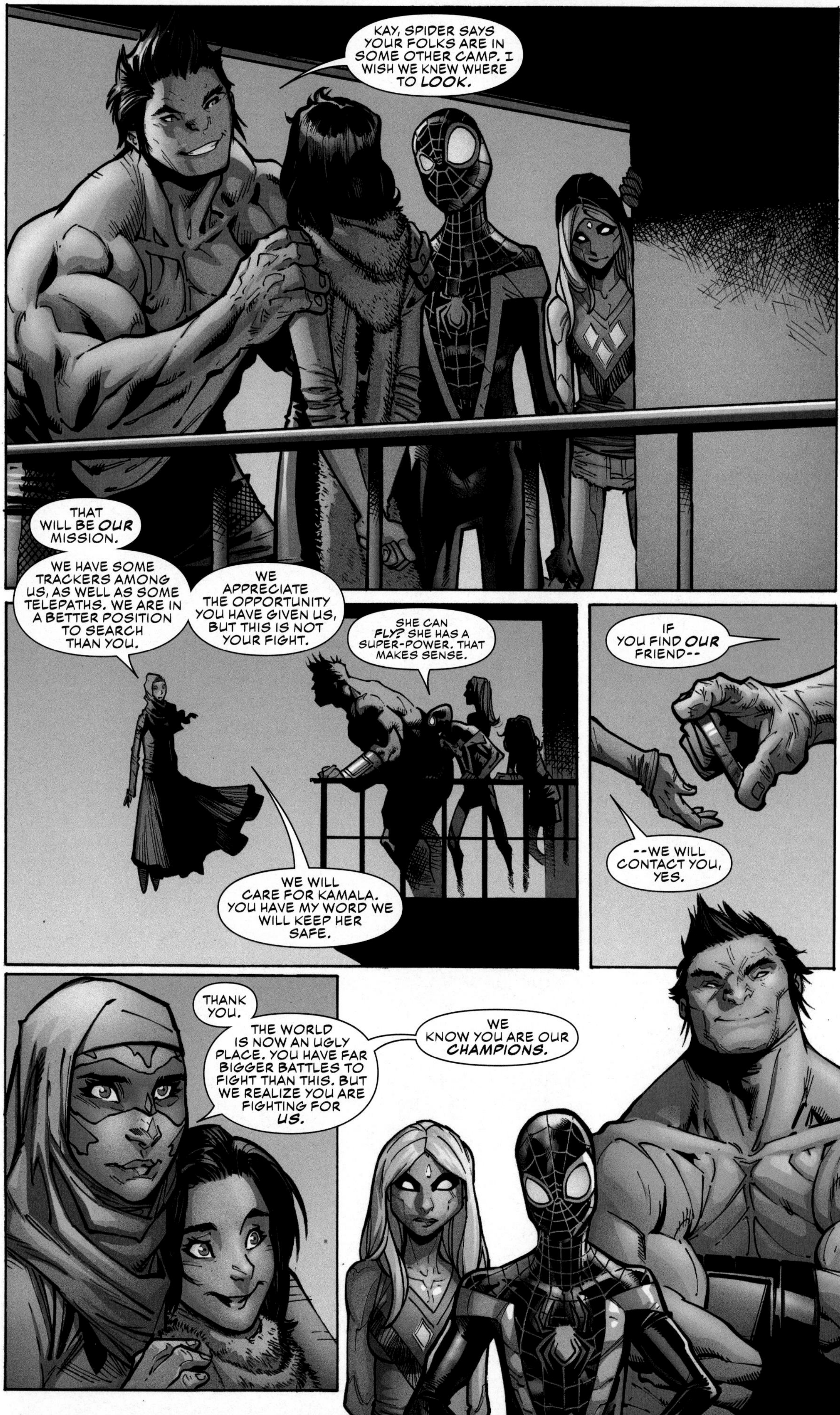
KAY, SPIDER SAYS YOUR FOLKS ARE IN SOME OTHER CAMP. I WISH WE KNEW WHERE TO LOOK.
THAT WILL BE OUR MISSION.
WE HAVE SOME TRACKERS AMONG US, AS WELL AS SOME TELEPATHS. WE ARE IN A BETTER POSITION TO SEARCH THAN YOU.
WE APPRECIATE THE OPPORTUNITY YOU HAVE GIVEN US, BUT THIS IS NOT YOUR FIGHT.
SHE CAN FLY? SHE HAS A SUPER-POWER. THAT MAKES SENSE.
WE WILL CARE FOR KAMALA. YOU HAVE MY WORD WE WILL KEEP HER SAFE.
IF YOU FIND OUR FRIEND--
--WE WILL CONTACT YOU, YES.
THANK YOU.
THE WORLD IS NOW AN UGLY PLACE. YOU HAVE FAR BIGGER BATTLES TO FIGHT THAN THIS. BUT WE REALIZE YOU ARE FIGHTING FOR US.
WE KNOW YOU ARE OUR CHAMPIONS.

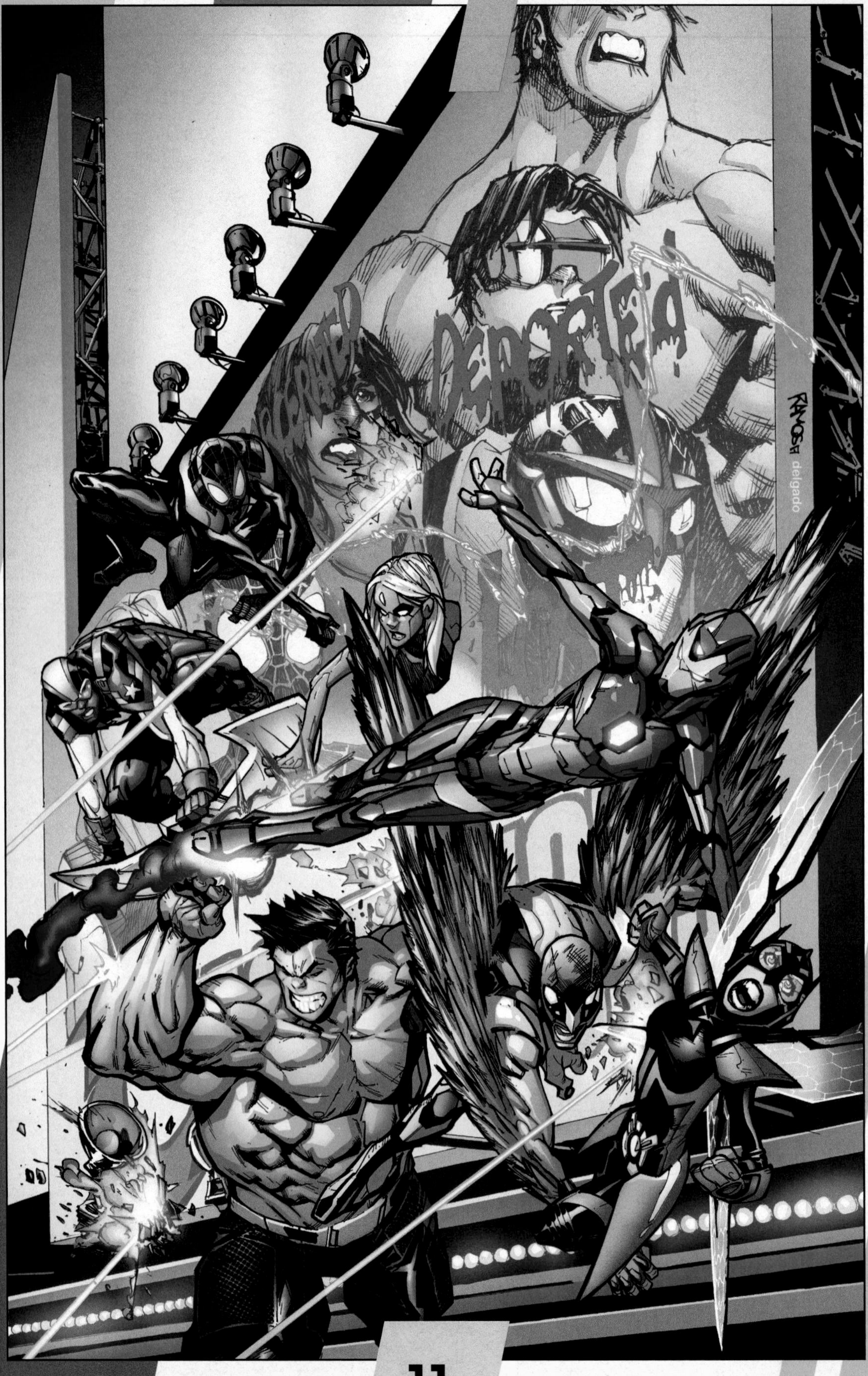
DEPORTED
RAMOS
delgado

11

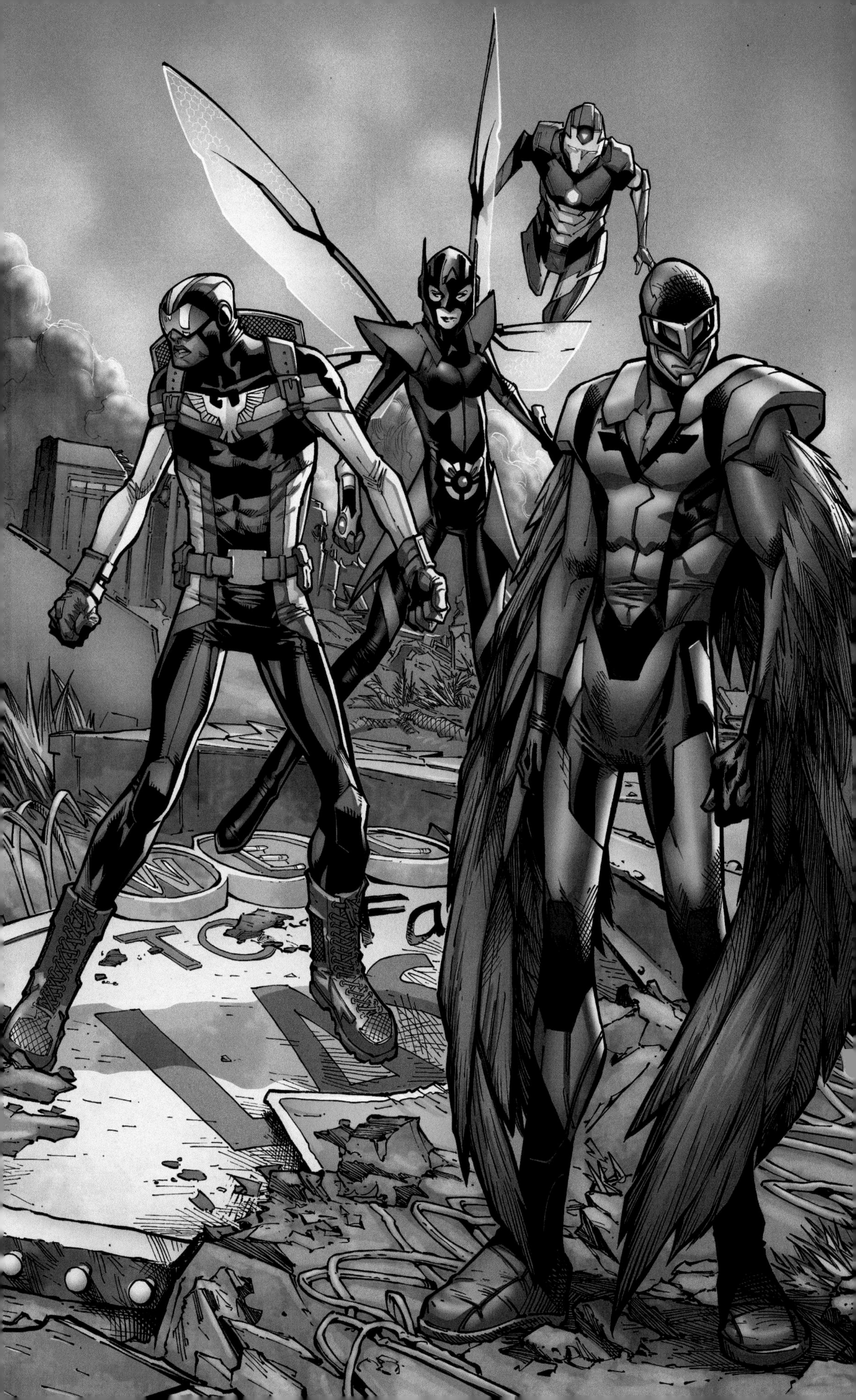

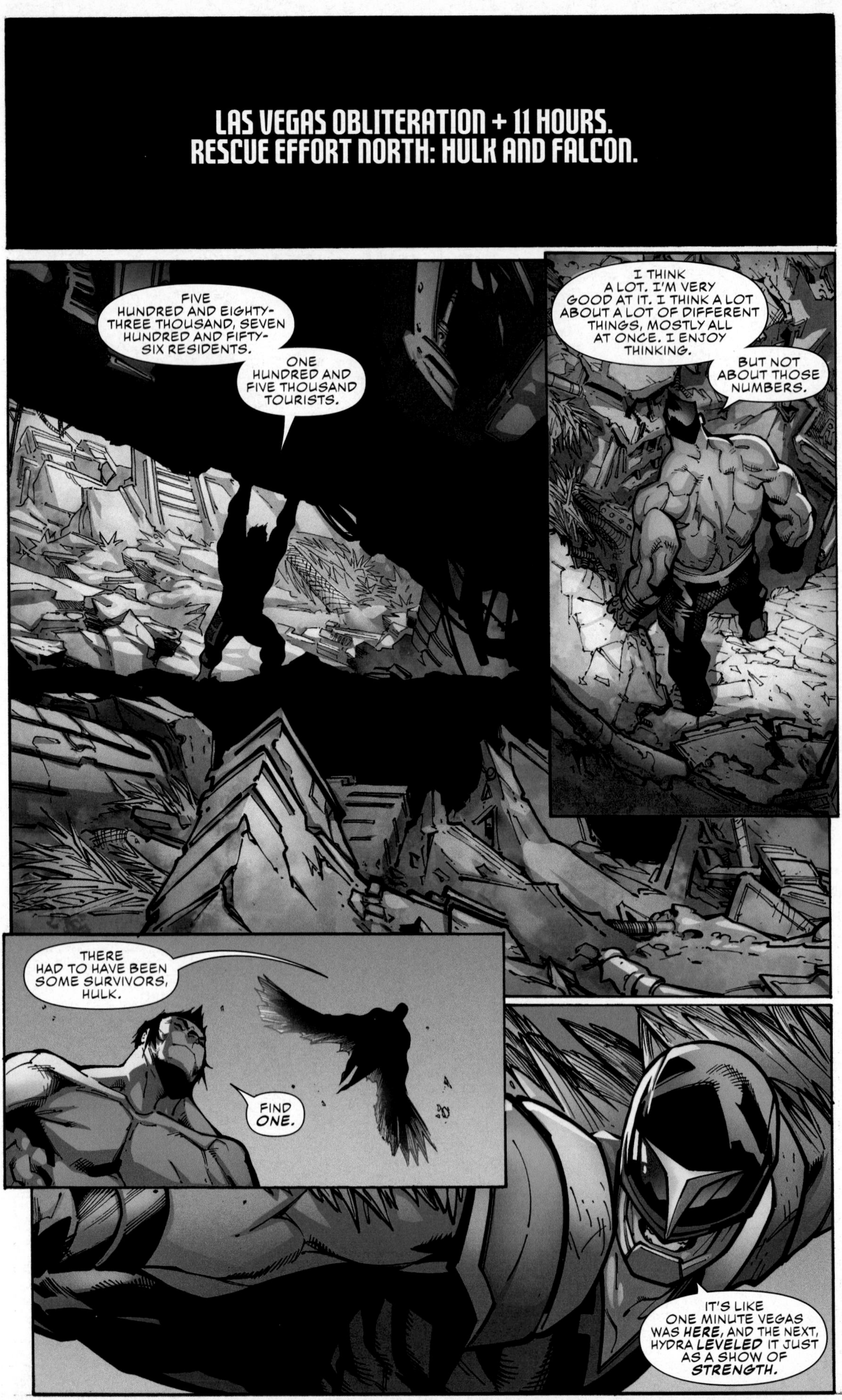
LAS VEGAS OBLITERATION + 11 HOURS.
RESCUE EFFORT NORTH: HULK AND FALCON.
FIVE HUNDRED AND EIGHTY-THREE THOUSAND, SEVEN HUNDRED AND FIFTY-SIX RESIDENTS.
ONE HUNDRED AND FIVE THOUSAND TOURISTS.
I THINK A LOT. I'M VERY GOOD AT IT. I THINK A LOT ABOUT A LOT OF DIFFERENT THINGS, MOSTLY ALL AT ONCE. I ENJOY THINKING.
BUT NOT ABOUT THOSE NUMBERS.
THERE HAD TO HAVE BEEN SOME SURVIVORS, HULK.
FIND *ONE.*
IT'S LIKE ONE MINUTE VEGAS WAS *HERE*, AND THE NEXT, HYDRA *LEVELED* IT JUST AS A SHOW OF *STRENGTH.*

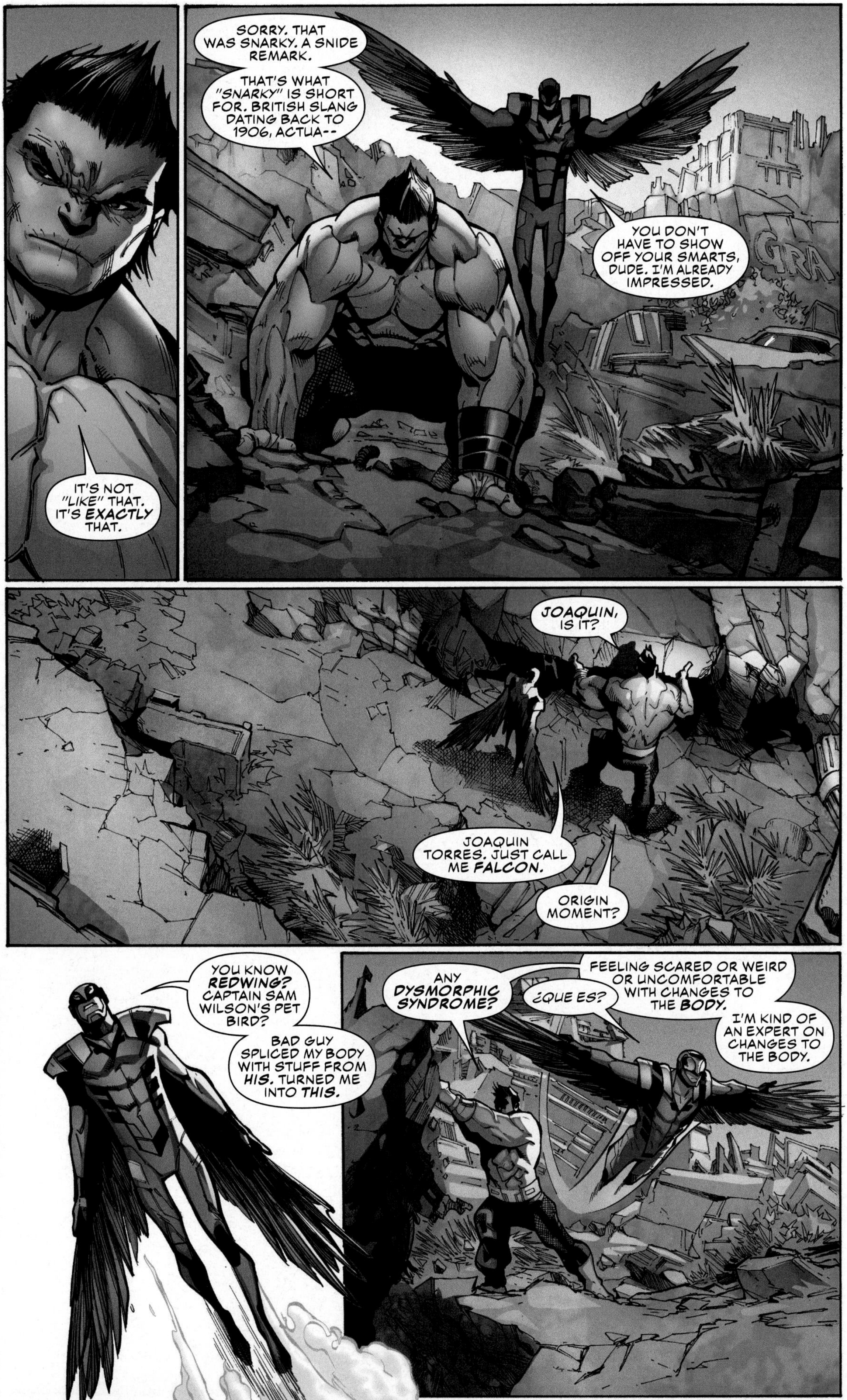
SORRY. THAT WAS SNARKY. A SNIDE REMARK.
THAT'S WHAT "SNARKY" IS SHORT FOR. BRITISH SLANG DATING BACK TO 1906, ACTUA--
YOU DON'T HAVE TO SHOW OFF YOUR SMARTS, DUDE. I'M ALREADY IMPRESSED.
IT'S NOT "LIKE" THAT. IT'S EXACTLY THAT.
JOAQUIN, IS IT?
JOAQUIN TORRES. JUST CALL ME FALCON.
ORIGIN MOMENT?
YOU KNOW REDWING? CAPTAIN SAM WILSON'S PET BIRD?
BAD GUY SPLICED MY BODY WITH STUFF FROM HIS. TURNED ME INTO THIS.
ANY DYSMORPHIC SYNDROME?
¿QUE ES?
FEELING SCARED OR WEIRD OR UNCOMFORTABLE WITH CHANGES TO THE BODY.
I'M KIND OF AN EXPERT ON CHANGES TO THE BODY.

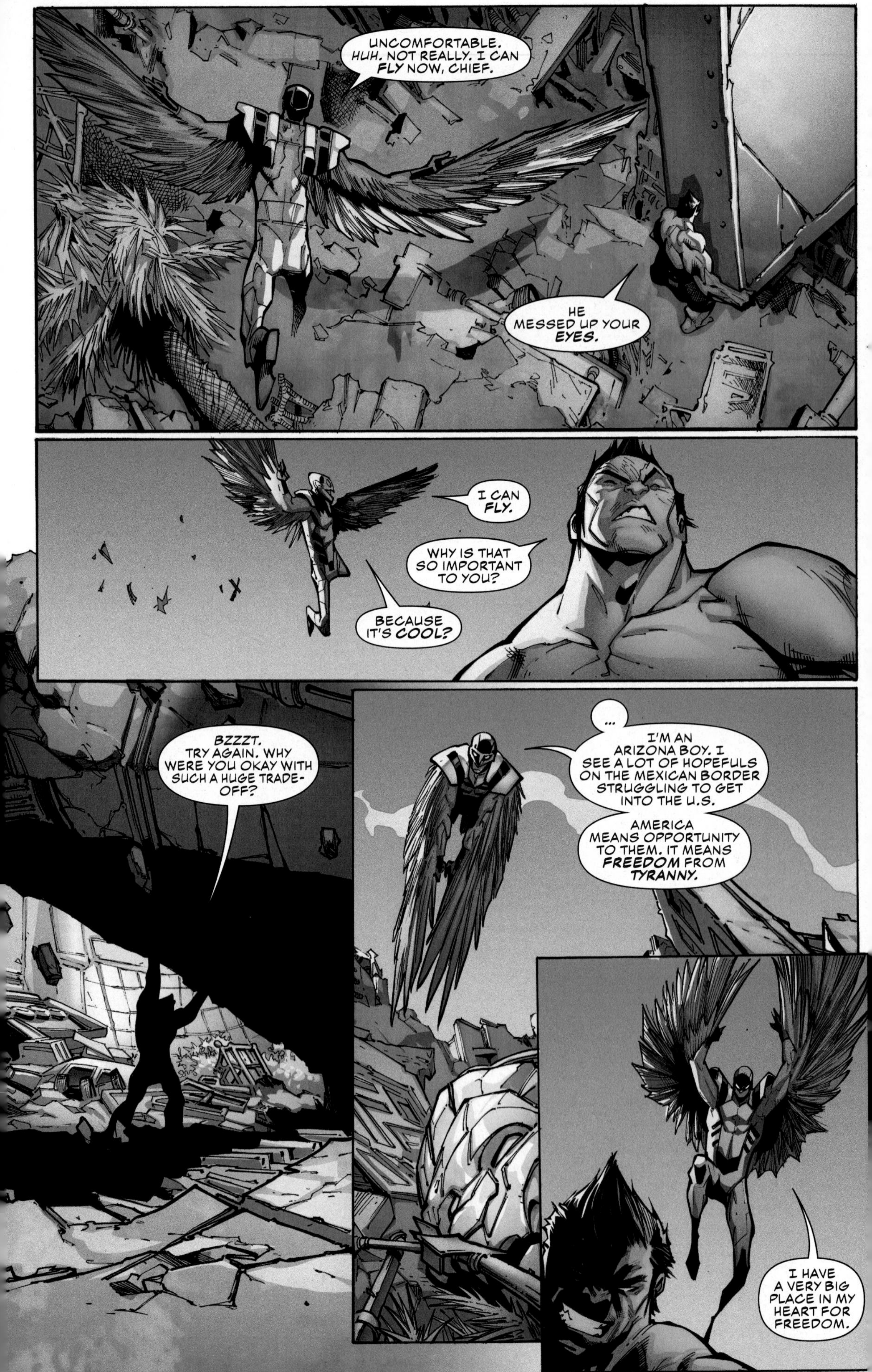
UNCOMFORTABLE. HUH. NOT REALLY. I CAN FLY NOW, CHIEF.
HE MESSED UP YOUR EYES.
I CAN FLY.
WHY IS THAT SO IMPORTANT TO YOU?
BECAUSE IT'S COOL?
BZZZT. TRY AGAIN. WHY WERE YOU OKAY WITH SUCH A HUGE TRADE-OFF?
...
I'M AN ARIZONA BOY. I SEE A LOT OF HOPEFULS ON THE MEXICAN BORDER STRUGGLING TO GET INTO THE U.S.
AMERICA MEANS OPPORTUNITY TO THEM. IT MEANS FREEDOM FROM TYRANNY.
I HAVE A VERY BIG PLACE IN MY HEART FOR FREEDOM.

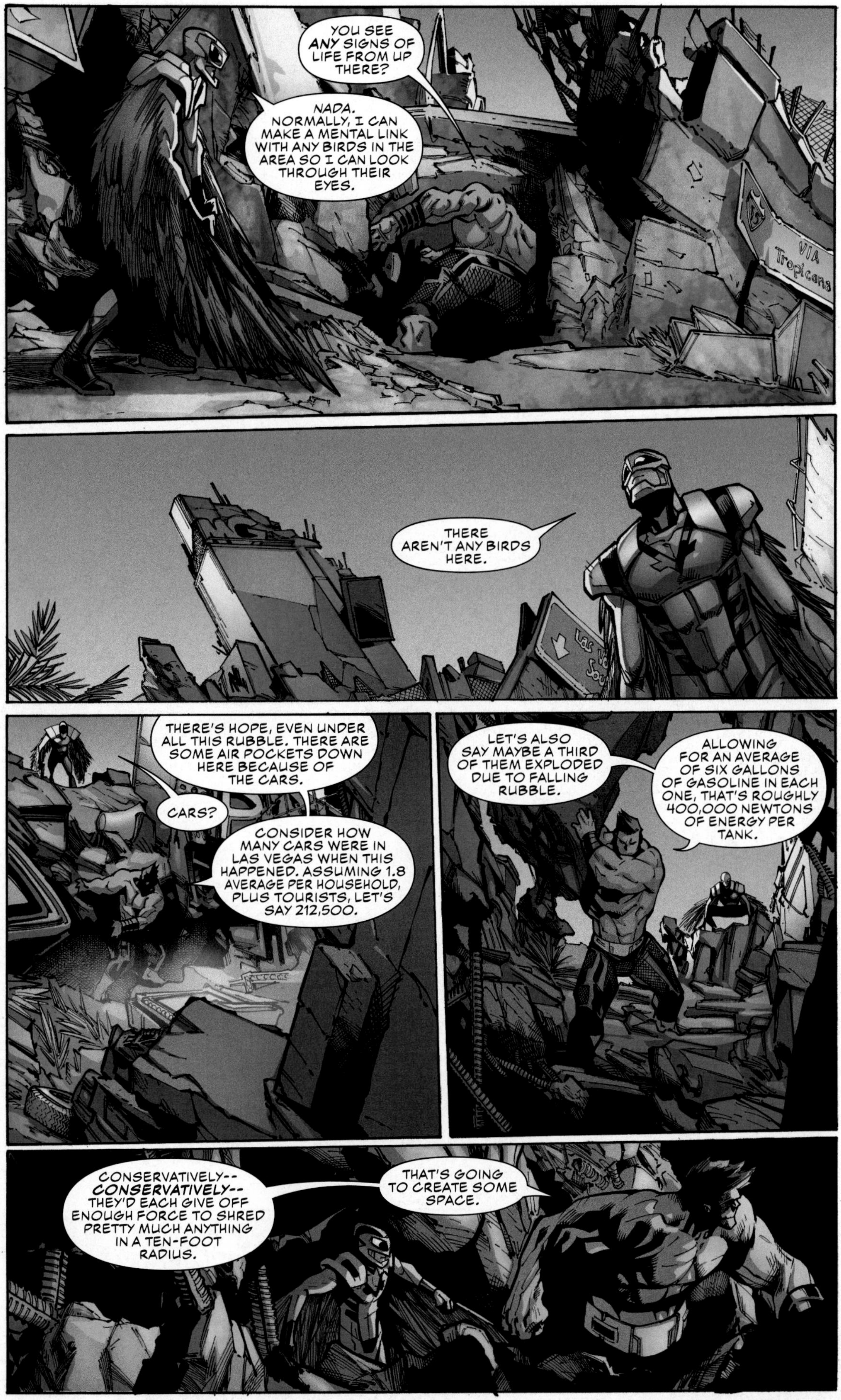
YOU SEE ANY SIGNS OF LIFE FROM UP THERE?
NADA. NORMALLY, I CAN MAKE A MENTAL LINK WITH ANY BIRDS IN THE AREA SO I CAN LOOK THROUGH THEIR EYES.
VIA Tropicana
THERE AREN'T ANY BIRDS HERE.
THERE'S HOPE, EVEN UNDER ALL THIS RUBBLE. THERE ARE SOME AIR POCKETS DOWN HERE BECAUSE OF THE CARS.
CARS?
CONSIDER HOW MANY CARS WERE IN LAS VEGAS WHEN THIS HAPPENED. ASSUMING 1.8 AVERAGE PER HOUSEHOLD, PLUS TOURISTS, LET'S SAY 212,500.
LET'S ALSO SAY MAYBE A THIRD OF THEM EXPLODED DUE TO FALLING RUBBLE.
ALLOWING FOR AN AVERAGE OF SIX GALLONS OF GASOLINE IN EACH ONE, THAT'S ROUGHLY 400,000 NEWTONS OF ENERGY PER TANK.
CONSERVATIVELY-- CONSERVATIVELY-- THEY'D EACH GIVE OFF ENOUGH FORCE TO SHRED PRETTY MUCH ANYTHING IN A TEN-FOOT RADIUS.
THAT'S GOING TO CREATE SOME SPACE.

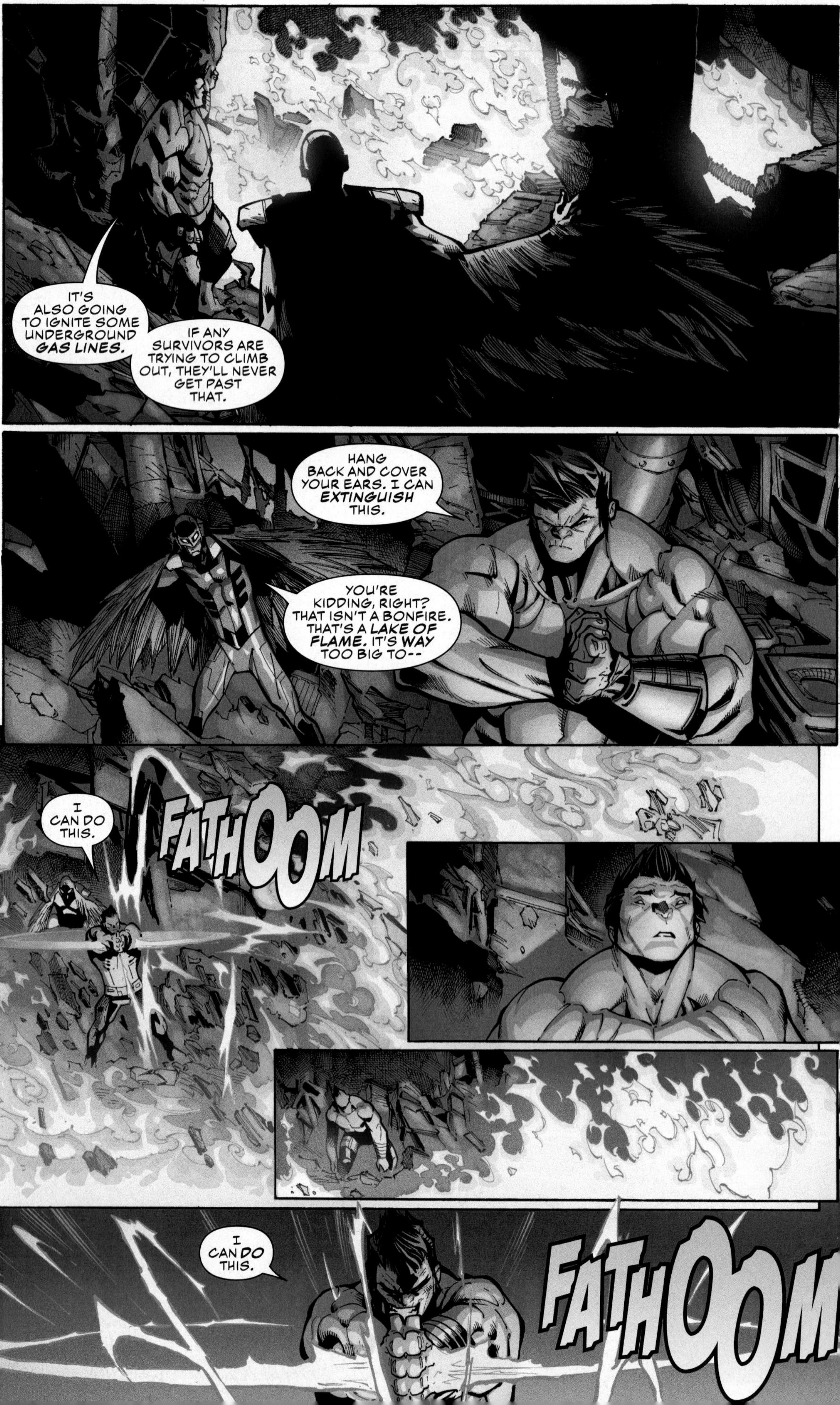
IT'S ALSO GOING TO IGNITE SOME UNDERGROUND GAS LINES.
IF ANY SURVIVORS ARE TRYING TO CLIMB OUT, THEY'LL NEVER GET PAST THAT.
HANG BACK AND COVER YOUR EARS. I CAN EXTINGUISH THIS.
YOU'RE KIDDING, RIGHT? THAT ISN'T A BONFIRE. THAT'S A LAKE OF FLAME. IT'S WAY TOO BIG TO--
I CAN DO THIS.
FATHOOM
I CAN DO THIS.
FATHOOM

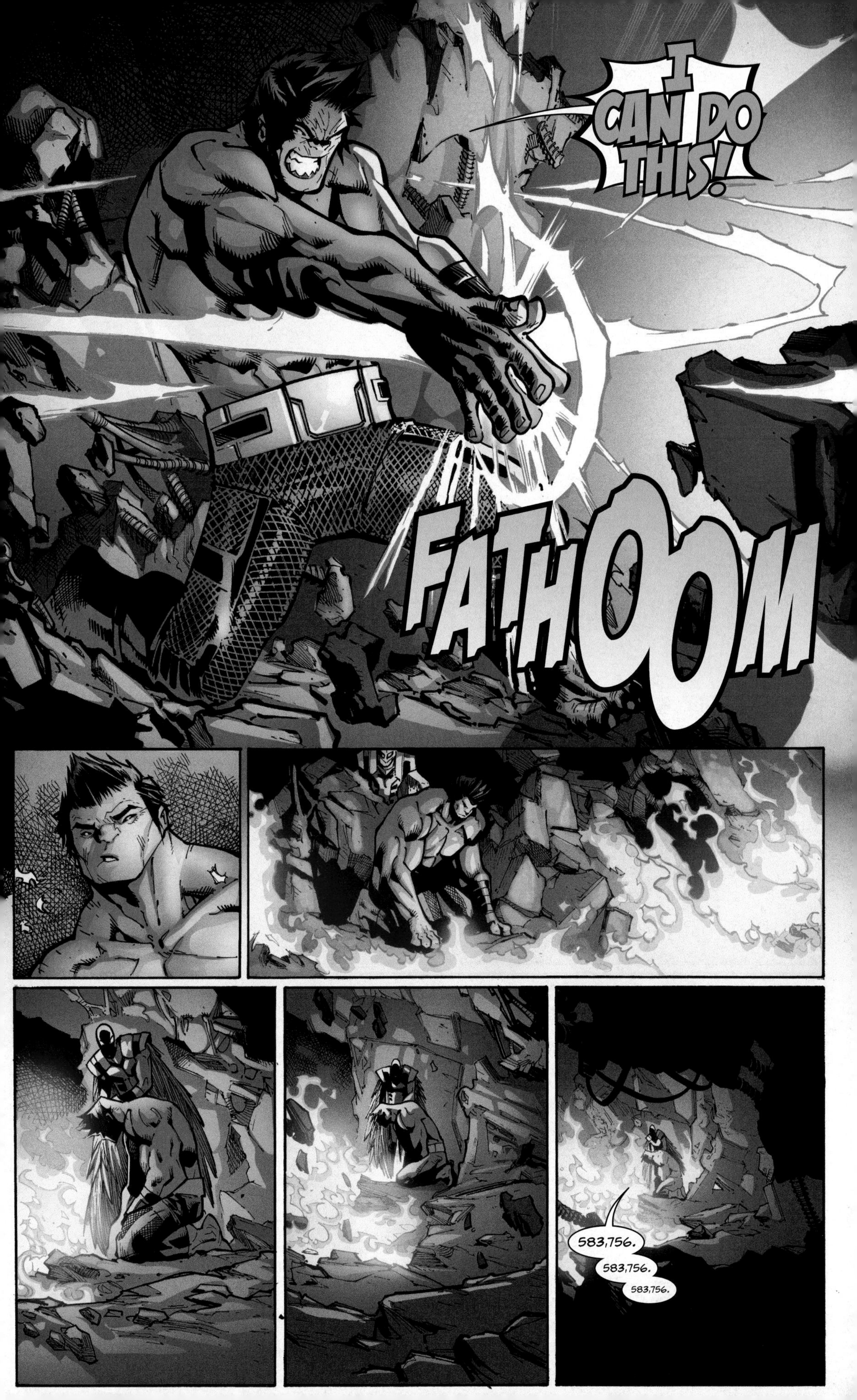
I CAN DO THIS!
FATHOOM
583,756.
583,756.
583,756.

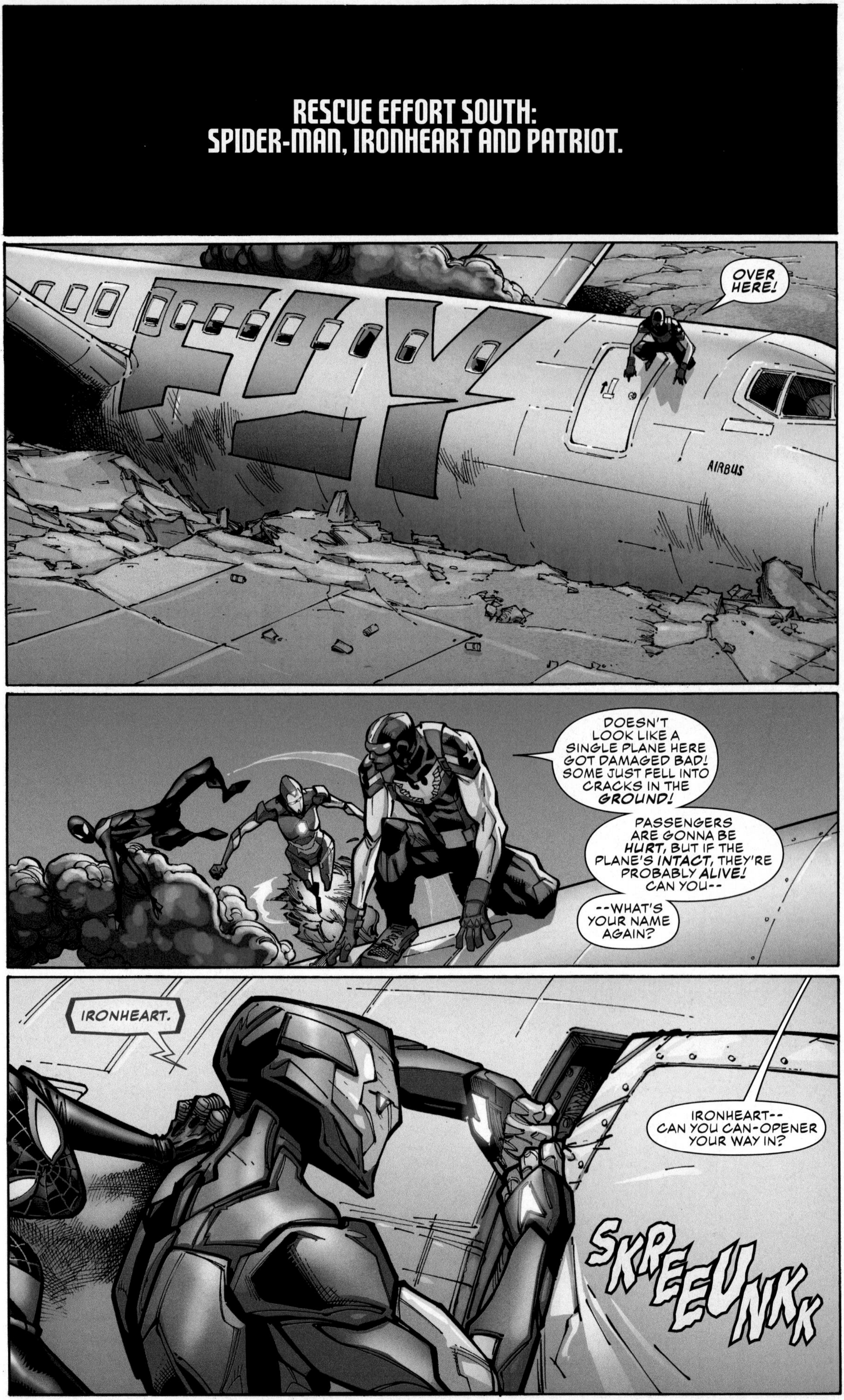
RESCUE EFFORT SOUTH:
SPIDER-MAN, IRONHEART AND PATRIOT.
OVER HERE!
DOESN'T LOOK LIKE A SINGLE PLANE HERE GOT DAMAGED BAD! SOME JUST FELL INTO CRACKS IN THE GROUND!
PASSENGERS ARE GONNA BE HURT, BUT IF THE PLANE'S INTACT, THEY'RE PROBABLY ALIVE! CAN YOU--
--WHAT'S YOUR NAME AGAIN?
IRONHEART.
IRONHEART-- CAN YOU CAN-OPENER YOUR WAY IN?
SKREEUNKK

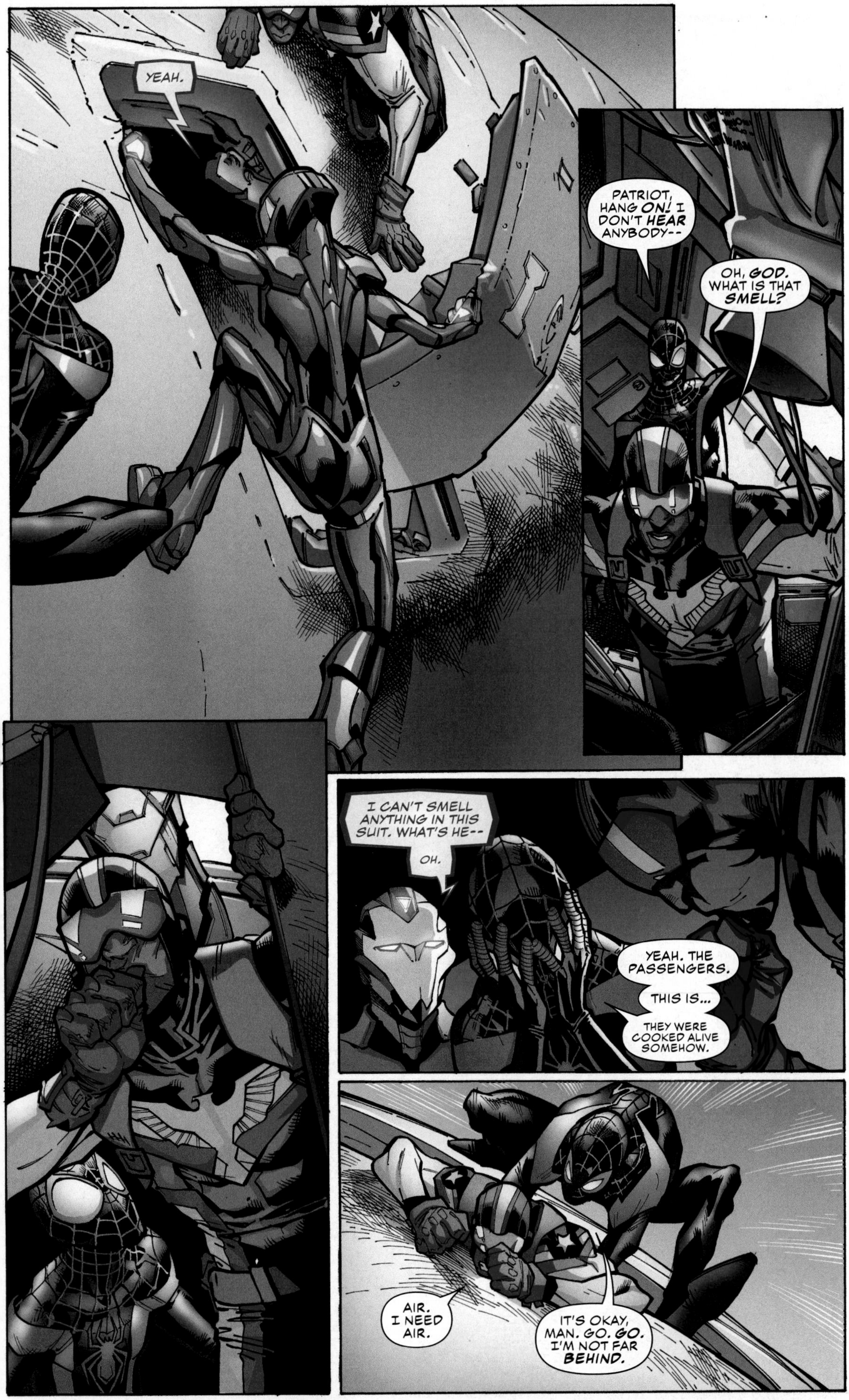
YEAH.
PATRIOT, HANG ON! I DON'T HEAR ANYBODY--
OH, GOD. WHAT IS THAT SMELL?
I CAN'T SMELL ANYTHING IN THIS SUIT. WHAT'S HE--
OH.
YEAH. THE PASSENGERS.
THIS IS...
THEY WERE COOKED ALIVE SOMEHOW.
AIR. I NEED AIR.
IT'S OKAY, MAN. GO. GO. I'M NOT FAR BEHIND.

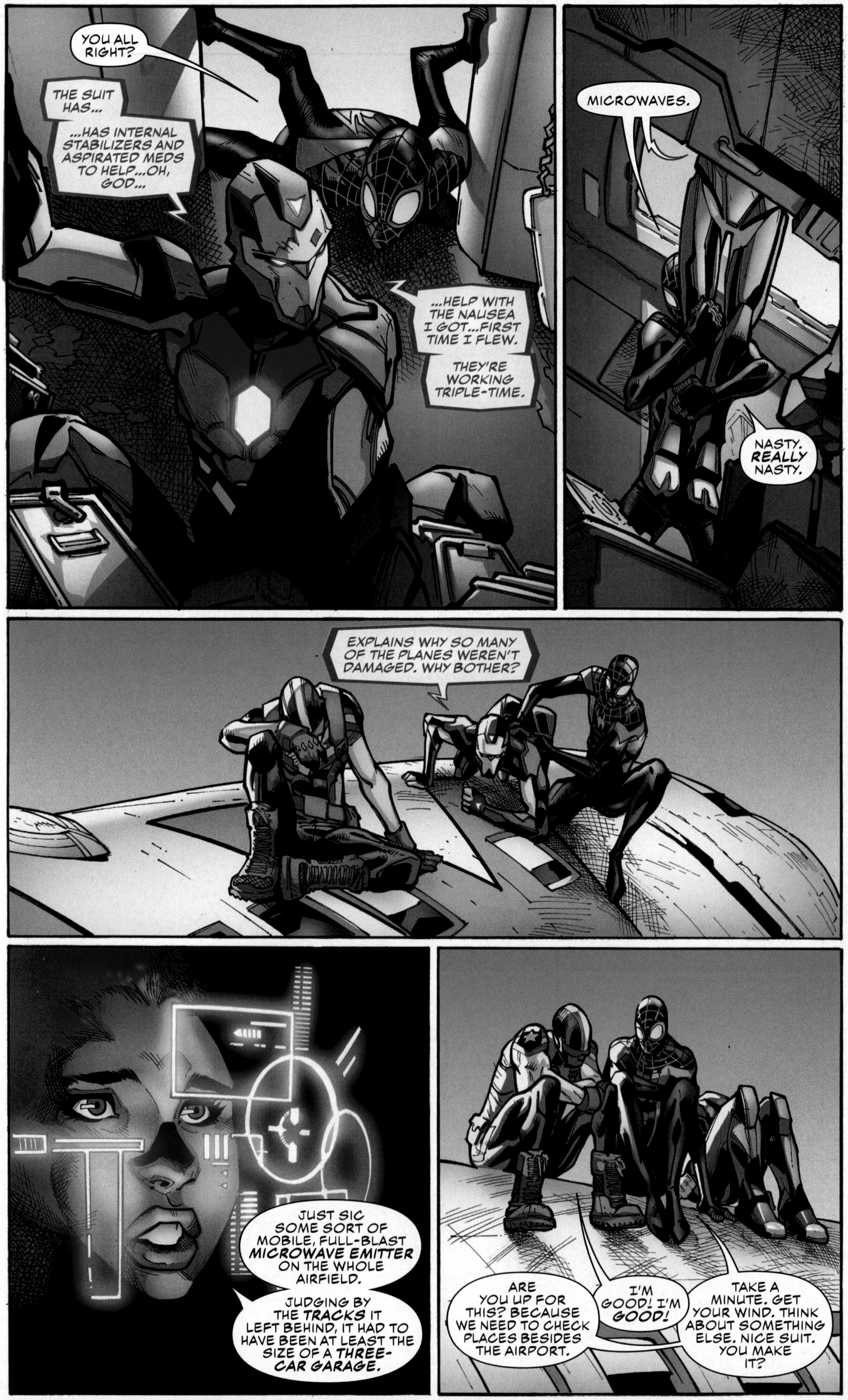
YOU ALL RIGHT?
THE SUIT HAS...
...HAS INTERNAL STABILIZERS AND ASPIRATED MEDS TO HELP...OH, GOD...
...HELP WITH THE NAUSEA I GOT...FIRST TIME I FLEW.
THEY'RE WORKING TRIPLE-TIME.
MICROWAVES.
NASTY. REALLY NASTY.
EXPLAINS WHY SO MANY OF THE PLANES WEREN'T DAMAGED. WHY BOTHER?
JUST SIC SOME SORT OF MOBILE, FULL-BLAST MICROWAVE EMITTER ON THE WHOLE AIRFIELD.
JUDGING BY THE TRACKS IT LEFT BEHIND, IT HAD TO HAVE BEEN AT LEAST THE SIZE OF A THREE-CAR GARAGE.
ARE YOU UP FOR THIS? BECAUSE WE NEED TO CHECK PLACES BESIDES THE AIRPORT.
I'M GOOD! I'M GOOD!
TAKE A MINUTE. GET YOUR WIND. THINK ABOUT SOMETHING ELSE. NICE SUIT. YOU MAKE IT?

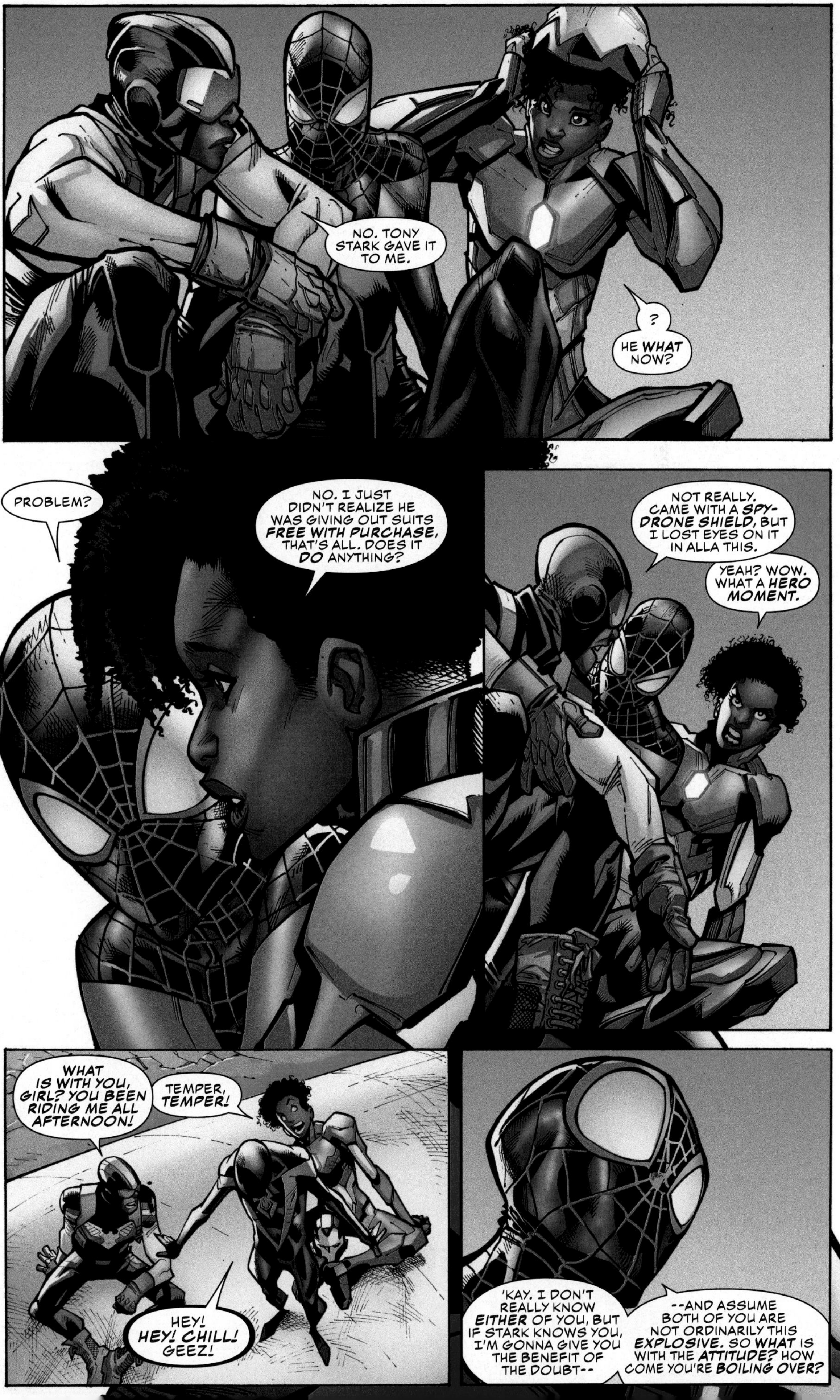
NO. TONY STARK GAVE IT TO ME.
?
HE WHAT NOW?
PROBLEM?
NO. I JUST DIDN'T REALIZE HE WAS GIVING OUT SUITS FREE WITH PURCHASE, THAT'S ALL. DOES IT DO ANYTHING?
NOT REALLY. CAME WITH A SPY-DRONE SHIELD, BUT I LOST EYES ON IT IN ALLA THIS.
YEAH? WOW. WHAT A HERO MOMENT.
WHAT IS WITH YOU, GIRL? YOU BEEN RIDING ME ALL AFTERNOON!
TEMPER, TEMPER!
HEY! HEY! CHILL! GEEZ!
'KAY. I DON'T REALLY KNOW EITHER OF YOU, BUT IF STARK KNOWS YOU, I'M GONNA GIVE YOU THE BENEFIT OF THE DOUBT--
--AND ASSUME BOTH OF YOU ARE NOT ORDINARILY THIS EXPLOSIVE. SO WHAT IS WITH THE ATTITUDE? HOW COME YOU'RE BOILING OVER?

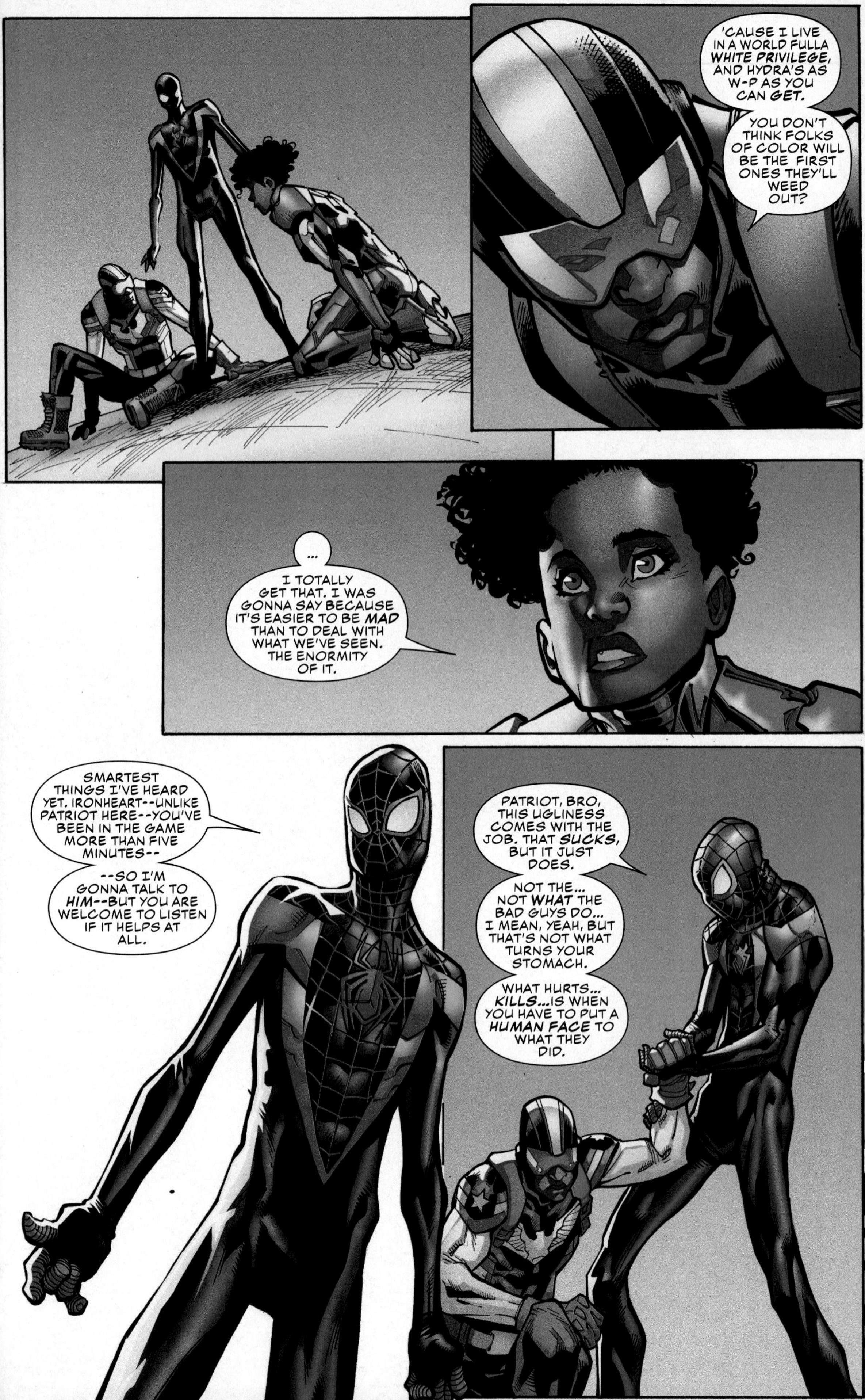
'CAUSE I LIVE IN A WORLD FULLA WHITE PRIVILEGE, AND HYDRA'S AS W-P AS YOU CAN GET.
YOU DON'T THINK FOLKS OF COLOR WILL BE THE FIRST ONES THEY'LL WEED OUT?
...
I TOTALLY GET THAT. I WAS GONNA SAY BECAUSE IT'S EASIER TO BE MAD THAN TO DEAL WITH WHAT WE'VE SEEN. THE ENORMITY OF IT.
SMARTEST THINGS I'VE HEARD YET. IRONHEART--UNLIKE PATRIOT HERE--YOU'VE BEEN IN THE GAME MORE THAN FIVE MINUTES--
--SO I'M GONNA TALK TO HIM--BUT YOU ARE WELCOME TO LISTEN IF IT HELPS AT ALL.
PATRIOT, BRO, THIS UGLINESS COMES WITH THE JOB. THAT SUCKS, BUT IT JUST DOES.
NOT THE... NOT WHAT THE BAD GUYS DO... I MEAN, YEAH, BUT THAT'S NOT WHAT TURNS YOUR STOMACH.
WHAT HURTS... KILLS...IS WHEN YOU HAVE TO PUT A HUMAN FACE TO WHAT THEY DID.

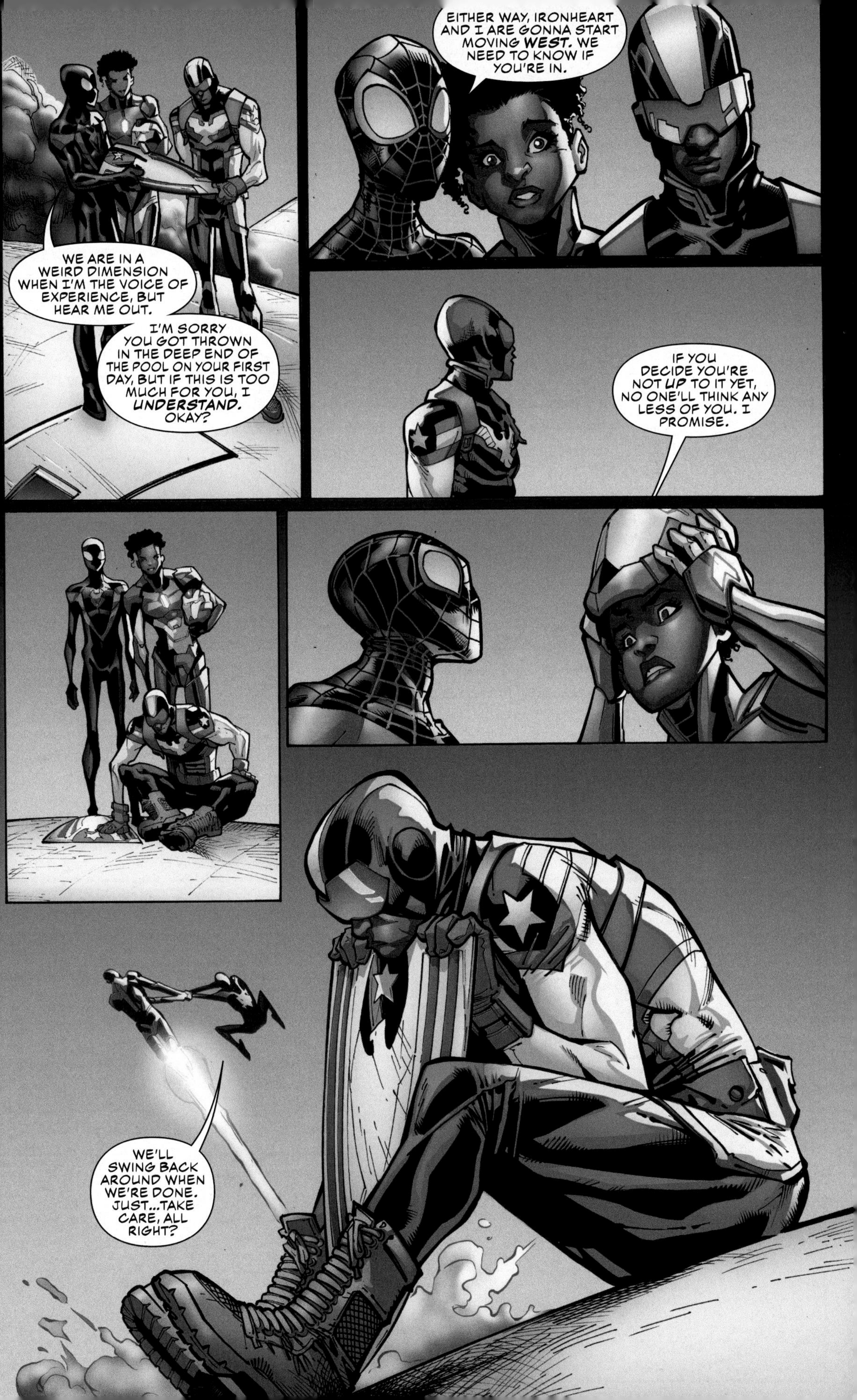
WE ARE IN A WEIRD DIMENSION WHEN I'M THE VOICE OF EXPERIENCE, BUT HEAR ME OUT.
I'M SORRY YOU GOT THROWN IN THE DEEP END OF THE POOL ON YOUR FIRST DAY, BUT IF THIS IS TOO MUCH FOR YOU, I *UNDERSTAND.* OKAY?
EITHER WAY, IRONHEART AND I ARE GONNA START MOVING *WEST.* WE NEED TO KNOW IF YOU'RE IN.
IF YOU DECIDE YOU'RE NOT *UP* TO IT YET, NO ONE'LL THINK ANY LESS OF YOU. I PROMISE.
WE'LL SWING BACK AROUND WHEN WE'RE DONE. JUST...TAKE CARE, ALL RIGHT?

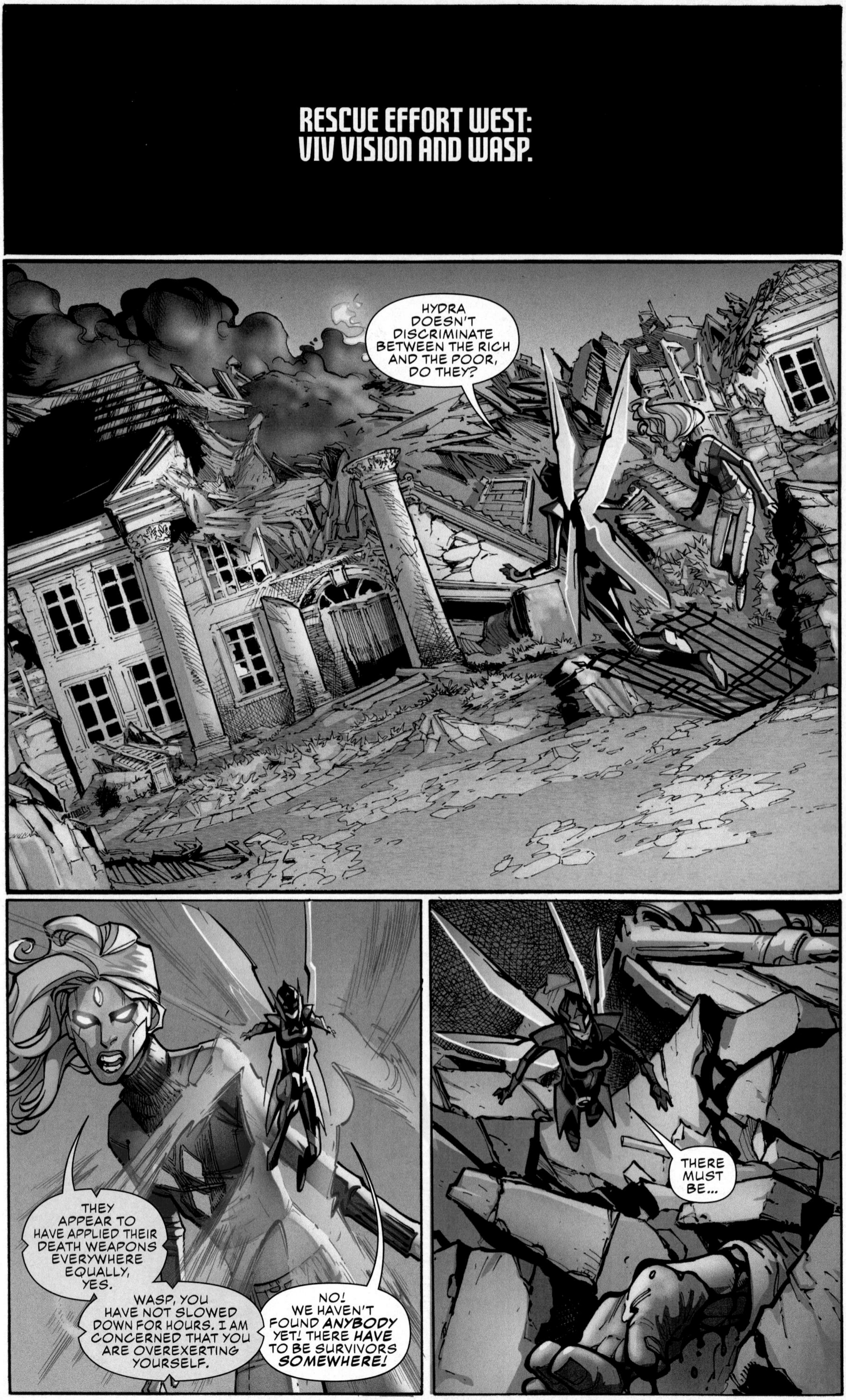

RESCUE EFFORT WEST:
VIV VISION AND WASP.
HYDRA DOESN'T DISCRIMINATE BETWEEN THE RICH AND THE POOR, DO THEY?
THEY APPEAR TO HAVE APPLIED THEIR DEATH WEAPONS EVERYWHERE EQUALLY, YES.
WASP, YOU HAVE NOT SLOWED DOWN FOR HOURS. I AM CONCERNED THAT YOU ARE OVEREXERTING YOURSELF.
NO! WE HAVEN'T FOUND ANYBODY YET! THERE HAVE TO BE SURVIVORS SOMEWHERE!
THERE MUST BE...

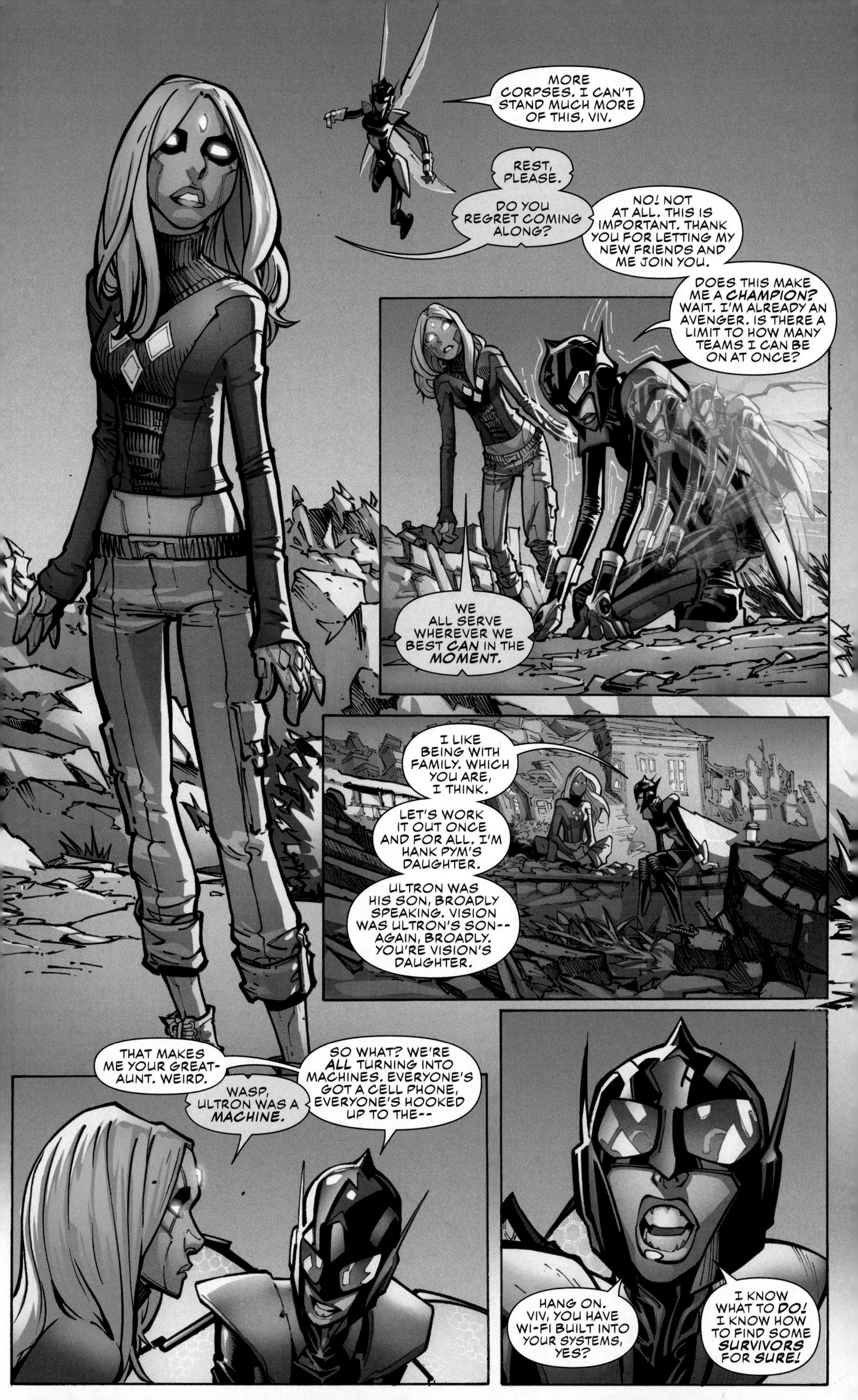

MORE CORPSES. I CAN'T STAND MUCH MORE OF THIS, VIV.
REST, PLEASE.
DO YOU REGRET COMING ALONG?
NO! NOT AT ALL. THIS IS IMPORTANT. THANK YOU FOR LETTING MY NEW FRIENDS AND ME JOIN YOU.
DOES THIS MAKE ME A CHAMPION? WAIT. I'M ALREADY AN AVENGER. IS THERE A LIMIT TO HOW MANY TEAMS I CAN BE ON AT ONCE?
WE ALL SERVE WHEREVER WE BEST CAN IN THE MOMENT.
I LIKE BEING WITH FAMILY. WHICH YOU ARE, I THINK.
LET'S WORK IT OUT ONCE AND FOR ALL. I'M HANK PYM'S DAUGHTER.
ULTRON WAS HIS SON, BROADLY SPEAKING. VISION WAS ULTRON'S SON-- AGAIN, BROADLY. YOU'RE VISION'S DAUGHTER.
THAT MAKES ME YOUR GREAT-AUNT. WEIRD.
WASP, ULTRON WAS A MACHINE.
SO WHAT? WE'RE ALL TURNING INTO MACHINES. EVERYONE'S GOT A CELL PHONE, EVERYONE'S HOOKED UP TO THE--
HANG ON. VIV, YOU HAVE WI-FI BUILT INTO YOUR SYSTEMS, YES?
I KNOW WHAT TO DO! I KNOW HOW TO FIND SOME SURVIVORS FOR SURE!

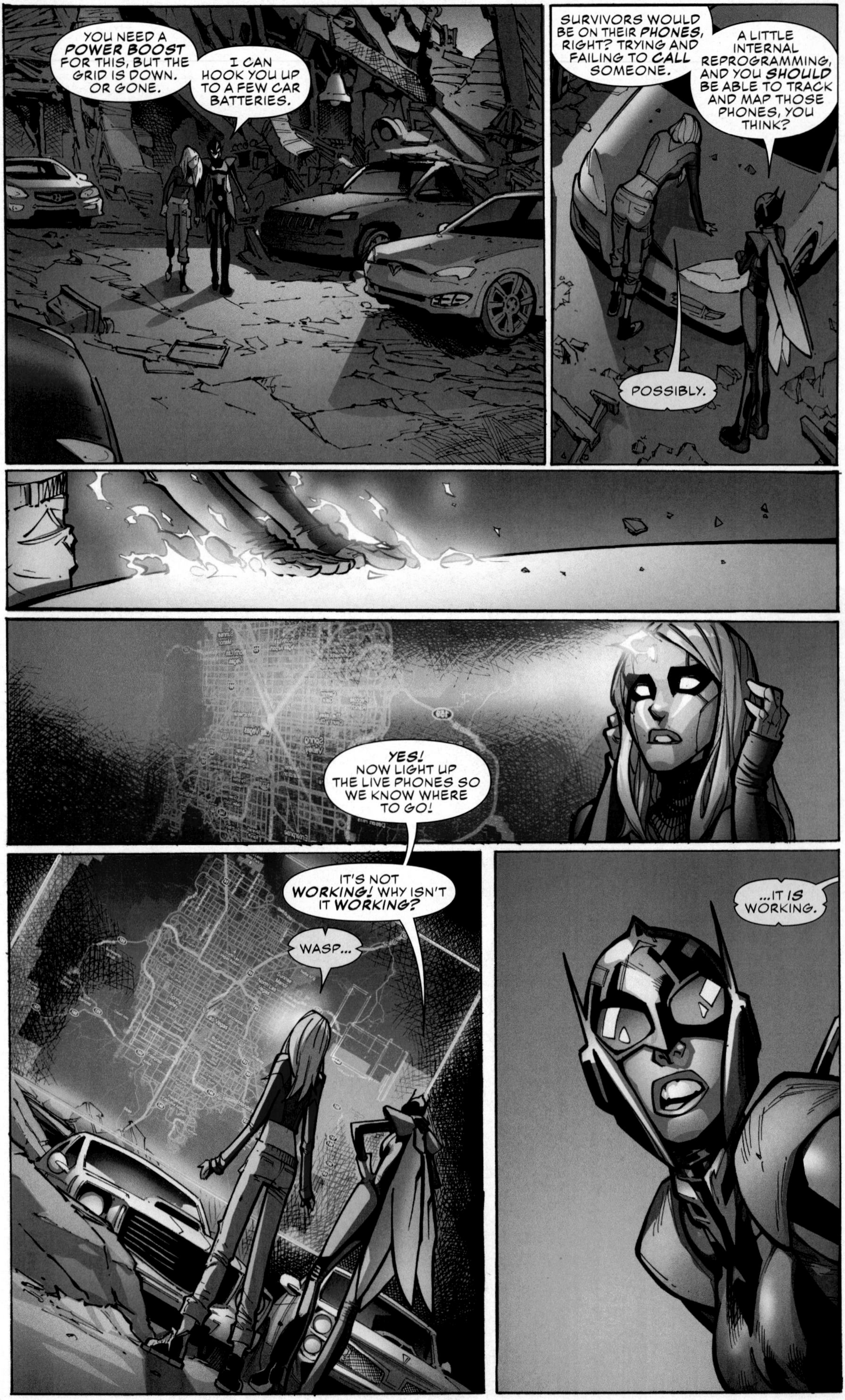

YOU NEED A POWER BOOST FOR THIS, BUT THE GRID IS DOWN. OR GONE.
I CAN HOOK YOU UP TO A FEW CAR BATTERIES.
SURVIVORS WOULD BE ON THEIR PHONES, RIGHT? TRYING AND FAILING TO CALL SOMEONE.
A LITTLE INTERNAL REPROGRAMMING, AND YOU SHOULD BE ABLE TO TRACK AND MAP THOSE PHONES, YOU THINK?
POSSIBLY.
YES! NOW LIGHT UP THE LIVE PHONES SO WE KNOW WHERE TO GO!
IT'S NOT WORKING! WHY ISN'T IT WORKING?
WASP...
...IT IS WORKING.

RESCUE EFFORT CONCLUSION: CHAMPIONS.

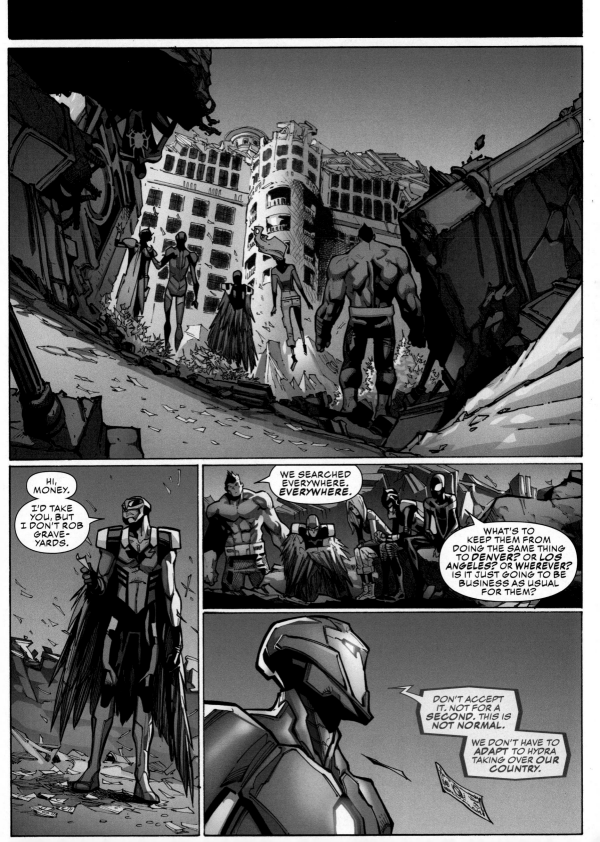

HI, MONEY.

I'D TAKE YOU, BUT I DON'T ROB GRAVEYARDS.

WE SEARCHED EVERYWHERE. EVERYWHERE.

WHAT'S TO KEEP THEM FROM DOING THE SAME THING TO *DENVER?* OR *LOS ANGELES?* OR *WHEREVER?* IS IT JUST GOING TO BE BUSINESS AS USUAL FOR THEM?

DON'T ACCEPT IT. NOT FOR A *SECOND.* THIS IS NOT NORMAL.

WE DON'T HAVE TO ADAPT TO HYDRA TAKING OVER OUR COUNTRY.

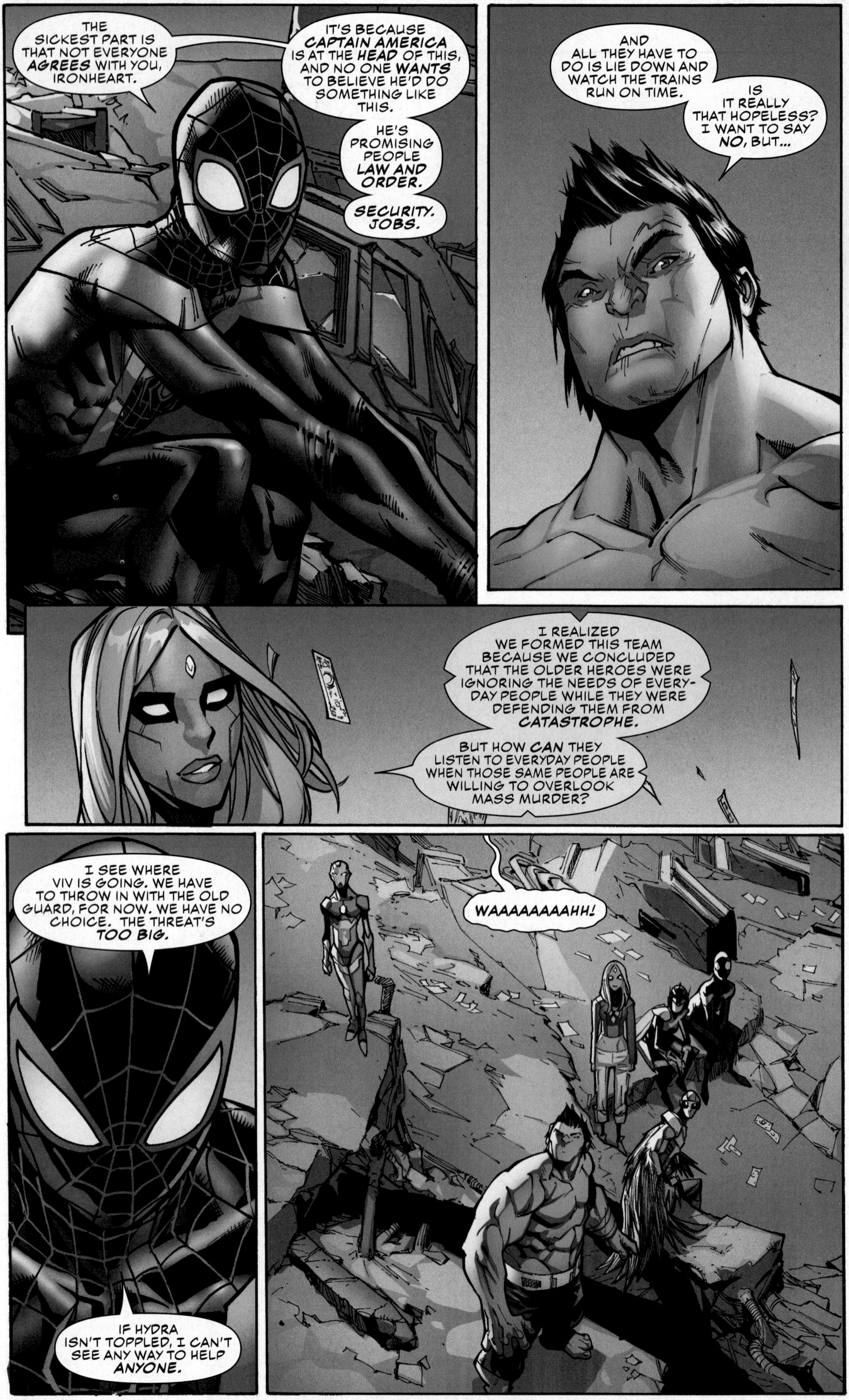
THE SICKEST PART IS THAT NOT EVERYONE AGREES WITH YOU, IRONHEART.
IT'S BECAUSE CAPTAIN AMERICA IS AT THE HEAD OF THIS, AND NO ONE WANTS TO BELIEVE HE'D DO SOMETHING LIKE THIS.
HE'S PROMISING PEOPLE LAW AND ORDER.
SECURITY. JOBS.
AND ALL THEY HAVE TO DO IS LIE DOWN AND WATCH THE TRAINS RUN ON TIME.
IS IT REALLY THAT HOPELESS? I WANT TO SAY NO, BUT...
I REALIZED WE FORMED THIS TEAM BECAUSE WE CONCLUDED THAT THE OLDER HEROES WERE IGNORING THE NEEDS OF EVERY-DAY PEOPLE WHILE THEY WERE DEFENDING THEM FROM CATASTROPHE.
BUT HOW CAN THEY LISTEN TO EVERYDAY PEOPLE WHEN THOSE SAME PEOPLE ARE WILLING TO OVERLOOK MASS MURDER?
I SEE WHERE VIV IS GOING. WE HAVE TO THROW IN WITH THE OLD GUARD, FOR NOW. WE HAVE NO CHOICE. THE THREAT'S TOO BIG.
IF HYDRA ISN'T TOPPLED, I CAN'T SEE ANY WAY TO HELP ANYONE.
WAAAAAAAAAHH!

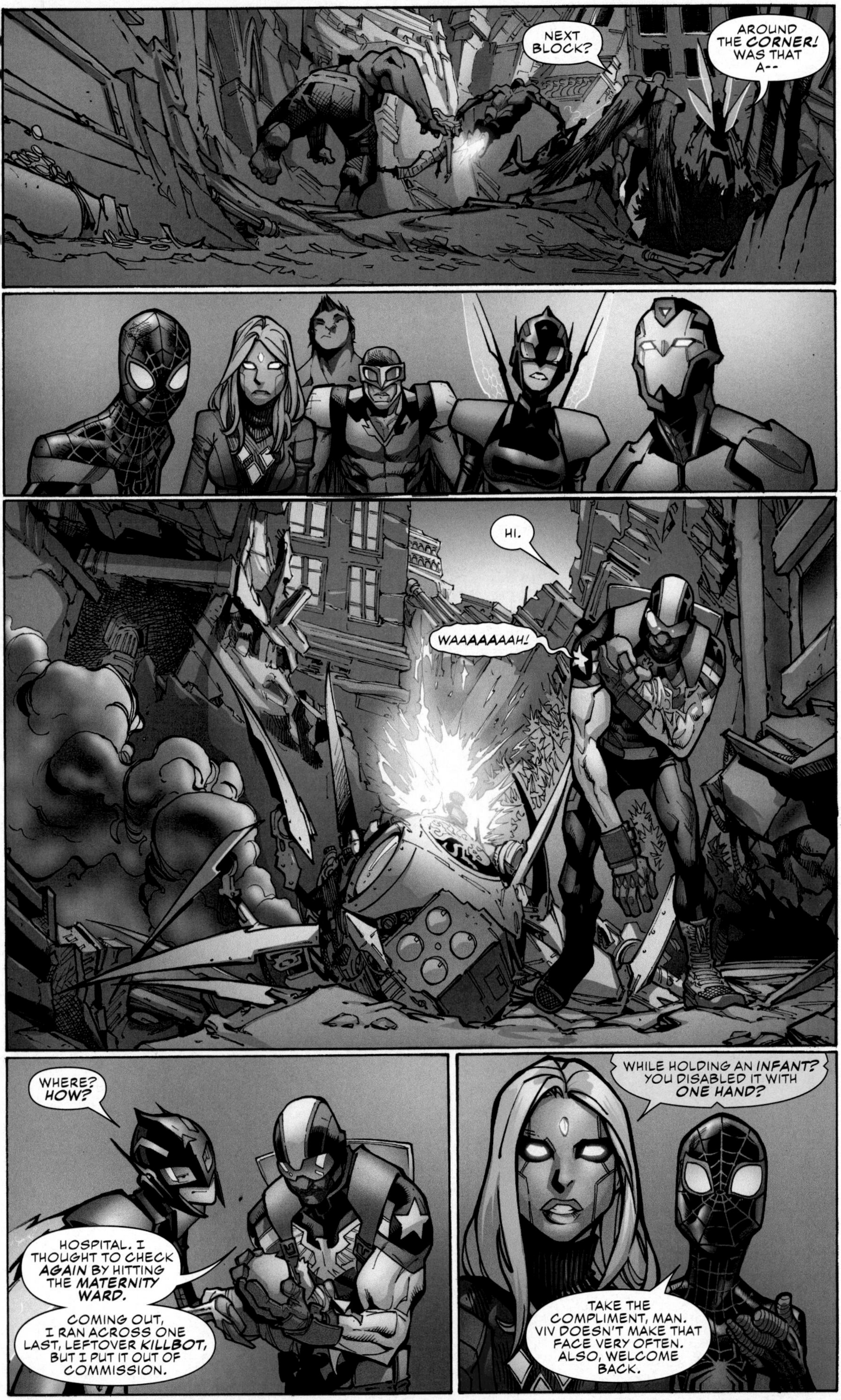
NEXT BLOCK?
AROUND THE CORNER! WAS THAT A--
HI.
WAAAAAAAH!
WHERE? HOW?
HOSPITAL. I THOUGHT TO CHECK AGAIN BY HITTING THE MATERNITY WARD.
COMING OUT, I RAN ACROSS ONE LAST, LEFTOVER KILLBOT, BUT I PUT IT OUT OF COMMISSION.
WHILE HOLDING AN INFANT? YOU DISABLED IT WITH ONE HAND?
TAKE THE COMPLIMENT, MAN. VIV DOESN'T MAKE THAT FACE VERY OFTEN. ALSO, WELCOME BACK.

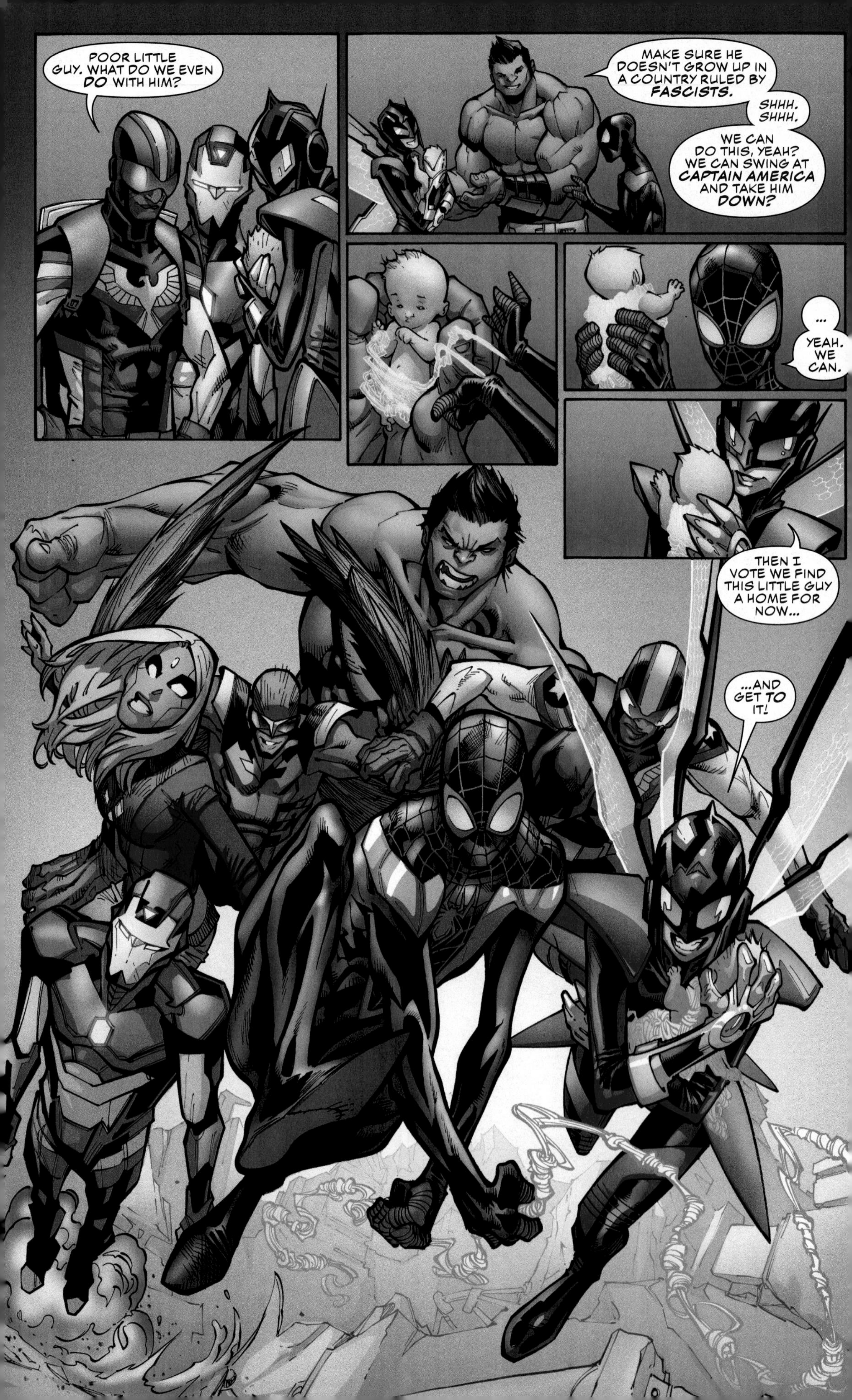
POOR LITTLE GUY. WHAT DO WE EVEN DO WITH HIM?
MAKE SURE HE DOESN'T GROW UP IN A COUNTRY RULED BY FASCISTS.
SHHH. SHHH.
WE CAN DO THIS, YEAH? WE CAN SWING AT CAPTAIN AMERICA AND TAKE HIM DOWN?
... YEAH. WE CAN.
THEN I VOTE WE FIND THIS LITTLE GUY A HOME FOR NOW...
...AND GET TO IT!

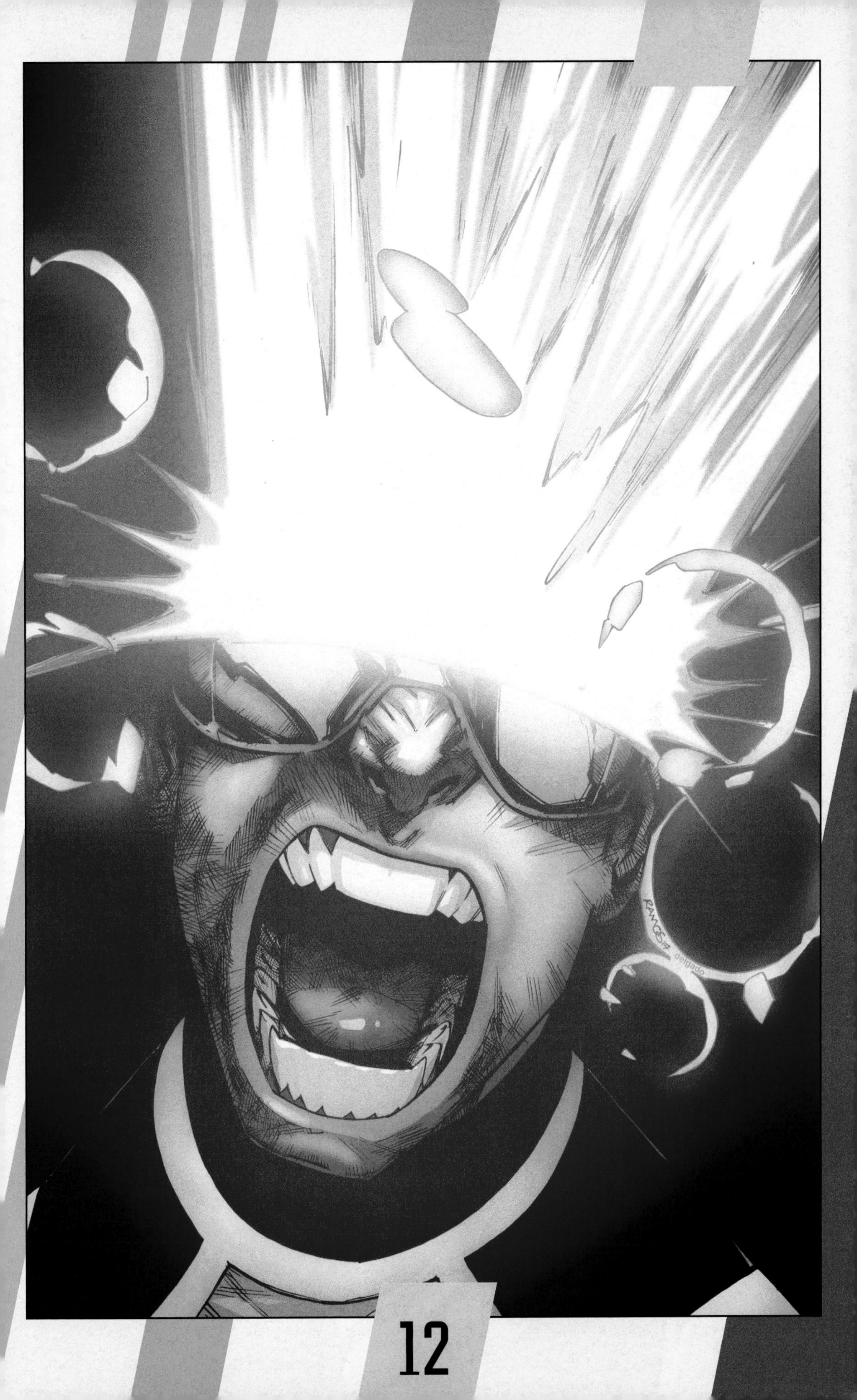
12

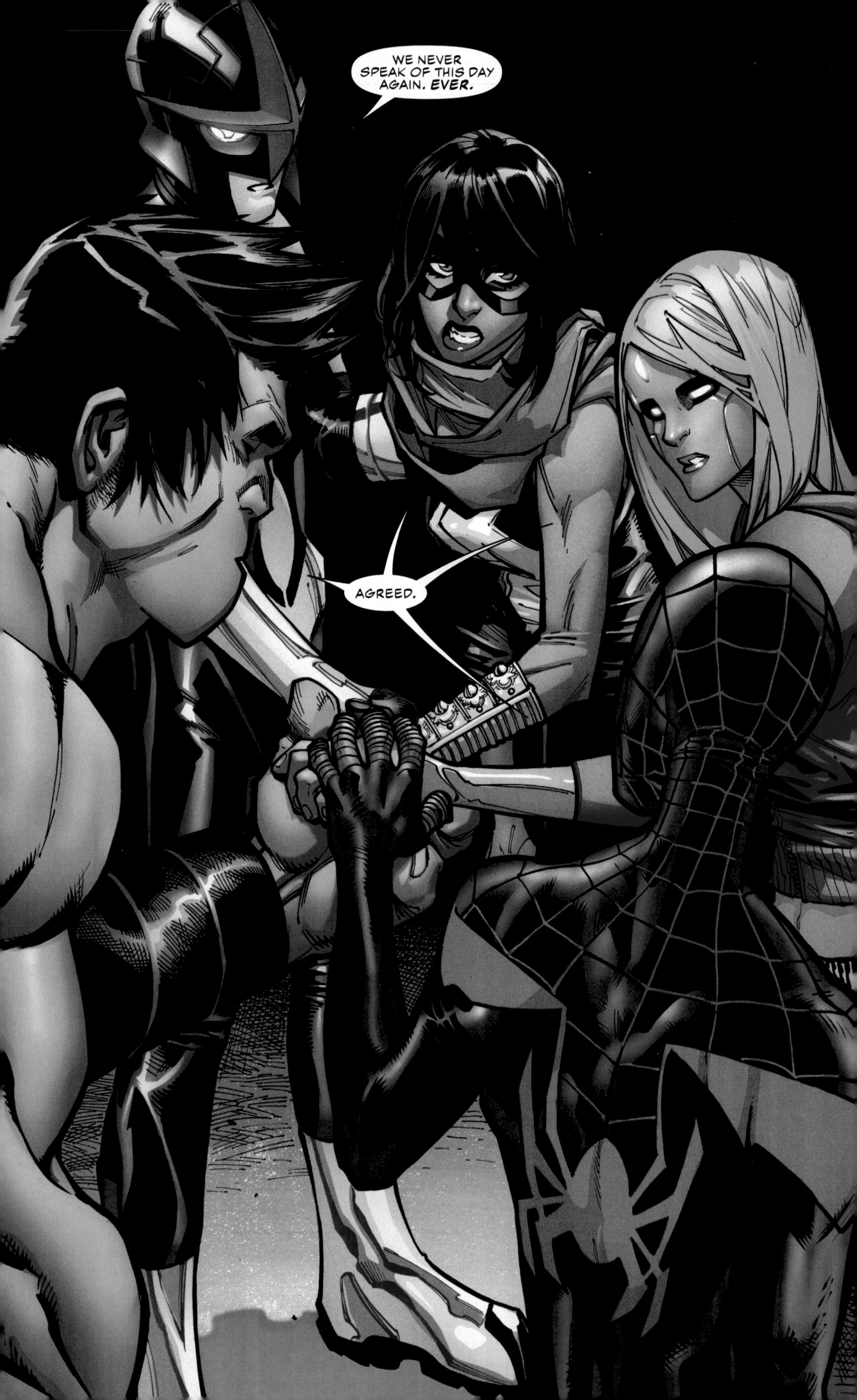
WE NEVER SPEAK OF THIS DAY AGAIN. EVER.
AGREED.

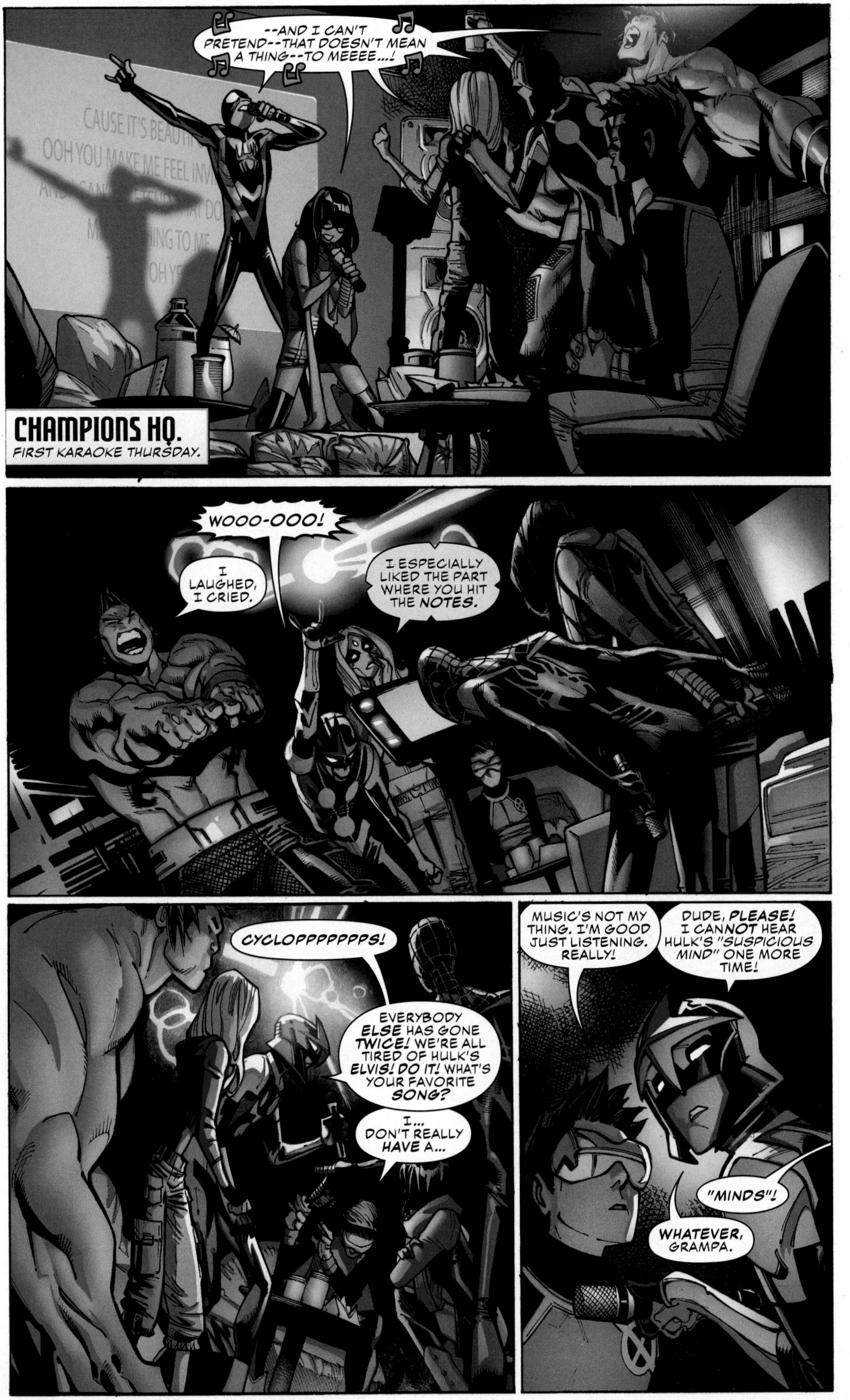
--AND I CAN'T PRETEND--THAT DOESN'T MEAN A THING--TO MEEEE...!
CAUSE IT'S BEAUTIF
OOH YOU MAKE ME FEEL INVI
CHAMPIONS HQ.
FIRST KARAOKE THURSDAY.
WOOO-OOO!
I LAUGHED, I CRIED.
I ESPECIALLY LIKED THE PART WHERE YOU HIT THE NOTES.
CYCLOPPPPPPPS!
EVERYBODY ELSE HAS GONE TWICE! WE'RE ALL TIRED OF HULK'S ELVIS! DO IT! WHAT'S YOUR FAVORITE SONG?
I... DON'T REALLY HAVE A...
MUSIC'S NOT MY THING. I'M GOOD JUST LISTENING. REALLY!
DUDE, PLEASE! I CANNOT HEAR HULK'S "SUSPICIOUS MIND" ONE MORE TIME!
"MINDS"!
WHATEVER, GRAMPA.

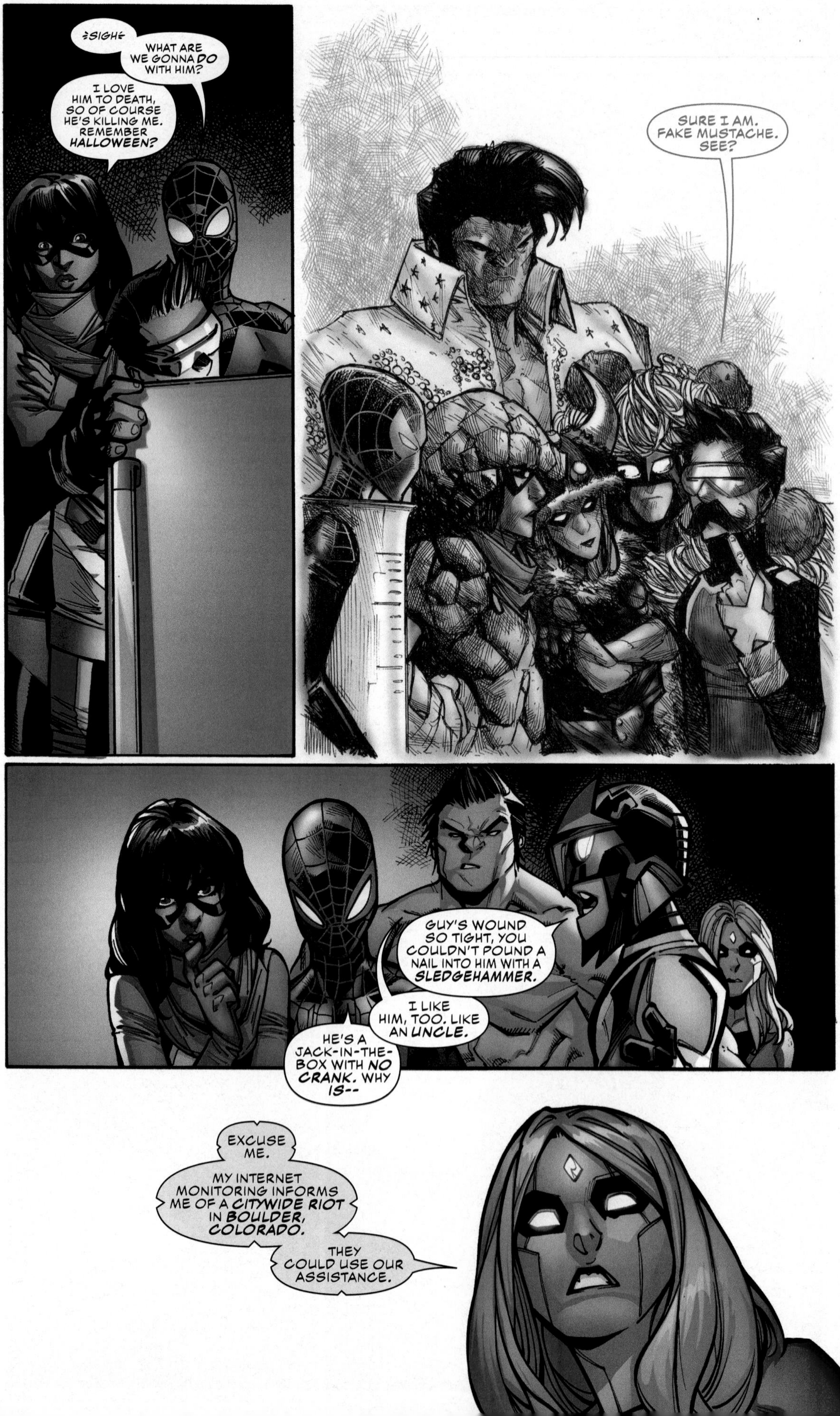

SIGH
WHAT ARE WE GONNA DO WITH HIM?
I LOVE HIM TO DEATH, SO OF COURSE HE'S KILLING ME. REMEMBER HALLOWEEN?
SURE I AM. FAKE MUSTACHE. SEE?
GUY'S WOUND SO TIGHT, YOU COULDN'T POUND A NAIL INTO HIM WITH A SLEDGEHAMMER.
I LIKE HIM, TOO. LIKE AN UNCLE.
HE'S A JACK-IN-THE-BOX WITH NO CRANK. WHY IS--
EXCUSE ME.
MY INTERNET MONITORING INFORMS ME OF A CITYWIDE RIOT IN BOULDER, COLORADO.
THEY COULD USE OUR ASSISTANCE.

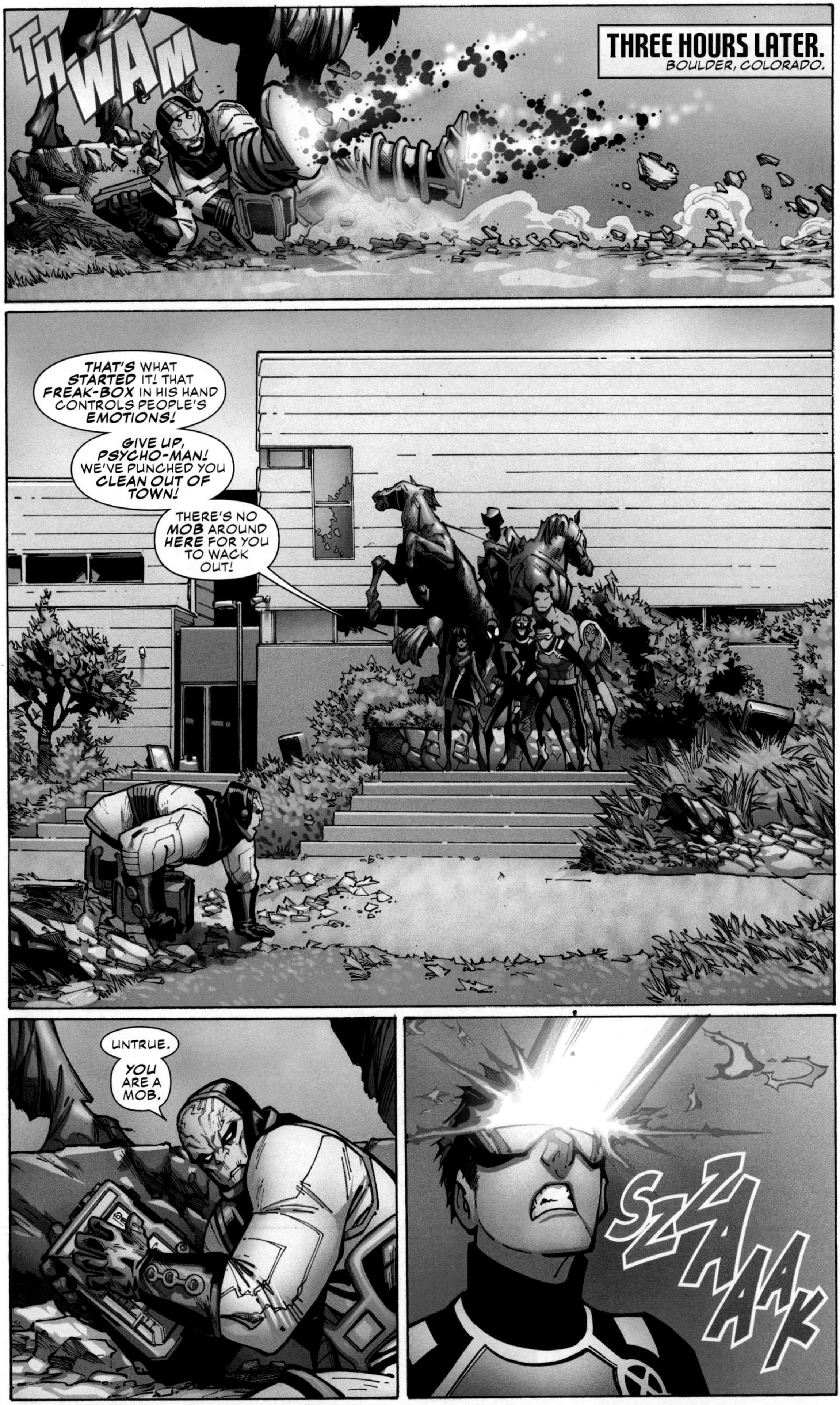
THWAM
THREE HOURS LATER.
BOULDER, COLORADO.
THAT'S WHAT STARTED IT! THAT FREAK-BOX IN HIS HAND CONTROLS PEOPLE'S EMOTIONS!
GIVE UP, PSYCHO-MAN! WE'VE PUNCHED YOU CLEAN OUT OF TOWN!
THERE'S NO MOB AROUND HERE FOR YOU TO WACK OUT!
UNTRUE. YOU ARE A MOB.
SZZAAK

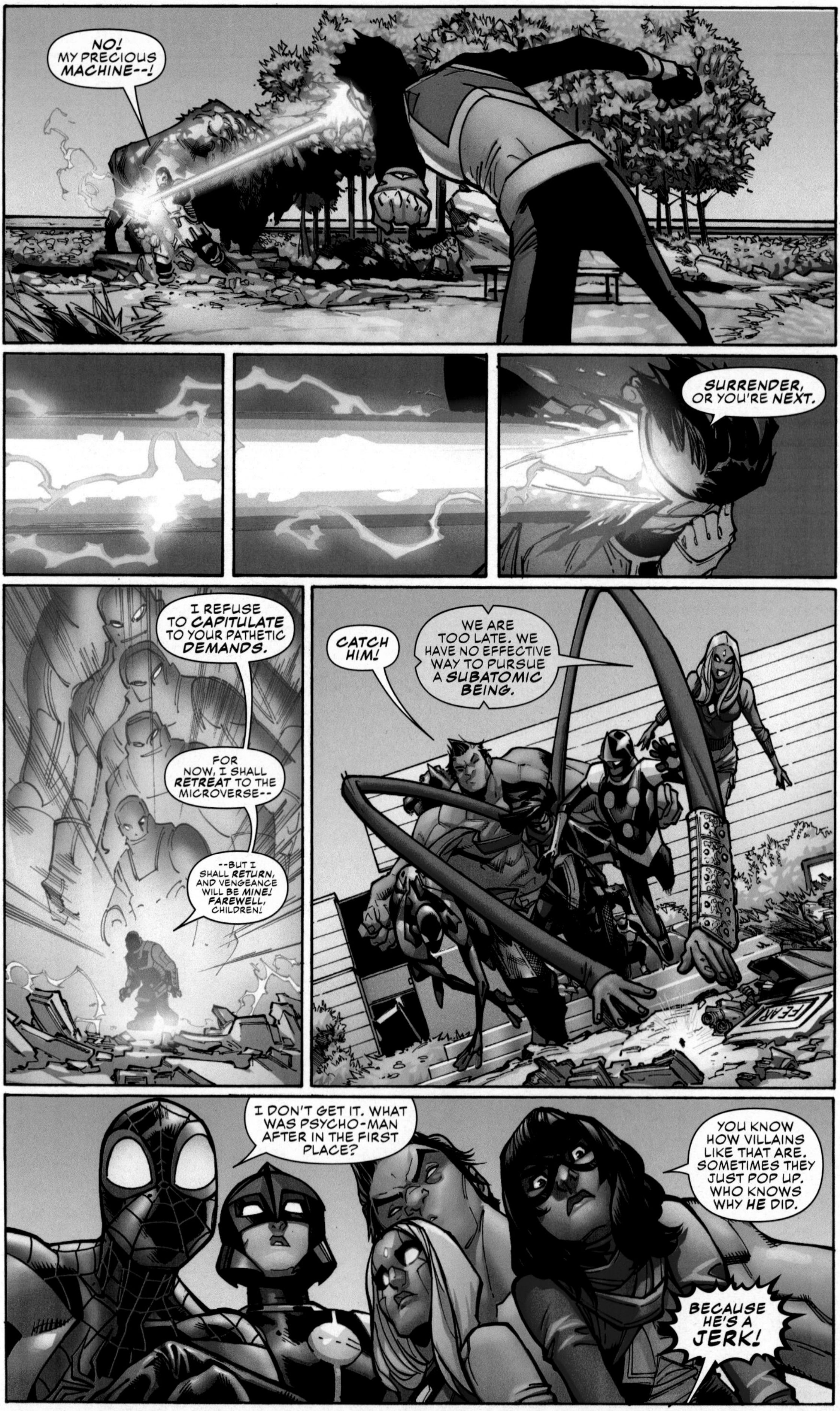
NO! MY PRECIOUS MACHINE--!
SURRENDER, OR YOU'RE NEXT.
I REFUSE TO CAPITULATE TO YOUR PATHETIC DEMANDS.
FOR NOW, I SHALL RETREAT TO THE MICROVERSE--
--BUT I SHALL RETURN, AND VENGEANCE WILL BE MINE! FAREWELL, CHILDREN!
CATCH HIM!
WE ARE TOO LATE. WE HAVE NO EFFECTIVE WAY TO PURSUE A SUBATOMIC BEING.
FEAR
I DON'T GET IT. WHAT WAS PSYCHO-MAN AFTER IN THE FIRST PLACE?
YOU KNOW HOW VILLAINS LIKE THAT ARE. SOMETIMES THEY JUST POP UP. WHO KNOWS WHY HE DID.
BECAUSE HE'S A JERK!

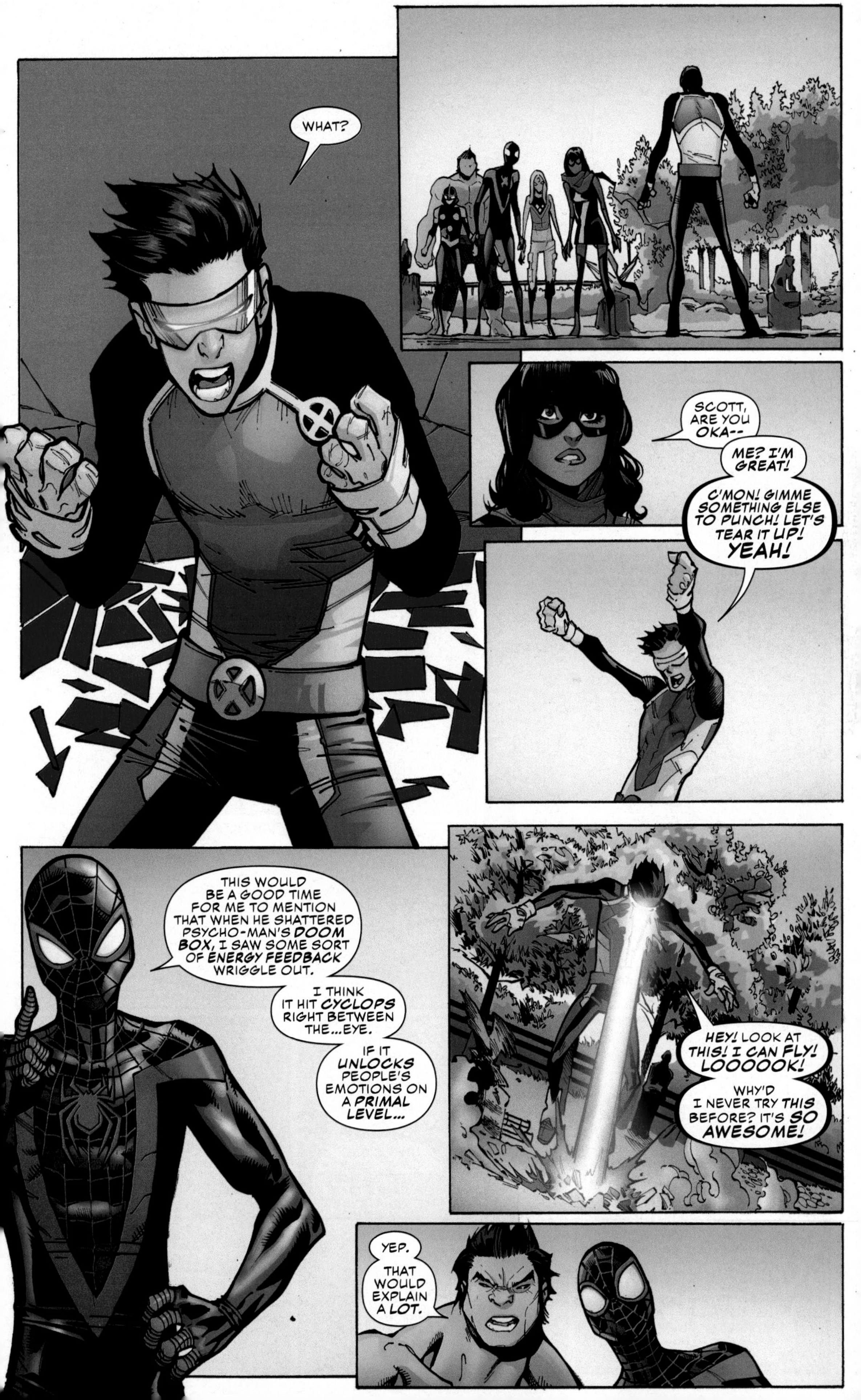
WHAT?
SCOTT, ARE YOU OKA--
ME? I'M GREAT!
C'MON! GIMME SOMETHING ELSE TO PUNCH! LET'S TEAR IT UP! YEAH!
THIS WOULD BE A GOOD TIME FOR ME TO MENTION THAT WHEN HE SHATTERED PSYCHO-MAN'S DOOM BOX, I SAW SOME SORT OF ENERGY FEEDBACK WRIGGLE OUT.
I THINK IT HIT CYCLOPS RIGHT BETWEEN THE...EYE.
IF IT UNLOCKS PEOPLE'S EMOTIONS ON A PRIMAL LEVEL...
HEY! LOOK AT THIS! I CAN FLY! LOOOOOK!
WHY'D I NEVER TRY THIS BEFORE? IT'S SO AWESOME!
YEP.
THAT WOULD EXPLAIN A LOT.

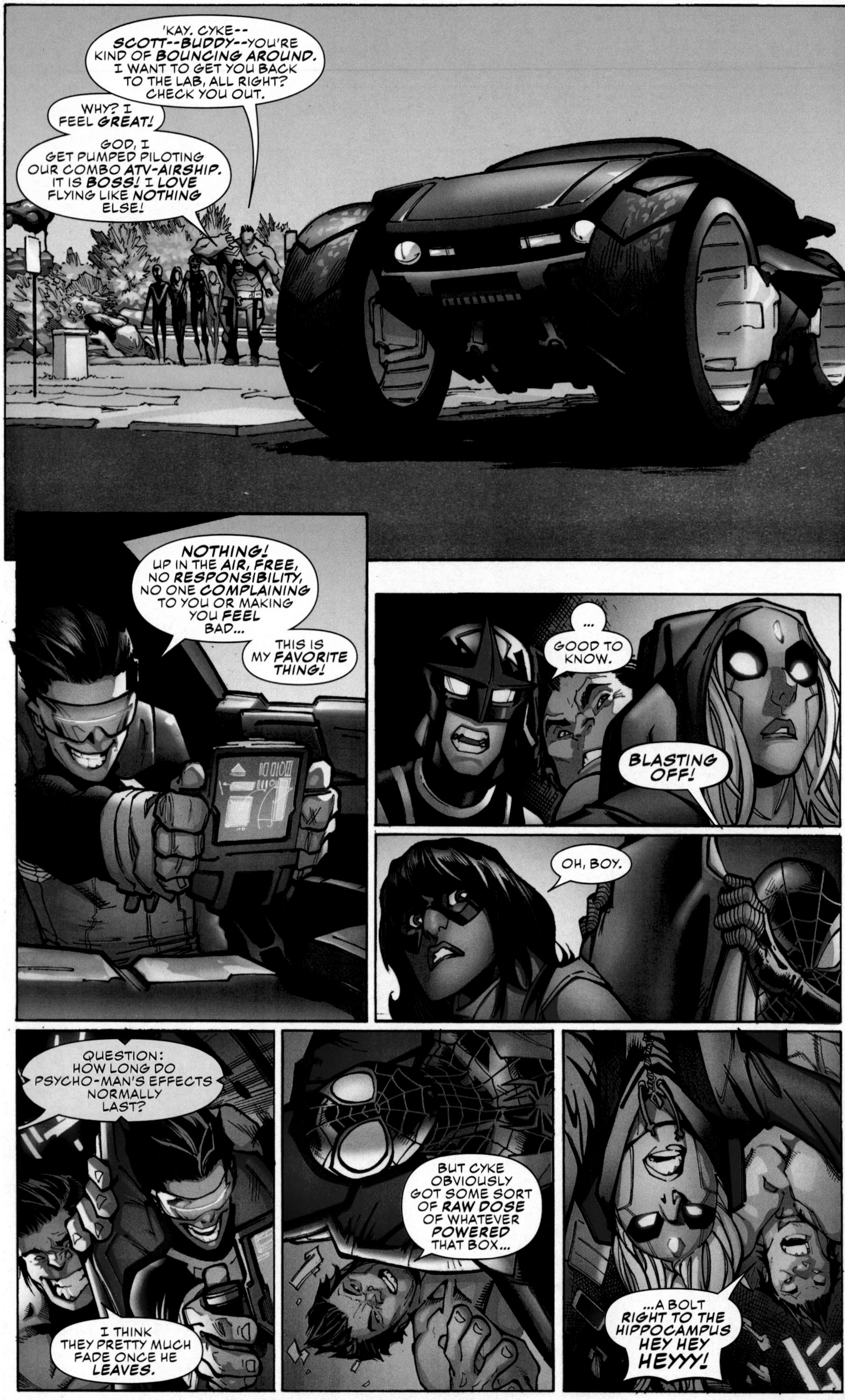
'KAY. CYKE-- SCOTT--BUDDY--YOU'RE KIND OF BOUNCING AROUND. I WANT TO GET YOU BACK TO THE LAB, ALL RIGHT? CHECK YOU OUT.
WHY? I FEEL GREAT!
GOD, I GET PUMPED PILOTING OUR COMBO ATV-AIRSHIP. IT IS BOSS! I LOVE FLYING LIKE NOTHING ELSE!
NOTHING! UP IN THE AIR, FREE, NO RESPONSIBILITY, NO ONE COMPLAINING TO YOU OR MAKING YOU FEEL BAD...
THIS IS MY FAVORITE THING!
... GOOD TO KNOW.
BLASTING OFF!
OH, BOY.
QUESTION: HOW LONG DO PSYCHO-MAN'S EFFECTS NORMALLY LAST?
I THINK THEY PRETTY MUCH FADE ONCE HE LEAVES.
BUT CYKE OBVIOUSLY GOT SOME SORT OF RAW DOSE OF WHATEVER POWERED THAT BOX...
...A BOLT RIGHT TO THE HIPPOCAMPUS
HEY HEY HEYYY!

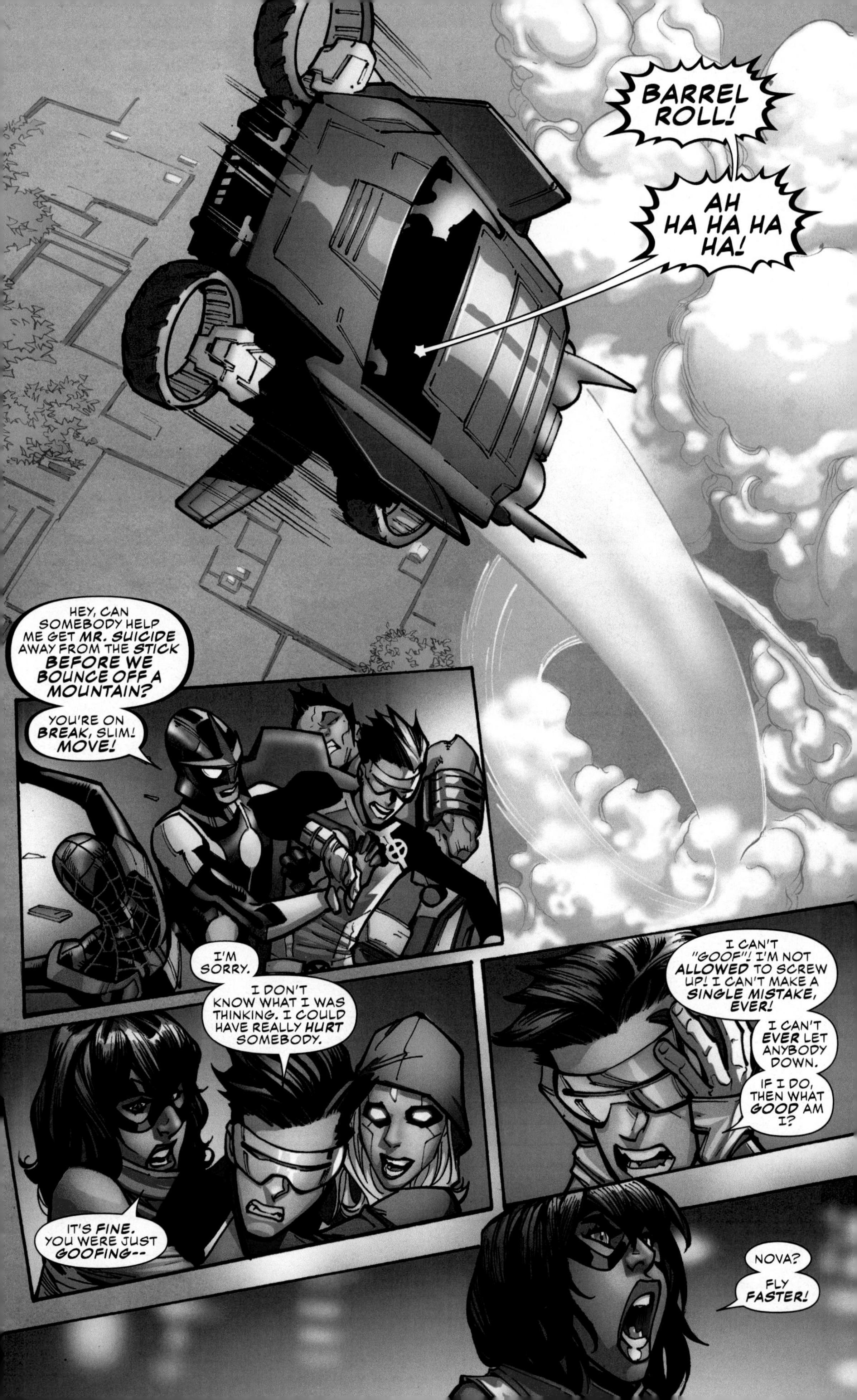
BARREL ROLL!
AH HA HA HA HA!
HEY, CAN SOMEBODY HELP ME GET MR. SUICIDE AWAY FROM THE STICK BEFORE WE BOUNCE OFF A MOUNTAIN?
YOU'RE ON BREAK, SLIM! MOVE!
I'M SORRY.
I DON'T KNOW WHAT I WAS THINKING. I COULD HAVE REALLY HURT SOMEBODY.
IT'S FINE. YOU WERE JUST GOOFING--
I CAN'T "GOOF"! I'M NOT ALLOWED TO SCREW UP! I CAN'T MAKE A SINGLE MISTAKE, EVER!
I CAN'T EVER LET ANYBODY DOWN.
IF I DO, THEN WHAT GOOD AM I?
NOVA?
FLY FASTER!

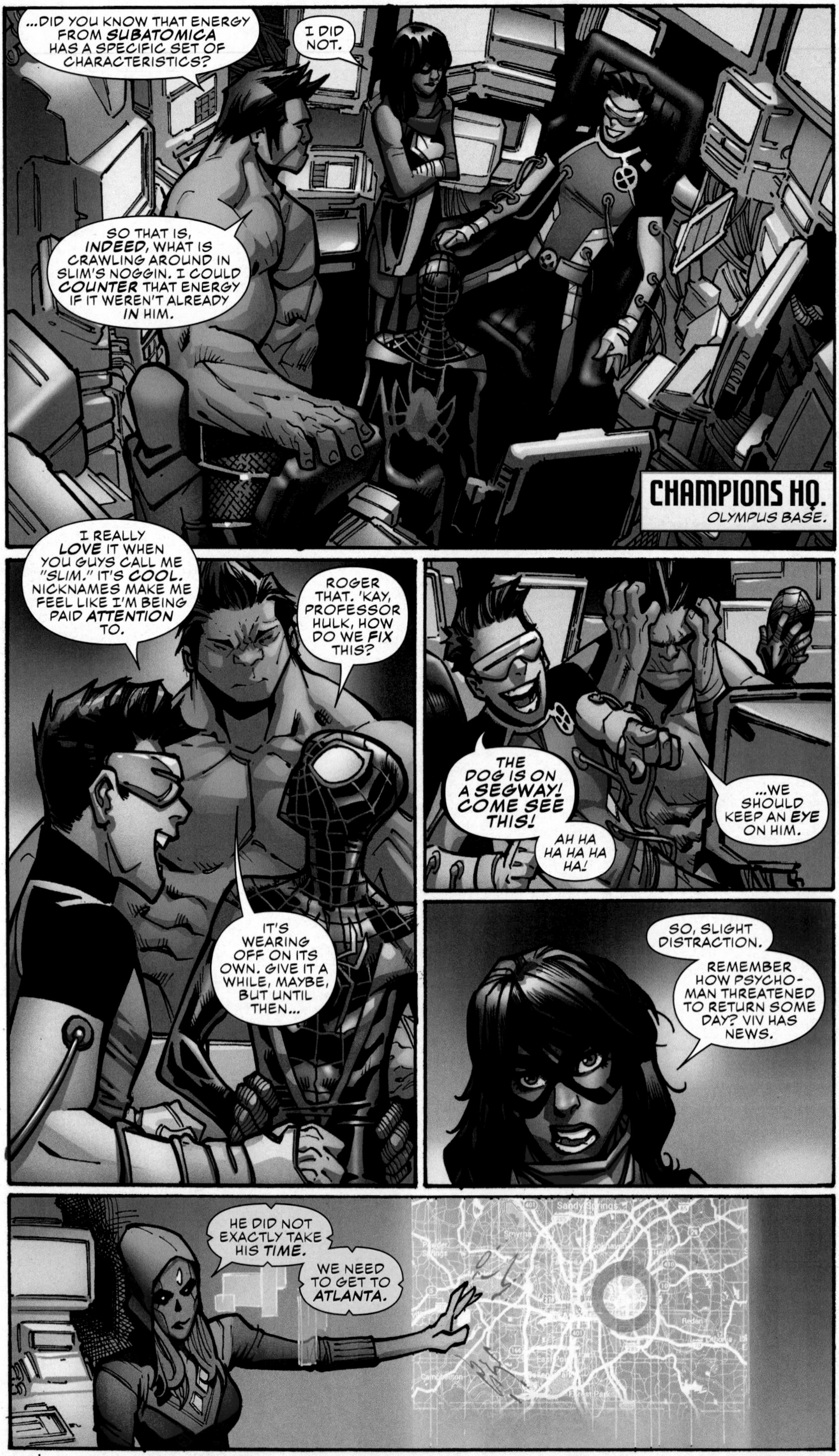
...DID YOU KNOW THAT ENERGY FROM SUBATOMICA HAS A SPECIFIC SET OF CHARACTERISTICS?
I DID NOT.
SO THAT IS, INDEED, WHAT IS CRAWLING AROUND IN SLIM'S NOGGIN. I COULD COUNTER THAT ENERGY IF IT WEREN'T ALREADY IN HIM.
CHAMPIONS HQ.
OLYMPUS BASE.
I REALLY LOVE IT WHEN YOU GUYS CALL ME "SLIM." IT'S COOL. NICKNAMES MAKE ME FEEL LIKE I'M BEING PAID ATTENTION TO.
ROGER THAT. 'KAY, PROFESSOR HULK, HOW DO WE FIX THIS?
IT'S WEARING OFF ON ITS OWN. GIVE IT A WHILE, MAYBE, BUT UNTIL THEN...
THE DOG IS ON A SEGWAY! COME SEE THIS!
AH HA HA HA HA HA!
...WE SHOULD KEEP AN EYE ON HIM.
SO, SLIGHT DISTRACTION.
REMEMBER HOW PSYCHO-MAN THREATENED TO RETURN SOME DAY? VIV HAS NEWS.
HE DID NOT EXACTLY TAKE HIS TIME.
WE NEED TO GET TO ATLANTA.

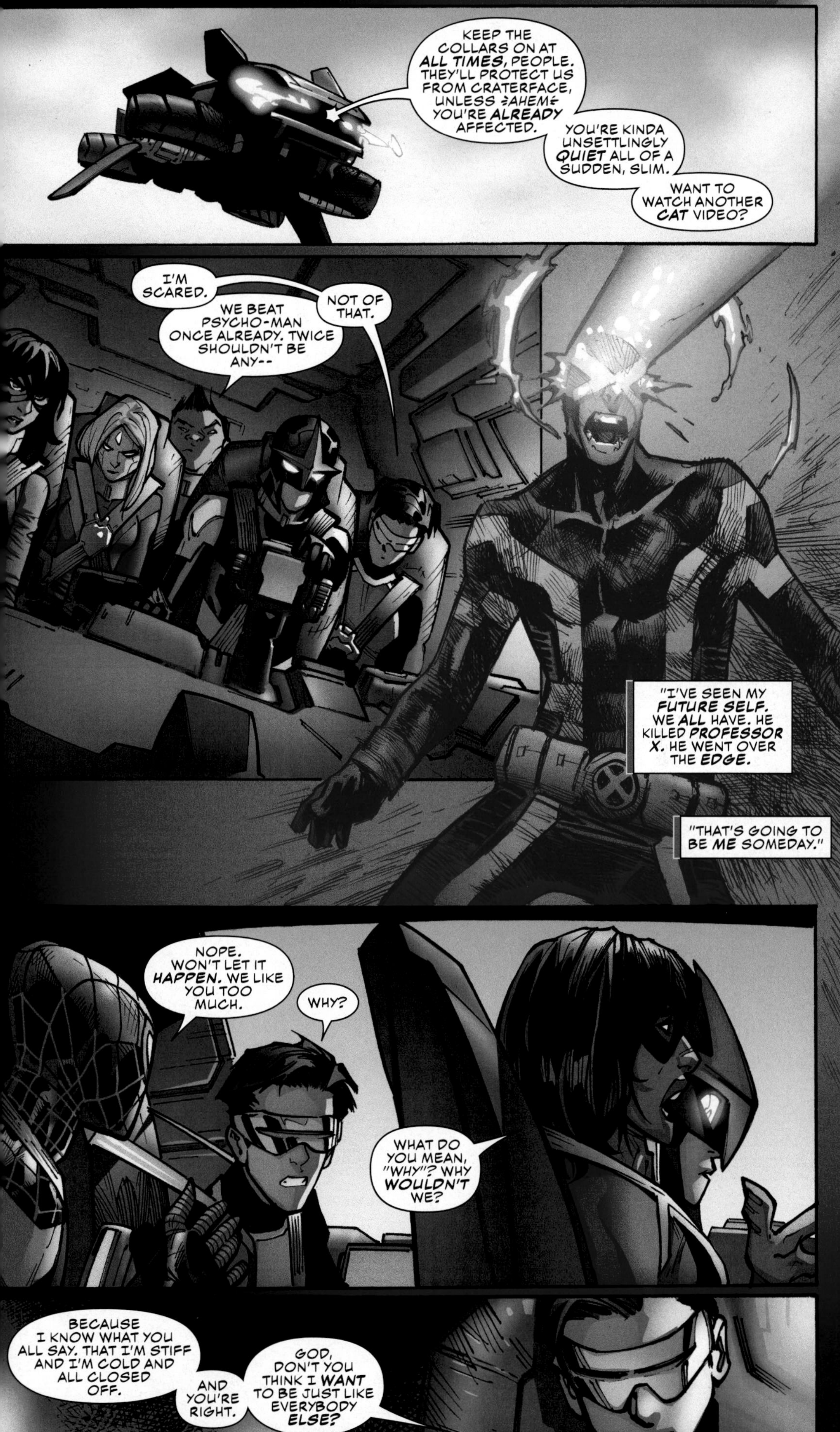

KEEP THE COLLARS ON AT ALL TIMES, PEOPLE. THEY'LL PROTECT US FROM CRATERFACE, UNLESS ≥AHEM≤ YOU'RE ALREADY AFFECTED.
YOU'RE KINDA UNSETTLINGLY QUIET ALL OF A SUDDEN, SLIM.
WANT TO WATCH ANOTHER CAT VIDEO?
I'M SCARED.
WE BEAT PSYCHO-MAN ONCE ALREADY. TWICE SHOULDN'T BE ANY--
NOT OF THAT.
"I'VE SEEN MY FUTURE SELF. WE ALL HAVE. HE KILLED PROFESSOR X. HE WENT OVER THE EDGE.
"THAT'S GOING TO BE ME SOMEDAY."
NOPE. WON'T LET IT HAPPEN. WE LIKE YOU TOO MUCH.
WHY?
WHAT DO YOU MEAN, "WHY"? WHY WOULDN'T WE?
BECAUSE I KNOW WHAT YOU ALL SAY. THAT I'M STIFF AND I'M COLD AND ALL CLOSED OFF.
AND YOU'RE RIGHT.
GOD, DON'T YOU THINK I WANT TO BE JUST LIKE EVERYBODY ELSE?

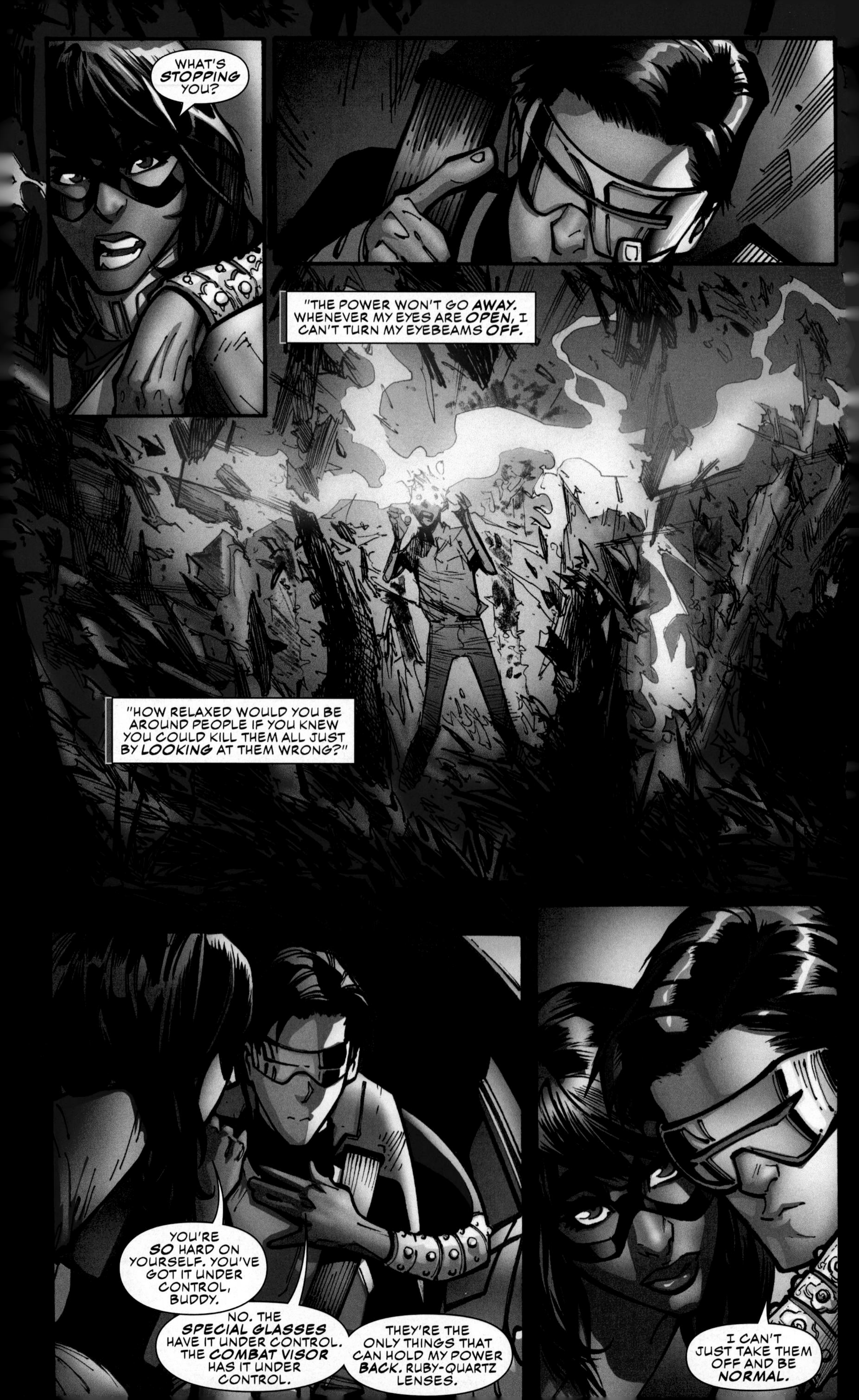
WHAT'S STOPPING YOU?
"THE POWER WON'T GO AWAY. WHENEVER MY EYES ARE OPEN, I CAN'T TURN MY EYEBEAMS OFF.
"HOW RELAXED WOULD YOU BE AROUND PEOPLE IF YOU KNEW YOU COULD KILL THEM ALL JUST BY LOOKING AT THEM WRONG?"
YOU'RE SO HARD ON YOURSELF. YOU'VE GOT IT UNDER CONTROL, BUDDY.
NO. THE SPECIAL GLASSES HAVE IT UNDER CONTROL. THE COMBAT VISOR HAS IT UNDER CONTROL.
THEY'RE THE ONLY THINGS THAT CAN HOLD MY POWER BACK. RUBY-QUARTZ LENSES.
I CAN'T JUST TAKE THEM OFF AND BE NORMAL.

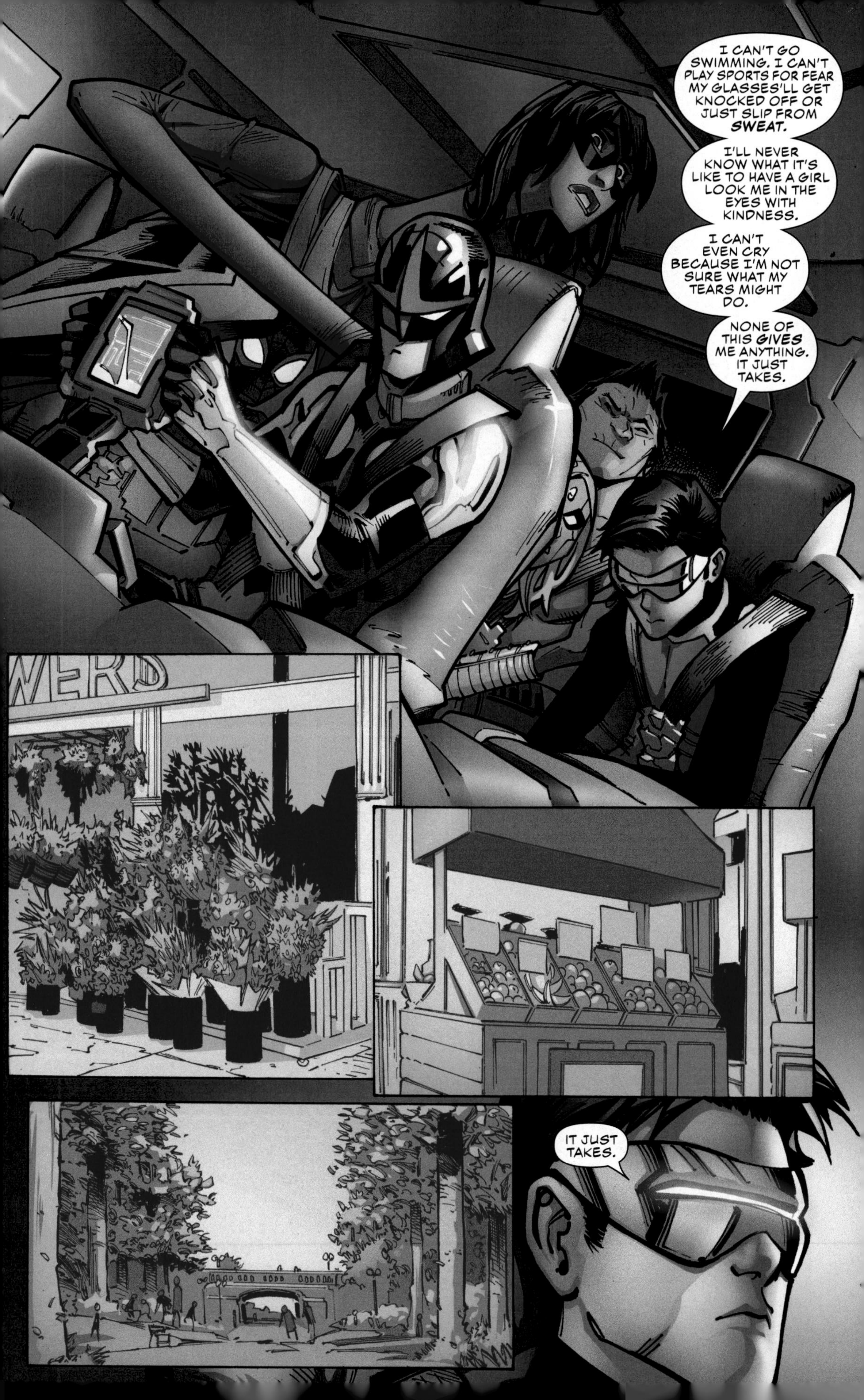
I CAN'T GO SWIMMING. I CAN'T PLAY SPORTS FOR FEAR MY GLASSES'LL GET KNOCKED OFF OR JUST SLIP FROM **SWEAT.**
I'LL NEVER KNOW WHAT IT'S LIKE TO HAVE A GIRL LOOK ME IN THE EYES WITH KINDNESS.
I CAN'T EVEN CRY BECAUSE I'M NOT SURE WHAT MY TEARS MIGHT DO.
NONE OF THIS **GIVES** ME ANYTHING. IT JUST TAKES.
IT JUST TAKES.

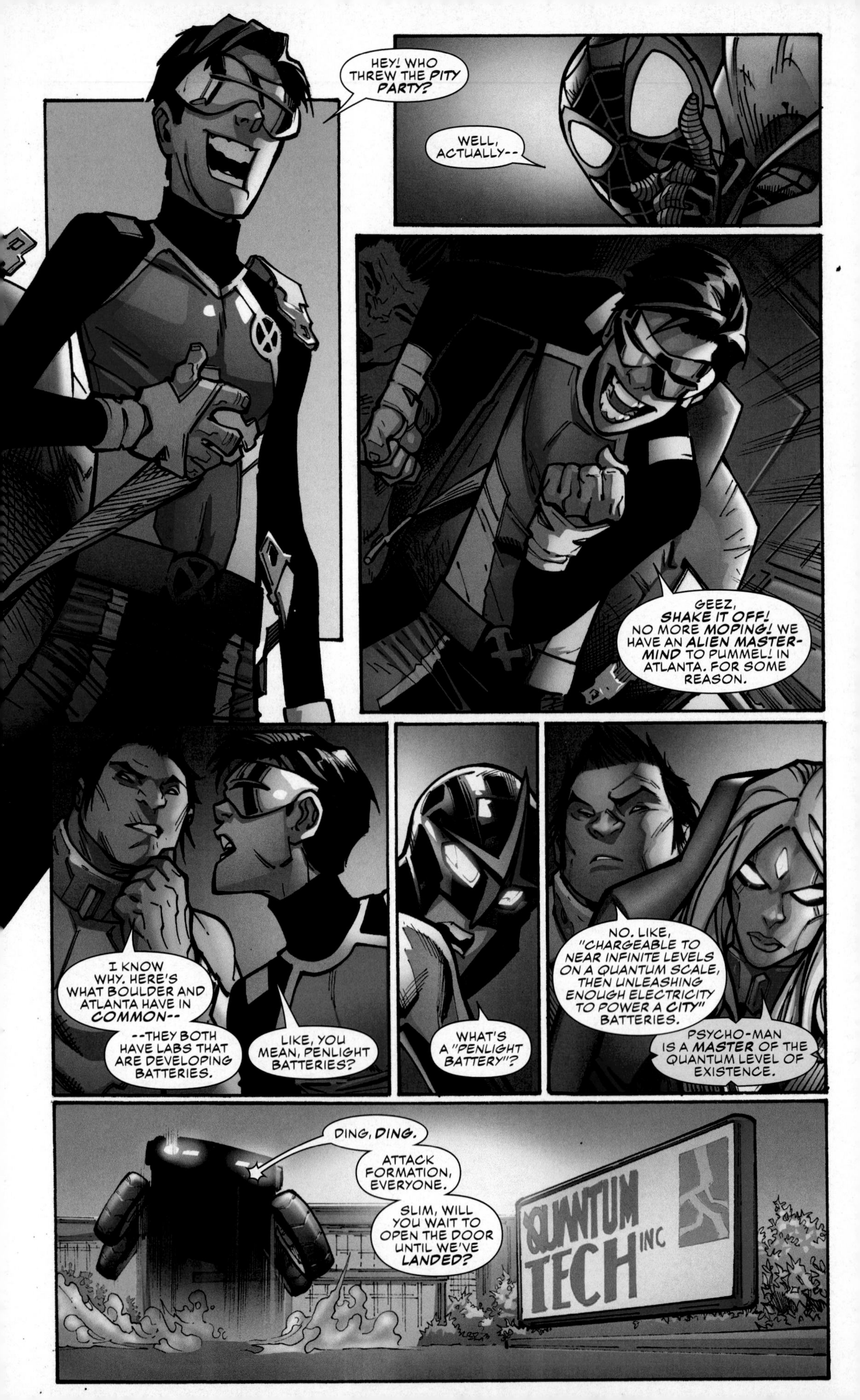
HEY! WHO THREW THE PITY PARTY?
WELL, ACTUALLY--
GEEZ, SHAKE IT OFF! NO MORE MOPING! WE HAVE AN ALIEN MASTER-MIND TO PUMMEL! IN ATLANTA. FOR SOME REASON.
I KNOW WHY. HERE'S WHAT BOULDER AND ATLANTA HAVE IN COMMON--
--THEY BOTH HAVE LABS THAT ARE DEVELOPING BATTERIES.
LIKE, YOU MEAN, PENLIGHT BATTERIES?
WHAT'S A "PENLIGHT BATTERY"?
NO. LIKE, "CHARGEABLE TO NEAR INFINITE LEVELS ON A QUANTUM SCALE, THEN UNLEASHING ENOUGH ELECTRICITY TO POWER A CITY" BATTERIES.
PSYCHO-MAN IS A MASTER OF THE QUANTUM LEVEL OF EXISTENCE.
DING, DING.
ATTACK FORMATION, EVERYONE.
SLIM, WILL YOU WAIT TO OPEN THE DOOR UNTIL WE'VE LANDED?
QUANTUM TECH INC

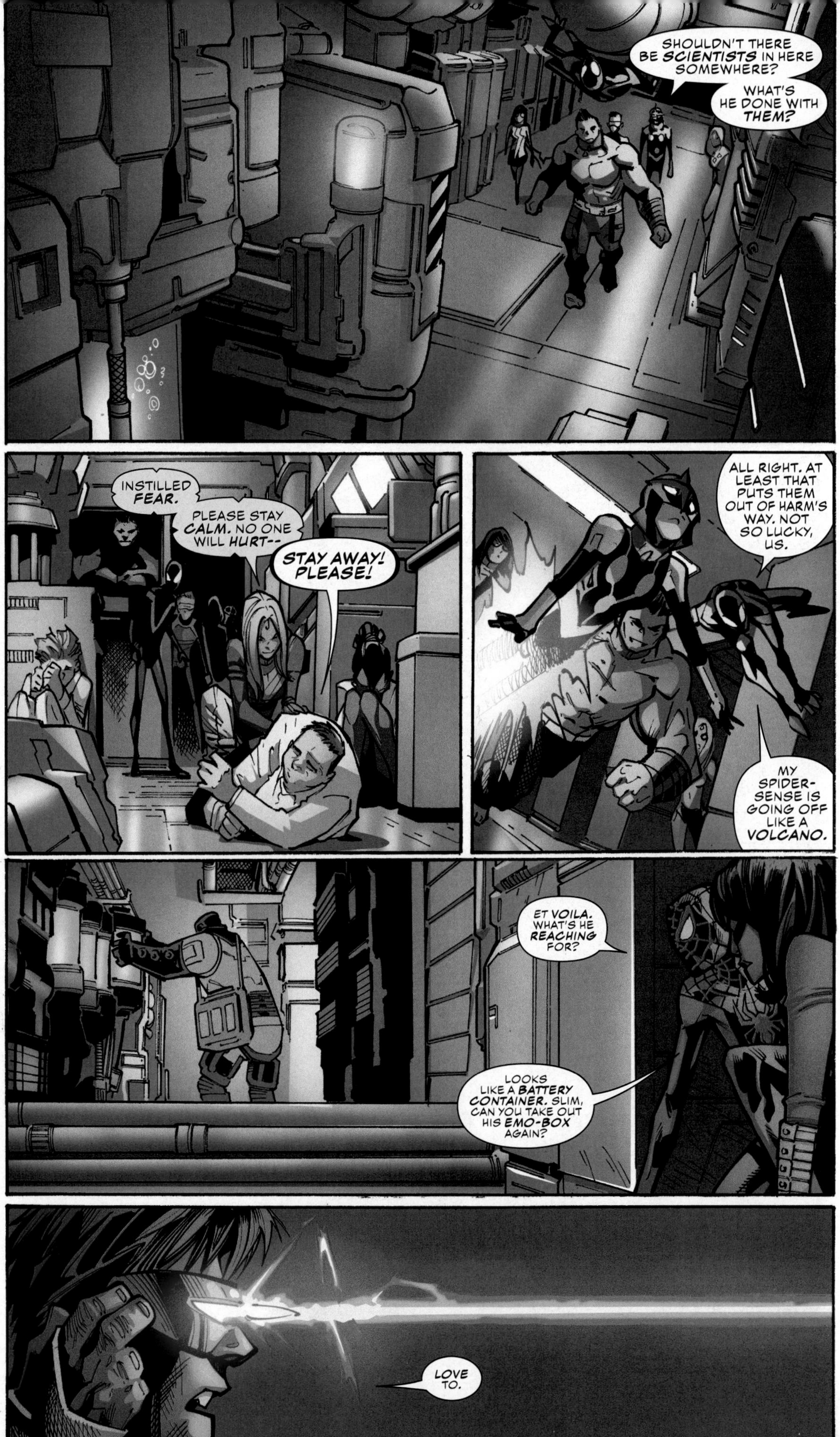
SHOULDN'T THERE BE SCIENTISTS IN HERE SOMEWHERE?
WHAT'S HE DONE WITH THEM?
INSTILLED FEAR.
PLEASE STAY CALM. NO ONE WILL HURT--
STAY AWAY! PLEASE!
ALL RIGHT. AT LEAST THAT PUTS THEM OUT OF HARM'S WAY. NOT SO LUCKY, US.
MY SPIDER-SENSE IS GOING OFF LIKE A VOLCANO.
ET VOILA. WHAT'S HE REACHING FOR?
LOOKS LIKE A BATTERY CONTAINER. SLIM, CAN YOU TAKE OUT HIS EMO-BOX AGAIN?
LOVE TO.

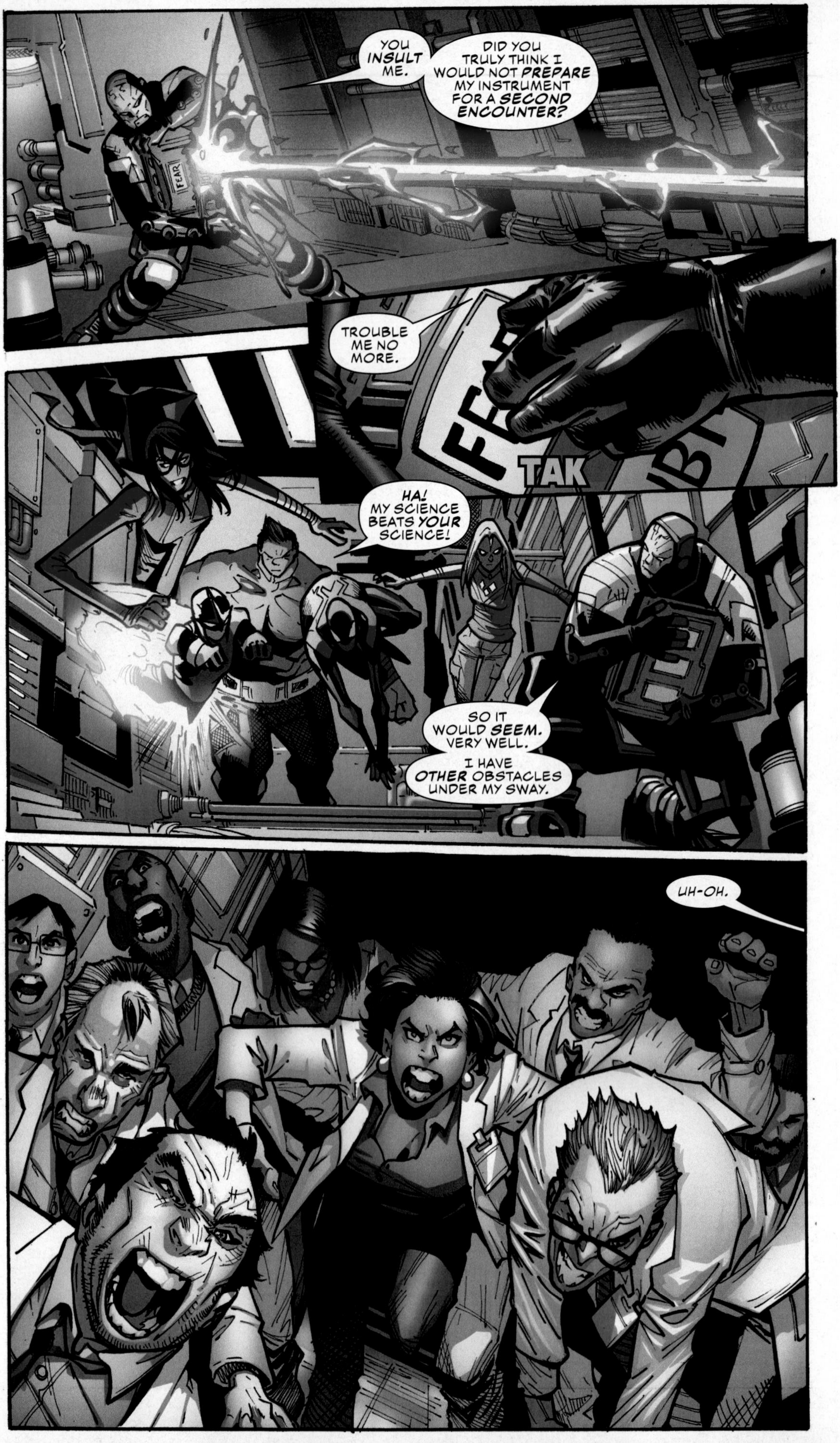

YOU INSULT ME.
DID YOU TRULY THINK I WOULD NOT PREPARE MY INSTRUMENT FOR A SECOND ENCOUNTER?
TROUBLE ME NO MORE.
TAK
HA! MY SCIENCE BEATS YOUR SCIENCE!
SO IT WOULD SEEM. VERY WELL.
I HAVE OTHER OBSTACLES UNDER MY SWAY.
UH-OH.

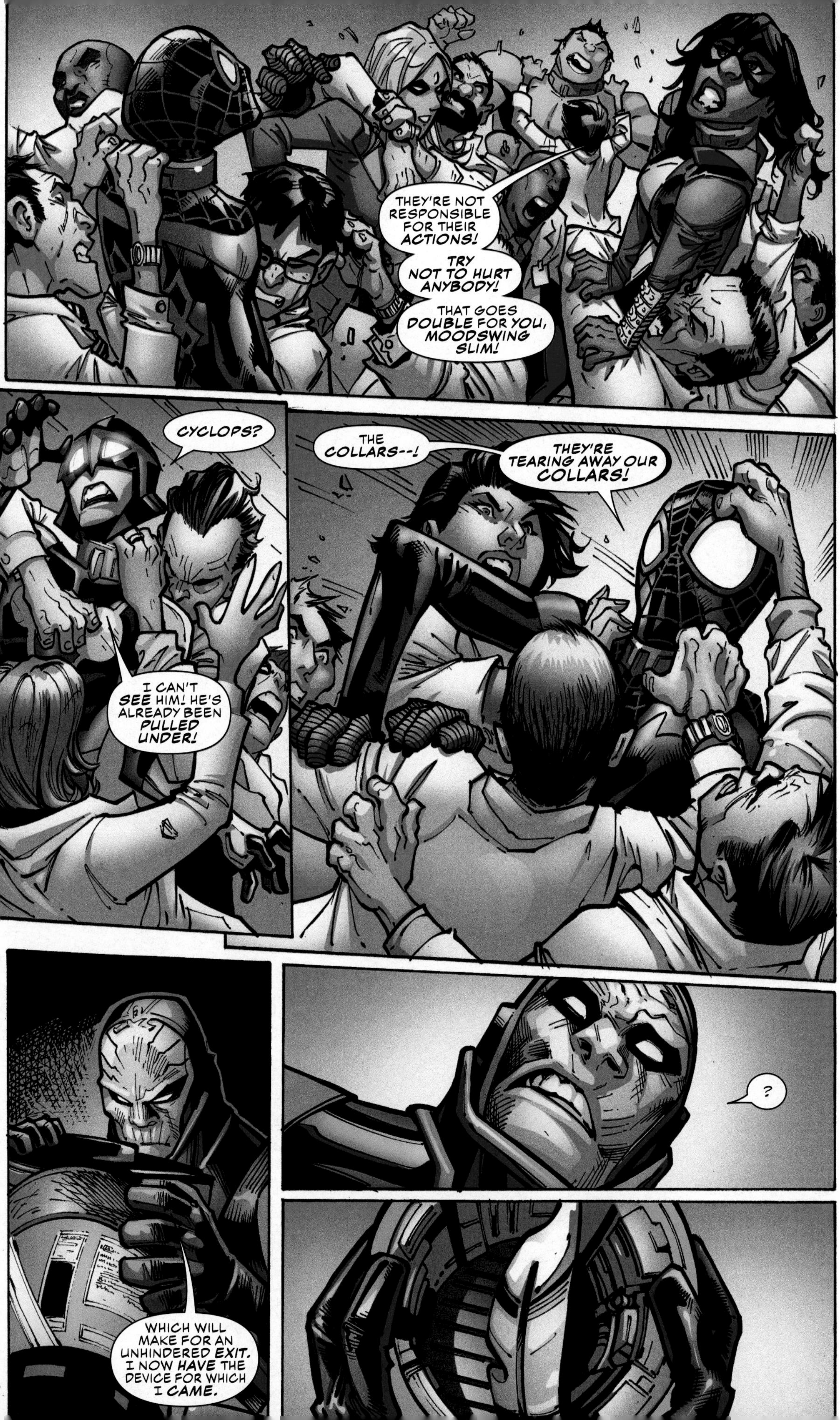

THEY'RE NOT RESPONSIBLE FOR THEIR ACTIONS!
TRY NOT TO HURT ANYBODY!
THAT GOES DOUBLE FOR YOU, MOODSWING SLIM!
CYCLOPS?
I CAN'T SEE HIM! HE'S ALREADY BEEN PULLED UNDER!
THE COLLARS--!
THEY'RE TEARING AWAY OUR COLLARS!
WHICH WILL MAKE FOR AN UNHINDERED EXIT. I NOW HAVE THE DEVICE FOR WHICH I CAME.
?

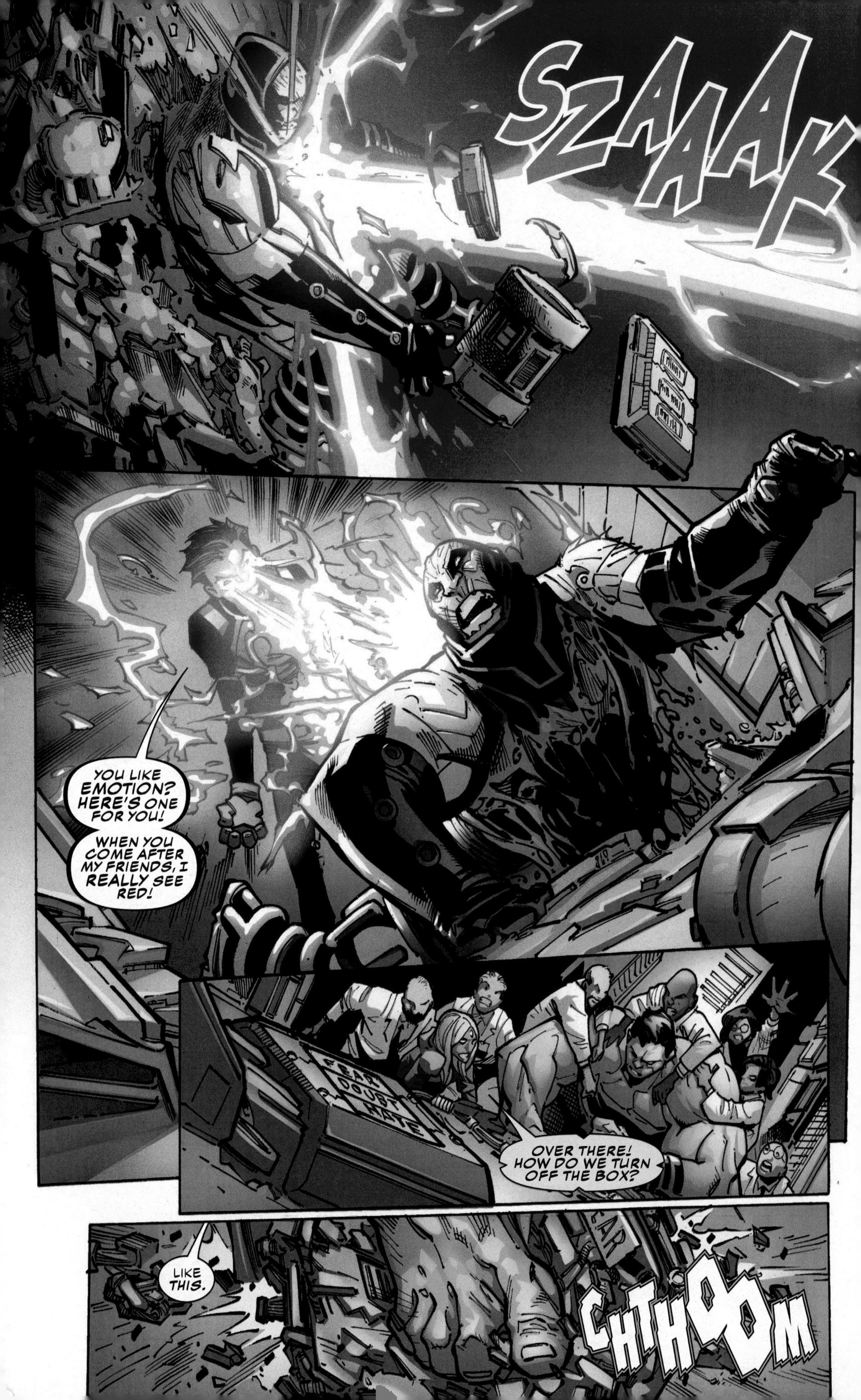
SZAAAK
YOU LIKE EMOTION? HERE'S ONE FOR YOU!
WHEN YOU COME AFTER MY FRIENDS, I REALLY SEE RED!
FEAR
DOUBT
HATE
OVER THERE! HOW DO WE TURN OFF THE BOX?
LIKE THIS.
CHTHOOM

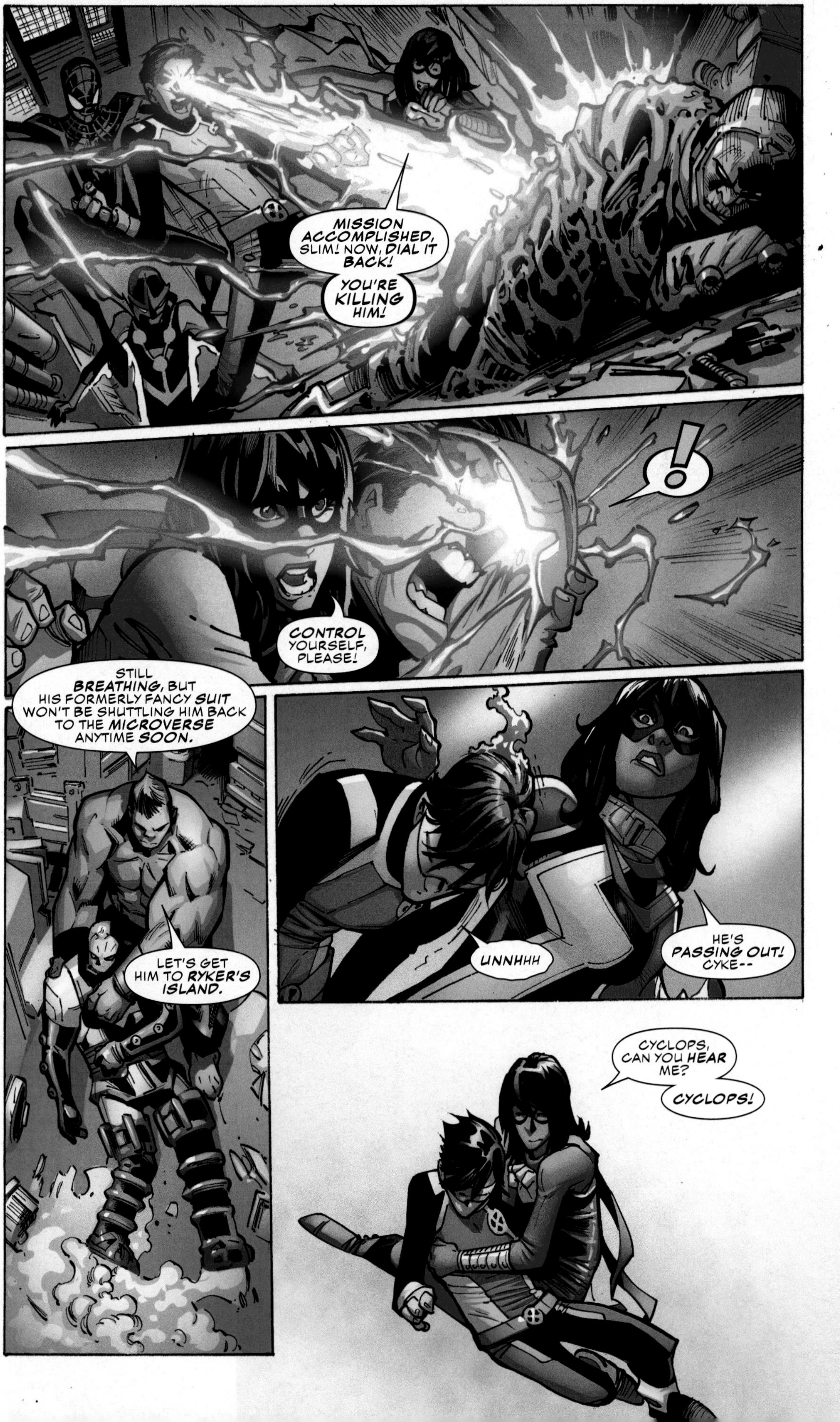
MISSION ACCOMPLISHED, SLIM! NOW, DIAL IT BACK!
YOU'RE KILLING HIM!
!
CONTROL YOURSELF, PLEASE!
STILL BREATHING, BUT HIS FORMERLY FANCY SUIT WON'T BE SHUTTLING HIM BACK TO THE MICROVERSE ANYTIME SOON.
LET'S GET HIM TO RYKER'S ISLAND.
UNNHHH
HE'S PASSING OUT! CYKE--
CYCLOPS, CAN YOU HEAR ME?
CYCLOPS!

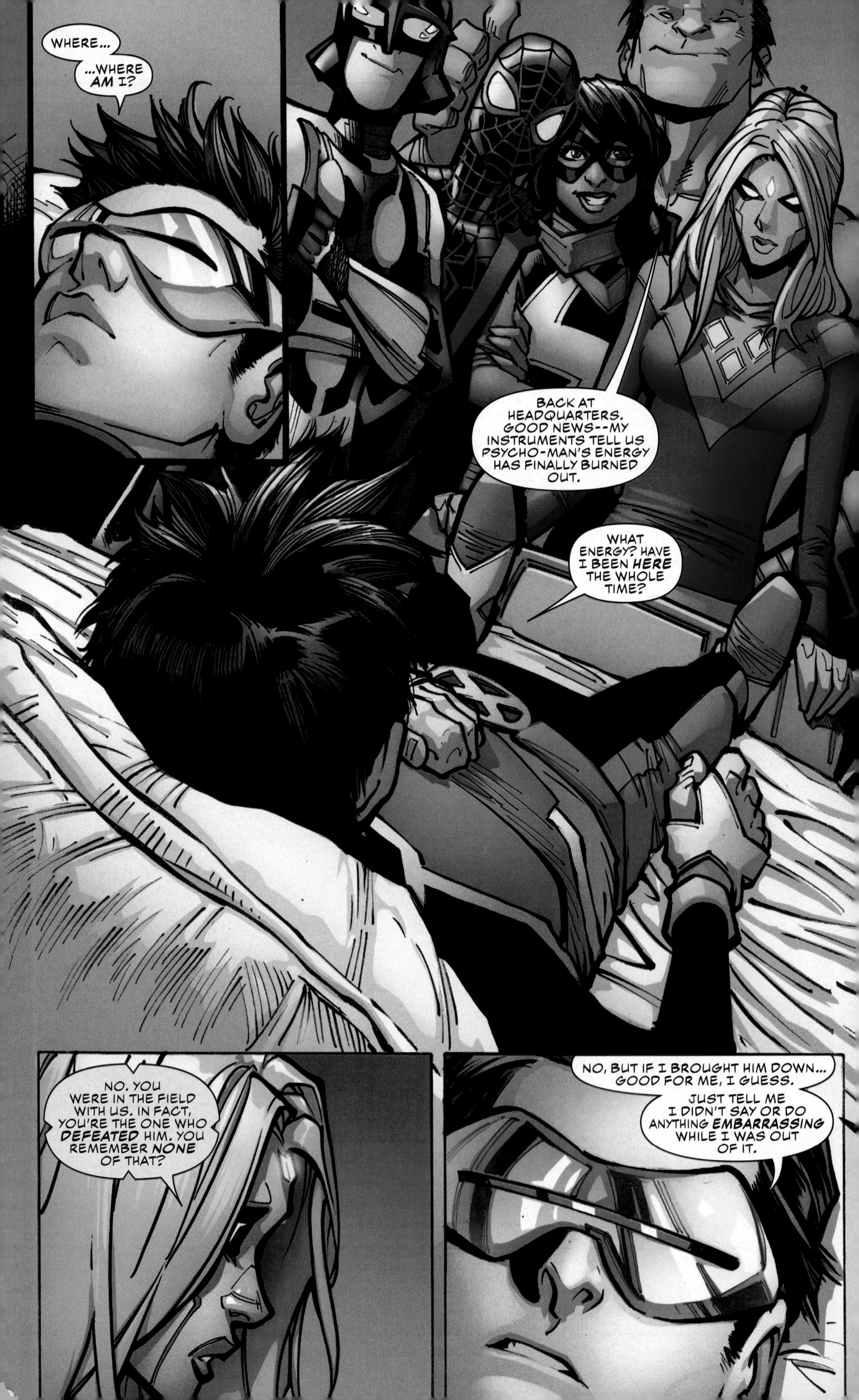
WHERE...
...WHERE AM I?
BACK AT HEADQUARTERS. GOOD NEWS--MY INSTRUMENTS TELL US PSYCHO-MAN'S ENERGY HAS FINALLY BURNED OUT.
WHAT ENERGY? HAVE I BEEN HERE THE WHOLE TIME?
NO. YOU WERE IN THE FIELD WITH US. IN FACT, YOU'RE THE ONE WHO DEFEATED HIM. YOU REMEMBER NONE OF THAT?
NO, BUT IF I BROUGHT HIM DOWN... GOOD FOR ME, I GUESS.
JUST TELL ME I DIDN'T SAY OR DO ANYTHING EMBARRASSING WHILE I WAS OUT OF IT.

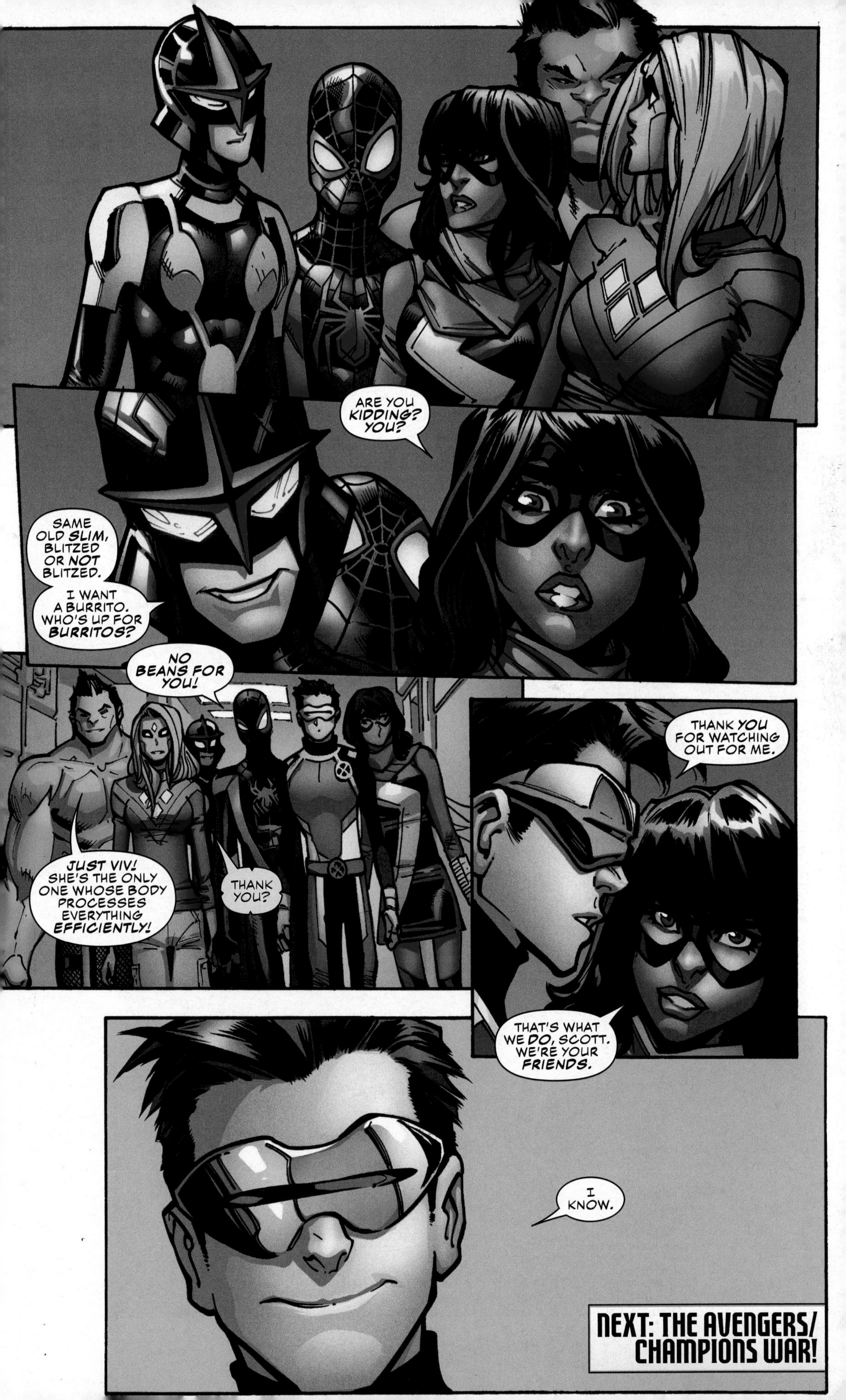
ARE YOU KIDDING? YOU?
SAME OLD SLIM, BLITZED OR NOT BLITZED.
I WANT A BURRITO. WHO'S UP FOR BURRITOS?
NO BEANS FOR YOU!
JUST VIV! SHE'S THE ONLY ONE WHOSE BODY PROCESSES EVERYTHING EFFICIENTLY!
THANK YOU?
THANK YOU FOR WATCHING OUT FOR ME.
THAT'S WHAT WE DO, SCOTT. WE'RE YOUR FRIENDS.
I KNOW.
NEXT: THE AVENGERS/ CHAMPIONS WAR!

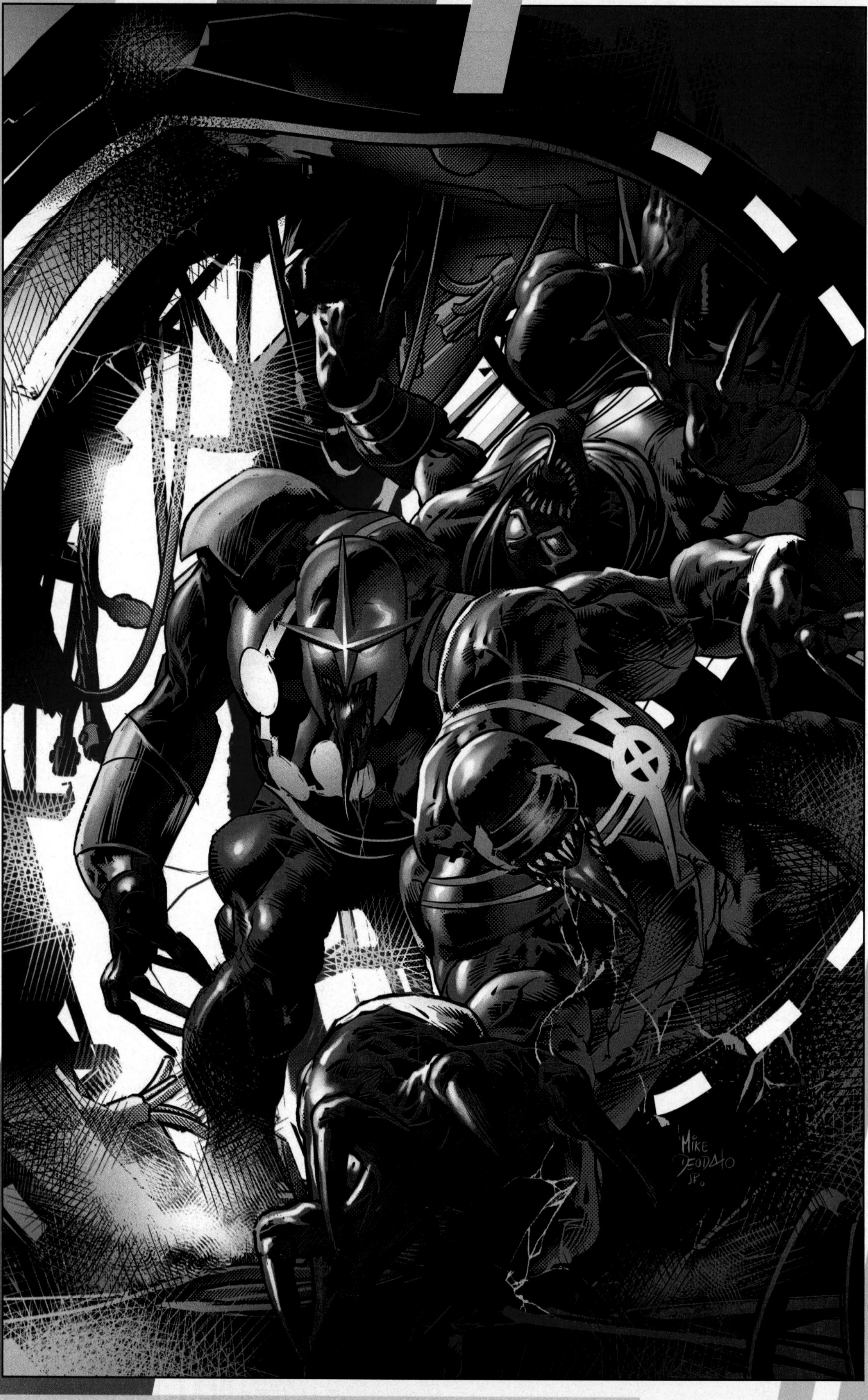

#6 VENOMIZED VARIANT BY **MIKE DEODATO JR. & RAIN BEREDO**

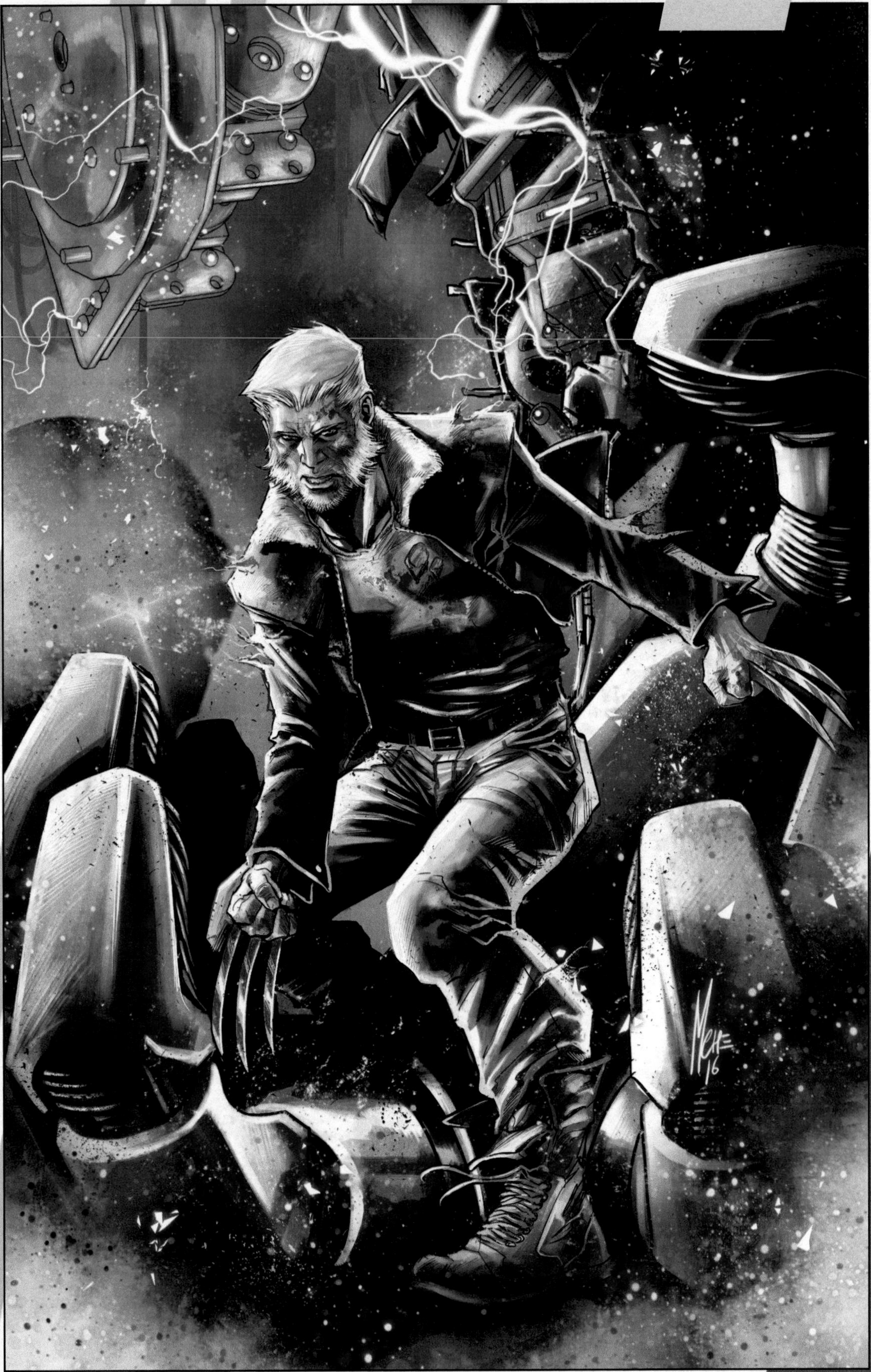
MCHE
16

#7 RESSURXION VARIANT BY **MARCO CHECCHETTO**

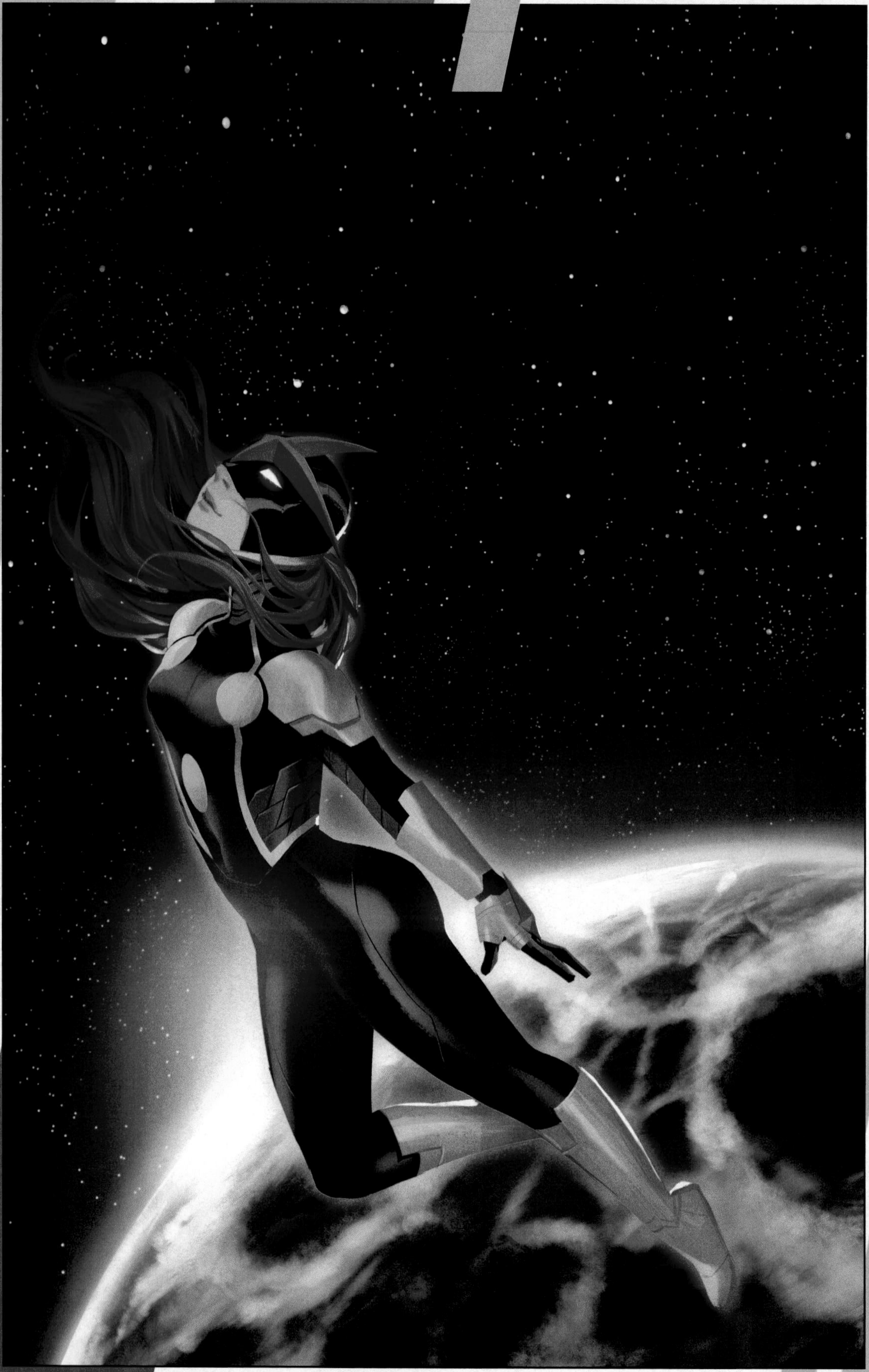

#9 MARY JANE VARIANT BY **HELEN CHEN**

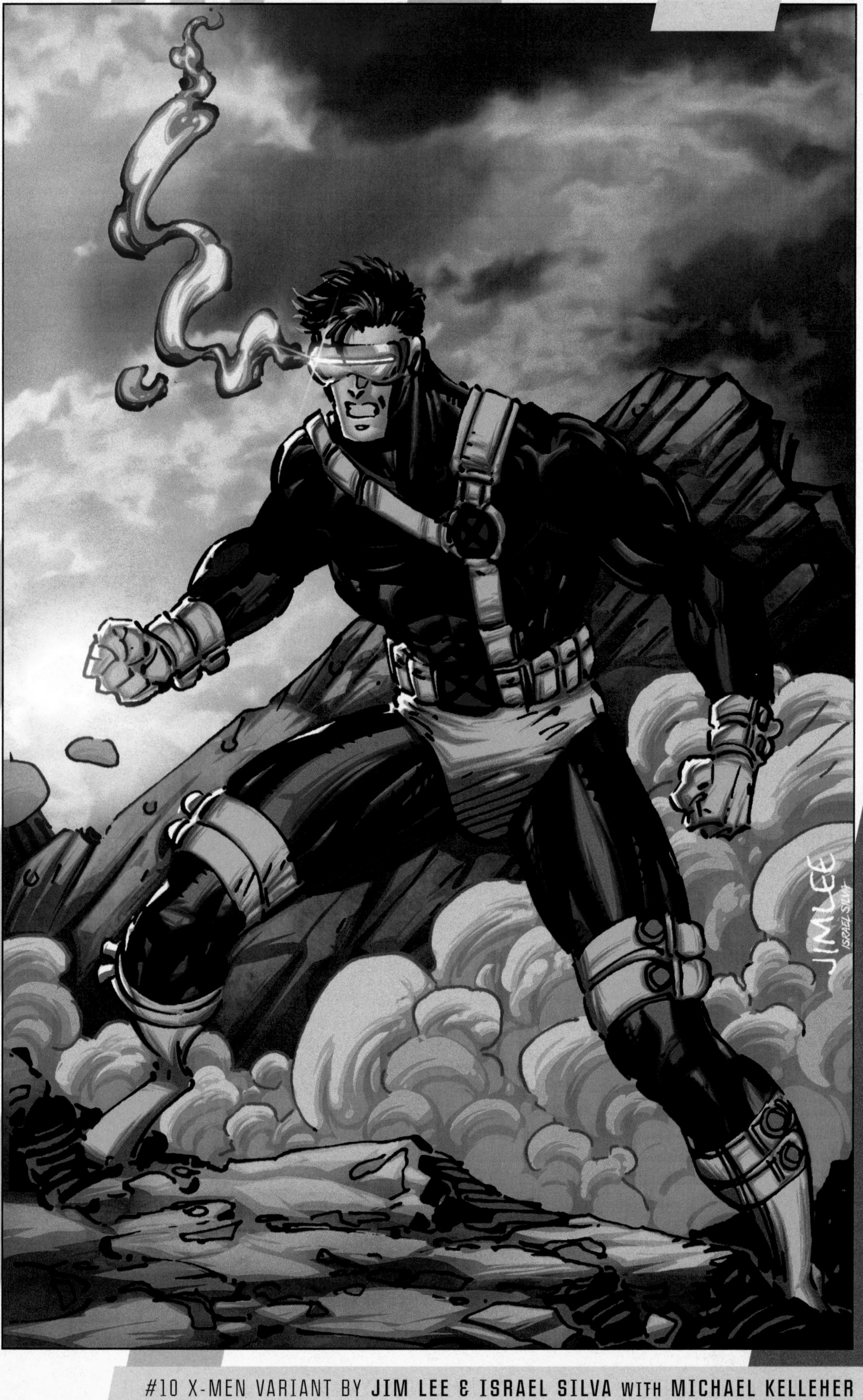

#10 X-MEN VARIANT BY **JIM LEE & ISRAEL SILVA** WITH **MICHAEL KELLEHER**

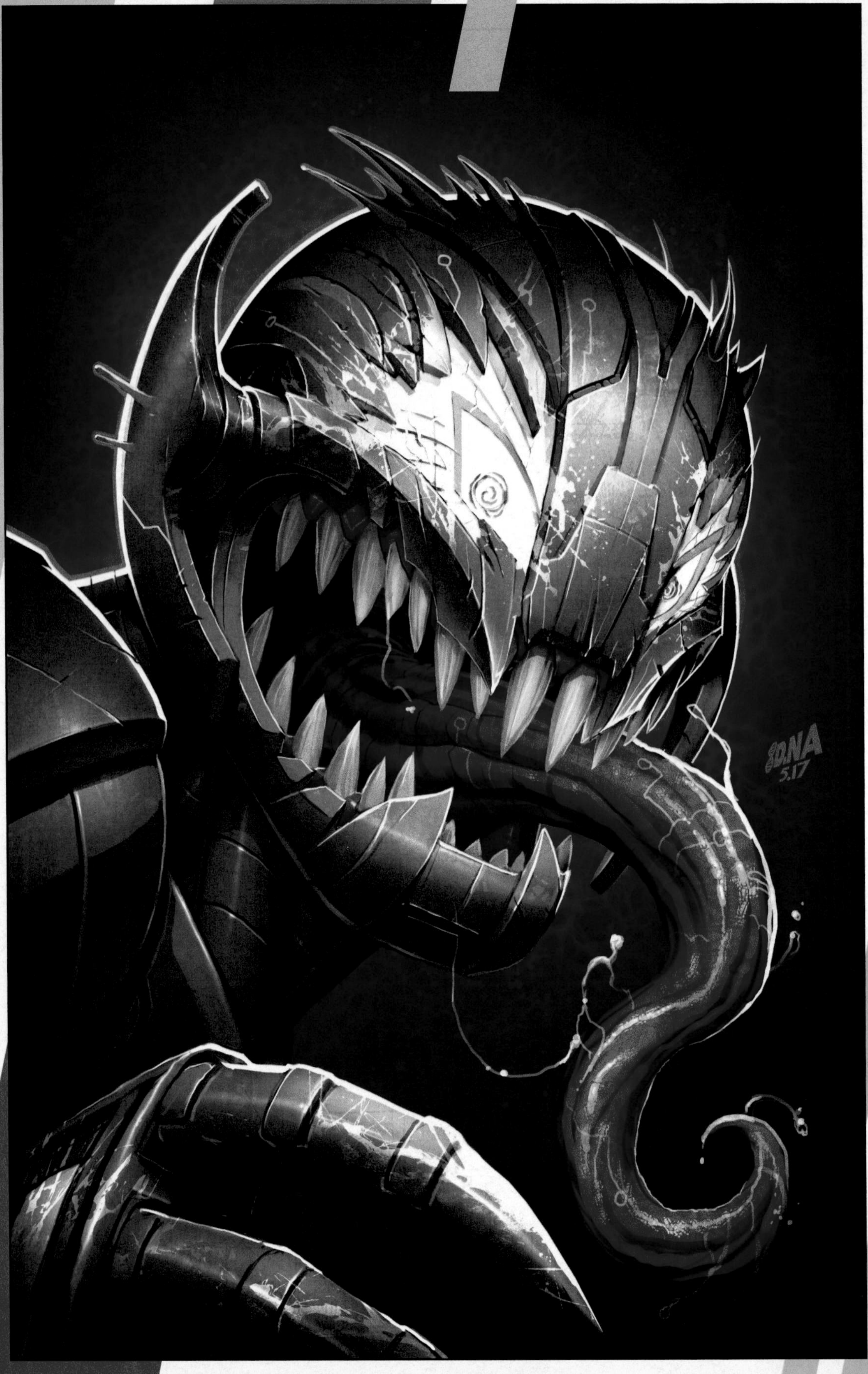
D.NA
5.17

#12 VENOMIZED VILLAINS VARIANT BY **DAVID NAKAYAMA**

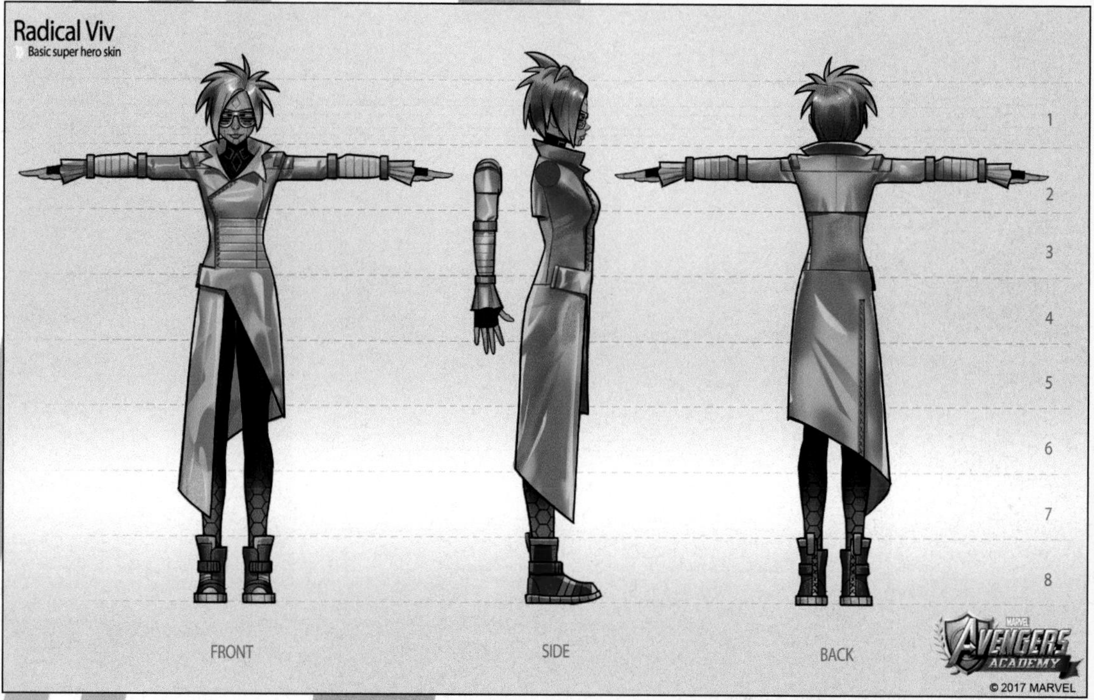
Radical Viv
Basic super hero skin
1
2
3
4
5
6
7
8
FRONT
SIDE
BACK
MARVEL
AVENGERS
ACADEMY
© 2017 MARVEL

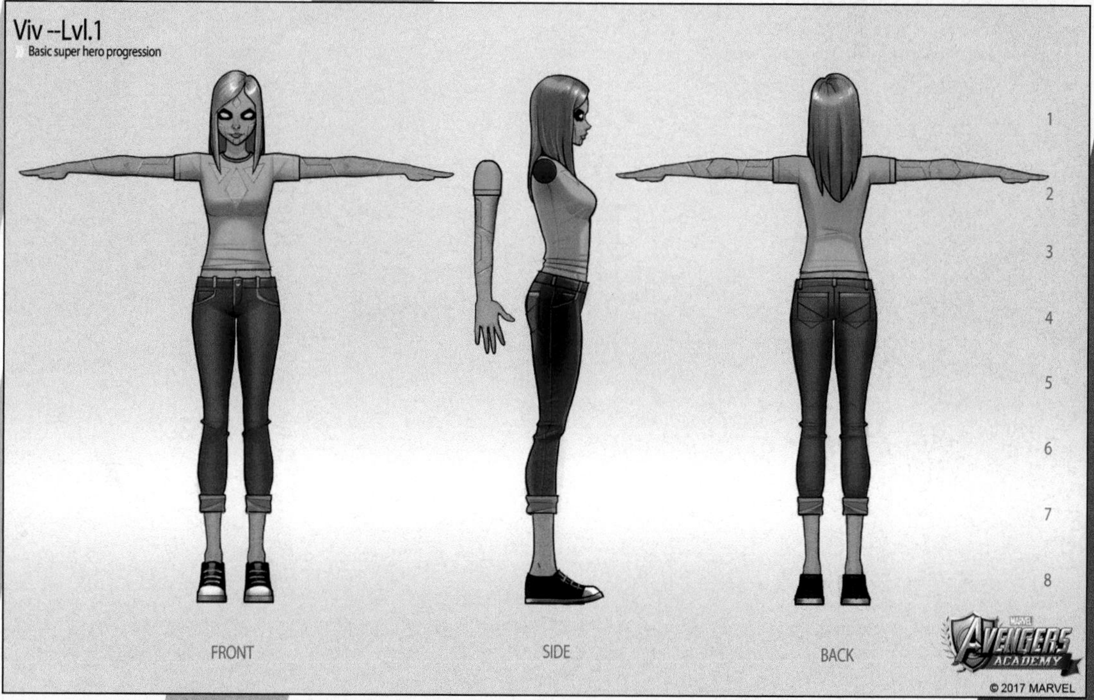
Viv --Lvl.1
Basic super hero progression
1
2
3
4
5
6
7
8
FRONT
SIDE
BACK
MARVEL
AVENGERS
ACADEMY
© 2017 MARVEL

VIV VISION CHARACTER DESIGNS FROM THE *AVENGERS ACADEMY* MOBILE GAME

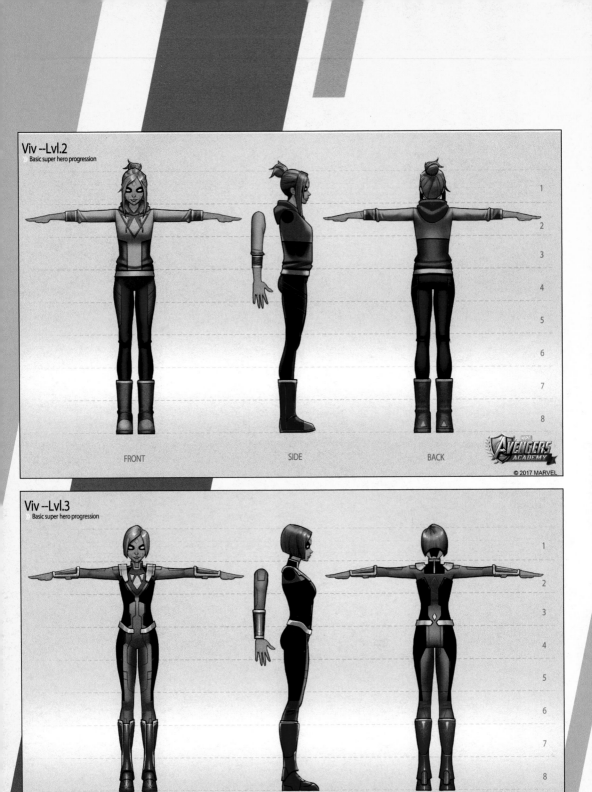

Viv --Lvl.2
Basic super hero progression

FRONT   SIDE   BACK

© 2017 MARVEL

Viv --Lvl.3
Basic super hero progression

FRONT   SIDE   BACK

© 2017 MARVEL

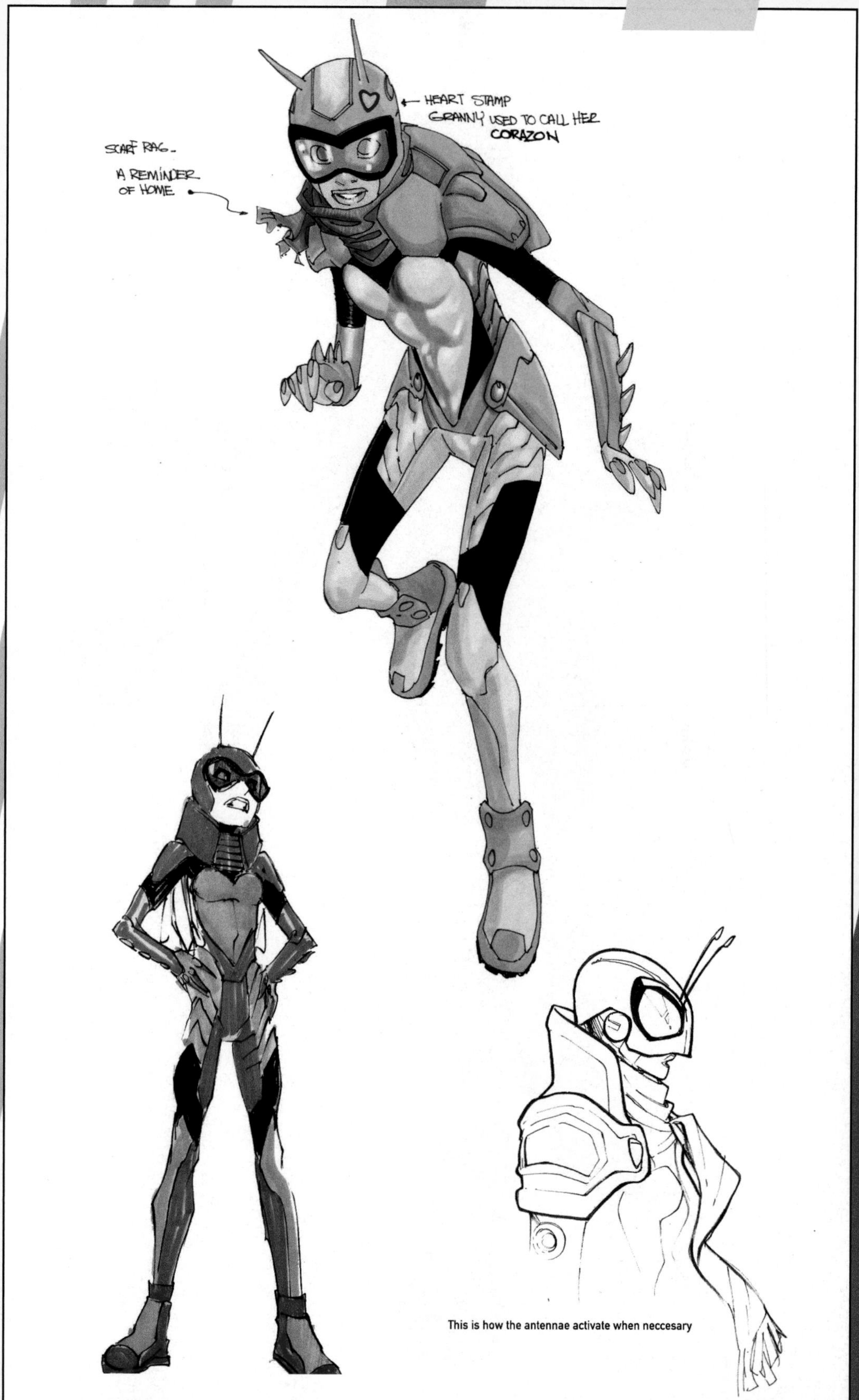
HEART STAMP
GRANNY USED TO CALL HER CORAZON
SCARF RAG -
A REMINDER OF HOME
This is how the antennae activate when neccesary

RED LOCUST DESIGNS BY **HUMBERTO RAMOS**

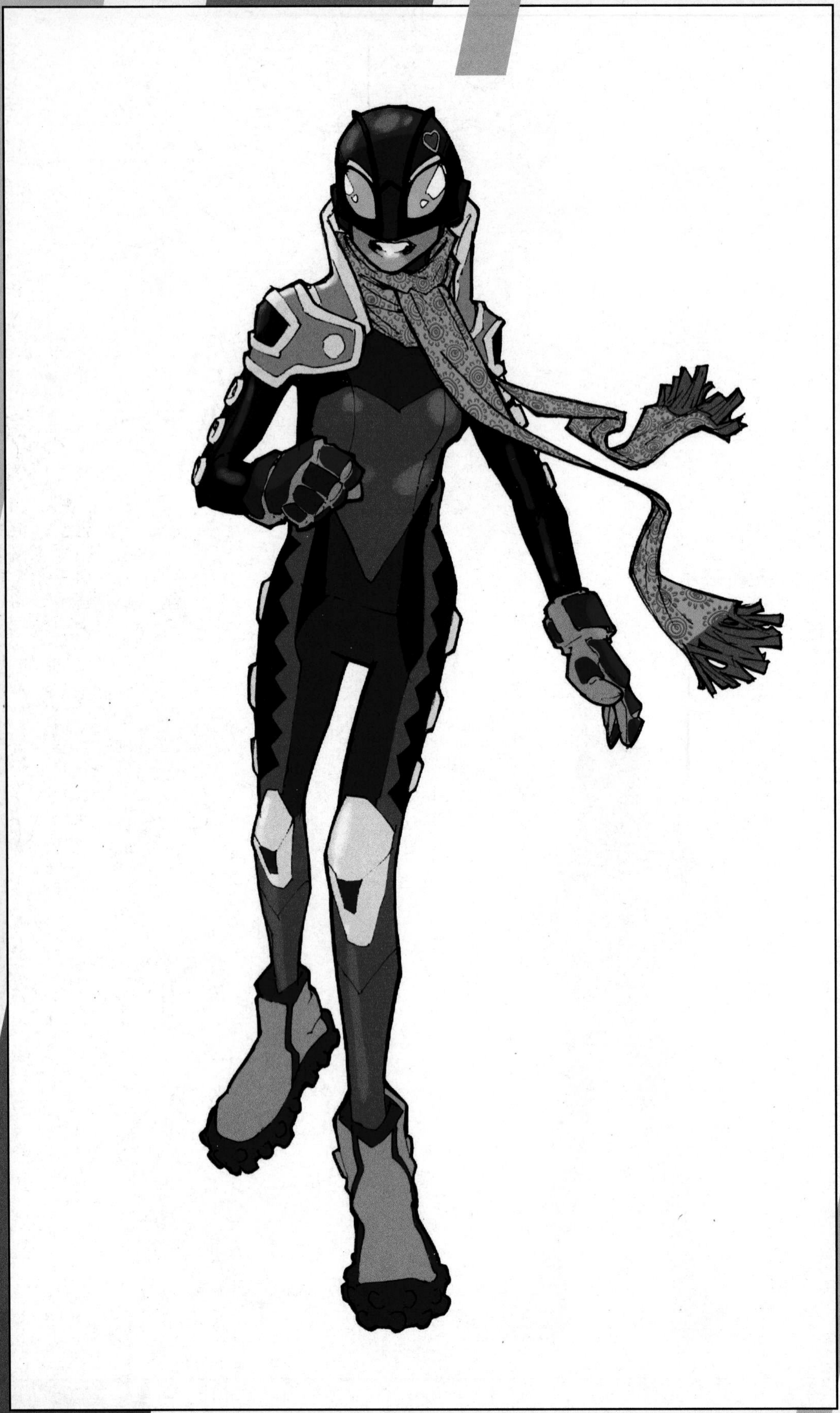